DECKER'S COMPLETE HANDBOOK

ON

MORMONISM

ED DECKER

HARVEST HOUSE PUBLISHERS
Eugene, Oregon 97402

DECKER'S COMPLETE HANDBOOK ON MORMONISM

Copyright © 1995 by Harvest House Publishers
Eugene, Oregon 97402

Library of Congress Cataloging-in-Publication Data

Decker, Ed.
    [Complete handbook on Mormonism]
    Decker's complete handbook on Mormonism / Ed Decker.
        p.   cm.
    ISBN 1-56507-012-7
        1. Church of Jesus Christ of Latter-day Saints—Controversial literature.   2. Mormon Church—
    Controversial literature.   I. Title.
    BX8645.D37   1995   94-44253
    289.3—dc20   CIP

Printed in the United States of America.

95   96   97   98   99   00   01 — 10   9   8   7   6   5   4   3   2   1

I dedicate this book to the many thousands of truth-seeking Mormons who have heard the truth of the biblical gospel and have chosen Jesus over Joseph—and to those Christians who cared enough, loved enough to bring that truth to them. May this process never stop as long as we are living on this side of heaven.

Acknowledgments

This book could not have been brought to print without the continued commitment and efforts by the staffs of Saints Alive, Christian Research Institute, and Harvest House Publishers.

I am especially grateful for the help of Bill Schnoebelen, who was my personal assistant and a sounding board during much of the time this book was being written.

I am also grateful for the love and understanding of my wife and family, all of whom learned to live with the back of my head facing them for great lengths of time as my face remained focused on my computer screen.

Foreword

by *Hank Hanegraaff*

For 20 years Ed Decker served as a missionary *for* the Mormon church.[1] For 20 more, he has served as a missionary *to* the Mormon church. Thus, he is uniquely qualified to equip committed Christians to use the deviations of Mormonism as opportunities for sharing the gospel of grace. While he considers himself a soldier rather than a scholar, in this volume he has distinguished himself as both. From the "restoration" of the Aaronic priesthood to the "restoration" of Zion in Jackson County, Missouri, Decker covers Mormonism from A to Z.

The saga of Mormonism began in 1820, when a young man named Joseph Smith, Jr. purportedly experienced a spectacular vision. Two celestial personages appeared to him, claiming *all* existing churches were wrong, *all* their creeds were an abomination, and *all* their professors were corrupt.[2] These beings made it clear to Joseph that he had been chosen to *restore*, rather than *reform*, a church that had disappeared from the face of the Earth.

In 1823 the angel Moroni was said to have visited young Joseph and divulged the location of gold plates containing the "fulness of the everlasting gospel." These plates—abridged by Moroni and his father, Mormon,[3] 1400 years earlier—were written in "reformed Egyptian hieroglyphics." Smith supposedly found, buried along with the plates, a pair of magical eyeglasses[4] that he used to translate the cryptic writing into English. The result was a new revelation called the *Book of Mormon*[5] and a new religion called Mormonism.

Organizationally, Mormonism began when John the Baptist allegedly ordained Smith and Oliver Cowdery (a schoolteacher who assisted Smith by transcribing the inscriptions on the gold plates) to the Aaronic priesthood. Subsequent to the appearance of John the Baptist, the apostles Peter, James, and John were said to have conferred the Melchizedek priesthood and apostleship on Smith and Cowdery, giving them the authority to act on behalf of Jesus Christ in this last dispensation.[6] On April 6, 1830, the Mormon church was officially launched.

Revelations in Mormonism are not relegated to personal appearances by angels like Moroni[7] or apostles like Peter. However, the Mormon church claims three volumes of scripture, or "standard works," in addition to the Bible. The foremost of these revelations is the *Book of Mormon*, purportedly *"the record of God's dealings with the ancient inhabitants of the Americas"* which *"contains, as does the Bible, the fulness of the everlasting gospel."*[8] Mormons believe the prophet Ezekiel was talking about the *Book of Mormon* when he alluded to the stick of Joseph (Ezekiel 37:16ff.).[9]

How millions can take the *Book of Mormon* seriously is almost beyond comprehension. While Smith referred to it as "the most correct of any book on earth, and the keystone of our religion,"[10] its flaws run the gamut from the serious to the silly. In the category of serious we find that Ether 3:14 ("Behold, I am Jesus Christ. I am the Father and the Son") is modalistic and militates against trinitarian theology, while Alma 11:44 ("Christ the Son, and God the Father, and the Holy Spirit, which is one Eternal God") is basically consistent with the biblical doctrine of the Trinity.

In the category of silly is the account in Alma 44 of a man who becomes irate after being scalped and stirs up his soldiers to fight "more powerfully." And in Ether 15 we read of a man who struggles to catch his breath after having his head cut off! The *Book of Mormon* has now been altered over 4000 times to compensate for Smith's poor command of English, as well as for the numerous errors and inconsistencies it presented.

The second volume of Mormon scripture is the *Doctrine and Covenants*—a compilation of alleged divine revelations given to the Mormon church—is equally problematic. Among the farfetched revelations it has foisted on humanity is the doctrine of polygamy. It was not until the Mormons were threatened with exile that their president, Wilford Woodruff, received a revelation relegating polygamy to the afterlife.

The third extrabiblical revelation in the Mormon canon—namely, *The Pearl of Great Price*—is no less troubling. It was used for years by Mormons to prevent African Americans from entering their priesthood and, consequently, from being exalted to godhood in the system's celestial kingdom. Mormon prophet Brigham Young went so far as to declare that the reason "Negroes" have a "flat nose and black skin" is because God had put a curse on them.[11] While these and other aberrations pose a serious threat to Mormon credibility, it is the organization's deviations from essential Christian doctrine which ultimately define it as a non-Christian cult.

Major Mormon theological travesties begin with the *denial of Christ's deity*. In fact, Christ, according to Mormon theology, has the dubious distinction of being Lucifer's spirit-brother. In addition, Mormonism denies:

- the doctrine of original sin, teaching instead that men and women are, in reality, gods in embryo;

- Christ's preservation of His church, teaching instead that the true church vanished from the earth after the death of the apostles, and that Joseph Smith had to restore it with his "latter-day saints";

- the Trinity, affirming instead that God the Father and Jesus have bodies of "flesh and bone," that the Holy Spirit is "a personage of Spirit,"[12] and that the Trinity is pagan in origin;

- the inerrancy of Scripture, teaching instead that the Bible can be trusted only "as far it is translated correctly"[13];

- Christ was begotten by the Holy Ghost in His incarnation, teaching instead that God the Father had sex with Mary,[14] "instead of letting any other man do it";[15]

- the immutability of God, affirming instead that God was "perhaps once child, and mortal like we ourselves";[16]

- the biblical concept of hell, teaching that all can be rescued, except for "sons of perdition"—who may include those who, like the author of this volume, are apostate Mormons.

Oath-taking is yet another problem with Mormonism. Temple Mormons, for example, once swore never to reveal their secret rituals on penalty that "our throats be cut from ear to ear and our tongues torn out by their roots." Although this and other violent oaths were altered during the first half of the twentieth century, and removed from the ritual just recently, they are an enduring reminder of the ferocious secrecy in which Mormon temple rituals are shrouded.

The "new and everlasting covenant" of plural marriage is perhaps the best example of Mormon equivocation. In 1890, under threat of exile to Mexico, Mormons officially abolished polygamy in the earthly realm. However, in secret temple ceremonies, Mormon males continue to be sealed to multiple wives—in the heavenly realm.[17] Thus, the earthly practice of polygamy, publicly promoted by Brigham Young (who personally had 27 wives and 52 children), is now promised to those who attain the highest level of the celestial kingdom. Like their heavenly Father, Mormon males may hope to one day, too, rule their own personal planets and enjoy endless, celestial sex with multiple goddess wives.

Even this cursory overview of Mormon history and theology should make it abundantly clear that while Mormons use Christian terminology, both the *roots* and *fruits* of their religion are decidedly unbiblical. It is crucial that Christians learn to scale the Mormon language barrier. In this comprehensive work by Ed Decker, you will be equipped to do just that. It is my prayer that in the process you will become so familiar with the truth that, when counterfeits loom on the horizon, you will be able to recognize them instantaneously.

A Note from the Author

This book is the fruit of my almost 40 years of involvement with Mormonism. For the first 20 years I was a member of the church; and like many members, I was a temple Mormon, an elder in the Melchizedek priesthood, a teacher, and one who held positions of some authority at the local level. For the past 20 years, I have been a born-again Christian with a burden and a zeal to reach my lost brothers and sisters in the LDS church with the joy of the true gospel of Jesus Christ.

This work comes from a collection of research notes, files, and teachings that I have done at seminars and churches in far more places than I can even remember. It includes data that has piled up in computers, boxes, and drawers at the ministry of Saints Alive over the last 18 years or so. Getting it all into one book has been a miracle in itself.

As you use this information, you will see that I have kept the Mormon references down to a minimum for simplicity's sake and hopefully to the benefit of anyone trying to follow through the actual references themselves. References to the book *Mormon Doctrine* by the late LDS apostle and church theologian Bruce R. McConkie appear throughout the text for that reason. His work is an ideal composite of official LDS doctrine.

I pray that this book will be used as an active tool in the evangelism of the Mormon people.

DECKER'S COMPLETE HANDBOOK

ON

MORMONISM

AARON

The LDS Position

The LDS church teaches much of what the Bible affirms about Aaron, the brother of Moses, the son of Amram and Jochebed of the tribe of Levi (see Exodus 4:14; 6:20; 15:20). It acknowledges him as the first high priest of the Levitical priesthood under Moses (*Encyclopedia*, 1:1).

The problem arises in what Joseph Smith added to the scriptural information about Aaron, and especially the information concerning his priestly legacy. Mormons assert that there is an Aaronic priesthood functioning in the world today and that they alone possess it (see also *Aaronic Priesthood*).

Mormons also believe their priesthood is called of God through a prophet, in accord with Hebrews 5:4 (*Encyclopedia*, 1:1). Mormons assert that the clergy of other faiths are not called in this fashion and thus have no authority to officiate in the ordinances of "the gospel."

The Biblical View

The LDS church espouses this teaching about a present-day Aaronic priesthood even though the Old Testament clearly says that only direct descendants of the tribe of Levi and the house of Aaron may hold this priesthood (Exodus 28:1; Numbers 18:1-7; Leviticus 6:19-23; Nehemiah 7:61-65). It is evident from these Scriptures and others that God wanted only direct descendants of

Aaron in the priesthood, and even that intermarriage with non-Aaronic wives could foul the priestly line.

Since there are few Jewish Mormons and fewer still that would claim Levitical descent, this leaves the Mormon church in a biblical dilemma. Most Mormons, including Joseph Smith himself, claim to be descended from the House of Ephraim (*Encyclopedia*, 2:461), another Jewish tribe. They are told this frequently when they receive their "Patriarchal blessings" (ibid., p. 462). (See also *Patriarchal Blessings*).

Yet Ephraim had no right to any priesthood. This means that most LDS men, including Joseph Smith, would be cursed if they tried to usurp the priesthood (Numbers 16:1-3,16-21; 1 Kings 13:33, 34).

Second, in insisting upon an exact correspondence between the "calling" of Aaron and the "calling" of LDS priesthood holders, the LDS church immediately runs aground on the shoals of biblical truth. In examining the way in which Aaron was called, we find this simple verse: "And take thou unto thee Aaron thy brother, and his sons with him, from among the children of Israel, that he may minister unto me in the priest's office" (Exodus 28:1).

It is obvious from the context that the Lord is speaking directly to Moses (Exodus 33:11; see also Deuteronomy 34:10). Yet virtually *no* LDS priesthood holders are called by an audible voice of God! Indeed, it is the testimony of many former LDS Melchizedek priesthood holders that most such callings are given in committee meetings between ward or stake leaders, much as leaders are chosen in most churches. Even most honest LDS priesthood holders would have to admit that they do not hear the audible voice of God speaking to them face-to-face.

Beyond that, if you examine what followed Aaron's calling in the book of Exodus, it is clear that virtually none of the things which were done to him at the command of the Lord were or are being done to LDS priesthood holders. In Exodus 29:4-27, we find many requirements for those called to be in the Aaronic priesthood. They include:

1. They must be washed with water (this is not done at the ordination of Aaronic priesthood holders, at least not until they attend the temple and take out their endowments).

2. They must be anointed with oil (also not done until years later when they attend the temple).

3. They must lay their hands on a bullock (not done).

4. The bullock must be killed and its blood poured out (obviously not done).

5. The animal's innards must be burnt on an altar, and its hide burnt with fire outside the camp (not done in Mormonism).

6. The priesthood candidate must lay his hands on the head of a ram (not done).

7. The ram should be killed and its blood sprinkled around the altar.

This list could be expanded by another half-dozen or more examples, but the point is clear. If Mormons insist their Aaronic priesthood parallels that of Aaron, then why are virtually *none* of the requirements for Aaron's sacerdotal office being fulfilled in their church? Remember as well that most LDS Aaronic priesthood holders are young boys from 12–17.

Mormons may protest that these are all Old Testament rituals which no longer apply, but that is precisely the point of the Book of Hebrews. The entire Aaronic priesthood is Old Testament; it is not part of the new covenant of Jesus Christ. The Aaronic priesthood is no longer relevant. It was done away with when God ripped the veil on the temple in Jerusalem as Jesus died on Calvary (Matthew 27:51).

This new covenant is based upon new and better promises (Hebrews 7:19-22; 8:6; 12:24) and it has only *one* high priest, Jesus Christ (Hebrews 7:23,24).

AARON, THE GIFT OF

The LDS Position

The phrase "gift of Aaron" is found in the standard works of the LDS church, though it is nowhere mentioned in the Bible. In *Doctrine and Covenants* 8, there is a "revelation" to Oliver Cowdery, who was then serving as Joseph Smith's scribe in the "translation" of the *Book of Mormon* in April 1829.

The commentary on the text says that Cowdery desired to be endowed with the gift of translation from God, and that the subsequent revelation was given by the Lord in response to this supplication. After being promised that the Holy Ghost would come and dwell in his heart and that this was the spirit of revelation, Cowdery was told this:

> And this is not all thy gift; for you have another gift, which is the gift of Aaron; behold, it has told you many things. Behold, there is no other power, save the power of God, that can cause this gift of Aaron to be with you. Therefore, doubt not, for it is the gift of God; and you shall hold it in your hands, and do marvelous works; and no power shall be able to take it away out of your hands, for it is the work of God. And, therefore, whatsoever you shall ask me to tell you by that means, that will I grant unto you, and you shall have knowledge concerning it (vv. 6-9).

Examining the Claim

This sounds pious enough—so why has this "divine revelation" been greatly edited? In the original edition (1833) of the *Book of Commandments*, which was the predecessor of *Doctrine and Covenants*, this revelation is titled "Chapter VII: A Revelation given to Oliver, in Harmony, Pennsylvania, April, 1829." Here is the 1833 version of the same passage:

> Now this is not all, for you have another gift, which is the gift of working with the rod: behold it has told you things: behold there is no other power save God, that can cause this rod of nature to work in your hands, for it is the work of God: and, therefore, whatsoever you shall ask me to tell you by that means, that will I grant unto you, and you shall know (#3).

Since 1833 the passage has swollen from 76 words to 118 words. This is a peculiar way to treat a revelation from God! Imagine if someone were to add 42 words to John 3:16 without any explanation—would not people begin to question which was actually the true revelation from God?

Beyond that issue, we must also ask why the words "working with the rod" and "the rod of nature" were changed. The answer becomes clear when we recall that Joseph Smith and his entire family were deeply involved in occult practices (see also *Occult*). Joseph Smith, Sr. was in fact a worker of a divining rod (or as it is more commonly known today, a dowsing rod).

A dowsing or divining rod is an occult implement. The *Encyclopedia Brittanica* (1982) defines *dowsing* as "the use of a forked piece of hazel, rowan or willow wood . . . to detect such hidden substances as water, minerals, treasure, archaeological remains, and even dead bodies" (*Micropedia*, III, p. 649).

It further defines *divination* as "the alleged art or science of foretelling the future by various natural, psychological and other techniques. Found in all civilizations—both ancient and modern, primitive and sophisticated, and in all areas—it is known in the Western world primarily in the form of horoscopic astrology" (ibid., p. 582).

An earlier encyclopedia more contemporary to Joseph Smith, the *Encyclopedia Americana* (1830), makes it clear that the divining rod is associated with the god Mercury and is a rod, either single or curved or with two branches like a fork, made of wood, brass, or other metal and empowered by certain superstitious ceremonies (vol. 4, p. 258).

In *The Encyclopedia of Occult Sciences* we are informed that "the rod, also called Caduceus, divining Rod, Rod of Aaron, staff of Jacob, etc., was known in all times. . . . As to the discovery of treasures, according to the author it must be assumed that the rod correctly handled is sensitive to metallic emanations, and he gives a list of mines found by this means" (p. 322). Thus we see that the phrase "Rod of Aaron" is, in fact, a code word for the divining or dowsing rod used by sorcerers throughout the Middle Ages and into the twentieth century.

According to LDS historian D. Michael Quinn, Joseph Smith, Sr.'s brother, Jesse, had embraced biblical Protestantism and condemned his brother for having a wand or rod like Jannes and Jambres who withstood Moses in Egypt: "that he can tell the distance from India to Ethiopia . . . another fool story, many other things alike ridiculous" (Quinn, 1987, p. 28).

This takes on a great deal more meaning when one recalls that both Joseph Smith, Sr. and Jr. evidently were involved in finding buried treasure for many local citizens (see the above definition of *dowsing*) and in fact supported themselves by claiming to be able to find treasures—Joseph, Sr. with his rod, and Joseph, Jr. with his "seer stone" (see also *Seer Stones*).

Additionally, Quinn reports that an entire sect of divining rodsmen existed near where Oliver Cowdery was raised in Vermont. This sect, called the "Wood Scrape," was six miles from the Cowdery home and only 50 miles from the home where Joseph Smith, Jr. was raised (Quinn, p. 31). Its leader, Nathaniel Wood, taught his followers that "they were descendants of the ancient Jews, and lawful inheritors of the whole country." The Wood Scrape practiced the occult sciences of alchemy and "used a cleft stick or rod" to discover "the hidden treasures of the earth." They received instructions from their rods, including a revelation that they must build a temple (ibid.).

Note that this strange theology is perilously close to that supposedly revealed anew to Joseph Smith, Jr. by God. It may well be that the phrases "rod of nature" and "rod of Aaron" were carefully edited out of the later editions of *Doctrine and Covenants* to cover up the Smith and Cowdery families' involvement in the occult and to conceal where Joseph Smith got some of his bizarre theology.

It would not do for a "prophet of God" to be caught plagiarizing his revelations from other sources, nor to be involved in practices clearly forbidden by the Lord in the Bible. Yet certainly Joseph Smith was involved in occultism and may also have been involved in plagiarism.

AARONIC PRIESTHOOD

The LDS Position

The LDS church functions under two priestly classifications. The first, or lesser priesthood (see *Doctrine and Covenants* 85:11) is called the Aaronic priesthood, which includes the Levitical priesthood (see *Doctrine and Covenants* 107:1,6).

Mormons believe that the priesthood conferred upon Aaron functioned through the time of John the Baptist. They teach that it was restored to the Earth on May 15, 1829. The introduction and single verse of *Doctrine and Covenants* 13 describe the supposed event:

Ordination of Joseph Smith and Oliver Cowdery to the Aaronic Priesthood along the bank of the Susquehanna River, near Harmony, Pennsylvania, May 15, 1829 (*History* 1:39-42). The ordination was done by the hands of an angel, who announced himself as John, the same that is called John the Baptist in the New Testament. The angel explained that he was acting under the direction of Peter, James and John, the ancient apostles. . . .

"Upon you my fellow servants, in the name of Messiah I confer the Priesthood of Aaron, which holds the keys of the ministering of angels and of the gospel of repentance, and of baptism by immersion for the remission of sins; and this shall never be taken again from the earth, until the sons of Levi do offer again an offering unto the Lord in righteousness."

In function, the Aaronic priesthood is said to be for the ministry of the temporal needs of the church. Bruce R. McConkie in his book *Doctrine* describes it this way (p. 11):

Perfection does not come by the Levitical order, and this lesser priesthood is not received with an oath (Hebrews 7:11,21; *Teachings*, p. 323). But it is a preparatory priesthood, the Priesthood of Elias, the schooling ministry, which prepares its worthy and faithful ministers for the oath and covenant and perfection that appertain to the Melchizedek order.

In practice, the LDS church brings up its male youth through this priesthood. The priesthood has three offices or levels within it, the offices of deacon, teacher, and priest. The *General Handbook of Instructions* (1976 edition, p. 40) describes the process of ordination in this manner:

Those who are worthy may be ordained to offices in the Aaronic Priesthood at the following minimum ages: Deacon, age 12; Teacher, age 14; Priest, age 16. . . .

The Aaronic Priesthood is conferred and brethren are ordained to offices therein under the direction of the Bishop. . . .

Newly baptized male members over the age of 12 should receive the appropriate Aaronic Priesthood office shortly after baptism. Adults may be ordained Priests and considered to be prospective Elders. If they are worthy of baptism, they are worthy of holding the priesthood.

Much of the special work of the Aaronic priesthood supports the Melchizedek priesthood. In a small congregation, an elder may assign a youngster to help with his home teaching. Deacons or other members of the Aaronic order are assigned to collect fast offerings on the first Sunday of each month. It is customary for the teachers to prepare and clear the sacrament elements and table. The deacons usually pass the sacrament each service, while the priests are normally appointed to officiate at the sacrament table. Worthy priests in the Aaronic order may perform the ordinance of baptism.

The LDS church uses this priesthood to groom its young men and new male members for the "higher priesthood." In the *Handbook* (p. 40), the bishop is given a 13-step test of worthiness with which to judge each candidate for advancement. These range from simple instructions to "speak and act honestly" to one that requires the young man to "pay a full tithing" or to a more open-ended one that requires he "do his duty in the Church and live in accordance with its rules and doctrines."

The Biblical View

We must ask, "Is this Aaronic priesthood valid?" Let's go back to the start of the story. Joseph claimed that John the Baptist descended in the flesh, with all parts of his body reattached, restoring the Levitical priesthood of Aaron and conferring it upon Joseph and Oliver. This can only lead one to believe that Joseph Smith had little or no knowledge of Bible history and tradition.

First, Mormon priesthood procedure is very simple in its order of authority. No one who does not hold a priesthood office (or one higher) can ordain or assist in the ordination of any LDS priesthood office. No one—not even Joseph Smith or Oliver Cowdery—could be ordained to the Melchizedek priesthood without first being raised up in the Aaronic. That in itself makes the entire system without merit.

First, Jesus Himself never held the Levitical priesthood, yet the Mormon church agrees that Jesus was our high priest "after the order of Melchizedek." How would this be possible?

As a Restorationist movement, the LDS church has put itself in a box. In its hurry to "restore" the purity of the priesthood order, it left out the Head of the church Himself!

Second, John the Baptist never held the Levitical priesthood and could not restore and pass on something he never had. John wore the skins of an animal and ate food considered unclean to the Levitical priests. He functioned among the people, calling them to repent and be baptized. The Levitical priests functioned within the temple, at the altar. Yet, members of the LDS Levitical priesthood are denied entrance to the LDS temples except to be "sealed" to their parents and to be baptized by proxy for the dead. In these functions, young women (without the priesthood) have equal access.

If the real John the Baptist were a priest, why did the Levite leaders know nothing of it? When Christ challenged them to identify the source of John's authority, they were ignorant that John held any such office (Matthew 21:23-27). Further, the "priesthood" that functions in the LDS church does not deal with the key functions of the Levitical priesthood: the offering of gifts according to the law (Hebrews 8:4).

The Bible declares that if Jesus were on Earth He would not be a priest, since their function was to offer gifts according to the law. Jesus put an end to the law and has given us a better covenant, established upon better promises, and has made the old to vanish away (Hebrews 8:3,6,7,13).

The Bible admonishes that "the deacons be the husbands of one wife, ruling their children and their own houses well" (1 Timothy 3:12). Yet in Mormonism the deacon is a 12-year-old child.

The whole idea of priesthood is upside down in Mormonism. In the Bible the priesthood was to function on behalf of sinful man before God. In Mormonism its function is to act on behalf of God.

ABRAHAM

The LDS Position

The new LDS *Encyclopedia* affirms that the church's approach to the Bible hero Abraham is "unique" among all religions (*Encyclopedia*, 1:7). This is because the LDS founder, Joseph Smith, added a great deal of extra-biblical material about Abraham and his life to the LDS canon of Scripture.

Chief among this pseudepigraphal material is the Book of Abraham, allegedly translated by Joseph Smith from an ancient

Egyptian papyrus (see also *Book of Abraham*). It supposedly recounts the patriarch's adventures in Egypt, including an incident where he nearly became a human sacrifice himself. This account also alleges that Abraham received an ordination to the priesthood (Abraham 2:9-11) and that he saw the Lord, who gave him promises not contained in the Genesis account.

The Biblical View

In the Book of Abraham, God commands Abraham to lie about Sarah in Egypt (Abraham 2:22-25), in contradiction of His nature (Numbers 23:19) and His commandments (Exodus 20:16). Then He bestows upon him a bizarre, ecstatic experience in which Abraham sees the entire universe, including the central planetary system around the throne of God, Kolob (see also *Kolob*). Indeed, many of the stranger LDS doctrines emerge from this book, which has no basis in archaeological, historical, or biblical reality.

Additional distortions of the Genesis account were created by Smith to justify his involvement in fornication and plural marriage. Abraham's taking of his wife's maidservant Hagar is made to seem a virtuous act in LDS scriptures (see *Doctrine and Covenants* 132:34,35).

To the contrary, the biblical accounts make it clear that Abraham's involvement with Hagar was a carnal act designed to "force the hand" of God and bring him an heir, instead of waiting for the child of promise. The fact that Hagar's son Ishmael fathered a race which has been in unceasing conflict with the chosen people indicates how "virtuous" Abraham's choice was.

Additionally, Joseph Smith claimed that Melchizedek taught Abraham about Jesus Christ (*Teachings*, pp. 322-23) and that Melchizedek gave Abraham the Melchizedek priesthood (Genesis 14:18-20; Alma 13:17-19) with all the accompanying temple ordinances. There is, of course, no biblical basis for any of this, and certainly no evidence of godly temple worship in Abraham's day. Indeed, the tabernacle in the wilderness—the first kind of temple to the true God—was raised up centuries after the time of Abraham.

Mormonism begins with a biblical character and proceeds to overlay him with all sorts of unhistorical nonsense until the original character and the message God intended to convey is all but obscured.

ADAM-GOD DOCTRINE

The LDS Position

The Adam-God doctrine is an extension of the law of eternal progression. In the early days of the church, Brigham Young often made comments about "our father, Adam." From there the comments drifted into a teaching that Adam was really God, who came to the Earth to begin the human race with one of his celestial wives, Eve.

The theory was that if Adam was the father of all men and women (which he is), then he is, in Brigham Young's words, "the only God with whom we have to do." Obviously, Adam had a heavenly "Father" also, but he would be off somewhere else; and the most immediate "god of this world," as the Mormons like to put it, would be "Father Adam." Of course, today the LDS leaders repudiate this doctrine as false; but Brigham *did* teach it as a "prophet of God."

Brigham Young taught some interesting things on the subject of Adam. Perhaps the one most often quoted by those who minister to Mormons is the Michael quote:

> Now hear it, O inhabitants of the earth, Jew and Gentile, Saint and sinner! When our father Adam came into the garden of Eden, he came into it with *a celestial body*, and brought Eve, *one of his wives* with him. He helped to make and organize this world. He is MICHAEL, the *Archangel*, the ANCIENT OF DAYS! about whom holy men have written and spoken—HE *is our* FATHER *and our* GOD, *and the only God with whom* WE have to do. Every man upon the earth, professing Christian or nonprofessing, must hear it, and *will know it sooner or later* (*Journal of Discourses* 1:50, emphasis in original).

Of course, there was all but open revolt among the saints and even a general authority or two. A little later on, some of Brigham's statements were less direct and somewhat softer on just who Adam was:

> *Adam and Eve*—Mankind is composed of two distinct elements; the first is a spiritual organization in eternity, the second is a natural organization on this earth, formed out of the

material of which this earth is composed. Man is first spiritual, then temporal.

These spirits I shall leave for the present, and refer to our first parents, Adam and Eve, who were found in the Garden of Eden, tempted and overcome by the power of evil, and consequently subject to evil and sin, which was the penalty of their transgression. They were now prepared, as we are, to form bodies or tabernacles for the reception of pure and holy spirits (*Journal of Discourses*, 18:257).

When Father Adam came to assist in organizing the earth out of the crude material that was found, an earth was made upon which the children of men could live. After the earth was prepared Father Adam came and stayed here, and there was a woman brought to him. There was a certain woman brought to Father Adam whose name was Eve, because she was the first woman, and she was given to him to be his wife (*Journal of Discourses*, 16:167).

Still, Brigham preached a sermon in 1873 that declared "Adam is our Father and God," referring to his statement as a "doctrine" (*Deseret News*, June 18, 1873).

Today the LDS people vehemently deny that their church ever believed the doctrine that Adam was the Ancient of Days, our heavenly Father. It is a battle you need not fight. The stories about Adam God abound, but dealing with them is pretty futile and will lead no one into the saving knowledge of the real God of the Bible.

The Mormon doctrine on Adam being the god of this world simply turns in upon itself. One is left to wonder how a church that once held this to be an essential doctrine of faith can so easily walk away from it, when it had rejected so many who would not receive it as truth.

More subtle than the Adam-God doctrine is the underlying doctrine stated above that all things are created first in the spiritual before becoming temporal.

The Biblical View

Brigham Young had to throw out a great deal of Scripture to make his claim about Adam being God. To be God, Adam had to exist prior to creation itself, yet the Bible clearly shows that Adam (and Eve) were part of the creation. They were created by the God who was God before creation began. That truth carries throughout the Scriptures, but let's just look at a few verses of the Genesis narrative.

> And God said, Let us make man in our image, after our likeness: and let them have dominion over the fish of the sea, and over the fowl of the air, and over the cattle, and over all the earth, and over every creeping thing that creepeth upon the earth. So God created man in his own image, in the image of God created he him; male and female created he them (Genesis 1:26,27).
> And the LORD God formed man of the dust of the ground, and breathed into his nostrils the breath of life; and man became a living soul. And the LORD God planted a garden eastward in Eden; and there he put the man whom he had formed (Genesis 2:7,8).
> And Adam gave names to all cattle, and to the fowl of the air, and to every beast of the field; but for Adam there was not found an help meet for him. And the LORD God caused a deep sleep to fall upon Adam, and he slept: and he took one of his ribs, and closed up the flesh instead thereof; and the rib, which the LORD God had taken from man, made he a woman, and brought her unto the man. And Adam said, This is now bone of my bones, and flesh of my flesh: she shall be called Woman, because she was taken out of Man (Genesis 2:20-23).

The LDS doctrine that all things are created first in the spiritual is tied to the LDS doctrine that man himself is created as a spirit being (see *Preexistence*) before coming to earth to gain a body. The Bible simply and clearly refutes that.

> So also is the resurrection of the dead. It is sown in corruption; it is raised in incorruption: it is sown in dishonour; it is raised in glory: it is sown in weakness; it is raised in power: it is sown a natural body; it is raised a spiritual body. There is a natural body, and there is a spiritual body. And so it is written, The first man Adam was made a living soul; the last Adam was made a quickening spirit. Howbeit that was not first which is spiritual, but that which is natural; and afterward that which is spiritual.
> The first man is of the earth, earthy: the second man is the Lord from heaven. As is the earthy, such are they also that are earthy: and as is the heavenly, such are they also that are heavenly. And as we have borne the image of the earthy, we shall also bear the image of the heavenly (1 Corinthians 15:42-49).

ADAM-ONDI-AHMAN

The LDS Position

In May of 1838, Mormon prophet Joseph Smith and several companions traveled some miles from Far West to a place near Wight's Ferry called Spring Hill. His goal was to lay claim to this site for the purpose of platting a new city. It was there that Joseph informed his brethren that they had come upon a very special place. It was, he said, the place where Adam and his posterity dwelt after Adam and Eve were cast out from the Garden of Eden. It was the very place where Adam gathered his righteous posterity before his death and blessed them and where "the Lord appeared unto them and they rose up and blessed Adam, and called him *Michael, the prince, the archangel.* And the Lord administered comfort unto Adam" (*Doctrine and Covenants* 107:53-56).

Although the local brethren called it Spring Hill, Joseph informed them that "by the mouth of the Lord it was named Adam-Ondi-Ahman, because, said He, it is the place where Adam shall come to visit his people, or the ancient of days shall sit, as spoken of by Daniel the Prophet" (*History*, 3:35).

Heber C. Kimball described his visit there with the prophet Brigham Young and some others. They went to the site where Joseph showed them:

> the ruins of three altars built of stone, one above the other, like unto the pulpits in the Kirkland Temple, representing the order of three grades of priesthood; "There," said Joseph, "is the place where Adam offered sacrifice after he was cast out of the garden." The altar stood at the highest point of the bluff. I went and examined the place several times while I remained there (Doxey, *LDS Prophets and the Doctrine and Covenants*, vol. 4, p. 155).

What may slip by the casual reader is the monumental fact that this place, sitting in the middle of Missouri, is believed by Mormons to be the actual site of the Garden of Eden, the birthplace of mankind. LDS apostle Bruce R. McConkie states it clearly:

> The early brethren of this dispensation taught that the Garden of Eden was located in what is known to us as the land of Zion, an area for which Jackson County, Missouri, is the center

place. In our popular Latter-day Saint hymn which begins, *"Glorious things are sung of Zion, Enoch's city of old,"* we find William W. Phelps preserving the doctrine that *"In Adam-Ondi-Ahman, Zion rose where Eden was"* (*Doctrine*, p. 20).

Later prophet and church president Joseph Fielding Smith confirmed that this was true.

Garden of Eden and City of Zion Same Place

In accord with the revelations given to the prophet Joseph Smith, we teach that the Garden of Eden was on the American continent located where the City Zion, or the New Jerusalem, will be built. When Adam and Eve were driven out of the Garden, they eventually dwelt at a place called Adam-Ondi-Ahman, situated in what is now Davies County, Missouri" (Smith, *Doctrines of Salvation*, vol. 3, p. 74).

A further look at Adam-Ondi-Ahman reveals that Joseph Smith also taught it will be the place where all the things of this last dispensation will wind down. Adam was, in fact, not only Michael the Archangel, but the Ancient of Days spoken of in Daniel 7.

Later prophet and president of the LDS church, Joseph Fielding Smith, taught that:

Not many years hence there shall be another gathering of high priests and righteous souls in this same valley of Adam-Ondi-Ahman. At this gathering Adam, the Ancient of Days will again be present. At this time, the vision which Daniel saw will be enacted. The Ancient of Days will sit (Daniel 7:9-14). There will stand before him those who have held the keys of all dispensations, who shall render up their stewardships to the first Patriarch of the race, who holds the keys of salvation. This shall be a day of judgment and preparation. . . .

He [Daniel] saw the Son of Man come to the grand council, as he did to the first grand council in the valley of Adam-Ondi-Ahman [presumably the one where he blessed Adam] and there he received the keys from Adam. . . . In this council Christ will take over the reigns [sic] of government, officially, on this earth" (Doxey, *LDS Prophets and the Doctrine and Covenants*, vol. 4, pp. 156-57).

The Biblical View

Several things jump out here to the Christian apologist. First, the Mormon church locates the events of the first section of the Book of Genesis right here in America, instead of in the Middle East where everyone else places it. As in most other things, Joseph Smith was operating with a severely limited knowledge of both the Bible and Mideast geography. His "revelation" placing the Garden of Eden in mid-America flies in the face of clear biblical teaching. Today it is doctrinally and geographically absurd for the LDS church to cling to such foolishness. Contrary to Smith's prophetic proclamation, the biblical passages about Eden's location are specific and rooted in genuine, historic landmarks which appear on any world atlas! Genesis says:

> And a river went out of Eden to water the garden; and from thence it was parted, and became into four heads. The name of the first is Pison: that is it which compasseth the whole land of Havilah, where there is gold; and the gold of that land is good: there is bdellium and the onyx stone. And the name of the second river is Gihon: the same is it that compasseth the whole land of Ethiopia. And the name of the third river is Hiddekel: that is it which goeth toward the east of Assyria. And the fourth river is Euphrates (Genesis 2:10-14).

Second, Mormonism claims Adam was also Michael the archangel, as well as the Ancient of Days. This is quite a workload for a man who was also revealed by Brigham Young to be God (Elohim)! (See also *Adam-God Doctrine.*) Although official Mormondom today frowns upon the Adam-God doctrine, the teaching that Adam is the Ancient of Days seems to be the last remaining vestige of it. But the LDS church cannot have it both ways. The biblical Ancient of Days is God the Father.

Third, Mormonism teaches that Christ will "return" to Missouri, where He will rule over the Earth for a thousand years through the management expertise of the LDS priesthood. Mormon theologians claim that Daniel was prophesying about the Latter-day Saints when he said, "Until the Ancient of days came, and judgment was given to the saints of the most High; and the time came that the saints possessed the kingdom" (Daniel 7:22).

The average reader might conclude that these are quaint

teachings or doctrines, silly but hardly serious. While I agree with such an evaluation, I have to say that they are textbook examples of the deceiving powers of Mormonism.

How can any logical, thinking person accept the headship of a theocratic organization that has moved the Garden of Eden halfway around the world? The Scriptures tell us how they came to such a place:

> Because that, when they knew God, they glorified him not as God, neither were thankful; but became vain in their imaginations, and their foolish heart was darkened. Professing themselves to be wise, they became fools, and changed the glory of the uncorruptible God into an image made like to corruptible man, and to birds, and fourfooted beasts, and creeping things (Romans 1:21-23).

ADAMIC LANGUAGE

The LDS Position

Mormonism teaches that Adam spoke a true and pure language, given to him by God. They believe this language has been lost to man and will again be restored in the millennial reign of Christ. Joseph Smith used it in numerous cases in giving names to special people and places.

> Therefore, verily I say unto you, that it is expedient for my servants *Alam* [Edward Partridge] and *Ahashdah* [Newel K. Whitney], *Mahalaleel* [A. Sidney Gilbert] and *Pelagoram* [Sidney Rigdon], and my servant *Gazelam* [Joseph Smith], and *Horah* [John Whitmer] and *Olihah* [Oliver Cowdery], and *Shalemanasseh* [W.W. Phelps] and *Mahemson* [Martin Harris] to be bound together by a bond and covenant that cannot be broken by transgression, except judgment shall immediately follow, in your several stewardships—To manage the affairs of the poor, and all things pertaining to the bishopric both in the land of Zion and in the land of *Shinehah* [Kirtland] (*Doctrine and Covenants* 82:11,12).

In the LDS scripture *The Pearl of Great Price*, it is mentioned in the Book of Moses:

29

And a book of remembrance was kept, in the which was recorded, in the language of Adam, for it was given unto as many as called upon God to write by the spirit of inspiration; and by them their children were taught to read and write, having a language which was pure and undefiled (Moses 6:5,6).

Wherefore teach it unto your children, that all men, everywhere, must repent, or they can in nowise inherit the kingdom of God, for no unclean thing can dwell there, or dwell in his presence; for, in the language of Adam, Man of Holiness is his name, and the name of his Only Begotten is the Son of Man, even Jesus Christ, a righteous Judge, who shall come in the meridian of time (v. 57).

Joseph Smith discovered a place in Missouri that he called "the altar of Adam." He named it "Adam-Ondi-Ahman" and said that it was the place's name in the pure Adamic language.

Evaluation

Those special names today are rarely used and have all but disappeared. It may be that none of those phrases is as identifiable as the words *pay lay ale*. These words were found until recently in the LDS temple ritual.

The meaning of *pay lay ale* in the temple rites has been an item of considerable speculation and controversy. Since the phrase was deleted without explanation from the temple endowment (as of April 1990), it becomes a bit academic.

Temple patrons were told that *pay lay ale* was the words, "O God, hear the words of my mouth" in the true language of Adam. The ritual showed Adam calling out those words at his altar in "the lone and dreary world" portion of the ceremony. The person who answers that cry in the temple drama is Lucifer, however, and thus we have always felt the phrase was out of order. There has been much controversy over what the words actually meant and numerous opinions were given, especially within the ex-Mormon groups.

It is a difficult and tangled situation, but perhaps the best proof of the evil nature of the "pay lay ale" cry is the fact that the church mysteriously deleted it without explanation. If it simply meant "O God, hear the words of my mouth," why remove such a harmless or even noble exclamation? This is a question every thinking Mormon needs to confront.

AGE OF ACCOUNTABILITY

The LDS Position

There is an old Mormon adage which I remember from my years in the church that goes something like this: "Adam fell that men might be, and men are that they might have joy." Mormons do not teach the doctrine of original sin or infant baptism, but do believe in baptismal regeneration—that baptism is for the remission of sins and must be done by those in authority (that is, the LDS priesthood).

This background helps to explain why Mormons have established an actual age of accountability. Bruce R. McConkie states:

> When a child reaches the age at which he has sufficient mental, spiritual, and physical maturity to be held accountable before God for his acts, he is said to have arrived at the years of accountability. He then knows right from wrong and can exercise his agency to do good or evil. Accordingly he must pay the penalty for his sins, unless he gains a remission of them through repentance and baptism (*Doctrine*, p. 853).

McConkie uses the LDS scriptures for his reference source:

> For all men must repent and be baptized, and not only men, but women, and children who have arrived at the years of accountability (*Doctrine and Covenants* 18:42).

> No one can be received into the church of Christ unless he has arrived unto the years of accountability before God, and is capable of repentance (*Doctrine and Covenants* 20:71).

Another LDS scripture reference to note regarding the accountability of children is as follows:

> But behold, I say unto you, that little children are redeemed from the foundation of the world through mine Only Begotten; wherefore, they cannot sin, for power is not given unto Satan to tempt little children, until they begin to become accountable before me (*Doctrine and Covenants* 29:46-47).

What is the actual year of LDS accountability?

And again, inasmuch as parents have children in Zion, or in any of her stakes which are organized, that teach them not to understand the doctrine of repentance, faith in Christ the Son of the living God, and of baptism and the gift of the Holy Ghost by the laying on of the hands, when eight years old, the sin be upon the heads of the parents. For this shall be a law unto the inhabitants of Zion, or in any of her stakes which are organized.

And their children shall be baptized for the remission of their sins when eight years old, and receive the laying on of the hands (*Doctrine and Covenants* 68:25-27).

The Biblical View

The Bible clearly teaches that baptism is for every Christian. Jesus Himself was baptized by John. The core of the biblical doctrine for baptism is this: 1. One must be a believer. 2. One must repent of sin.

Peter, preaching to a multitude of new believers, declared: "Repent, and be baptized every one of you in the name of Jesus Christ for the remission of sins" (Acts 2:38).

To the committed Christian, the act of baptism has a significance that goes beyond the remission of sin. Christ went into the waters of baptism Himself. Obviously, He did not need to repent of sin, but He did act out His own death to self—a pointer to His death and resurrection.

One of my favorite Scriptures is Galatians 2:20: "I am crucified with Christ: nevertheless I live; yet not I, but Christ liveth in me: and the life which I now live in the flesh I live by the faith of the Son of God, who loved me, and gave himself for me."

The Scriptures also tell us:

Know ye not, that so many of us as were baptized into Jesus Christ were baptized into his death? Therefore we are buried with him by baptism into death: that like as Christ was raised up from the dead by the glory of the Father, even so we also should walk in newness of life. For if we have been planted together in the likeness of his death, we shall be also in the likeness of his resurrection: knowing this, that our old man is crucified with him, that the body of sin might be destroyed, that henceforth we should not serve sin (Romans 6:3-6).

It's clear that we need to understand what we are doing in the act of baptism. That requires an independent thought process that is not found in infants or the very young. At what age is it appropriate for a child to be baptized? That seems to be a private matter for the parents to decide.

I have had the joy of baptizing both children and grandchildren. In every case, the baptism was performed on the basis of their *declared* desire to be dead to the flesh and alive in Christ.

AHMAN

The LDS Position

This is believed by Mormons to be the name of God the Father in the "pure language spoken by Adam . . . and which will be spoken again during the millennial era" (*Doctrine*, p. 29). It is said the name is to be translated "Man of Holiness" (see *Pearl of Great Price*, Moses 6:57).

McConkie says the name comes from an unpublished revelation mentioned by LDS apostle Orson Pratt in *Journal of Discourses*, 2:342:

It is given in questions and answers. The first question is, "What is the name of God in the pure language?" The answer says, "Ahman." "What is the name of the Son of God?" Answer, "Son Ahman—the greatest of all the parts of God excepting Ahman." "What is the name of men?" "Sons Ahman," is the answer. "What is the name of angels in the pure language?" "Anglo-man."

McConkie also notes something which has interesting implications for the spiritual origins of Mormonism. As is well known among ancient historians, one of the chief names of the pagan Egyptian sun-god was Ammon. It is also sometimes rendered Amun or Amun-Ra. McConkie writes,

[Ammon] was first worshipped as the local deity of Thebes; he was shown as a ramheaded god of life and reproduction. Later, united with the sun-god to become a supreme deity, he was known as Amen-Ra, with other gods as his members or parts (ibid., p. 30).

Evidently, McConkie feels this somehow supports the truth of Mormonism; but we must look to the Bible to evaluate this strange concept.

The Biblical View

A homonym for Ahman, similar to what McConkie describes, is found in Genesis 19:38. It is Ammon, a name of one of the sons of Lot incestuously conceived by his own daughters following the destruction of Sodom. Ammon, or the "children of Ammon" (Ammonites), are mentioned 85 times in the Bible, and virtually never in any sort of positive way. The hermeneutical principle of the law of first reference implies that it is highly unlikely there is anything holy or sacred about the name since Ammon was conceived in a cursed manner.

Additionally, Ammon and his brother, Moab, both quickly produced idolatrous tribes—the Ammonites and the Moabites—which worshiped the false gods Molech and Chemosh and practiced child sacrifice (Leviticus 18:21; 1 Kings 11:7; Jeremiah 32:35). The true biblical God decreed the death penalty for anyone who worshiped the god of Ammon (Leviticus 20:2-5), and tore the kingdom of Israel away from Solomon for worshiping Ammon's god (1 Kings 11).

Although there are many wonderful names given in the Bible for God, Ahman is never one of them. It would be very difficult to imagine that the true "pure language" name of God would also be the name of one of the most cursed tribes in history.

ANGEL OF LIGHT

The LDS Position

In searching the standard works of Mormonism and the works of Joseph Smith, we find a consistent pattern to the definition of the term "angel of light." In every single case it means an evil angel, the devil himself. The *Book of Mormon* talks about that angel of light:

> O the wisdom of God, his mercy and grace! For behold, if
> the flesh should rise no more our spirits must become subject to

that angel who fell from before the presence of the Eternal God, and became the devil, to rise no more. And our spirits must have become like unto him, and we become devils, angels to a devil, to be shut out from the presence of our God, and to remain with the father of lies, in misery, like unto himself; yea, *to that being who beguiled our first parents, who transformeth himself nigh unto an angel of light, and stirreth up the children of men unto secret combinations of murder and all manner of secret works of darkness* (2 Nephi 9:8-9, emphasis added).

We read about this same evil character in the *Doctrine and Covenants*:

> And again, what do we hear? Glad tidings from Cumorah! Moroni, an angel from heaven, declaring the fulfillment of the prophets—the book to be revealed. A voice of the Lord in the wilderness of Faith, Seance county, declaring the three witnesses to bear record of the book! *The voice of Michael on the banks of the Susquehanna, detecting the devil when he appeared as an angel of light!* The voice of Peter, James, and John in the wilderness between Harmony, Susquehanna county, and Collusive, Broom county, on the Susquehanna river, declaring themselves as possessing the keys of the kingdom, and of the dispensation of the fulness of times! (*Doctrine and Covenants* 128:20).
>
> When a messenger comes saying he has a message from God, offer him your hand and request him to shake hands with you. If he be an angel he will do so, and you will feel his hand. If he be the spirit of a just man made perfect he will come in his glory; for that is the only way he can appear—Ask him to shake hands with you, but he will not move, because it is contrary to the order of heaven for a just man to deceive; but he will still deliver his message.
>
> *If it be the devil as an angel of light, when you ask him to shake hands he will offer you his hand, and you will not feel anything; you may therefore detect him.* These are three grand keys whereby you may know whether any administration is from God (Section 129:4-9, emphasis added).

Joseph Smith talked about this angel of light a number of times:

> *The devil may appear as an angel of light.* Ask God to reveal it; if it be of the devil, he will flee from you; if of God, He will manifest Himself, or make it manifest (*Teachings*, p. 162).

There have also been ministering angels in the Church which were of Satan appearing as an angel of light. A sister in the state of New York had a vision, who said it was told her that if she would go to a certain place in the woods, an angel would appear to her. She went at the appointed time, and saw a glorious personage descending, arrayed in white, with sandy colored hair; he commenced and told her to fear God, and said that her husband was called to do great things, but that he must not go more than one hundred miles from home, or he would not return; whereas God had called him to go to the ends of the earth, and he has since been more than one thousand miles from home, and is yet alive.

Many true things were spoken by this personage, and many things that were false. *How, it may be asked, was this known to be a bad angel? By the color of his hair; that is one of the signs that he can be known by, and by his contradicting a former revelation* (*Teachings*, pp. 214-15, emphasis added).

Evaluation

These are pretty interesting statements from a prophet who claimed he was called of God by an angel who fits the very description he here details! Joseph didn't even challenge or test him, as suggested above.

Is it just a strange coincidence? We doubt it. Listen to how McConkie defines it. Under the heading "Angel of Light," he says, "See Devil." Under the heading "Devil," he says:

See Abaddon, Adversary, Agency, Angel of the Bottomless Pit, Apollyon, Beelzebub, Belial, Cain, Church of the Devil, Common Enemy, Demons, Destroyer, Devils, Dragon, Evil One, God of This World, Hell, Lucifer, Master Mahan, Perdition, Prince of Devils, Prince of Power of the Air, Prince of This World, Satan, Serpent, Son of the Morning, Sons of Belial, Sons of Perdition, Spiritual Death, Tempter. The devil (literally meaning "slanderer") is a spirit son of God who was born in the morning of pre-existence (*Doctrine and Covenants* 76:25-26). Endowed with agency, the free power of choice, he chose the evil part from the beginning, thus placing himself in eternal opposition to the divine will. He was "a liar from the beginning" (*Doctrine and Covenants* 93:25) (*Doctrine*, p. 192).

Nowhere does McConkie clearly attribute anything to the name "angel of light" except a direct reference to Satan himself.

36

Yet, read what has been hidden away all these years in the introduction to the *Doctrine and Covenants*—a secret that reveals the true identity of one of the main characters in the story of Mormonism.

> This [the first vision] took place in the early spring of 1820. In September, 1823, and at later times, Joseph Smith received visitations from *Moroni, an angel of light* [emphasis added], who revealed the resting place of the ancient record from which The Book of Mormon was afterward translated [explanatory introduction to the *Doctrine and Covenants*, page iii. The introduction is no longer found in current editions of *Doctrine and Covenants*].

There is no doubt that Joseph Smith knew what an angel of light was and there is no doubt Mormonism's leaders know today. Moroni was, indeed, an angel of light. Yet, if Moroni was an angel of light—as he is acknowledged to be above—then the gospel and *Book of Mormon* which he revealed would have to be of the devil.

But what of the first vision? Look at it again from the "angel of light" viewpoint:

> So, in accordance with this [the determination to "ask of God"], I retired to the woods to make the attempt. It was on the morning of a beautiful, clear day, early in the spring of eighteen hundred and twenty. It was the first time in my life that I had made such an attempt, for amidst all my anxieties I had never as yet made the attempt to pray vocally.
>
> After I had retired to the place where I had previously designed to go, having looked around me, and finding myself alone, I kneeled down and began to offer up the desires of my heart to God. I had scarcely done so, when immediately I was seized upon by some power which entirely overcame me, and had such an astonishing influence over me as to bind my tongue so that I could not speak. Thick darkness gathered around me, and it seemed to me for a time as if I were doomed to sudden destruction.
>
> But, exerting all my powers to call upon God to deliver me out of the power of this enemy which had seized upon me, and at the very moment when *I was ready to sink into despair and abandon myself to destruction—not to an imaginary ruin, but to the power of some actual being from the unseen world, who had such marvelous power as I had never before felt in any being—just at this*

37

moment of great alarm, I saw a pillar of light exactly over my head, above the brightness of the sun, which descended gradually until it fell upon me.

It no sooner appeared than I found myself delivered from the enemy which held me bound. When the light rested upon me I saw two Personages, whose brightness and glory defy all description, standing above me in the air. One of them spake unto me, calling me by name and said, pointing to the other—This is My Beloved Son. Hear Him *(Pearl of Great Price,* Joseph Smith— History: 14-17, emphasis added).

The Biblical View

In the Bible, we read:

For I am jealous over you with godly jealousy: for I have espoused you to one husband, that I may present you as a chaste virgin to Christ. But I fear, lest by any means, as the serpent beguiled Eve through his subtilty, so your minds should be corrupted from the simplicity that is in Christ. For if he that cometh preacheth another Jesus, whom we have not preached, or if ye receive another spirit, which ye have not received, or another gospel, which ye have not accepted, ye might well bear with him. . . .

For such are false apostles, deceitful workers, transforming themselves into the apostles of Christ. And no marvel; for *Satan himself is transformed into an angel of light. Therefore it is no great thing if his ministers also be transformed* as the ministers of righteousness; whose end shall be according to their works (2 Corinthians 11:2-4,13-15, emphasis added).

Remember that Joseph Smith and his family were already dabbling in Ab Brac, in folk magic. He understood mysticism; he played around in it. Yet he described this "actual being from the unseen world" as "having such marvelous power as he had never felt in any being." And at the moment of succumbing fully to it, he sees this pillar of light, in which come two beings "whose brightness and glory defy all description."

Did Joseph actually succumb to this power from the unseen world? Was he actually delivered *to* it rather than *from* it? Check out what the two personages tell him and notice how closely they fit the description Smith later used to describe bad angels.

Many true things were spoken by this personage, and many things that were false. How, it may be asked, was this known to be a bad angel? By the color of his hair; that is one of the signs that he can be known by, and by his contradicting a former revelation (*Teachings*, pp. 214-15).

These beings certainly delivered some information that directly contradicts Christian orthodoxy.

No sooner, therefore, did I get possession of myself, so as to be able to speak, than I asked the Personages who stood above me in the light, which of all the sects was right (for at this time it had never entered into my heart that all were wrong)—and which I should join.

I was answered that I must join none of them, for they were all wrong; and the Personage who addressed me said that all their creeds were an abomination in his sight; that those professors were all corrupt; that: "they draw near to me with their lips, but their hearts are far from me, they teach for doctrines the commandments of men, having a form of godliness, but they deny the power thereof." He again forbade me to join with any of them; and many other things did he say unto me (*Pearl of Great Price*, Joseph Smith—History: 18-20).

Something is deeply amiss here. Both the first vision and the Moroni visits fit the angel of light scenario to a tee and fly in the face of biblical truth.

Doctrine and Covenants, section 93, talks about the Mormon Jesus. Yet, McConkie has it as a reference to the devil. Here is the context:

And I, John, bear record that I beheld his glory, as the glory of the Only Begotten of the Father, full of grace and truth, even the Spirit of truth, which came and dwelt in the flesh, and dwelt among us.

[12]And I, John, saw that he received not of the fulness at the first, but received grace for grace;

[13]And he received not of the fulness at first, but continued from grace to grace, until he received a fulness;

[14]And thus he was called the Son of God, because he received not of the fulness at the first.

¹⁵And I, John, bear record, and lo, the heavens were opened, and the Holy Ghost descended upon him in the form of a dove, and sat upon him, and there came a voice out of heaven saying: This is my beloved Son.

¹⁶And I, John, bear record that he received a fulness of the glory of the Father;

¹⁷And he received all power, both in heaven and on earth, and the glory of the Father was with him, for he dwelt in him.

¹⁸And it shall come to pass, that if you are faithful you shall receive the fulness of the record of John.

¹⁹I give unto you these sayings that you may understand and know how to worship, and know what you worship, that you may come unto the Father in my name, and in due time receive of his fulness.

²⁰For if you keep my commandments you shall receive of his fulness, and be glorified in me as I am in the Father; therefore, I say unto you, you shall receive grace for grace.

²¹And now, verily I say unto you, I was in the beginning with the Father, and am the Firstborn;

²²And all those who are begotten through me are partakers of the glory of the same, and are the church of the Firstborn.

²³Ye were also in the beginning with the Father; that which is Spirit, even the Spirit of truth;

²⁴And truth is knowledge of things as they are, and as they were, and as they are to come;

²⁵And whatsoever is more or less than this is the spirit of that wicked one who was a liar from the beginning.

This is an unbelievable revelation! The lie from the very pit of hell is right here in the middle of this hodgepodge of insane prattle. It is the same lie that Lucifer laid at the feet of Adam and Eve in the Garden of Eden: the lie that we shall be as gods. The same lie these "glorious beings" brought forth through Joseph Smith!

Another lie: that Jesus Christ was not God within the bosom of God from before time began. This is the Mormon Jesus who went from grace to grace, who did not have the fulness of God, who was "called the Son of God, because he received not of the fulness at the first."

The final word twist, the final play on the minds of men comes in the words, "And truth is knowledge of things as they are, and as they were, and as they are to come; and whatsoever is more or less than this is the spirit of that wicked one who was a liar from the beginning."

Work your way through that one. Mormonism gives us a knowledge of things not as they were, are, or will be, but as they have been given to them by their angel of light—who is "that wicked one who was a liar from the beginning."

ANIMAL SACRIFICES

The LDS Position

Mormons seem to partly understand the saving power of the atonement of Christ, yet have a hard time dealing with the general act of animal sacrifices. Joseph Smith taught:

It is generally supposed that sacrifice was entirely done away when the great sacrifice, the sacrifice of the Lord Jesus was offered up, and that there will be no necessity for the ordinance of sacrifice in the future; but those who assert this are certainly not acquainted with the duties, privileges and authority of the priesthood, or the prophets.

The offering of sacrifice has ever been connected and forms a part of the duties of the priesthood. It began with the priesthood and will be continued until after the coming of Christ, from generation to generation.

These sacrifices, as well as every ordinance belonging to the priesthood will, when the Temple of the Lord shall be built, and the sons of Levi be purified, be fully restored and attended to in all their powers, ramifications and blessings. This ever did and ever will exist when the powers of the Melchizedek Priesthood are sufficiently manifest; else how can the restitution of all things spoken of by the holy prophets be brought to pass. It is not to be understood that the law of Moses will be established again with all its rites and variety of ceremonies; this has never been spoken of by the prophets; but those things which existed prior to Moses' day, namely sacrifice, will be continued.

It may be asked by some, what necessity for sacrifice, since the Great Sacrifice was offered? In answer to which, if repentance, baptism, and faith existed prior to the days of Christ, what necessity for them since that time? (*Teachings*, pp. 172-73).

Bruce R. McConkie tied this right in to the Garden of Eden and referenced LDS scriptural support to show the Lord gave them the order to sacrifice when He cast them from the Garden and the reason for it (*Doctrine*, pp. 664-65):

> The Lord gave them commandments that they should worship the Lord their God and should offer the firstlings of their flocks. . . . And after many days an angel of the Lord appeared unto Adam saying: "Why dost thou offer sacrifices unto the Lord?" (Moses 5:5-8).

The angel then claims that this is to be done as a similitude of the sacrifice of Christ.

The Biblical View

The real power of Christ's sacrifice is lost by McConkie and the rest of the Mormon world. The Bible is clear in the matter. Jesus was our sin offering, our sacrifice, offered once for all. Hebrews 8:4 says that were He on earth today, He would not be a priest, offering gifts according to the law. Remember that He fulfilled the law. It was ended in His sacrifice.

> But Christ being come an high priest of good things to come, by a greater and more perfect tabernacle, not made with hands, that is to say, not of this building; neither by the blood of goats and calves, but by his own blood he entered in once into the holy place, having obtained eternal redemption for us. For if the blood of bulls and of goats, and the ashes of an heifer sprinkling the unclean, sanctifieth to the purifying of the flesh: how much more shall the blood of Christ, who through the eternal Spirit offered himself without spot to God, purge your conscience from dead works to serve the living God? And for this cause he is the mediator of the new testament, that by means of death, for the redemption of the transgressions that were under the first testament, they which are called might receive the promise of eternal inheritance (Hebrews 9:11-15).

The doctrine of the continuation of animal sacrifice as promised by the LDS prophet is a sound example of the unbiblical foundation of Mormonism.

APOLOGETICS

There are those within both the Mormon community and the Christian community who say that we should not confront the Mormons with the errors of their doctrines, but that we should minister only through love and example. They say that we are being contentious and nonbiblical in our behavior, that we are too polemic in our approach. Let's take a look at that problem and see what the biblical position really is in this very important matter.

The word *apologetics* comes from the Greek *apo* ("for") and *logeo* ("to speak"). Webster defines it as a "systematic argumentative discourse in defense (as of a doctrine). Defense of the faith."

Webster says the word *polemics* means "an aggressive attack on or refutation of the opinions or principles of another (as in denouncing heresy)."

The Bible tells us in Jude 3: "Beloved, when I gave all diligence to write unto you of the common salvation, it was needful for me to write unto you, and exhort you that ye should earnestly contend for the faith which was once [for all] delivered unto the saints."

Paul tells us in Philippians 1:7: "Inasmuch as both in my bonds, and in the defence and confirmation of the gospel, ye are all partakers of my grace."

In 2 Timothy 2:15, Paul says, "Study to shew thyself approved unto God, a workman that needeth not to be ashamed, rightly dividing the word of truth."

Further, he says, "Preach the word; be instant in season, out of season [when convenient, when not convenient]; reprove, rebuke, exhort, with all longsuffering and doctrine" (2 Timothy 4:2).

With these exhortations in mind, we must seek to fulfill our commission from the Lord to witness to Mormons and other cultists, as well as to all other people lost in spiritual darkness. That is the biblical pattern.

Defending the Faith in Israel

In the biblical account of Elijah's encounter with the prophets of Baal, we find that Baal worship has been introduced into Israel. Elijah stands before the people and cries: "How long halt ye between two opinions? If the LORD be God, follow him: but if Baal, then follow him" (1 Kings 18:21).

43

He then challenges the prophets of Baal to call down fire from Baal upon the sacrifice that they had prepared. Although they call on Baal from morning to evening, leaping upon the altar and slashing themselves, nothing happens. Elijah derides them: "Cry aloud: for he is a god; either he is talking, or he is pursuing, or he is in a journey, or peradventure he sleepeth, and must be awaked" (1 Kings 18:27).

Then Elijah calls down fire from God which consumes not only the sacrifice, but also the altar stones and the water in the ditch around the altar.

What Did Jesus Say?

In Matthew 12:34,39, Jesus Himself spoke of the false religious leaders of His day: "O generation of vipers, how can ye, being evil, speak good things? . . . An evil and adulterous generation seeketh after a sign."

In Matthew 13:15, He says: "For this people's heart is waxed gross, and their ears are dull of hearing, and their eyes they have closed; lest at any time they should see with their eyes, and hear with their ears, and should understand with their heart, and should be converted, and I should heal them."

In Matthew 15:7, Jesus calls the scribes and Pharisees "hypocrites" and in verse 9 says: "In vain they do worship me, teaching for doctrines the commandments of men."

In Matthew chapter 21, He tells the parable of wicked husbandmen against the religious leaders of Israel. In Matthew 23:23, 24,27,28,33 He says:

> Woe unto you, scribes and Pharisees, hypocrites! For ye pay tithe of mint and anise and cummin, and have omitted the weightier matters of the law, judgment, mercy, and faith: these ought ye to have done, and not to leave the other undone. Ye blind guides, which strain at a gnat and swallow a camel. . . . Woe unto you, scribes and Pharisees, hypocrites! For ye are like unto whited sepulchres, which indeed appear beautiful outward, but are within full of dead men's bones, and of all uncleanness. Even so ye also outwardly appear righteous unto men, but within ye are full of hypocrisy and iniquity. . . . Ye serpents, ye generation of vipers, how can ye escape the damnation of hell?

So many are willing to hear the Jesus of peace and faith, but are reluctant to hear the Jesus who upbraids those teachers who lead their followers into darkness ("blind leaders of the blind"—Matthew 15:14).

The Apostles Speak Out

Next we find the defenders of the faith, the "apologists": Peter in Acts 2:14-41; 3:12-26; 4:8-12; and Stephen in Acts 6:8,10; 7:1-60 speak forcefully against the Jews. In Acts 13:8-12, Paul condemned sorcery, and he spoke against the Jews in Acts 13:16-46; 14:1-4; 17:1-4. Also in Acts 17:16-34, Paul contended with the Jews and then against paganism with the Greeks. Then to the Galatians he defended his apostleship and the teaching of grace against the Judaizers.

The Early Church Fathers

After the apostles came great men of God to defend the church, even when it was considered illegal. First they had to defend the faith against the Jews and the early heretical movements. Afterward they fought against paganism and the many later heresies. The first of these were Quadratus (bishop of Athens) and Aristedes (philosopher of Athens), who wrote a defense of Christianity addressed to Emperor Hadrian c. A.D. 117. Between A.D. 117 and 138, Hegesippus wrote about the heresies of Simeon, Cleobus, Gorthoeus, Masbotheus, Menander, Marcion, Carpocrates, Valentinus, Basilides and Saturnilius and also the Jewish heresies of the Essenes, Galileans, Hemereobaptists, Samaritans, Saducees, and Pharisees.

Later, Justin Martyr wrote his first apology to Emperor Antonius Pius c. A.D. 138. Tatian wrote against the Greeks c. A.D. 163. Justin wrote his second apology to the emperors, his dialogue with Trypho (to the Jews), and his hortatory address to the Greeks. At about this time Athenagoras and Tatian wrote their apologies.

Melito of Sardis wrote a discourse to Emperor Antonius around A.D. 166. During the same period, Dionysius of Corinth and Philip of Gortyna wrote against Marcion, and Theophilus of Antioch wrote against Marcion and others. Apollinaris, bishop of Hierapolis, wrote five books against the Greeks, two books against the Jews, and another against the Phrygian heresy and Montanus.

Musanus Modestus (disciple of Justin) wrote an elegant work to some of the brethren who had swerved from the truth and had embraced the heresy of the Encratites and Tatianus.

Irenaeus, Tertullian, and Origen

Between 170 and 220, Irenaeus, bishop of Lyons, wrote "On Knowledge" against the Greeks and "Against Heresies" or "Overthrow of False Doctrine" in which he outlines and refutes the doctrines of the Gnostics, including Simon Magus, Cerinthus, Valentinus, Marcion, and others. Approximately A.D. 180, Rhoto, a disciple of Tatian, wrote against Marcion and other false teachers. Miltiades wrote against Montanus and the Paraphrygian heresy of Montanism. Apollonius of Rome wrote against the Phrygian heresy and Montanus. Serapion, bishop of Antioch, wrote against the Phrygians.

Around 194, Tertullian wrote his apology and in A.D. 205, Clement of Alexandria refuted the Greek heresiarchs. Between A.D. 205-250, Origen had discourse with Beryllus, winning him back from heresy to the truth. He wrote a reply against Celsus the Epicurian, called "The True Doctrine," and is also credited with debating the Arabians and later the Helcisaites, leading many of these back to orthodoxy. Between A.D. 250-256, Cyprian of Carthage wrote against Novatus and Cornelius of Rome wrote against Novatus and the heresies of the Cathari.

Apologetics in the Councils

During this same period, Dionysius, bishop of Alexandria, wrote against the Novatians, the Sabellians, and later against the schism of Nepos. At the Council of Antioch, a former Sophist refuted Paul of Samosata. In A.D. 314 the Council of Arles was held against the Donatists, and in A.D. 325 the Council of Nicea was held to deal with the Arian heresy.

These are just some of the Church Fathers up to Nicea that defended the faith against the Jews, paganism, and heresies. Had it not been for their polemic and apologetic works, we would know little indeed of these great men from the first four centuries of Christianity. This sort of defense of the faith makes up the greater part of their extant writings.

God Calls the Great Reformers

In addition to these, a host of great men from every age such as Augustine, Martin Luther, and others have spoken out against heresies, excesses, and misuse of power inside and outside the church. Not a few of them died martyr's deaths to defend the faith. Among the tenets they so vigorously defended were the deity of Christ, the Trinity, the sovereignty of God, the inerrancy of Scripture, the depravity of man, the certainty of final retribution, and the heresy of Gnosticism, which is again creeping into Christian doctrine.

Apologists in Our Time

In our own age, men such as Charles Finney (who spoke out against Freemasonry in the church and immorality) have taken a strong stand for the faith. No stronger defender of the faith in modern times has arisen than the late Dr. Walter Martin, founder of the Christian Research Institute, who publicly challenged, rebuked, and debated the false cults and false teachers of the last generation.

We stand therefore with those who have gone before us and say, "Knowing therefore the terror of the Lord, we persuade men" (2 Corinthians 5:11). "Wherefore come out from among them, and be ye separate, saith the Lord, and touch not the unclean thing; and I will receive you, and will be a Father unto you, and ye shall be my sons and daughters, saith the Lord Almighty" (2 Corinthians 6:17,18).

APOSTASY, THE GREAT

The LDS Position

Implicit in the doctrine of Restorationism is the need for something to have been lost or taken away before it can be restored.

Mormonism denies all the central creeds of historic Christianity and has done so from its very inception. Joseph Smith claimed that when he went to a nearby grove of trees to pray and ask God which church was true, God Himself and Jesus Christ both appeared to him:

47

I saw two Personages, whose brightness and glory defy all description, standing above me in the air. One of them spake unto me, calling me by name and said, pointing to the other— This is My Beloved Son. Hear Him!

My object in going to inquire of the Lord was to know which of all the sects was right, that I might know which to join. No sooner, therefore, did I get possession of myself, so as to be able to speak, than I asked the Personages who stood above me in the light, which of all the sects was right (for at this time it had never entered into my heart that all were wrong)—and which I should join.

I was answered that I must join none of them, for they were all wrong; and the Personage who addressed me said that all their creeds were an abomination in his sight; that those professors were all corrupt; that: "they draw near to me with their lips, but their hearts are far from me, they teach for doctrines the commandments of men, having a form of godliness, but they deny the power thereof" (*Pearl of Great Price*, Joseph Smith—History 1:17-19).

The word *abomination* refers to something that stinks in God's nostrils; it's about as severe a word as you can find in the Bible. Yet it's how the LDS church officially characterizes our different denominations. It *is* Mormon doctrine, however much in recent times they may want to cover it up. Even the *Book of Mormon* teaches it:

Behold, there are save *two churches only*; the one is the church of the Lamb of God, and the other is the church of the devil; wherefore, *whoso belongeth not to the church of the Lamb of God belongeth to that great church, which is the mother of abominations*; and she is the whore of all the earth (1 Nephi 14:10, emphasis added).

To the Mormon, only the Mormon church is true; therefore all other churches are "great and abominable." If Mormonism is true, then all other Christian bodies are false. Mormons teach that the power and authority was taken away from earth and was not restored until Joseph Smith made physical contact in a grove of trees with the almighty God, Creator of heaven and earth.

Implicit in the LDS church's argument is the idea that the church collapsed (or apostasized) soon after the death of the apostles and the world was separated fully from God. Bruce R. McConkie in *Doctrine*, pp. 43-44, puts that situation into Mormon perspective:

> This universal apostasy began in the days of the ancient apostles themselves (2 Peter 2:1-2); and it was known to and foretold by them. Paul recorded specifically that the Second Coming would not be until this great falling away took place (2 Thessalonians 2:1-12). He warned of the "perilous times" that should come "in the last days"; times when men would have "a form of godliness," but would deny "the power thereof"; times when they would be "Ever learning, and never able to come to the knowledge of the truth" (2 Timothy 3:1-7); times in which they would be turned "from the truth unto fables" (2 Timothy 4:1-4). Our Lord foretold the perplexities, calamities, and apostate wickedness of these same days (Matthew 24; Mark 13; Luke 21).
>
> With the loss of the gospel, the nations of the earth went into a moral eclipse called the Dark Ages. Apostasy was universal. "Darkness covereth the earth, and gross darkness the minds of the people, and all flesh has become corrupt before my face" (*Doctrine and Covenants* 112:23). And this darkness still prevails except among those who have come to a knowledge of the restored gospel (*Doctrines of Salvation*, vol. 3, pp. 265-326).

The Biblical View

All this contradicts the Bible, for Jesus said He would be "with you alway, even unto the end of the world" (Matthew 28:20), and also that "upon this rock I will build my church; and the gates of hell shall not prevail against it" (Matthew 16:18). The divinely inspired Paul also wrote, "Unto him be glory in the church by Christ Jesus throughout all ages, world without end. Amen" (Ephesians 3:21).

Now if Jesus promised He would be with us always and that the gates of hell could never prevail against His church, how could there have been such a universal apostasy as Joseph Smith taught? How could Jesus be glorified by His church "throughout all ages" if from A.D. 300-1830 it was drowning in apostasy? Certainly there have been times when the church was not all it should be, but Jesus was still with it totally and prevented hell from crushing it.

No real Christian church believes that it is the "one true church." The true church is an organism, not an organization. It is the body of Christ, made up of Baptists, Presbyterians, Pentecostals, etcetera, all of whom worship the same God and believe the same essential truths. They may differ in minor things, but in the essentials they are one. They are the living body of Christ and always have been.

APOSTATE

The word *apostate* in LDS circles comes with a tone of dread. To the Mormon, the Great Apostasy following the death of the original apostles brought with it an age of darkness and the absence of God. For a Mormon, to be labeled an apostate is perhaps the worse curse that could be put upon a living person.

For an active, believing member of the Mormon church to turn from it, even to become a member of a strict, Bible-believing church, the end is eternal death. Here is the word of the Mormon god on the subject:

> Thus saith the Lord concerning all those who know my power, and have been made partakers thereof, and suffered themselves through the power of the devil to be overcome, *and to deny the truth and defy my power*—they are they who are the sons of perdition, of whom I say that it had been better for them never to have been born; for they are vessels of wrath, doomed to suffer the wrath of God, with the devil and his angels in eternity; *concerning whom I have said there is no forgiveness in this world nor in the world to come* [emphasis added].
>
> Having denied the Holy Spirit after having received it, and having denied the Only Begotten Son of the Father, having crucified him unto themselves and put him to an open shame. These are they who shall go away into the lake of fire and brimstone, with the devil and his angels—and the only ones on whom the second death shall have any power; yea, verily, the only ones who shall not be redeemed in the due time of the Lord, after the sufferings of his wrath (*Doctrine and Covenants* 76:31-38).

The apostate who leaves the church through the door of the excommunication process does have a way back through that same door. He can return through the same church courts, following the steps of repentance and rebaptism and eventual restoration to full fellowship.

On the other hand, the one who is called a "son of perdition" is the one who leaves the church and begins to "deny the truth and defy my power"—the ex-Mormon who becomes an anti-Mormon. Here is what the church's encyclopedia says about such a person:

> Apostates sometimes become enemies of the Church. Leaving the Church, which claims to be God's official church, containing the fulness of the gospel, often results in feelings of guilt. While many return, others develop a need to defend their actions, "disprove" the Church, or become hostile enemies. The fruits of apostasy are generally bitter (*Encyclopedia*, vol. 1, p. 59).

Citing myself as an example of an apostate Mormon who has also become an anti-Mormon, the writers say this:

> A current example of ridicule and distortion of Latter-day Saint beliefs comes from Edward Decker, an excommunicated Mormon and co-founder of Ex-Mormons for Jesus, now known as Saints Alive in Jesus. Professing love for the Saints, Decker has waged an attack on their beliefs. Latter-day Saints see his film and book, both entitled *The God Makers*, as a gross misrepresentation of their beliefs, especially the *temple ordinances* (ibid., p. 51).

It is to this type of ex-member that the LDS god sent a strong word of warning to Joseph Smith:

> Hearken and hear, O ye my people, saith the Lord and your God, ye whom I delight to bless with the greatest of all blessings, ye that hear me; and ye that hear me not will I curse, that have professed my name, with the heaviest of all cursings (*Doctrine and Covenants* 41:1).

Joseph also applied Hebrews 6:4-6 to this class of men:

> For it is impossible for those who were once enlightened, and have tasted of the heavenly gift, and were made partakers of the Holy Ghost, and have tasted the good word of God, and the powers of the world to come, if they shall fall away, to renew them again unto repentance, seeing they crucify to themselves the Son of God afresh, and put Him to an open shame (*Teachings*, p. 339).

This means there is absolutely no room for negotiation for the Mormon who becomes a born-again Christian and wants to actively attend a different church. He is excommunicated and cast off as apostate. While it should not concern a Christian to be cast out from a cult, there can be serious emotional and financial problems involved.

If the one cast out is married to a Mormon (which is usually the case), the family erupts into chaos. When children are involved, it gets even worse. Add to that the good possibility that other Mormon influences are involved such as parents, brothers and sisters, and business relationships. The ex-member may be employed by another Mormon who must separate from the apostate.

Recently a young student at Brigham Young University (BYU), Michelle Warner, had been attending the Evangelical Free Church in Orem. *The Salt Lake Tribune* reported (Saturday, March 20, 1993, C1) that: "Mormon students at BYU who leave the faith or affiliate with another religion will be barred permanently from the school under a new written policy governing such cases."

Only rebaptism in the LDS church will allow a student to return to the school. The paper reported that:

> A small but growing number of Mormon students had requested that their names be removed from church rolls. Others have just started attending other churches. . . . However, a recent case involving a holder of one of the school's most prestigious scholarships led to the written policy. Michelle Warner, a Benson scholar, was excommunicated from the church in January for requesting that her name be struck from church rolls, and was barred immediately from BYU.

Michelle, like so many other Mormons, had found the peace that comes with making Jesus Christ her Lord and Savior. It is ironic that the church that calls itself by His own name would cast her out from among them for this great "heresy."

APRONS, TEMPLE

The LDS Position

Special aprons are worn as part of the ceremonial temple robes in the LDS church. They are made of green satin or other cloth, with a design (of varying degrees of ornamentation) of fig leaves sewn into them. The aprons are about a foot and a half square and are tied about the waist.

Mormons are formally invested with these aprons in the temple endowment during the "Garden of Eden" scene (see also *Endowments*). They are intended to represent the fig-leaf aprons worn by Adam and Eve after their eating of the forbidden fruit. After the actors in the film or live performance have eaten the fruit and then hear "Father" (the LDS god) coming back down into the garden, Lucifer advises them, "See, you are naked. Take some fig-leaves and make you aprons. Father will see your nakedness. Quick! Hide!" (Sackett, p. 28).

Adam responds by agreeing with Lucifer and saying, "Come, let us hide." Immediately after this the narrative stops, and all temple patrons are advised to put on their aprons. This is the first item of ceremonial clothing put on in the endowment (other than the temple garment, which was added earlier in the initiatory work).

This apron is later removed and placed over the robes of the holy priesthood, which are pure white (Sackett, p. 37). It remains a striking, key feature of the priesthood robes worn by either men or women in the temple. Faithful temple Mormons are also buried in their robes, including the apron.

A strange, darker note is added to this scenario when we backtrack and realize that a satanic symbolism has been applied to the fig-leaf apron by the writers of the very endowment ritual itself. Just seconds before the point in the narrative just described, Adam and Eve begin to recognize the true identity of Lucifer. Eve says, "Thou art Lucifer, he who was cast out of Father's presence for rebellion" (Sackett, p. 28).

The sinister element is this: Lucifer also has been wearing an apron. In the few remaining LDS temples where the endowment ritual is performed with "live" actors instead of films, the actor playing Lucifer wears a blue apron of the same shape as the later fig-leaf model. The apron is covered with Masonic-looking markings (see *Endowment: Similarity to Masonry and Occultism*). In the film version, it is a plain, dark-blue apron, the same as the fig-leaf aprons revealed later.

In the endowment, Adam challenges Lucifer as to the nature of the apron he is wearing. Lucifer replies arrogantly that it is the "symbol of my power and Priesthoods." This is key, because LDS theology knows of only two priesthoods, the Aaronic priesthood and the Melchizedek. Yet Lucifer is identifying these priesthoods as *his*. Adam seems as puzzled as the temple patrons are and asks, "Priesthoods?"

Lucifer simply replies with enigmatic finality: "Yes. Priesthoods," as if that answered all questions (Sackett, p. 28). Of course, all it does is raise serious questions. If Lucifer is fallen, what is he doing with an emblem of the priesthood? Supposedly, in LDS doctrine, no unrighteous person can hold the priesthood (*Doctrine and Covenants* 121:34-37), and yet here it seems that the most unrighteous one of all is holding it. Additionally, no one can hold the priesthood without a physical tabernacle (body), yet Lucifer has been eternally denied a tabernacle of flesh. Why does the Lord allow him to wear an apron, which is the symbol of his priesthoods? These are not easy questions for the temple patron to answer.

Within seconds of this dialogue, temple patrons are asked to put on aprons which are identical to Lucifer's except for color and to continue to wear them as part of their "garments of the holy priesthood." It is no wonder some temple patrons come away a bit uneasy with the entire episode.

Additionally, it is undeniable that this kind of apron has a long and very dubious history as a central artifact in Freemasonry, ceremonial magic, and occultism (Schnoebelen & Spencer, 1987, pp. 20-23). This is just one more indication of the deceptive and occult roots of the supposedly sacred LDS temple ceremonies.

The Biblical View

The strange doctrinal elements in all this are apparent from the biblical account of the Garden of Eden scene and also from the internal logic of the temple endowment itself. It is clear from the Genesis account that although Adam and Eve did indeed make fig-leaf aprons, God immediately rejected them. Instead, He made them "coats of skin" (Genesis 3:21). These skins were obviously of animals, perhaps even from a lamb, and thus could only have been made by the Lord through the shedding of blood.

The fig-leaf aprons clearly represent a bloodless attempt to cover sin, an effort involving human effort and artifice. On the other hand, God Himself made the skin coverings for our first parents, shedding innocent blood to do it. Thus the garments made by the Lord are a clear type of the covering of the blood of the Lamb of God, provided without human works (see Ephesians 2:8,9).

It is an ironic commentary on the biblical ignorance of Mormon leaders and the flawed nature of their "gospel plan" that they have chosen to retain the fig-leaf apron—a symbol of works-salvation which God rejected—as a prominent emblem in the temple regalia.

Although most temple Mormons have learned to live with the ambiguity of the apron's place in the endowment rite, its inversion of key biblical doctrine is clear and very disturbing.

ARTICLES OF FAITH

The LDS Position

The LDS church has issued a statement of its creed for the general public. Although it has been changed at least once, this statement is regarded as "Scripture" and is published as part of *The Pearl of Great Price*.

The Articles of Faith were originally published by the LDS church as part of the *Book of Commandments* in 1833. Originally there were 14 of them, but today there are only 13. The missing article is a statement about belief in the literal resurrection of the body. No "official" explanation has ever been offered by the church as to why the number was pared to 13.

The Articles of Faith are a masterpiece of saying as little as possible while seeming to say everything. Even McConkie (*Doctrine*, p. 53) admits that almost none of the major doctrines of Mormonism are contained therein: "The Articles of Faith are silent on such things as celestial marriage, salvation for the dead, temple work in all its phases, the resurrection, and degrees of glory in the eternal worlds."

Until recently, LDS leaders made no mention of the Mormon doctrine of eternal progression, certainly a central doctrine of the church. Investigators are now given a pamphlet titled "Eternal Progression," but "becoming a god" is not mentioned. Instead, investigators are told how they might "become like our Heavenly Father." It is evident that the Articles were designed for non-LDS consumption and thus studiously downplay any of the controversial or distinctive doctrines of Mormonism.

Nevertheless, one must read through the Articles of Faith with a careful eye for definitions of terms. Affirmations which on the surface seem impeccably orthodox actually reflect doctrines which are anything but biblical. A good example of this is the first Article: "We believe in God, the Eternal Father, and in His Son Jesus Christ, and in the Holy Ghost."

It is almost necessary to apply LDS "subtitles" to the statement in order to understand what the LDS church really believes about the Godhead:

"We believe in God, the Eternal Father...

[who is not Almighty God, because there is a Father God over him, and a Grandfather over him, etc.; He is not eternal, because eternal means everlastingly unchangeable (Malachi 3:6), and the LDS "Father" has evolved into a god from manhood. His "fatherhood" is of an unbiblical variety. Mormons believe Heavenly Father conceived all of us through sex in the spirit world between himself and one of his goddess wives. He has a finite, physical body and is neither all-present, nor all-powerful, nor all-knowing.]

... and in His Son Jesus Christ...

[who is not Almighty God either in the way confessed since New Testament times (John 1:1-14; 8:58; 10:30; Colossians 1:15-19; 2:9; 1 Timothy 3:16; 1 John 2:22; 4:1-3; Revelation 1:7,8; 22:13-16); this Jesus is our elder brother, and there is no qualitative difference between him and Lucifer, or even between him and you and me. He is just a little better, a little older, and a little wiser. He also was not born of a virgin and did not die to save us from our sins.]

... and in the Holy Ghost."

[who is not Almighty God either. By LDS standards, he really can't be any kind of god since he doesn't have a physical body, but is only a spirit. This Holy Ghost cannot really regenerate or sanctify us, neither is he omniscient nor omnipresent. Additionally, LDS doctrine replaces the Trinity with the idea of a three-god committee. Thus, Mormons are polytheists.]

Similar explanatory notes should be added to virtually all the Articles of Faith:

Article 2: We believe that men will be punished for their own sins, and not for Adam's transgression.

[This subtly denies the Christian doctrine of original sin (1 Kings 8:46; Psalm 51:5; Isaiah 53:6; 64:6; Matthew 15:19; Romans 3:23) which Mormons reject, and also denies that Adam really sinned. He only "transgressed."]

Article 3: We believe that through the Atonement of Christ all mankind may be saved, by obedience to the laws and ordinances of the [Mormon] Gospel.

[This denies the biblical doctrine of salvation by grace without works (John 6:29; Romans 3:27; Galatians 2:16; 3:2; Ephesians 2:8,9) and affirms that only through membership in the LDS church and obedience to the laws and ordinances established by them can people be truly saved.]

Article 4: We believe that the first principles and ordinances of the Gospel are: first, Faith in the Lord Jesus Christ; second, repentance; third, Baptism by immersion for the remission of sins; fourth, laying on of hands for the gift of the Holy Ghost.

[Same critique as for Article 3. Additionally, it is faith in another Jesus (2 Corinthians 11:4); it is the teaching of the unscriptural doctrine of baptismal regeneration, and that *only* a baptism performed by a LDS priesthood holder is valid.]

Article 5: We believe that a man must be called of God, by prophecy, and by the laying on of hands by those who are in authority, to preach the Gospel and administer in the ordinances thereof.

[This is a subtle denial of the validity of the callings of all Christian pastors and evangelists. The phrase "by those in authority" means only those who hold the LDS Melchizedek priesthood. Yet there is *no scriptural warrant* for the necessity of "laying on of hands" in order to be a preacher. There is no biblical record that Jesus ever laid hands on any of the apostles to "ordain" them to any priesthood whatever.]

Article 6: We believe in the same organization that existed in the Primitive Church, namely, apostles, prophets, pastors, teachers, evangelists, and so forth.

[Mormons do not tell you that they also have a large number of offices never mentioned in the New Testament, such as the LDS First Presidency, stake presidents, branch presidents, and even 12-year-old deacons. They also do not tell you that there is no evidence in the New Testament for a hierarchical Christian priesthood structure underneath a First Presidency which owns and controls all the corporate assets. In fact, nowhere in the New Testament or in contemporary, historic writings do we see either the actual office of such a trio or the function of the office described.]

Article 7: We believe in the gift of tongues, prophecy, revelation, visions, healing, interpretations of tongues, and so forth.

[They do not tell you that they define these terms differently from biblical Christians, or that they refuse to submit their "prophecies and visions" to the test of biblical scrutiny according to Isaiah 8:20 and 1 Corinthians 14:29.]

Article 8: We believe the Bible to be the word of God as far as it is translated correctly; we also believe the Book of Mormon to be the word of God.

[This denies the biblical teaching that the Bible has been faithfully transmitted to us down through the centuries by the power of the Holy Spirit (Matthew 5:18; 1 Peter 1:25; Isaiah 40:8; 51:6; Psalm 119:89; 12:6,7; 19:7,8; Luke 16:17). There is no biblical evidence of the need for additional "scriptures" such as the *Book of Mormon.*]

Article 9: We believe all that God has revealed, all that He does now reveal, and we believe that He will yet reveal many great and important things pertaining to the Kingdom of God.

[This denigrates the all-sufficient, definitive power of biblical revelation to give us the knowledge we need to be saved (Hebrews 1:1,2; Acts 20:27). It legitimizes the Mormon latter-day "prophecies" and prepares the believer for the continuation of such utterances from the mouths of their "living oracles" as though they speak the words of God Himself. It also makes no provision for testing or checking these "great and important things."]

Article 10: We believe in the literal gathering of Israel and in the restoration of the Ten Tribes; that Zion (the New Jerusalem) will be built upon the American continent; that Christ will reign personally upon the earth; and that the earth will be renewed and receive its paradisical glory.

[Eschatalogical material is harder to pin down biblically; but there is certainly no biblical evidence for the New Jerusalem being established in America.]

Article 11: We claim the privilege of worshipping Almighty God according to the dictates of our own conscience, and allow men the same privilege, let them worship how, where or what they may.

[Mormons don't worship "Almighty God" at all, but just a mythical, extraterrestrial superhuman being who has gods above him. They also send out over 40,000 missionaries to tell people that the church they attend is wrong, abominable, and corrupt.]

Article 12: We believe in being subject to kings, presidents, rulers, and magistrates, in obeying, honoring, and sustaining the law.

[Except when it interferes with LDS practices, as in the many years of illegal polygamy practiced in Utah.]

Article 13: We believe in being honest, true, chaste, benevolent, virtuous, and in doing good to all men; indeed, we may say that we follow the admonition of Paul—We believe all things, we hope all things, we have endured many things, and hope to be able to endure all things. If there is anything virtuous, lovely or of good report or praiseworthy, we seek after these things.

[This is often true and often not true, since it is hard to maintain such high standards as this without the help of a regenerated heart and the grace of the Holy Spirit.]

AUTHORITY: Who in Mormonism Is Authoritative?

Very often, a Mormon witnessing to a Christian friend will give away some interesting LDS book, tape, or video to encourage the friend to look deeper into their faith. But when a Christian uses that or some other material to question the Mormon regarding nonorthodox doctrine, the Mormon will usually claim that the referenced material is not authorized. The Mormon will say that the authority being quoted is speaking for himself and not for the church. We are often told that the only material by which the church can be judged are the *Standard Works* and formal, direct statements from the First Presidency. Anything that would change eternal doctrine would have to come as a revelation and be voted on in General Conference.

This is an easy "out." Most of the nonorthodox practices of Mormonism are found in none of the "official places." For example, the details of the sacred LDS temple ritual are found nowhere in these documents. Nor was there any *official* announcement of recent revisions to the temple ritual. Nowhere is there a word in *official* documents about temple garments.

If you are a Christian who has hit this wall in attempting to dialogue with a Mormon, you need to understand something. The LDS church tends to deceive its own people as well as the general populace by not laying all its cards on the table—particularly those who are recent converts to the LDS Church and who have yet to be *fully instructed* are not immediately told the more odd doctrines of the church. They are *never* mentioned to investigators of the church. The material the investigator and the new convert hears about and from the general authorities is all the "good stuff," the faith-building stuff. The "bad stuff" we Christian apologists write about is hidden away from the new Mormons.

We often have to explain to these new converts what Mormonism really teaches in order to encourage them not to believe it. In fact, we are the first people to tell some Mormons about the bedrock doctrine of Mormonism: the law of eternal progression.

Once you get down to describing what their leaders have taught and still teach, you get right back to the problem of who and what are the real authorities of Mormonism.

Many of the blasphemies of early LDS "prophets" like Joseph Smith and Brigham Young are dismissed with a wave of the hand as the chatty musings of their leaders on an off day.

But the fact is, these prophets of Mormonism believed and clearly stated that the sermons they preached were utterly gospel truth! In fact, Brigham Young stated the following:

> I have never yet preached a sermon and sent it out to the children of men, that they may not call Scripture. Let me have the privilege of correcting a sermon, and it is as good Scripture as they deserve. The people have the oracles of God continually (*Journal of Discourses*, 13:950).
>
> The Lord almighty leads this Church, and he will never suffer you to be led astray if you are found doing your duty. You may go home and sleep as sweetly as a babe in its mother's arms as to any danger of your leaders leading you astray (ibid., 9:289).

Joseph Fielding Smith, another LDS "prophet," proclaimed:

> What is Scripture? When one of the brethren stands before a congregation of the people today and the inspiration of the Lord is upon him, he speaks that which the Lord would have him speak. It is just as much scripture as anything you will find in any of these records and yet we call these the standard works of the Church. We depend, of course, upon the guidance of the brethren, who are entitled to inspiration (Joseph Fielding Smith, *Doctrines of Salvation*, 1954, vol. 1, p. 186).
>
> Therefore it behooves us, as Latter-day Saints, to put our trust in the presiding authorities of the Church . . . no man ever went astray by following the counsel of the authorities of the Church (ibid., p. 243).

This clearly means that if Ezra Taft Benson, Brigham Young, Joseph Smith, or any other apostle (such as Bruce R. McConkie or Orson Pratt) have written something or preached something, it will be doctrinally correct and as authoritative as the Bible or the *Book of Mormon*, according to LDS theology.

One way to successfully respond to this is to point out that the item referenced was published in a book or magazine sold at LDS-owned bookstores and is the work of an official LDS general authority.

The question then must be asked and answered by the Mormon: Is the referenced leader telling the truth or is he lying? How could the church produce or sell the referenced item if it presented a doctrine that was opposite to the official doctrine?

BAAL

Baal is the false, pagan god of the Phoenicians and the Canaanites. Indeed, he was their supreme male deity. As in most pagan pantheons, Baal had a female consort (named Ashtoreth). In the Old Testament, Baal is one of the chief rival deities of the true God for the affections of the people of Israel. He first shows up in Numbers 22:41 and is probably mentioned more by name than any other false god in the Old Testament. His name is literally translated as "lord" or "sun."

It was with Baal that the climactic battle on Mount Carmel took place, when Elijah, God's true prophet, challenged the 400 prophets of Baal to a duel (1 Kings 18). At the time, God's chosen people seem to have been given over to the Baal cult because of the influence of King Ahab and his vile, heathen wife Jezebel (within whose name the name Baal, or Bel can be found). Thus, Baal worship remains a substantial biblical metaphor for false religion of any kind.

Bruce R. McConkie (*Doctrine*, p. 68) substantially agrees with the above information in his work and gives a cross-reference to the entry "False Gods." There, more useful information is available:

> As pertaining to this universe, there are three Gods: the Father, Son, and Holy Ghost. All other supposed deities are false gods.

However, the mere worship of a god who has the proper scriptural names does not assure one that he is worshipping the true and living God. The true names of Deity, for instance, are applied to the false concepts of God found in the apostate creeds of the day. "There is but one only living and true God who is infinite in being and perfection," the Presbyterian Confession of Faith correctly recites, and then proceeds to describe a false god who is "without body, parts, or passions, immutable, immense, eternal, incomprehensible," and so forth (*Doctrines of Salvation*, vol. 1, p. 2).

From the beginning of history the great masses of men have worshipped false gods. Those who believe the creeds of Christendom profess to worship an incomprehensible, unknowable, immaterial essence that fills the immensity of space and is everywhere and nowhere in particular present. Heathen and pagan peoples in all ages have worshipped idols; the liberal Athenian philosophers paid homage to what they called, "The Unknown God" (Acts 17:22-31). There are those who set their whole hearts on learning, money, power, and the like, until these things become in effect their god. There is no salvation in the worship of false gods. For such false worship the Lord imposed the death penalty in ancient Israel (Deuteronomy 13:6-11) (pp. 269-70).

It needs to be pointed out here that McConkie describes as false the God of historic orthodoxy (as described in the Presbyterian confession). This is especially ironic because the very qualities which he rejects—pure Spirit, omniscient, omnipresent, incomprehensible—are the qualities which set apart the God of the Bible from Baal and his ilk.

It is evident both from the Bible and from history that Baal was an anthropomorphic (man-shaped) god. Just like the god of Mormonism, he came fully equipped (to be delicate about it) with "body, parts, and passions." Idols of Baal emphasize his fertility and reproductive prowess. This is exactly like the Mormon god, who comes equipped with a full set of reproductive organs and reproduces sexually. The biblical God is a Spirit (John 4:24) and not manlike (Numbers 23:19), and it is ludicrous to think He reproduces sexually.

Like Baal, the Mormon god has a consort known as the "Heavenly Mother" (see also *Heavenly Mother*). The biblical God has *no* consort, and the idea of Asherah (plural of Ashtoreth) or "queens of heaven" is soundly condemned as abominable in the Old Testament (see Jeremiah 7:18 and elsewhere).

Like the Mormon god, Baal is limited by a body. He cannot be in more than one place at one time. Even Elijah, in the Mount Carmel episode, mocks this limiting feature of Baal. When the prophets of Baal cannot get their god to respond, "Elijah mocked them, and said, Cry aloud: for he is a god; either he is talking, or he is pursuing, or he is in a journey, or peradventure he sleepeth, and must be awaked" (1 Kings 18:27).

This is exactly like the LDS god, who might be "out of the office" at the moment because he cannot be omnipresent. Thus, the very traits McConkie denigrates as those of false gods are those which distinguish the truth of the God of the Bible from the falsity of Baal (and the Mormon "Elohim").

BABYLON

Babylon (originally known as Babel, "gate of God") was a mighty capital built on the plains of Shinar (see Genesis 10:10). It was built on the Euphrates River about 2600 B.C. and measured a vast square of 56 miles in circumference. Legend, with considerable biblical basis, attributes its construction and subsequent prominence to Nimrod.

Babylon's architecture and famed "hanging gardens" were said to be one of the seven wonders of the ancient world. Under the reign of Nebuchadnezzar, it became one of the most persistent persecutors of the kingdom of Judah. Because of its opposition to Israel, the Lord ultimately allowed Babylon's utter destruction, first under Darius the Mede; then through Cyrus, king of Persia; and ultimately by Alexander the Great (Daniel 5:30,31).

LDS author Bruce R. McConkie puts a uniquely Mormon spin on this history:

As the seat of world empire, Babylon was the persistent persecutor and enemy of the Lord's people. It was to escape the imminent destruction of Jerusalem by Nebuchadnezzar's Babylonian hordes *that Lehi and his family were led to the new world.* To the Lord's people anciently, Babylon was known as the center of iniquity, carnality, and worldliness. Everything connected with it was in opposition to all righteousness and had the effect of leading men downward to the destruction of their souls.

It was natural, therefore, for the apostles and inspired men of New Testament times to apply the name Babylon to the forces organized to spread confusion and darkness in the realm of spiritual things (Revelation 17; 18; *Doctrine and Covenants* 29:21; Ezekiel 38; 39). In a general sense, the wickedness of the world generally is Babylon (*Doctrine and Covenants* 1:16; 35:11; 64:24; 133:14).

As Babylon of old fell to her utter destruction and ruin, so the great and abominable church together with all wickedness shall be utterly destroyed when the Lord comes. Before that great day the servants of the Lord are calling, "Go ye out from Babylon" (*Doctrine and Covenants* 133:5,7), for the time is not far distant when "BABYLON THE GREAT, THE MOTHER OF HARLOTS AND ABOMINATIONS OF THE EARTH" (Revelation 17:5) shall receive her foreordained doom, and an angel shall proclaim the fateful judgment: "Babylon is fallen, is fallen, that great city, because she made all nations drink of the wine of the wrath of her fornication (Revelation 14:8, emphasis added) (*Doctrine*, p. 68).

Although much of this is in substantial agreement with the biblical truths concerning Babylon's typology, many of the details are pure Mormon fiction—and conflict with the Bible. "Lehi" is a character from the *Book of Mormon*. By leaving Jerusalem and taking his family to the New World, he would have been substantially out of the revealed will of the Lord, according to the Book of Jeremiah.

Also, the "great and abominable church" mentioned above means, to Mormons, all Christian churches that do not accept the "restored gospel" of Joseph Smith. Indeed, one of the pillars upon which Mormonism stands is the idea of the unique truth of its revelation and the utter corruption of all other churches. In *The Pearl of Great Price* (*History* 1:19) we still read as "inspired scripture" the following statement about Christian churches:

I [Joseph Smith] was answered that I must join none of them, for they were all wrong; and the Personage [Jesus] who addressed me said that all their creeds were an abomination in his sight; that those professors were all corrupt; that: "they draw near to me with their lips, but their hearts are far from me, they teach for doctrines the commandments of men, having a form of godliness, but they deny the power thereof."

Thus, despite all the earnest and warm dialogue about ecumenism lately coming from the LDS church, we who are historic, biblical Christians are "Babylon" to devout Mormons. Hence the celebrated line from the LDS hymnal: "O Babylon, O Babylon, we bid thee farewell; we're going to the mountains of Ephraim to dwell."

BAPTISM FOR THE DEAD

The LDS Position

One of the most distinctive elements of LDS doctrine is its teaching on baptism for the dead, as well as all the other ordinances of the church applied to the departed.

Mormons do not physically baptize dead people, but worthy Mormon members stand in as proxies for the departed person and are baptized, given their endowments (see also *Endowments*), and sealed in eternal marriage. This doctrine is outlined most clearly in *Doctrine and Covenants* 124:28-36; 127; 128.

The LDS answer to the classic question "What happens to those good people who die without hearing the gospel?" is that when a person dies outside of the LDS church through no fault of their own, they go to a spirit prison. There they are visited by LDS spirit missionaries—very much like the physical missionaries we see here going door-to-door.

These missionaries preach the LDS gospel to this dead person in the spirit prison. The spirit then has the opportunity to reject or accept the message and ask for church membership. But since there is no water in spirit prison (or anywhere else around there), the spirit cannot be baptized if it wishes to join the LDS church.

This is where the Mormon temples and the rites of vicarious ordinances—baptism, priesthood ordination (only for men), endowment, and sealing in eternal marriage—come into play. Though this is not well known, the vast majority of work done in the mysterious temples is done for and on behalf of dead people. These proxy rites are believed to be possible only in the temple.

Mormons are taught that they have a primary obligation to "redeem their dead." This means that they must go back and accumulate thorough genealogical information on all their ancestors, at least to the fourth generation. This includes information on dates of birth and death, children, and weddings.

All of this information is sent into the huge genealogical library in Salt Lake City. After it is processed, the Mormon can use it to go to the temple and stand in as proxy for their departed loved ones. Men must stand in for men and women must stand in for women. So important is this task that it is felt to be one of the three major missions of the church:

1. Preach the gospel.
2. Perfect the saints.
3. Redeem the dead.

Mormons believe that once they have done their four generations, they must continue to go to the temple and do proxy work for the thousands of names which church genealogical staffers acquire from public records, church rolls, and even graveyards. They believe that ultimately every man and woman from the time of Adam to the present must have their proxy work done for them. Once the work is done in the temple, the spirit in prison is able to become a full-fledged member of the church and leave their prison.

In doing this, Mormons believe they are "Saviors on Mount Zion" (*Mormon Doctrine*, pp. 677-78). They believe that when they die and go to wherever they go, many people will come up and kiss their feet and thank them for doing their proxy work for them. To this end, faithful Mormons spend hundreds of hours trying to track down their genealogy and then going to the temple to do proxy work for their ancestors or other dead people.

The Biblical View

There are serious problems with this teaching, theologically speaking. First, nowhere does the Bible indicate that anything done for the dead by the living can have any impact upon the dead. There is no substantial difference between the LDS doctrine and the Catholic doctrine of purgatory. Both are without biblical support.

Mormons will cite 1 Corinthians 15:29 as their sole scriptural warrant for all their effort: "Else what shall they do which are baptized for the dead, if the dead rise not at all? why are they then baptized for the dead?" Yet nowhere in the passage does Paul indicate that he is talking about a *Christian* practice.

To the contrary, there is ample evidence that there was a pagan cult in the city of Corinth familiar to the readers of Paul's epistle. This cult did baptize for the dead. Note two important facts: 1. This is the only verse in the Bible which even mentions baptizing the dead; and 2. Paul nowhere in this verse says that "we" (the Christians at Corinth) baptize the dead.

It is bad hermeneutics (the science of biblical interpretation) to take any one verse and build a doctrine out of it in isolation. This is especially true if there are other verses elsewhere which teach something quite different. The Bible commands that "at the mouth of two witnesses, or at the mouth of three witnesses, shall the matter be established (Deuteronomy 19:15b, see also Numbers 35:30; Deuteronomy 17:6,7).

Mormons quote this verse to try and prove the *Book of Mormon.* So they should also be required to produce two or three verses if they want to teach us to baptize for the dead, which they cannot.

Second, Paul invariably talks about the church of Jesus Christ as "we" or "us" or "our." There is no biblical reason to assume that in 1 Corinthians 15:29 he was talking about a Christian practice.

On the other hand, the Bible elsewhere clearly teaches that the state of a person at the moment of death is fixed and cannot be changed after death. The entire account which Jesus gives of the rich man and Lazarus (nowhere is it said to be a parable) in Luke 16 makes it clear that the rich man's fate is sealed.

Additionally, there is Hebrews 9:27: "And as it is appointed unto men once to die, but after this the judgment."

Paul also warns his Corinthian readers: "Behold, now is the accepted time; behold, now is the day of salvation" (2 Corinthians 6:2).

Now is the time for repentance! There is no chance after death. The LDS program for evangelizing the dead, ambitious as it is, is a fool's errand.

As if that weren't enough, Paul even condemns the researching of genealogies: "Neither give heed to fables and endless genealogies, which minister questions, rather than godly edifying which is in faith: so do" (1 Timothy 1:4). And he further commands in Titus 3:9: "But avoid foolish questions, and genealogies, and contentions, and strivings about the law; for they are unprofitable and vain."

The program for baptism for the dead keeps Mormons very busy—perhaps too busy to realize that they cannot be "Saviors on Mt. Zion." Indeed, they cannot even save themselves. The moment of death will be too late for them to discover this spiritual truth.

BELIEF

Mormons place a great deal of emphasis on belief or faith in the acceptance of their religion. It is one of the "first principles of the gospel" that one must have faith. One cannot join the LDS church without faith.

Of course, this is also true of historic Christianity. Heartfelt faith in the death, resurrection, and saving work of Jesus Christ (Romans 10:9-13) is essential to salvation in all Christian fellowships.

But like everything else in Mormonism, these evident resemblances are deceptive and need to be examined. While both Mormons and Christians ask belief of their converts, a deeper question is, In *what* or *whom* must that belief be placed?

LDS apostle and theologian Bruce R. McConkie makes it clear that "belief in Christ is essential to salvation" (*Doctrine*, p. 78). Yet the LDS version of Christ is not the biblical version (see also *Jesus*) and McConkie does not stop there. He goes beyond what historic Christianity professes and the Bible teaches and continues:

> Belief in the various truths that must be accepted if salvation is to be won, cannot be parceled out in such a way as to accept one essential truth and reject another. All phases of the doctrines of salvation are so intertwined with each other that it is not possible to believe one part without also believing all parts of which knowledge has been gained. Thus no one can believe in Christ without believing in his Father also (Matthew 11:27; John 5:23; 6:44; 12:44-46; 14:1,6). *And no one can accept Christ without accepting the prophets who testify of him* (p. 79, emphasis added).

A quantum leap has been taken here. Suddenly we have moved from faith in Jesus and the Father, two divine Persons, into faith in human beings. All prophets, even biblical giants like Isaiah, are only human beings. McConkie quotes 2 Chronicles 20:20 and John 15:1-11 as support for his strange thesis. But the John passage says nothing about prophets and the 2 Chronicles passage refers to belief in what the prophets are saying, not belief in them as objects of faith. The Bible knows nothing of people standing up and "bearing their testimony" of a prophet. No one ever stood up and said, "I bear you my testimony that God lives and that Isaiah is a prophet of God."

Naturally, McConkie lays down further faith requirements beyond believing in Mormon "prophets":

> No one in our day who has an understanding of the *Book of Mormon* can believe in Christ *unless he also believes the Book of Mormon*. . . . Similarly, people who have an understanding of both the *Book of Mormon* and the Bible cannot believe the one without believing the other also. In speaking of the Bible and *Book of Mormon*, the Prophet Mormon said, "If ye believe that ye will believe this also" (Mormon 7:8,9, ibid.).

This is, of course, another mighty leap of fancy. Of course there can be no Bible verse cited for this strange doctrine, for nowhere does the Bible insist that we must believe anything other than its own inspired words. McConkie offers no further explanation for why belief in the Bible necessitates belief in the *Book of Mormon*—except for quotations from the *Book of Mormon*. But that is circular reasoning. You cannot logically prove the truth of the *Book of Mormon* by quoting that document itself.

McConkie then says that belief in Joseph Smith as a prophet is also an essential for salvation. He quotes a lengthy passage from Brigham Young which says, in part:

> There is not that being that ever had the privilege of hearing the way of life and salvation set before him as it is written in the New Testament, and in the *Book of Mormon*, and in the book of Doctrine and Covenants, by a Latter-day Saint, that can say that Jesus lives, that his gospel is true, and at the same time say that Joseph Smith was not a Prophet of God. That is strong testimony, but it is true (*Doctrine*, p. 79).

Saying a thing does not make it true. Mormons are required to believe these kinds of statements without a stitch of biblical support to hang them on. Mormons are required to believe many idiosyncratic doctrines on the basis of little or no biblical, historical, or common-sense reasons.

But merely having more things to believe does not make a church a better church—unless those things are also true. As we have seen, there is no biblical basis for believing any of the unique LDS doctrines.

BELIEVING BLOOD

This term is used to describe certain people who seem to receive the LDS "plan of salvation" with greater readiness than others. They receive the missionary discussions of the church with less resistance and may actually leap at the chance of being baptized. Such people are said to have or be of "believing blood" (see *Doctrine*, p. 81).

Though this doctrine seems to mirror in some sense the Christian doctrine held by Calvinists that certain people are sovereignly elected by God to be saved before birth, there is really little of Calvinism in this. Mormons are taught that there is a preexistence (see also *Preexistence*) where souls interact with each other and God before coming to Earth.

More "worthy" or spiritually mature spirits from that preexistent state are sent to earth in the lineage of Jacob (i.e., Israel). They are born into families where they have Jewish (or at least Israelite) blood ancestry. Since Mormons believe the ten "lost tribes" are scattered (partially) among descendants of northern European nations, they think that many people are of the stock of the lost tribes without even knowing they are of Abraham's lineage.

Thus, anyone with this blood is specially attuned to spiritual truth and would much more readily accept and believe the strange principles of the LDS "gospel" than would others. People who join the church quickly when they receive the missionary lessons and then who succeed and advance swiftly in the social and religious hierarchy of the church are usually felt to be some of those who have "believing blood."

BIBLE

The LDS Position

The Bible is one of the published standard works of the Mormon church and is thus a part of the canon of scripture for the LDS faith. On the surface, the Christian can breathe a sigh of relief that even though Mormons claim other additional works of scripture, the Bible is still recognized as authoritative. Would that this were true!

Let's look at what they really say about the Bible. The first bit of theological sidestepping comes with the official church statement in the LDS eighth Article of Faith: "We believe the Bible to be the word of God *as far as it is translated correctly* [our emphasis]; we also believe the Book of Mormon to be the word of God."

The key phrase here is "as far as it is translated correctly." As long as there is some doubt about the Bible, there is need for other Scripture that is more "pure" than the suspect Bible. That, of course, is stated in the second half of the eighth Article: "We also believe the Book of Mormon to be the word of God." The statement says there is no such problem of translation with the *Book of Mormon*; therefore, one can assume that it is the full Word of God, to be trusted above the Bible.

Mormons are not instructed to test all things by the biblical Word of God but to lean on the LDS scriptures and prophets to guide them. That is the first major step down the road to heresy. New converts have stepped away from a foundation of solid rock and stand upon the shifting sands of Mormonism, its strange dogma, and the ever-progressing revelations of the "prophets."

Orson Pratt, comparing the Bible and the *Book of Mormon*, made this comment:

> What shall we say then, concerning the Bible's being a sufficient guide? Can we rely upon it in its present known corrupted state, as being a faithful record of God's word? We all know that but a few of the inspired writings have descended to our times, which few quote the names of some twenty other books which are lost, and it is quite certain that there were many other inspired books that even the names have not reached us. What few have come down to our day, have been mutilated, changed and corrupted, in such a shameful manner that not two manuscripts agree. Verses and even whole chapters have been added by unknown persons; and even we do not know the authors of some whole books; and we are not certain that all those which we do know, were written by inspiration. Add all this imperfection to the uncertainty of translation, and who, in his right mind, could,

for one moment, suppose the Bible in its present form to be a perfect guide? *Who knows that even one verse of the whole Bible has escaped pollution, so as to convey the same sense now that it did in the original?* (Orson Pratt, *Divine Authenticity of the Book of Mormon*, chapter 3: section 48, 1991, ICD Corporation, Provo, Utah—emphasis added).

Joseph Smith was like-minded. In fact, under "divine guidance" he rewrote much of the Bible and produced *The Inspired Version of the Bible*. Smith told his followers: "I believe the Bible as it read when it came from the pen of the original writers. Ignorant translators, careless transcribers, or designing and corrupt priests have committed many errors" (*Teachings*, p. 327).

Bringing the LDS case against the Bible to the present day, Bruce R. McConkie maintained the same theme:

> That portion of the writings of inspired men in the old world which, in the providences of the Almighty, has been handed down from age to age until modern times is called the Bible. These writings in their original form were perfect scripture; they were the mind and will of the Lord, his voice to his chosen people and to all who would hear it (*Doctrine and Covenants* 68:4). *That they have not come down to us in their perfect form is well known in the Church and by all reputable scholars. Only a few fanatics among the sects of Christendom close their eyes to reality and profess to believe in what they call verbal revelation, that is, that every word and syllable in some version or other of the Bible is the exact word spoken by Deity* (*Doctrine*, p. 82, emphasis added).

How do we deal with this? Nothing on earth is as precious to the believer as the Word of God. One of the sure signs of a cult is how that holy Word is presented. Mormons might want to soften the blow and not come right out and say that the Bible is a polluted work, but it surely is such to them.

The August 1992 edition of *The Ensign Magazine* let the cat out of the bag when it published the following article, titled "First Presidency Statement on the King James Version of the Bible." In part, it says:

> The Bible, as it has been transmitted over the centuries, has suffered the loss of many plain and precious parts. . . . Many

versions of the Bible are available today. Unfortunately, no original manuscripts of any portion of the Bible are available for comparison to determine the most accurate version. However, the Lord has revealed clearly the doctrines of the gospel in these latter-days. *The most reliable way to measure the accuracy of any biblical passage is not by comparing different texts, but by comparison with the Book of Mormon and modern-day revelations* (p. 80, emphasis added).

The article then says that the LDS edition of the Bible, supplemented and clarified with its approved footnotes, study aids, and cross-references, is really the only one to use.

Can you see the terrible spiritual danger here? Something is seriously out of order. *The Mormon church has taken the very document of God by which they must be judged and have instead become its judge.*

We have seen what the Mormons have done to the Word of God. Let's look at the Bible itself and see if what they say really holds true.

The Biblical View

Mark 13:31—"Heaven and earth shall pass away, but my words [*logoi mou*] shall not pass away."

Matthew 5:18—"For verily I say unto you, till heaven and earth pass, one jot or one tittle shall in no wise pass from the law [*tou nomon*], till all be fulfilled" (see also Luke 16:17).

1 Peter 1:25—"But the word [*rhema*] of the Lord endureth forever [*tou aiwna*]."

Hebrews 4:12—"For the word [*logos*] of God is quick, and powerful, and sharper than any twoedged sword, piercing even to the dividing asunder of soul and spirit, and of the joints and marrow, and is a discerner of the thoughts and intents of the heart."

2 Timothy 3:16—"All scripture [*pasa graphe*] is given by inspiration of God [*theopneustos*], and is profitable for doctrine, for reproof, for correction, for instruction in righteousness."

1 Kings 8:56—"There hath not failed one word [*dabar*] of all his good promise, which he promised by the hand of Moses his servant."

Psalm 12:6,7—"The words [*'imrah*] of the LORD are pure words: as silver tried in a furnace of earth, purified seven times. Thou shalt keep them, O LORD, thou shalt preserve them from this generation for ever."

Psalm 18:30—"As for God, his way is perfect: the word [*'imrah*] of the LORD is tried: he is a buckler to all those that trust in him."

Psalm 19:7,8—"The law [*torah*] of the LORD is perfect, converting the soul: the testimony [*'eduwth*] of the LORD is sure, making wise the simple. The statutes of the LORD are right, rejoicing the heart: the commandment of the LORD is pure, enlightening the eyes."

Psalm 33:4—"For the word [*dabar*] of the LORD is right; and all his works are done in truth."

Psalm 33:6—"By the word [*dabar*] of the LORD were the heavens made; and all the host of them by the breath of his mouth."

Psalm 119:89—"For ever, O LORD, thy word [*dabar*] is settled in heaven."

Psalm 119:140—"Thy word [*'imrah*] is very pure: therefore thy servant loveth it."

Proverbs 30:5—"Every word [*'imrah*] of God is pure: he is a shield unto them that put their trust in him."

Isaiah 8:19,20—"And when they shall say unto you, Seek unto them that have familiar spirits, and unto wizards that peep, and that mutter: should not a people seek unto their God? for the living to the dead? To the law [*torah*] and to the testimony [*t'uwdah*]: if they speak not according to this word, it is because there is no light in them."

Isaiah 45:19b—"I the LORD speak [*dabar*] righteousness, I declare things that are right."

Ezekiel 12:25—"For I am the LORD: I will speak, and the word [*dabar*] that I shall speak shall come to pass; it shall be no more prolonged: for in your days, O rebellious house, will I say the word [*dabar*], and will perform it, saith the Lord GOD."

Let's simplify this by doing a brief word study on these terms. Fortunately, although there are 17 Scripture passages, only a few words in the original Greek and Hebrew are used.

1. *Logos* (#3056 in *Strong's Concordance*). The word is defined as "intelligence, word as the expression of that intelligence" (Spiros Zodhiates, *The Hebrew Greek Study Bible*, Baker Book House, 1984, p. 1707). It may thus be said to be "God's intelligence."

   "The Word is the distinct and superfinite Personality of Jesus. . . . His was the Shekinah glory in open manifestation. John 1:18 makes clear that the Word (logos) is the Son's revelation of the Father, the personal manifestation, not a part of the Divine nature, but of the whole Deity!" (*Vine's Expository Dictionary of New Testament Words*, p. 1253). Thus, the *logos* in the above verses may be taken as an essential expression of the nature of God.

2. *Rhema* (#4487 in *Strong's Concordance*). From *rheo*, "to speak"—a word spoken or uttered. "Rhema stands for the subject matter of the word, the thing which is spoken about; and frequently denotes the operative or all powerful word of God" (Zodhiates, p. 1727).

   "The significance of rhema (as distinct from logos) is exemplified in the injunction in Ephesians 6:17. . . . Here the reference is not to the whole Bible as such, but to the individual scripture which the Spirit brings to our remembrance for use in time of need" (*Vine's*, p. 1253).

   Thus, *logos* refers to the essential expression of the nature of God, while *rhema* refers more to individual "words" of God for specific occasions.

Therefore, in Mark 13:31, the expositors agree that when Jesus says "my words," He means *the* Word of God—not just what He happened to be saying at that occasion. The same Word (*logos*) is said to be "quick, and powerful, and sharper than any twoedged sword" (Hebrews 4:12). It is a living, vital, and powerful expression of the intelligence of God. It is "God-breathed" (*theopneustos*), as 2 Timothy 3:16 puts it. If God speaks, who can disannul it?

3. *Tou nomon* (#3551 in *Strong's Concordance*). "The law" reads: "2) most frequently, the divine law given by Moses, whether moral, ceremonial or judicial. Sometimes it means the books of Moses or the Pentateuch containing the

law. . . . 3) the Gospel of gospel method of justification is called 'the law of faith'" (Zodhiates, p. 654).

Thus we see that Jesus is teaching here (Matthew 5:18) that the law of Moses will not be permanently altered in the *tiniest* way. This means that the entire Pentateuch, at the very least, must be accepted as it stands—including the warnings against polytheism, idolatry, and false prophecy.

4. *Ton aona* (#165 in *Strong's Concordance*). Universally recognized as meaning "eternity, whether past or to come" (Zodhiates, p. 1660). Thus if something is said to endure forever, it means that it will continue to exist for eternity.

5. *Pasa graphay* (#1124 in *Strong's Concordance*). Used as a plural in the New Testament for the entire Holy Scriptures, or in the singular for a part of it. The Holy Scriptures are everywhere termed as *hay* (the) *graphay* (Scripture), giving it authority (ibid., p. 1676).

Pasa literally means "every" (*The Discovery Bible*, New American Standard New Testament, Moody Press, 1987, p. 425, note b). The definitive *Vine's* concurs, saying that the plural usage means the whole Scriptures (*Vine's*, p. 1011). Vine writes, "The Scripture . . . stands for its Divine Author with an intimation that it remains perpetually characterized as the living voice of God" (ibid., p. 1012). Again, the idea is clear that all or every Scripture is God-breathed—that God Himself inspired the authors to write down exactly what they wrote; and that His power preserves the text.

Now, in the Hebrew, we have these terms:

1. *Dabar* (#1697 in *Strong's Concordance*). Essentially means "word" and appears more than 1400 times in the Old Testament. "The word of the LORD" was a technical expression for prophetic revelation 225 times in the singular form (Zodhiates, p. 1586).

It is translated in the Septuagint (LXX—Greek Old Testament) as *logos*, indicating its affinity with John's "Word made flesh." "This term we know is applied to the Son of God in the NT, and has been so understood by the ancient Jews. It is a remarkable circumstance that the expression 'word's sake' in 2 Samuel 7:21 is changed in 1 Chronicles 17:19 to 'servant's sake.'" (William Wilson, *Old Testament Word Studies*, MacDonald's Pub., n.d., p. 488). Thus, the term *word* means essentially the same thing in the Old Testament as in the New Testament.

2. *'Imrah* (#565 in *Strong's Concordance*). Means an utterance or speech. Nineteen of the word's 36 uses are in Psalm 119, and it occurs only ten times outside of the Psalms (Zodhiates, p. 1579). It is used more often in a *poetic* manner of God's Word (Wilson, p. 488).

3. *Torah* (#8451 in *Strong's Concordance*). Often has the definite article affixed to it when referring to the law of Moses. This important Hebrew noun occurs about 220 times in the Old Testament. The essential meaning is "teaching," whether it is the wise man who gently instructs his own son, or God patiently teaching Israel. Eventually it became synonymous with the Pentateuch (Zodhiates, p. 1652).

4. *'Eduwth* (#5715 in *Strong's Concordance*). Means "testimony, witness," especially the Ten Commandments. It is clearly associated with the law in Psalm 19 and Psalm 119 (ibid., p. 1620).

Thus we see that the Bible makes little or no distinction in the original manuscript between the various *words* or forms of *Scripture* or *law* of which Jesus, the apostles, or the Old Testament writers spoke. *All* seem equal; all are a vital, living part of the very essence of God. It is evident that *both* the individual *words* (*rhema*) and the collective *word* (*logos*) of Jesus are said to be eternal and to endure forever. No tampering has been successful in permanently altering the biblical text. That would seem to preclude the kind of tampering which Joseph Smith claimed had occurred.

BIBLE: Are There Books Missing from the Bible?

The LDS Position

Along with the Mormon position that there were many "plain and precious things" removed from the original Bible, the LDS church also teaches that whole books are missing as well. All this, of course, only adds to the fallibility of God's true Word and forces the LDS believer to rely even more on LDS scripture and its prophets.

Although it may not be consciously articulated as such by the Mormon, the underlying LDS concept is that the Bible—because of lost books, poor translations, and the removal of precious doctrine—is finally only a *human* book, not a *divine* book. Joseph Smith had this to say about the character of the Bible: "I believe the Bible as it read when it came from the pen of the original writers. Ignorant translators, careless transcribers, or designing and corrupt priests have committed many errors" (*Teachings*, p. 327).

Bruce R. McConkie comments further on the authenticity of the Bible:

> One of the great heresies of modern Christendom is the unfounded assumption that the Bible contains all of the inspired teachings now extant among men. Foreseeing that Satan would darken the minds of men in this way, and knowing that other scripture would come forth in the last days, Nephi prophesied that unbelieving Christians would reject the new revelation with the cry: "A Bible! A Bible! We have got a Bible, and there cannot be any more Bible" (*Doctrine*, p. 83).

If the Bible is merely a fallible, human book, then of course things can be missing and left out, either accidentally or on purpose. This would be *especially* true if the Bible never claimed to be divinely preserved, or to be the perfect Word of God.

Not even the *Book of Mormon* claims to be the perfect, inerrant, inspired Word of God. See the frontispiece of the modern (1981) Book of Mormon, which says, "Now, *if there be faults* [in the record] they are the mistakes of men; wherefore condemn not the things of God, that ye may be found spotless at the judgment-seat of Christ."

Also, on the page near the beginning (no number) titled "A Brief Explanation about the Book of Mormon," you will find this final paragraph added by the Mormon church: "About this edition: Some *minor errors* in the text have been perpetuated in past editions of the Book of Mormon. This edition contains corrections that *seem* appropriate to bring the material into conformity with prepublication manuscripts and early editions edited by the Prophet Joseph Smith."

That "*seem* appropriate"? A church with a "living prophet" should be able to do better than that! From these two texts alone it is clear that we are not dealing with a perfect, inerrant, or infallible text.

The Biblical View

The Bible, on the other hand, claims that it cannot be permanently altered:

> As for God, his way is perfect; the word of the LORD is tried: he is a buckler to all them that trust in him (2 Samuel 22:31).
> The law of the LORD is perfect, converting the soul: the testimony of the LORD is sure, making wise the simple. The statutes of the LORD are right, rejoicing the heart: the commandment of the LORD is pure, enlightning the eyes (Psalm 19:7,8)
> But the word of the Lord endureth for ever. And this is the word which by the gospel is preached unto you (1 Peter 1:25).
> For verily I say unto you, Till heaven and earth pass, one jot or one tittle shall in no wise pass from the law, till all be fulfilled (Matthew 5:18).

We all know how much reverence the name of God is due. We cannot take it in vain; we are not to use it in a profane or blasphemous manner. Yet, God tells us that His Word is just as important to Him as His name: "You have exalted above all things your name and your word" (Psalm 138:2b NIV).

Stop and think about that for a moment. God is saying that He has "exalted" (lifted up) His Word to the same level as His name. Now, if God thought enough of His name to put a strong prohibition against taking it in vain right in the Ten Commandments (Exodus 20:7), and if He ordered that His people were to be killed by stoning for misusing it, then imagine how God must watch over and protect His book!

This is even more true because the Bible is a *living* book! The author of Hebrews tells us that "the word of God is quick, and powerful, and sharper than any twoedged sword, piercing even to the dividing asunder of soul and spirit, and of the joints and marrow, and is a discerner of the thoughts and intents of the heart" (Hebrews 4:12).

The word *quick* means living. If God's book is alive, how could anyone permanently take something out of it? It would be like trying to remove your appendix without your permission!

God's Word also judges our reception of it. Jesus said, "He that rejecteth me, and receiveth not my words, hath one that judgeth him: *the word that I have spoken, the same shall judge him* in the last day" (John 12:48, emphasis added).

What a wonderful book the Lord has given us! How could a living book which actually "discerns" our thoughts and intents of the heart, and which will one day judge us—*how could such a book have missing parts?*

Matthew 5:18 especially shows us that Jesus Christ Himself (who certainly cannot lie) promised us that not the tiniest part of the law (i.e., at least the Old Testament), not even the crossing of a *t* or the dotting of an *i*, would be lost. Now if even a single letter could not be lost, how could an *entire book* be lost? Ask yourself if Jesus Christ has within Himself the power to enforce the promise that He made. If God promises something, then who on earth can prevent Him from keeping that promise?

This is highlighted when we consider the extreme care and reverence that both Jewish and Christian scribes took in copying the text of the Bible. They knew they were handling the very Word of God and behaved accordingly. Jewish copyists, especially, would take incredible pains to ensure that there was not even the tiniest error in their scrolls.

The scribes also were forbidden from copying more than one word from memory. They would perform tests at the end of a page to ensure it was perfect. They would count the number of letters on the page of the original and of the copy, and the numbers had to match. If they didn't, the scroll was immediately burned. They would count to see which word was the middle word on a page, and if there was a discrepancy, the new scroll was burned. These people were intensely serious because they knew they were handling God's very words. Now, with care like that, how could entire books be lost?

Still, we do need to examine verses in the Bible which might seem to indicate that there were books left out and see if there is any validity to this. Remember what we said at first, though: If the Bible doesn't clearly say something, we cannot assume that it is true, especially in the face of all the above verses which clearly teach the perfection and all-sufficiency of the book.

The first verse is "Wherefore it is said in the book of the wars of the LORD, What he did in the Red sea, and in the . . . brooks of Arnon" (Numbers 21:14).

What is this "book of the wars of the LORD"? We don't really know. But if you examine the entire passage surrounding this verse, you will see that nowhere does the Bible say this "book of the wars of the LORD" is the Word of the Lord. The Bible declares of itself hundreds of times that it is the Word of God. Yet this "missing" book is not said to be inspired, nor is it ever referred to as such by Christ or any of the New Testament writers.

It may have been merely a historical book recounting some of the battles, just like our modern history texts. There is no internal or external evidence from archaeology to support the idea that this is a missing book of the Bible.

"And the sun stood still, and the moon stayed, until the people had avenged themselves upon their enemies. Is not this written in the book of Jashar? So the sun stood still in the midst of heaven, and hasted not to go down about a whole day" (Joshua 10:13). The "book of Jashar" is the best-known of these so-called missing books, and usually the first one that a Mormon will mention as being "missing." But simply because it is well-known doesn't mean it is inspired or that God wanted it in the Bible. No orthodox rabbi or Jewish scribe today thinks it should be in the Bible; nor does any Christian Bible authority. Nothing in Joshua 10 says the book of Jashar is inspired or the Word of God. Thus, it is merely another historical book.

Yet most LDS bookstores sell a volume purported to be the *Book of Jashar*. One would think that the LDS prophet would have had that book placed into the canon of Scripture. The truth seems to be that even they do not believe it is Scripture, but use it only as a tool to discredit the authenticity of the Bible.

"And the men went and passed through the land, and described it by cities into seven parts in a book, and came again to Joshua to the host at Shiloh" (Joshua 18:9). Similar remarks apply.

This book seems to be something of a surveying document, almost like a modern land plat. It is nowhere referred to as an inspired book or as the Word of God.

"Then Samuel told the people the manner of the kingdom, and wrote it in a book, and laid it up before the LORD. And Samuel sent all the people away, every man to his house" (1 Samuel 10:25). It is highly unlikely that this is an inspired, missing book. God didn't even *want* the Jewish people to have a king! This was probably just a book of the rules about how a king should conduct himself. Nowhere does the passage say this book is something God considered important or inspired.

"Also he bade them teach the children of Judah the use of the bow: behold, it is written in the book of Jashar" (2 Samuel 1:18). The same comments as above apply—there's no internal or external evidence at all to support the idea that this is a missing book of the Bible.

"And the rest of the acts of Solomon, and all that he did, and his wisdom, are they not written in the book of the acts of Solomon?" (1 Kings 11:41). We do not know what this book is, although there are numerous pseudepigraphic (false Scripture) books attributed to Solomon, including medieval black magic books. Again, no evidence supports this as being a missing book. No doubt it was merely some historical account.

"Now the acts of David the king, first and last, behold, they are written in the book of Samuel the seer, and in the book of Nathan the prophet, and in the book of Gad the seer" (1 Chronicles 29:29). These books of Nathan the prophet and of Gad the seer are never said to be the Word of God or to be inspired writings. Even if they were written by prophets, that is no proof of their inspiration. Mormons today say that many of the writings of LDS "prophets" like Brigham Young or Joseph Smith aren't really Scripture, but mere speculation put down in writing. So if they say that can be true today, why couldn't it be true thousands of years ago?

"Now the rest of the acts of Solomon, first and last, are they not written in the book of Nathan the prophet, and in the prophecy of Ahijah the Shilonite, and in the visions of Iddo the seer against Jereboam the son of Nebat?" (2 Chronicles 9:29). The same comments as above apply. Nowhere are these books called inspired writing or God's Word.

"Now the acts of Rehoboam, first and last, are they not written in the book of Shemaiah the prophet, and of Iddo the seer concerning genealogies? And there were wars between Rehoboam and Jeroboam continually" (2 Chronicles 12:15). "Now the rest of the acts of Jehoshaphat, first and last, behold, they are written in the book of Jehu the son of Hanani, who is mentioned in the book of the kings of Israel" (2 Chronicles 20:34). The same comments as above apply. Nowhere are these books called inspired writing or God's Word.

"That search may be made in the book of the records of thy fathers: so shalt thou find in the book of the records, and know that this city is a rebellious city, and hurtful unto kings and provinces, and that they have moved sedition within the same of old time: for which cause was this city destroyed" (Ezra 4:15). This is obviously not an inspired book because it is part of the records of King Artaxerxes, a pagan ruler. This shows how ludicrous this kind of reasoning can be. Just because this book is mentioned in the Bible, does that mean it is inspired? Hardly.

"I wrote unto you in an epistle not to company with fornicators" (1 Corinthians 5:9). "And when this epistle is read among you, cause that it be read also in the church of the Laodiceans; and that ye likewise read the epistle from Laodicea" (Colossians 4:16). Since these words are from Paul's own hand, most Bible commentators do believe that there are other letters which are not in the New Testament. Paul probably wrote dozens of epistles to various churches, and yet only a few are preserved in the New Testament. While the epistle obviously had the same apostolic authority as did his other writings, we cannot assume that God wanted it in His book when there is no evidence that He did.

Mormons continue to assert that the writings of their apostles and prophets are not Scripture, so why should they demand that everything Paul wrote is Scripture? While we can assume that whatever Paul wrote outside the mantle of Scripture was in perfect harmony with Scripture, Mormons do not want to put their own prophets to such a test. Yet what is true for one should be true for the other.

The bottom line is that none of these passages intimate that there are inspired books missing from the canon of Scripture. We must remember that if Joseph Smith contradicts what God says, then "Yea, let God be true, but every man a liar" (Romans 3:4).

BIBLE: Does It Prophesy the *Book of Mormon?*

The LDS Position

One of the important missionary books of the Mormon church is *A Marvelous Work and a Wonder* by the late "apostle" LeGrand Richards. It is handed out by the tens of thousands to investigators of the church. It is what you might call "a great soft sell."

In it, Richards asks the reader to view the *Book of Mormon* as something that has come forth as a voice from the dust, the stick of Joseph as prophesied in the thirty-seventh chapter of Ezekiel. He states: "Until someone can explain where the record of Joseph is, the *Book of Mormon* stands unrefuted in its claim to be the 'stick of Joseph'" (*A Marvelous Work and a Wonder*, pp. 65-69).

This is a very important matter, for if the Mormon church can clearly show that the *Book of Mormon* is actually the fulfillment of Old Testament prophesies, it would take on a whole different light. Let's look at the passage in question:

> The word of the LORD came again unto me, saying, More-over, thou son of man, take thee one stick, and write upon it, For Judah, and for the children of Israel his companions: then take another stick and write upon it, For Joseph, the stick of Ephraim, and for all the house of Israel his companions: and join them one to another into one stick; and they shall be one in thine hand. And when the children of thy people shall speak unto thee, saying, Wilt thou not shew us what thou meanest by these? Say unto them, Thus saith the Lord GOD; Behold, I will take the stick of Joseph, which is in the hand of Ephraim, and the tribes of Israel his fellows, and will put them with him, even with the stick of Judah and make them one stick, and they shall be one in mine hand (Ezekiel 37:15-19).

The Mormon church interprets this as follows: The sticks are really scrolls, an ancient form of books. The stick of Judah is the Bible, the history of that tribe. The stick of Joseph is the *Book of Mormon*, the history of his "other sheep" who migrated to the Americas. This is a command to write these two records and, at a later date, they will be combined into one record. The joining into one stick refers to bringing the Bible and the *Book of Mormon* together.

The Biblical View

But is this really what the text says? This passage, like all other texts in the Bible, doesn't exist in a vacuum. It fits into a chapter, a book, and into the fabric of the Bible itself. In order to interpret it, we need to find and follow the context. In this case, we find that the context involves a specific time. Throughout chapters 34 to 48, Ezekiel is prophesying the return of Israel to her land after the captivity. This passage about the two sticks appears right in the middle of that segment.

At the time of Ezekiel, the Jews were split into two kingdoms, called Judah and Israel (1 Kings 12:16-24), each with its own king. As we see by closely reading the context, God was not finished speaking at the end of verse Ezekiel 37:19. Starting with verse 20, God Himself interprets the prophecy for us:

> And the sticks whereon thou writest shall be in thine hand before their eyes. And say unto them, Thus saith the Lord GOD; Behold, I will take the children of Israel from among the heathen, whither they be gone, and will gather them on every side, and bring them into their own land: and I will make them one nation in the land upon the mountains of Israel; and one king shall be king to them all: and they shall be no more two nations, neither shall they be divided into two kingdoms any more at all (Ezekiel 37:20-22).

First, God says that both sticks will be right there *at that time* in Ezekiel's hands. The *Book of Mormon,* or what the LDS calls the "stick of Joseph," wasn't completed until after the time of Christ. So the stick could not be the *Book of Mormon,* could it? Obviously, the Mormon interpretation does not fit with what God says.

What we really have is God instructing Ezekiel to apply a little theatrics to his prophecy, using two sticks to represent the two factions. Why is something so simple so difficult to get through to a Mormon? Because a grasp of this is important in understanding the Mormon mind-set, let's look even deeper.

When is a stick ever a scroll? Nowhere in the Bible is a stick used to symbolize a scroll. Ezekiel surely knew the difference between a scroll and a stick! He referred to a "roll of the book," meaning a scroll, in 2:9—the normal biblical phrase for a scroll. The Hebrew word used here, however, is *ates,* which is translated "stick" 14 times in the entire Old Testament, eight times right in this passage. It is the only word translated "stick" in the Bible, but it is also rendered in other ways. It is translated "planks" in Ezekiel 41:25 and as "timber" in Ezekiel 26:12. It is mostly rendered "tree" (163 times), as it is in Ezekiel 36:30. Of the more than 300 times it is used, it *never* refers to scrolls. It simply means "a piece of wood." Sadly, if *ates* had been translated simply as "wood," the LDS rendering of this prophecy would not even exist. Its whole interpretation is based solely on the English and has no support in the original Hebrew.

Further, for the LDS reading to be seriously considered, the Bible would have to deal solely with the tribe of Judah. Yet it clearly tracks the history of *all* the tribes of Israel. The story of the tribes is found in Genesis all the way through Kings. They are all seen, with Judah receiving no special attention.

But let's be fair about this. What if this *is* a prophecy of a second book of Scripture as the Mormons claim, despite all the problems? Does the *Book of Mormon* fulfill the specific requirements of the prophecy?

First, the *Book of Mormon* never calls itself the stick of Joseph. Wouldn't it be logical to expect the book to refer to itself as such at least once?

Second, if a stick is really a scroll as the Mormons claim, then wouldn't the prophecy require that the "stick of Joseph which is in the hand of Ephraim" also be a scroll? Yet the *Book of Mormon* was supposedly written on gold plates, not on scrolls.

LeGrand Richards uses another key verse or two to claim the *Book of Mormon* is prophesied by the Bible. Let's look briefly at his other "prophecy": "And thou shalt be brought down, and shalt speak out of the ground, and thy speech shall be low out of the dust, and thy voice shall be, as of one that hath a familiar spirit, out of the ground, and thy speech shall whisper out of the dust" (Isaiah 29:4).

Richards tells his readers that this passage refers to the *Book of Mormon* being brought out of the ground, a record of an ancient people speaking "out of the dust." The *Book of Mormon* even applies this prophecy to itself in Moroni 10:27. Also, "the *Book of Mormon* has a familiar spirit for it contains the words of long-dead prophets of God, like its counterpart, the Bible" (*A Marvelous Work and a Wonder*, pp. 67-68).

Once again, let's check the context. To whom is Isaiah speaking? Right away, we find this prophecy is being given to a city called

"Ariel" (Isaiah 29:1,2,7). Ariel ("hearth of God") is actually the city of Jerusalem. It is in no way referring to any distant people or a record they have buried, since Isaiah is pronouncing judgment on the city for trusting in Egypt rather than in God (chapters 30 and 31).

Most of the events he describes actually happened when Judah went into Babylonian captivity a few years later; therefore it cannot be applied to another later event. The context completely rules out the possibility that this refers to a branch of Israel in a distant land which had its record buried and later brought out of the dust on gold plates.

But let's take the position of the LDS church and assume for a moment that the prophecy *is* speaking of the *Book of Mormon*. What about this claim? What if it were true? Mormons testify that the *Book of Mormon* has a familiar spirit . . . and perhaps it does.

The Bible uses this term elsewhere, and we can learn a lot from how it is used. Look in Leviticus 19:31; 20:6,7; and Deuteronomy 18:9-12. Those references show that anyone or anything which has "a familiar spirit" is an abomination before God. A person with a familiar spirit is a medium—one who is on friendly terms with demons. Isaiah uses the phrase identically in Isaiah 8:19 and 19:3, so it is clear he fully understands what a familiar spirit was.

The Mormons may certainly claim that the *Book of Mormon* has a familiar spirit. But they shouldn't be hurt if for that reason Christians refuse to accept it as the Word of God.

BLASPHEMY AGAINST THE HOLY GHOST

The LDS Position

The LDS definition of *blasphemy* ends much like what a biblical Christian might formulate, but its beginning is a bit strange: "1. Speaking irreverently, evilly, abusively, or scurrilously against God or sacred things; or 2. Speaking profanely or falsely about Deity" (*Doctrine*, p. 90).

McConkie then begins to fill out what he means by this simple definition:

Among a great host of impious and sacrilegious speaking that constitute blasphemy are such things as: Taking the name of

God in vain; evil-speaking about the Lord's anointed; belittling
sacred temple ordinances, or patriarchal blessings, or sacramen-
tal administrations; claiming unwarranted divine authority; and
promulgating with profane piety a false system of salvation (ibid.).

Let's translate this into English. "Evil-speaking about the
Lord's anointed" means saying anything against the leaders of the
LDS church, even if they are wrong! Thus, even though Paul H.
Dunn was lying and exaggerating a few years back in telling his
faith-promoting stories, it would have been blasphemy for a Mormon to point that out to another Mormon, and especially to the
"Gentile" media. Fortunately, one did anyway. Such a belief effec-
tively squelches all criticism, justified or otherwise, of church
leaders.

"Belittling sacred temple ordinances"—in practice this means
even *talking* about the rituals when outside the temples. It obviously
precludes saying anything about the rituals being weird, medieval,
occult, or sexist.

"Claiming unwarranted divine authority"—this means thinking that you can read and understand the Bible without the help of
the brethren, or that you might have better ideas about how to do a
task in your local ward than the "divinely called" priesthood official
in charge of that task, who might very well be administratively
inept. It may even come to thinking that you can get truth from
God without the help of the church hierarchy. This is dangerous,
and can lead to . . .

"Promulgating with profane piety a false system of salvation"—translated, this means getting born again or saved through
the grace of Jesus flowing from the cross of Calvary. It means having
a personal relationship with Jesus. This is especially perilous and is a
"dangerous gospel hobby" (see also *Gospel Hobbies*). It can lead to
what McConkie calls "Blasphemy against the Holy Ghost—which
is falsely denying Christ after receiving a *perfect revelation of him
from the Holy Ghost*—[and] is the unpardonable sin (*Doctrine*, p.
91).

That means that no one can receive a perfect revelation of
Christ from the Holy Spirit outside of the Mormon church. Blasphemy against the Holy Ghost occurs when a temple Mormon
knowingly and decisively turns his back on Mormon doctrine after
getting born again. Hundreds of thousands have done just that,
praise the Lord.

The Biblical View

Obviously, no Christian approves of speaking evil against the Lord. However, New Testament Christianity leaves little place for "sacred *things*." A Christian might revere a Bible, but I do not believe they would call the book "sacred." That would be about the limit of what the vast majority of Christians today would consider as a "sacred thing." Having "holy" this and "sacred" that is more a holdover from the Old Testament priesthood, which is not carried through into the new covenant.

The Bible does warn against blasphemy against the Holy Ghost, however. Matthew told the people,

> Wherefore I say unto you, All manner of sin and blasphemy shall be forgiven unto men: but the blasphemy against the Holy Ghost shall not be forgiven unto men. And whosoever speaketh a word against the Son of man, it shall be forgiven him: but whosoever speaketh against the Holy Ghost, it shall not be forgiven him, neither in this world, neither in the world to come (Matthew 12:31,32).

The warning was repeated by Mark:

> Verily I say unto you, All sins shall be forgiven unto the sons of men, and blasphemies wherewith soever they shall blaspheme: but he that shall blaspheme against the Holy Ghost hath never forgiveness, but is in danger of eternal damnation: because they said, He hath an unclean spirit (Mark 3:28-30).

The sin of blasphemy against the Holy Ghost is obviously "the big one." It isn't just the words that are spoken, but the heart that is so firmly and eternally turned against God that there is nothing that even God can do to turn that bitter and contemptuous rebel back to Him.

BLESSING OF CHILDREN

Mormons are commanded to bring their children to the elders of the local church and have them blessed (usually before the entire congregation or ward) a few weeks after the birth of the child at the nearest fast and testimony meeting (see also *Fast and Testimony*

Meetings). *Doctrine and Covenants* tells us that: "Every member of the church of Christ [meaning the Mormon church] having children is to bring them unto the elders before the church, who are to lay their hands upon them in the name of Jesus Christ, and bless them in his name" (*Doctrine and Covenants* 20:70).

This is not believed by Mormons to be like a Catholic baptism, wherein the child is *saved*, but rather it is similar to the practice in many Protestant churches of "dedicating a baby to the Lord." Mormons do not believe that unbaptized infants or small children under the age of accountability (eight years old) can die and "be lost." In this they agree with most Christians.

At the fast and testimony meeting, the child is brought up to the front of the church and at the pulpit is held in a basket of hands in a center of a ring of "priesthood holders"—men who may be friends or relatives of the family, and usually the bishop. In most cases, the worthy father will pronounce the blessing. Afterward, the child is held up so that the entire ward congregation can see it.

At this time of blessing, the baby is formally given its name, which is then entered into the church's vast record-keeping system. This makes the child a "child of record." Mormons keep excellent records, believing as they do that this is necessary for complete accountability to God.

Additionally, LDS parents are encouraged to bless their children frequently. The father lays his hands on the child's head and pronounces a "father's blessing" over the child. This is often done during times when the child is sick [not the same as anointing the sick with oil], or before some important event in their life—going off to kindergarten or college, playing in an important sporting event, or leaving for a mission.

All of this is reasonably innocent and even laudable, except of course for the fact that all these blessings are being given by the power of the "holy Melchizedek priesthood" in the name of a false Jesus. This is a false priesthood which *no* Mormon (or any other human being) has the right to hold (see also *Priestcraft*). Quite often, the overall spiritual effect of these blessings is anything but salutary.

While the child might be heartened emotionally and psychologically by his father's prayers and concern, in many cases the spiritual impact of those prayers is the opposite of what was innocently intended. Because of the strong spiritual deception and demonic element of lying and deceitful spirits (1 Timothy 4:1) so present in Mormonism, frequently these blessings can be a source of grave spiritual oppression later in life.

This is an especially nasty trick that the devil is pulling on these parents, because they are acting out of the highest of motives. However, as we understand from the Bible, sincerity is not always a guarantee of spiritual truth (Proverbs 14:12). As these children grow into their teen years and attempt to struggle with the temptations of life, quite often they are hampered by the spirits of priestcraft which surround them because of their fathers' (and other priesthood holders') ministrations (see also *Laying on of Hands*).

Of course, this oppression is further magnified by patriarchal blessings (see also *Patriarchal Blessings*) and other blessings often given in the LDS church later on in the person's life, as well as visits to the LDS temple (see also *Endowments*).

BLOOD ATONEMENT DOCTRINE

The LDS doctrine of blood atonement is one of those central tenets of faith about which the early LDS church was extremely vocal and the LDS church of today would rather let quietly slip away. Great effort has been made to deny it ever existed, but that simply cannot be done.

Bruce R. McConkie in his encyclopedic work *Mormon Doctrine* states the case for the present church position:

> From the days of Joseph Smith to the present, wicked and evily-disposed persons have fabricated false and slanderous stories to the effect that the Church, in the early days of this dispensation, engaged in a practice of blood atonement whereunder the blood of apostates and others was shed by the Church as an atonement for their sins. These claims are false and were known by their originators to be false. There is not one historical instance of so-called blood atonement in this dispensation, nor has there been one event or occurrence whatever, of any nature, from which the slightest inference arises that any such practice either existed or was taught.
>
> There are, however, in the sermons of some of the early church leaders some statements about the true doctrine of blood atonement and of its practice in past dispensations, for instance, in the days of Moses. *By taking one sentence on one page and another*

from a succeeding page and even by taking a part of a sentence on one page and a part of another found several pages away—all wholly torn from context—dishonest persons have attempted to make it appear that Brigham Young and others taught things just the opposite of what they really believed and taught (pp. 92-93, emphasis added).

Before we wander too far away from that statement, let's look at just a few *in context, same page, same sentence* statements of several of the early Mormon prophets speaking to the saints from LDS pulpits.

The "prophet," Joseph Smith:

> In debate, George A. Smith said imprisonment was better than hanging. I replied, I was opposed to hanging, even if a man kill another, I will shoot him, or cut off his head, spill his blood on the ground, and let the smoke thereof ascend up to God; and if ever I have the privilege of making a law on that subject, I will have it so (*History*, vol. 5, p. 296, under the heading, "The Questions of 'Currency' and Blood Atonement, in the Nauvoo City Council").

The "prophet" Brigham Young, teaching from the pulpit of the Tabernacle in Salt Lake City on February 8, 1857, on the doctrine of blood atonement, and using the example of a fully knowledgeable saint who falls into sin, said:

> Suppose that he is overtaken in a gross fault, that he has committed a sin that he knows will deprive him of the exaltation which he desires, and that he cannot attain to it without the shedding of his blood, and also knows that by having his blood shed he will atone for that sin and be saved and exalted with the Gods, is there a man or woman in this house but would say, "shed my blood that I may be saved and exalted with the Gods"? (*Journal of Discourses*, vol. 4, p. 219).

I doubt that we could find a clearer statement on the subject. Later in the same teaching, Young added:

> I could refer you to plenty of instances where men have been righteously slain, in order to atone for their sins. . . . I have known a great many men who have left this Church for whom there is no chance whatever for exaltation, but if their blood had

been spilled, it would have been better for them. The wickedness and ignorance of the nations forbid this principle's being in full force, but the time will come when the law of God will be in full force.

This is loving our neighbor as ourselves; and if he needs help, help him; and if he wants salvation and it is necessary to spill his blood on the earth in order that he might be saved, spill it. Any of you who understand the principles of eternity, if you have sinned a sin requiring the shedding of blood, except the sin unto death, would not be satisfied nor rest until your blood be spilled, that you might gain that salvation you desire. That is the way to love mankind (ibid., p. 220).

Brigham Young was prone to talk about this "holy principle" from the pulpit. He felt it would solve a lot of the church's problems. Here are a few more of his thoughts on the matter:

"I say rather than that apostates should flourish here, I would unsheathe my bowie knife and conquer or die."

There was a great commotion in the congregation and a simultaneous burst of feelings assenting to the declaration.

"Now, you nasty apostates, clear out or judgment will be put on the line and righteousness to the plummet." [Voices generally, "Go it! Go it!"] "If you say it is right, raise your hands!" [All hands up.] "Let us call upon the Lord to assist us in this and every good work!" (Journal of Discourses, vol. 1, p. 83).

The Journal of Discourses article says that all hands went up. One would certainly expect so! Can you imagine being in that congregation and not raising your hand? On the subject of theft, Brigham had this to say: "If you want to know what to do with a thief that you find stealing, I say kill him on the spot and never suffer him to commit another iniquity" (Journal of Discourses, vol. 1, p. 108).

Back to McConkie's denial and grossly flawed apologetic on the subject: Again we read on pp. 92-93:

Raising the curtain of truth on this false and slanderous bluster of enemies of the Church who have thus willfully chose to fight the truth with outright lies of the basest sort, the true doctrine of blood atonement is simply this:
1. Jesus Christ worked out the infinite and eternal atonement by the shedding of his own blood. He came into the world for the

95

purpose of dying on the cross for the sins of the world. By virtue of that atoning sacrifice immortality came as a free gift to all men, and all who would believe and obey his laws would in addition be cleansed from sin through his blood (Mosiah 3:16-19; 3 Nephi 27:19-21; 1 John 1:7; Revelation 5:9,10).

2. But under certain circumstances there are some serious sins for which the cleansing of Christ does not operate, and the law of God is that men must have their own blood shed to atone for their sins. Murder, for instance, is one of these sins; hence we find the Lord commanding capital punishment. Thus, also, if a person has so progressed in righteousness that his calling and election has been made sure, if he has come to that position where he knows "by revelation and the spirit of prophecy, through the power of the Holy Priesthood" that he is sealed up unto eternal life (*Doctrine and Covenants* 131:5), then if he gains forgiveness for certain grievous sins, he must "be destroyed in the flesh," and "delivered unto the buffetings of Satan unto the day of redemption, saith the Lord God" (*Doctrine and Covenants* 132:19-27).

McConkie then cites President Joseph Fielding Smith on the subject, perhaps thinking that President Smith is helping his cause:

Man may commit certain grievous sins—according to his light and knowledge—that will place him beyond the atoning blood of Christ. If then he would be saved, he must make sacrifice of his own life to atone—so far as in his power lies—for that sin, for the blood of Christ alone under certain circumstances will not avail. . . . Joseph Smith taught that there were certain sins so grievous that man may commit, that they will place the transgressors beyond the power of the atonement of Christ. If these offenses are committed, then the blood of Christ will not cleanse them from their sins even though they repent. Therefore their only hope is to have their own blood shed to atone, as far as possible, in their behalf (*Doctrines of Salvation*, vol. 1, pp. 133-38).

Due to the sheer quantity of documentation on the blood atonement doctrine, we won't attempt to reference all that's available. Perhaps one other place in LDS scripture that shows the doctrine to be a cornerstone of LDS theology is in *Doctrine and Covenants* 132, the revelation that lays out the principle of plural marriage, or polygamy. Although they seem to be unrelated, the doctrines of blood atonement and polygamy are closely joined in Mormonism.

The two doctrines are dealt with together for two reasons. First, they have a common textual basis in *Doctrine and Covenants* 132, and second, they show that Mormonism is clearly nonbiblical and anti-Christian. Plural marriage and blood atonement are doctrines that Mormons would use to replace historic Christian orthodoxy! *Doctrine and Covenants* 132 lays out this law of polygamy and death for all to see. Take notice that in 1993 it is still in the LDS scripture, as given.

> [37]Abraham received concubines, and they bore him children; and it was accounted unto him for righteousness, because they were given unto him, and he bode in my law; as Isaac also and Jacob did none other things than that which they were commanded; and because they did none other things than that which they were commanded, they have entered into their exaltation, according to the promises, and sit upon thrones, and are not angels but are gods.
>
> [38]David also received many wives and concubines, and also Solomon and Moses my servants, as also many others of my servants, from the beginning of creation until this time; and in nothing did they sin save in those things which they received not of me.
>
> [39]David's wives and concubines were given unto him of me, by the hand of Nathan, my servant, and others of the prophets who had the keys of this power; and in none of these things did he sin against me save in the case of Uriah and his wife; and, therefore he hath fallen from his exaltation, and received his portion; and he shall not inherit them out of the world, for I gave them unto another, saith the Lord.
>
> [40]I am the Lord thy God, and I gave unto thee, my servant Joseph, an appointment, and restore all things. Ask what ye will, and it shall be given unto you according to my word (*Doctrine and Covenants* 132).

Verses 37 and 38 stress the right of Abraham to have concubines and explain how Moses, David, and Solomon all were blessed to have a plurality of wives and concubines. Then in verse 40 the

LDS god, speaking through Joseph Smith, gives Smith the appointment and authority to restore all these things.

Then the LDS god admonishes Emma, Smith's wife, to receive all those who have been given to Joseph or be destroyed (the doctrine of blood atonement being used to bring their women into line).

> And let mine handmaid, Emma Smith, receive all those that have been given unto my servant Joseph, and who are virtuous and pure before me; and those who are not pure, and have said they were pure, shall be destroyed, saith the Lord God.
>
> For I am the Lord thy God, and ye shall obey my voice; and I give unto my servant Joseph that he shall be made ruler over many things; for he hath been faithful over a few things, and from henceforth I will strengthen him.
>
> And I command mine handmaid, Emma Smith, to abide and cleave unto my servant Joseph, and to none else. But if she will not abide this commandment she shall be destroyed, saith the Lord; for I am the Lord thy God, and will destroy her if she abide not in my law (vv. 52-54).

In an earlier verse, the "Lord" warned all those—men and women alike—who had been through the temple and were being sealed up in this "holy principle" to watch out. The penalty for failure was death, blood atonement:

> [26]Verily, verily, I say unto you, if a man marry a wife according to my word, and they are sealed by the Holy Spirit of promise, according to mine appointment, and he or she shall commit any sin or transgression of the new and everlasting covenant whatever, and all manner of blasphemies, and if they commit no murder wherein they shed innocent blood, yet they shall come forth in the first resurrection, and enter into their exaltation; but they shall be destroyed in the flesh, and shall be delivered unto the buffetings of Satan unto the day of redemption, saith the Lord God.

Verse 64 also admonished the sisters that if a wife did not believe in the doctrine, she would be destroyed. Interestingly, Emma Smith was threatened with that very destruction—yet history shows that although she strongly resisted the doctrine of plural marriage, she lived to a very old age. Her "prophet" husband who

98

threatened her with destruction was dead within the year, shot by a mob after being imprisoned in Carthage jail for causing a riot in Nauvoo in which a printing press used to print material accusing Joseph of having more than one wife was destroyed. Historical irony, or the judgment of God?

The doctrine of blood atonement also carried some special coded meaning. To Mormons, murder was not killing. Killing was done to non-Mormons by Mormons; murder was done to Mormons by non-Mormons. Killing was done out of love to prevent people from going to hell. As Mark Twain said after visiting Salt Lake City, "Many a stranger has found himself down an alley happily awaiting a hearse, after making a few comments on polygamy" (see *Roughing It* by Twain).

Another element of blood atonement is found in the LDS temple rituals, even as recently as 1990. In their rites, temple Mormons swore not to reveal the secrets of the temple on penalty of having their lives taken.

Finally, one last quote from McConkie. After admitting it is a divine principle, that it was practiced in days of old (by Moses), and denying any latter-day part of it, he states, "This doctrine can only be practiced in its fulness in a day when the civil and ecclesiastical laws are administered in the same hands" (ibid.).

Many Mormons await the final days before the return of Christ, when this country's Constitution supposedly will hang by a thread and will be saved by the elders of the Mormon church. Then they hope to institute the kingdom of God, where this country will be governed by a Mormon prophet. Then, when "the civil and ecclesiastical laws are administered in the same hands," they can again restore the laws of the United Order (see *Oracles*), blood atonement, and polygamy.

BLOOD, CHANGED AT BAPTISM

As strange as it sounds, it is a tenet of LDS theology that if a person who converts to the LDS church is not of Jewish descent, then their blood is magically transformed into the blood of Abraham when they are immersed in the baptismal font at their Mormon baptism.

Joseph Smith taught:

As the Holy Ghost falls upon one of the literal seed of Abraham, it is calm and serene . . . while the effect of the Holy Ghost upon a Gentile is to purge out the old blood and make him actually of the seed of Abraham. That man that has none of the blood of Abraham (naturally) must have a new creation by the Holy Ghost (*History of the Church* 3:380).

Additionally, Brigham Young taught:

If a Gentile firmly believes the Gospel of Jesus Christ, and yields obedience to it, in such a case I will give you the words of the Prophet Joseph—"When the Lord pours out the Holy Ghost upon that individual he will have spasms, and you would think that he was going into fits." Joseph said that the Gentile blood was actually cleansed out of their veins, and the blood of Jacob made to circulate in them. . . . we are of the house of Israel, of the royal seed, of the royal blood (*Journal of Discourses* 2:268-69).

One big problem with this odd doctrine is that it never seems to happen. Though most converts to the LDS church (at least in America) are quite obviously not of Jewish descent, yet none of them have spasms or fits. Especially since the 1978 "revelation" which encouraged black people to join the LDS church, you would think spasms would be breaking out right and left. It is obvious that black people are not of Jewish descent!

Yet there has not, to our knowledge, been a single case of a person rising up out of the LDS baptismal fonts with fits and spasms. Nor is there any measurable incidence of Tay-Sachs disease (a disorder which seems to primarily afflict Jewish people) among Mormons.

This would be an excellent opportunity for the LDS church to prove the truth of its prophets, Joseph and Brigham. With the advent of DNA testing, blood samples could be taken from a person of Jewish descent and then before-and-after samples could be taken from an obviously non-Jewish LDS convert. If Joseph Smith is a true prophet and teacher, there should be a measurable difference. If he is wrong on this, then he is a false prophet, and following him would be spiritually dangerous.

BOOK OF ABRAHAM

The Book of Abraham is found in the LDS book of "scripture," *The Pearl of Great Price,* and is one of the standard works of the Mormon church. It is introduced as follows in its preface:

> *Translated from the papyrus, by Joseph Smith:* A Translation of some ancient Records, that have fallen into our hands from the catacombs of Egypt—The writings of Abraham while he was in Egypt, called the Book of Abraham, written by his own hand, upon papyrus. See *History of the Church,* vol. 2, pp. 235, 236, 348-51.

In going to the referenced pages of the *History,* Joseph Smith reported that on July 3, 1835, "Mr. Michael H. Chandler came to Kirtland to exhibit some Egyptian mummies. There were four human figures, together with some two or more rolls of papyrus covered with hieroglyphic figures and devices" (p. 235).

Smith states that he was able to translate some of the figures and was given a certificate of proof of that by Mr. Chandler (dated July 6) and that:

> Soon after this, some of the Saints at Kirtland purchased the mummies and papyrus, a description of which will appear hereafter, and with W. W. Phelps and Oliver Cowdery as scribes, I commenced the translation of some of the characters or hieroglyphics, and much to our joy, found that one of the rolls contained the writings of Abraham, another the writings of Joseph of Egypt, etc.—a more full account of which will appear in its place, as I proceed to examine or unfold them. Truly we can say, the Lord is beginning to reveal the abundance of peace and truth (p. 236).

McConkie reports on it as follows:

> Book of Abraham—This work was translated by the Prophet from a papyrus record taken from the catacombs of Egypt, a record preserved by the Lord to come forth in this day of restoration (Milton R. Hunter, *Pearl of Great Price Commentary,* pp. 6-35). Abraham was the original author, and the scriptural account contains priceless information about the gospel, preexistence, the nature of Deity, the creation, and priesthood, information which is not otherwise available in any other revelation now extant (*Doctrine,* p. 564).

While it is a small issue, Fawn Brodie in *No Man Knows My History* reported:

> "Joseph told Josiah Quincy in 1844 that his mother purchased them with her own money at a cost of Six Thousand dollars," although he wrote in his journal that they had been bought by some of the Saints in Kirtland (p. 170).
> The prophet never deciphered that papyrus which told the story of Joseph in Egypt, contenting himself with a translation of the writings of Abraham (p. 171).

For Mr. Chandler to give the "prophet" a certificate proving he had correctly translated the papyri was something of a miracle since the documents were all but indecipherable to the rest of the scholarly world. The breakthrough in translating Egyptian hieroglyphics did not come until 1837, when Champollion's work with the Rosetta stone was published in England (p. 170, footnote *).

In fact, the prophet "translated" it any way he wanted to, and in 1835 America there wasn't anyone who could argue the point.

This episode should have provided a golden opportunity to prove Joseph Smith's office of prophet, seer, and revelator, but it didn't. By the time information became available on a less spiritual form of translation, Joseph was long gone from the scene. It wasn't until 1861 that his less-than-accurate translation was questioned, when a Frenchman named Jules Remy published an exposé of the Book of Abraham in a book entitled *A Journey to Great Salt Lake* (Brodie, p. 175).

The papyri escaped further study for quite some time, and it was generally believed that they had been burned in the Chicago fire. But in 1967, 11 fragments of the papyri were discovered in the New York Museum of Art, some bearing the actual handwriting of Joseph Smith. They were soon turned over to the LDS church.

Here was the chance to prove to the whole world, once and for all, that Joseph Smith was a real prophet of God and Mormonism was the true and only kingdom of God on earth. Yet what surfaced was a confirmation of Remy's earlier claim that the scrolls were simple funeral documents found by the thousands all over Egypt (p. 175).

It is obvious that the book is of extreme importance because, true or false, it is the only LDS scripture that teaches some of the church's most nonorthodox beliefs. If genuine, it would be the earliest Jewish/Christian scriptural writing known to man. Yet, in spite of clear, unbiased scholarly tests that prove the Book of Abraham to be a complete fraud, the valiant, faithful members of the church continue to prefer to take the word of their prophet over valid scholarship.

It is interesting to look at what LDS scholars themselves say about the matter. Hugh Nibley's recent book *The Message of the Joseph Smith Papyri: An Egyptian Endowment* is a case in point. In studying the book and going back to the Book of Abraham, the reader will be astonished to find little to no correspondence between the way Joseph Smith had translated the text and the actual meaning of the Egyptian characters. The reproductions of facsimiles one through three, found with the Book of Abraham in the *Pearl of Great Price*, are prime examples of gross misinterpretations given by Smith in his fable.

When Dr. Nibley examined the recovered papyri in 1967, he admitted that "the papyrus scripts given to the Church *do not prove* the Book of Abraham is true" (from an article in the Brigham Young University newspaper, *The Daily Universe*, December 1, 1967). That was the understatement of the year.

Even his book does such a poor job in trying to defend Joseph Smith's "translation" that the church has been unwilling to endorse it, even though it is published by Deseret Publishing. In fact, Francis Gibbs (then secretary to the First Presidency) wrote the Baptist minister to Mormons John L. Smith and stated, "The writings of Dr. Hugh Nibley concerning the papyri scrolls have been done entirely on his own responsibility, and *do not have the official approval and sanction of the church*" (copy of letter on file).

In 1976, Nibley asked fellow LDS Egyptologist Dee Jay Nelson (who claimed to have a Ph.D.) to help translate the scrolls. Nelson concluded that Joseph *didn't get one character right* on the whole scroll, and that it had nothing to do with Abraham, but was a funeral text!

Although Mormon scholars originally stated that Nelson's "competence in both Egyptian and Semitic languages is unquestioned" (Richley H. Crapo, *Book of Abraham Symposium*, April 30, 1970, p. 27), it later developed that Nelson's doctorate was from a diploma mill in Seattle. When this was discovered, Mormon apologists tried to make a lot of mileage out of the fact that Nelson was "discredited." Yet although Nelson's academic credentials were discredited, his translation of the papyrus was not. In fact, it was said to be quite excellent!

The *Ogden Standard Examiner* investigated the controversy surrounding Nelson's credentials and competence. It contacted the leading U.S. expert on Egyptology, Dr. Klaus Baer of the University of Chicago's Oriental Institute. Dr. Baer was quoted as saying that although Nelson had no formal training in Egyptology, "he had certainly learned Egyptian somewhere" (*Ogden Standard Examiner*, March 29, 1980, article by Charles F. Trentelman).

He described Nelson as "having a good amateur knowledge of Egyptian. He can translate hieroglyphics, but not without error. . . . As to the papyri in question, Nelson's translation is 'essentially' correct" (ibid.).

That means that Joseph Smith's "translation" is essentially incorrect. Dr. Baer provided his own translation of the papyri, which was published in the "liberal" *Dialogue: A Journal of Mormon Thought* (Autumn 1968, pp. 119-20). Although too lengthy to quote here, it bears *no resemblance* to Smith's Book of Abraham.

Another Egyptologist, Dr. Richard A. Parker of Brown University, also published his translation, which almost totally agrees with Dr. Baer's and which bears zero resemblance to the Book of Abraham (Autumn 1968, pp. 119-20).

Both scholars' translations comprise only about 75 words. Compare that to Smith's Book of Abraham: It has *thousands* of words. Joseph somehow milked dozens of words out of a single Egyptian character. For example, one character in the papyri which resembles a backwards "E" is "translated" by Smith as Abraham 1:13-14. That is 76 words in those verses alone, including nine proper names and eight other nouns (Decker, *The Massive Mormon Scripture Mess* [Issaquah, WA: Saints Alive, 1987], p. 20).

This isn't an unusual example. Abraham 1:16-19 contains 177 words that Joseph Smith "translated" from a single character that represented the name of an Egyptian god named Khonso.

In the more than 20 years since the papyri came to light, not one LDS defender has been able to explain how Joseph Smith managed to derive the Book of Abraham from a 70-plus-word pagan funeral text. Clearly, Smith knew nothing of Egyptian and obviously had no divine help in translating the papyri. The Book of Abraham is a fraudulent work and it bears strong testimony to the deep spiritual blindness of the LDS people—a basically intelligent people who cannot allow themselves to look at reality in such a matter of faith.

BOOK OF LIFE

The LDS Position

Mormons have a unique approach to understanding the book of life. Of course, they do correctly identify it with the "Lamb's book of life" mentioned in Revelation 3:5; 13:8; 17:8; and 20:15. They believe, as do Christians, that this book contains the names of the redeemed. It is *how* they are redeemed that is the problem.

Yet there is also a real figurative sense in which they wish to define this book of life:

> The book of life is the record of the acts of men as such record is written in their own bodies. It is the record engraven on the very bones, sinews, and flesh of the mortal body. That is, every thought, word, and deed has an affect on the human body; all these leave their marks, marks which can be read by Him who is Eternal as easily as the words in a book can be read.
>
> By *obedience to telestial law* men obtain telestial bodies; terrestrial law leads to terrestrial bodies; and conformity to celestial law—because this law includes the sanctifying power of the Holy Ghost—results in the creation of a body which is clean, pure, and spotless, a celestial body (*Doctrine and Covenants* 88:16-32). When the book of life is opened in the day of judgment (Revelation 20:12-15), men's bodies will show what law they have lived. The Great Judge will then read the record of the book of their lives; the account of their obedience or disobedience will be written in their bodies (*Doctrine*, p. 97).

This is, of course, not a biblically warranted interpretation of what the book of life is. Of course, it endorses the LDS doctrine of salvation by works of obedience to their gospel law.

The Biblical View

The Bible tells us that the names of the redeemed were written in the book of life "from the foundation of the world" (Revelation

17:8). If that is true, then nothing we could do as Christians could impact that name being written, since it was done even before the world was made. It certainly could not be some reading of our human physiology as the teaching above states, for that physiology was not even created until millennia after our names were written in the book. Praise God, we are saved by His grace alone!

BOOK OF MORMON

The *Book of Mormon* is the keystone of the LDS church and its religious belief system. Though only a few of the unique LDS beliefs can be found in the *Book of Mormon*, that book is the supposed "proof" of Joseph Smith's prophetic calling. Smith himself taught:

> Take away the *Book of Mormon* and the revelations, and where is our religion? *We have none*; for without Zion, and a place of deliverance, we must fall; because the time is near when the sun will be darkened, and the moon turn to blood, and the stars fall from heaven, and the earth reel to and fro. Then, if this is the case, and if we are not sanctified and gathered to the places God has appointed, with all our former professions and our great love for the Bible, *we must fall; we cannot stand; we cannot be saved!* (*Teachings*, p. 71).

The centrality of this book makes it essential that we examine it. There are several entries under the *Book of Mormon* heading; this is only the introductory one. Others will examine the changes in the *Book of Mormon* text, its doctrinal problems, and its many errors in history, logic, science, consistency, etc. This section will serve as a brief introduction.

Mormons believe that the *Book of Mormon* is an abridged account of God's dealings with a group of Jewish people (and some others) who fled to the New World. It is said to span a period in pre-Columbian history from 2247 B.C. to A.D. 421. The original records which comprise the *Book of Mormon* were said to be written on plates of gold and brass by various prophets from this New World community.

A key feature of this book's narrative is a conflict between the descendants of two brothers, Nephi and Laman, who came with their father Lehi along with other members of their family from

Jerusalem around the time of the prophet Jeremiah in 600 B.C. Nephi, who was righteous and faithful to his father, produced a line of godly descendants who came to be known as Nephites. Laman, who was a churl, produced descendants who were sinners and evil before the Lord. These "Lamanites" (see also *Lamanites*) were smitten by God with the curse of a dark skin and they began to make war with the Nephites and persecute them.

A key selling point of the *Book of Mormon* (especially as it is presented today) is its teaching that, after His resurrection, Jesus Christ came in His glorified body to the Americas around A.D. 33. After first causing days of darkness to envelop the mystified populace and then bringing devastating earthquakes which wiped out many cities, Jesus supposedly descended in a pillar of light to receive the adulation of the (surviving) Nephites.

The *Book of Mormon* teaches that Jesus established another branch of His church in the Americas, complete with 12 disciples. He also preached sizable parts of the Sermon on the Mount and other things taken verbatim from the Gospel narrative. Then, after establishing His church, He ascended to heaven. This was followed by many years of idyllic peace between the Nephites and Lamanites, but ultimately apostasy occurred.

Around A.D. 400, a massive, genocidal war commenced which ended with the destruction of virtually all the Nephites. The few who survived were led by a prophet and general named Moroni. He took all the metallic plates containing the records of his people and hid them in a hill called Cumorah. This hill was supposedly located in what is today rural New York State near Palmyra. There they were hid from 421 to the early 1800s, when supposedly Moroni appeared to a youth named Joseph Smith and showed him where the plates were.

After three years, Smith was considered worthy to remove the plates, and then he began to translate them from "Reformed Egyptian"—supposedly a hitherto unknown ancient language used by the Hebrews in America—into English by the gift and power of God.

It is upon Smith's alleged finding of the plates and his supposed ability to translate them that the entire foundation of the LDS church rests. The *Book of Mormon* claims to be superior to the Bible because the plates have lain pristine for 1000 years under Hill Cumorah, untouched by human hands. The Bible, on the other hand, Mormons believe to have been tampered with by wicked monks and rabbis down through the centuries.

Mormons today call the *Book of Mormon* "Another Testament of Jesus Christ" and are trying their best to make it line up beside the New Testament. As we shall see, it falls far short of that lofty aspiration. It is, perhaps, fitting to close with the very title page of the *Book of Mormon* to point out the significant problems raised by this odd and disturbing piece of pseudepigrapha (false Scripture):

The
Book of Mormon
an account written by
The Hand of Mormon
upon plates
taken from the plates of Nephi

Wherefore, it is an abridgment of the record of the people of Nephi, and also of the Lamanites—Written to the Lamanites, who are a remnant of the house of Israel; and also to Jew and Gentile—Written by way of commandment, and also by the spirit of prophecy and of revelation—Written and sealed up, and hid up unto the Lord, that they might not be destroyed—To come forth by the gift and power of God unto the interpretation thereof—Sealed by the hand of Moroni, and hid up unto the Lord, to come forth in due time by way of the Gentile—The interpretation thereof by the gift of God.

An abridgment taken from the Book of Ether also, which is a record of the people of Jared, who were scattered at the time the Lord confounded the language of the people, when they were building a tower to get to heaven—Which is to show unto the remnant of the House of Israel what great things the Lord hath done for their fathers; and that they may know the covenants of the Lord, that they are not cast off forever—And also to the convincing of the Jew and Gentile that JESUS is the CHRIST, the ETERNAL GOD, manifesting himself unto all nations—And now, if there are faults they are the mistakes of men; wherefore, condemn not the things of God, that ye may be found spotless at the judgment-seat of Christ.

Unlike the Holy Bible, the *Book of Mormon* right up front admits that it may have "faults"—not a very promising beginning for a book that wishes to tower above the "monarch of books"!

BOOK OF MORMON, CHANGES IN

For most of the LDS church's 150-year history, church leaders staunchly maintained that there were no changes in the *Book of Mormon* of a doctrinal nature. Indeed, Joseph Fielding Smith warned in 1961:

> There was not one thing in the *Book of Mormon* or in the second edition or in any other edition since that in any way contradicts the first edition, and *such changes as were made* were made by the prophet Joseph Smith because under those adverse conditions the *Book of Mormon* was published. *But there was no change of doctrine.* Now, these sons of Belial who circulate these reports evidently know better. I will not use the word that is in my mind (*The Improvement Era*, December 1961, pp. 924-25).

As with everything else in Mormonism, these claims have changed over the years. Today, most Mormons will guardedly acknowledge that there have been *many* changes—and not all of them made only to the first edition. Yet they still maintain that not one doctrinally significant teaching has been changed.

There have been more than 4000 changes made to the *Book of Mormon*, and *not all of them are minor.* Although the recent "line" on the changes in the *Book of Mormon* from the LDS church is that they are unimportant, examination does not bear this out— especially when one considers the contention by *Joseph Smith himself* (see *Saint's Herald*, November 15, 1962, p. 16) that the golden plates were supposedly translated *letter-by-letter* "by the power of God" (*History of the Church*, pp. 54-55).

If this were true, why were any errors committed at all? Typographical errors are one thing; *profound* changes in doctrine and *major* errors in consistency and common sense are quite another. Here is a list of a few serious changes in the *Book of Mormon*. First we will reproduce the text from the 1830 edition; then we will list subsequent changes, with the changed parts highlighted.

Doctrinal Problems

1. Title page: (both versions)

    1830: ". . . by Joseph Smith, jr., *author* and proprietor"

Today: "*translated* by Joseph Smith, Jr."

2. First Book of Nephi, p. 25 (1830): "Behold, the virgin which thou seest, is *the mother of God,* after the manner of the flesh."

   Today: 1 Nephi 11:18: ". . . is the mother of *the Son of* God."

3. First Book of Nephi, p. 25 (1830): ". . . behold the lamb of God, yea, even the Eternal Father!"

   Today: 1 Nephi 11:21: "yea, even *the Son of* the Eternal Father!"

4. First Book of Nephi, p. 26 (1830): "And I looked and beheld the Lamb of God, that he was taken by the people; *yea, the Everlasting God* was judge of the world."

   Today: 1 Nephi 11:32: ". . . yea *the Son of* the Everlasting God was judged of the world."

5. First Book of Nephi, p. 32 (1830): ". . . that the Lamb of God is the Eternal Father and the Saviour of the world."

   Today: ". . . the Lamb of God *is the Son of* the Eternal Father and the Savior of the world."

6. Second Book of Nephi, p. 37 (1830): ". . . and the mean man boweth down, and the great man humbleth himself not" (cf. Isaiah 2:6-9).

   Today: 2 Nephi 12:9: "and the mean man boweth *not* down and the great man humbleth himself not."

7. Second Book of Nephi, p. 117 (1830): "and many generations shall not pass away among them, save they shall be a *white* and delightsome people."

   Today: 2 Nephi 30:6: "and many generations shall not pass away among them, save they shall be a *pure* and delightsome people."

8. Book of Alma, p. 236 (1830): "I know that Jesus Christ shall come; yea the Son of the only begotten of the Father."

   Today: Alma 5:48: "I know that Jesus Christ shall come; yea *the Son,[?] the only begotten* of the Father."

9. Book of Alma, p. 315 (1830): "But behold, as the seed swelleth and sprouteth and beginneth to grow, and then ye must needs say, That seed is good; for behold, it swelleth and sprouteth and beginneth to grow."

   Today: Alma 32:30: "But behold, as the seed swelleth and sprouteth and beginneth to grow, and then ye must needs say, That seed is good; for behold, it swelleth and sprouteth and beginneth to grow. *And now behold, will not this strengthen your faith? Yea, it will strengthen your faith: for ye will say that I know that this is a good seed; for behold, it sprouteth and beginneth to grow.*"

10. Book of Alma, p. 328 (1830): "yea, and that ye preserve these directors."

    Today: Alma 37:21: "yea, and that ye preserve these *interpreters.*"

11. Book of Alma, p. 328: (1830): "And now my son, these *directors* were prepared that the word of God might be fulfilled."

    Today: Alma 37:24: "And now my son, these *interpreters* were prepared that the word of God might be fulfilled."

Errors in Logic, Consistency, or Grammar

1. Book of Mosiah, p. 200 (1830): ". . . on learning from the mouth of Ammon that king *Benjamin* had a gift from God . . ."

   Today: Mosiah 21:28: ". . . on learning from the mouth of Ammon that king *Mosiah* had a gift from God. . . ."

   Benjamin (died c. 121 B.C.) was a *son* of a Mosiah (*Encyclopedia*, 1:99) who reigned for 40 years before Benjamin took over the throne (ibid., 2:959). Another Mosiah reigned c. 153-91 B.C. (ibid., 2:960). It is difficult to imagine how a "divine" book dictated line by line and word for word could have such a gross error. Mosiah is certainly spelled nothing like Benjamin, and the time frame is off! A book of divine origin would not get its characters so confused.

2. Book of Mosiah, p. 214 (1830): "My soul was *wrecked* with eternal torment."

Today: Mosiah 27:29: "My soul was *racked* with eternal torment."

3. Book of Alma, p. 260 (1830): "Behold, the Scriptures are before you; if ye will *arrest* them, it shall be to your own destruction" (also p. 336).

Today: Alma 13:20: "Behold, the Scriptures are before you; if ye will *wrest* them, it shall be to your own destruction."

4. Book of Alma, p. 270 (1830): "And it came to pass, when they had *arriven* in the borders of the land . . ." (also p. 433).

Today: Alma 17:13: "And it came to pass, when they had *arrived* in the borders of the land . . ."

5. Book of Alma, p. 278 (1830): "the multitude beheld that the man had *fell* dead . . ." (also p. 310).

Today: Alma 19:24: "the multitude beheld that the man had *fallen* dead . . ."

6. Book of Alma, p. 299 (1830): "Now when Ammon and his brethren saw this work of destruction among those *who* they so dearly beloved, and among those who had so dearly beloved them . . ."

Today: Alma 27:4: "Now when Ammon and his brethren saw this work of destruction among those *whom* they so dearly beloved, and among those who had so dearly beloved them . . ."

The previous five examples exhibit a misunderstanding of simple English usage—an error which God certainly would not commit.

7. Book of Alma, p. 351 (1830): ". . . he went forth among the people, *waving the rent of his garment* in the air, that all might see the writing which he *had wrote* upon the *rent* . . ."

Today: Alma 46:19: ". . . he went forth among the people, waving the *rent part* of his garment in the air, that all might see the writing which he *had written* upon the rent *part* . . ."

This reflects an error in logic. It is impossible to write on a "rent," since a rent is an absence of cloth. It is also hard to wave a "rent" in the air. Surely, if God had meant to say "rent part," He would have said it in the first edition.

8. Book of Alma, p. 353 (1830): "to remove the cause of diseases *which was subsequent* to men by the nature of the climate."

   Today: Alma 46:40: "to remove the cause of diseases *to which men were subject* by the nature of the climate."

   This obviously exhibits a misuse of simple English vocabulary—an error which God certainly would not commit.

9. Book of Alma, p. 388 (1830): "For behold, *Ammon* had sent to their support..."

   Today: Alma 57:17: "For behold, *Ammoron* had sent to their support..."

   Again, a confusion in "character" names which a novelist might make, but which God would certainly avoid.

Many other citations could be given. It is clear that although the LDS god supposedly dictated the *Book of Mormon* letter by letter, He could not spell, keep doctrine or historical characters straight, and even had serious problems with grammar and logic.

What is even more bizarre is that in the *Book of Mormon*, after all of these changes, several odd things still remain:

1. Jacob 7:27: "and to the reader I bid farewell, hoping that many of my brethren may read my words. Brethren, adieu."

   What is a French word doing in a document supposedly written by a Hebrew in America around 421 B.C.? This is almost a millennium before French existed as a language!

2. Helaman 9:6: "...when the judge had been murdered—he being stabbed by his brother *by a garb of secrecy*..."

   How can one be stabbed by a garb or garment? This is a logical absurdity.

3. Alma 13:1: ". . . my brethren, I would *cite your minds forward* to the time when the Lord gave these commandments unto his children . . ."

How can you "cite" someone's mind "forward" to something that happened in the past? Again, it is an absurd sentence.

4. Alma 24:19: ". . . they buried *their weapons of peace,* or they buried the weapons of war for peace."

What is a weapon of peace, and can it be the same as a weapon of war?

5. Alma 43:38: "they being shielded *from* the more vital parts of the body . . ."

This, again, is a biological oddity. How does one shield oneself from the vital parts of one's own body?

6. Ether 15:31: "And it came to pass that after *he had smitten off the head of Shiz, that Shiz raised up on his hands and fell; and after that he struggled for breath,* he died."

This obviously requires the violation of several biological realities involved in the decapitation of a person.

BOOK OF REMEMBRANCE

The book of remembrance is a treasured cultural icon within LDS culture. The keeping of a book of remembrance is a commandment of the church. It is loosely based on Malachi 3:16: "Then they that feared the LORD spake often one to another: and the LORD hearkened, and heard it, and a book of remembrance was written before him for them that feared the LORD, and that thought upon his name."

This is believed to be a book which records your family's history and especially your deeds of righteousness. It is believed that such books were kept by the saints in all ages (*Doctrine,* p. 100). The LDS church feels a mandate to keep vast and extensive records on

all members, past and present. This has led to the church's reputation as a "record-keeping people," which indeed it is, both indi-
vidually and corporately.

Of course, like anything else in Mormonism, sometimes the
book of remembrance gets lost in the thicket of thousands of other
good and worthy things which must be done. But many diligent
Mormons do keep journals and attempt to write (or maintain)
thorough and meticulous family histories and records. While all of
this makes for a fascinating hobby, it sadly does not prevent the
Mormon from going to hell without the true Jesus Christ.

It may, in fact, represent busywork which Satan has crafted to
keep the good Mormon people too occupied to sit back and reflect
upon the contradictions in their history and doctrine.

BORN AGAIN

The LDS Position

The meaning of the term "born again" is so central to the
heart of the Christian gospel that the way a church defines it sets it
either toward true biblical Christianity or toward false religion.

Christians, for the most part, see the new birth (or second
birth) as being very much like the first—it is a definitive event
which can often be identified with a particular time and place.
Thus, it is like the "first birth" or the physical birth of a baby.

Here, however, is the LDS definition of being born again:

> The second birth begins *when men are baptized in water by
> a legal administrator*; it is completed when they actually receive the
> companionship of the Holy Ghost, becoming new creatures by
> the cleansing power of that member of the Godhead.
> *Mere compliance with the formality of the ordinance of bap-
> tism does not mean that a person has been born again.* No one can be
> born again without baptism, but the immersion in water and the
> laying on of hands to confer the Holy Ghost do not of themselves
> guarantee that a person has been or will be born again. The new
> birth takes place only for those who actually enjoy the compan-
> ionship of the Holy Ghost, only for those who are fully converted,
> who have given themselves without restraint to the Lord. Thus

Alma addressed himself to his "brethren of the church," and pointedly asked them if they had "spiritually been born of God," received the Lord's image in their countenances, and had the "mighty change" in their hearts which always attends the birth of the Spirit (Alma 5:14-31).

Those members of the Church who have actually been born again are in a blessed and favored state. They have attained their position, not merely by joining the Church, but through *faith* (1 John 5:1), *righteousness* (1 John 2:29), *love* (1 John 4:7), and *overcoming the world* (*Doctrine*, p. 101).

By this definition, no average Mormon can ever be *truly certain* if he or she has been born again. Mormons can mark the beginning of their born-again experience when they are baptized by water "by a legal administrator," but they can never be certain if they fulfill all the other commands. This is why no Mormon has an assurance of his or her eternal destiny.

The Biblical View

This stands out in stark contrast to the clear teaching of the New Testament. Jesus teaches us that true believers in Him can have assurance of eternal life right now:

> Verily, verily, I say unto you, He that heareth my word, and believeth on him that sent me, *hath* everlasting life, and shall not come into condemnation; but *is* passed from death unto life (John 5:24).
> Verily, verily, I say unto you, He that believeth on me *hath* everlasting life (John 6:47).
> My sheep hear my voice, and I know them, and they follow me: and I *give* unto them *eternal life*; and *they shall never perish*, neither shall any man pluck them out of my hand. My father, which gave them me, is greater than all; and no man is able to pluck them out of my Father's hand (John 10:27-29).

It is easy to see the emphasis here in the present tense. Salvation is not just happening for a true Christian—it has happened! Another wonderful New Testament truth is that all true Christians are sealed unto eternity by God Himself:

116

And grieve not the holy Spirit of God, whereby ye are sealed unto the day of redemption (Ephesians 4:30).

That we should be to the praise of his glory, who first trusted in Christ. In whom ye also trusted, after that ye heard the word of truth, the gospel of your salvation: in whom also after that ye believed, ye were *sealed with that holy Spirit of promise, which is the earnest* of our inheritance until the redemption of the purchased possession, unto the praise of his glory (Ephesians 1:12-14).

Now he which stablisheth us with you in Christ, and hath anointed us, is God; who hath also *sealed* us, and given the *earnest* of the Spirit in our hearts (2 Corinthians 1:21,22).

The concept here is that the Lord has given us the Holy Spirit as "earnest money" or a security deposit, if you will, on our heavenly mansions. Just as you cannot lose a home you want if your earnest money is in the seller's hands, so the Holy Spirit is our personal promise of a complete, eternal reward. Again, note the tenses in these verses—this is the past tense, something which is already a "done deal," and not something which the believer has to work on or tinker with.

The Bible also teaches that real born-again people are *kept* by the power of God through faith unto salvation (1 Peter 1:5) and are told to "work out your own salvation with fear and trembling. For it is *God which worketh in you* both to will and to do of his good pleasure" (Philippians 2:12,13).

In all of this, it is what God is doing and has done, not anything the Christian can do. Finally, the most wonderful Bible truth which the Mormon is missing is the fact that they can *know* for certain that they have (present tense) eternal life: "These things have I written unto you that believe on the name of the Son of God; that ye may *know* that ye have eternal life, and that ye may believe on the name of the Son of God" (1 John 5:13).

To all of these simple promises, the poor Mormon adds requirements for water baptism by the "right" person in authority. This means that for a Mormon no non-LDS person can really be born again, in spite of his or her profession. Beyond that, the Mormon must be certain he has the right amount of faith, righteousness, and devotion to the Mormon church—and has overcome the world!

There can be no real "good news" in this LDS gospel, because no Mormon can ever rest in the Lord, secure that he has eternal life.

That is totally different from the simple message Paul preached. Thus, sadly, for all their efforts, Mormons have no real hope and no real salvation. They cannot really be born again through the LDS gospel.

BUFFETINGS OF SATAN

This is a term used by Mormons to describe the fate of those who have been disfellowshipped or excommunicated from the church for serious offenses. They believe that the church is a kind of protected space for people and that to have its protective umbrella withdrawn from a person is to leave him naked and exposed to anything which Satan wishes to inflict upon him. Bruce R. McConkie describes it thus:

> To be turned over to the buffetings of Satan is to be given into his hands; it is to be turned over to him with all the protective power of the priesthood, of righteousness, and of godliness removed, so that Lucifer is free to torment, persecute, and afflict such a person without let or hindrance. When the bars are down, the cuffs and curses of Satan, both in this world and in the world to come, bring indescribable anguish typified by burning fire and brimstone. The damned in hell so suffer.
> Those who broke their covenants in connection with the United Order in the early days of this dispensation were to "be delivered over to the buffetings of Satan until the day of redemption" (*Doctrine and Covenants* 78:12; 82:20-21; 104:9-10). A similar fate (plus destruction in the flesh) is decreed against those who have been sealed up unto eternal life so that their callings and elections have been made sure and who thereafter turn to grievous sin (*Doctrine and Covenants* 131:5; 132:19-26) (*Doctrine*, p. 108)

While the Bible does teach that Christian believers may be turned over to Satan for the "destruction of the flesh, that the spirit might be saved in the day of the Lord Jesus" (1 Corinthians 5:5), the Mormon understanding of what this entails is far from biblical.

First of all, no true Christian can ever be excommunicated from the body of Christ (Romans 8:37-39). For serious sins— especially for those which might cause public scandal—a Christian might be disfellowshipped from local church membership, but only as a last resort. Of course, Mormons equate membership in their church with salvation, so they practice excommunication as a last resort. But it is not biblical.

Even more problematic are McConkie's remarks in the second paragraph of his teaching. In the days of the United Order (and also in the times of Brigham Young's reign over Utah), severe *physical* penalties were inflicted upon "those who broke their covenants." Though today LDS leaders will deny it, there were marauding bands of theocratic vigilantes known as "Danites" or "Avenging Angels"— almost a Mormon Ku Klux Klan—who would often exact fearsome retribution upon any who were seen to be out of order with the rulers of the church.

The LDS doctrine of "blood atonement" (see also *Blood Atonement Doctrine*) demanded actual *death* for certain "sins" against the Lord and His church, such as "apostasy" (meaning disagreeing with church leaders) or adultery. Thus, unlike Paul, the Mormons were not content to leave vengeance to the Lord—they exacted it themselves.

BURNING IN THE BOSOM

The LDS Position

Rarely does a Mormon bear his/her testimony but that he/she will say, "I know the church is true. I know that Joseph Smith is a true prophet of God. I know that the *Book of Mormon* is true, that it's the perfect word of God."

When challenged to give stronger evidence than the simple statement, "I know..." invariably the inquirer will be told, "I prayed about it and God made it manifest to me beyond any doubt." How? "I received a burning in my bosom and I know it is true." End of conversation. The Mormon "burning in the bosom" strikes again.

This response relies upon a subjective feeling that supposedly represents a special moment when the LDS god *actually* touched them, personally and physically. It is a moment in life when God breathed His warmth upon them. It's probably the most untouchable part of their faith. You can ask a Mormon, "How can you trust your feelings?" and the response will be "This isn't a feeling. God physically touched me. I felt it in a real, tangible burning in my bosom." The "burning bosom" allegedly gives a very peaceful feeling, but what does it really prove?

A key part of the conversion strategy of LDS missionaries is to quote to the investigator out of Moroni 10:3-5, especially part of verse 4: "I would exhort you that ye would ask God, the Eternal Father, in the name of Christ, if these things are not true; and if you shall ask with a sincere heart, with real intent, having faith in Christ, he will manifest the truth of it unto you, by the power of the Holy Ghost."

They then team this verse with *Doctrine and Covenants* 9:8,9:

> Behold I say unto you, that you must study it out in your mind; then you must ask me if it be right, and if it be right I will cause that your bosom shall burn within you; therefore, you shall feel that it is right. (9) But if it be not right you shall have no such feelings, but you shall have a stupor of thought that shall cause you to forget the thing which is wrong; therefore you cannot write that which is sacred save it be given you from me.

Combining these two, the Mormons have come up with the idea that if the investigator reads the *Book of Mormon* and then "prays about it" and they get this mystical "burning bosom," then the *Book of Mormon* (and Joseph Smith and the Mormon church) must be true. The convert "knows" the message is true.

The Biblical View

This whole procedure is utterly without scriptural foundation. Nowhere in the Bible are we told that we can trust our feelings with important issues like our eternal destiny. We cannot use the *Book of Mormon* or other LDS scriptures to prove the validity of the burning bosom, because that would be circular reasoning. You cannot logically or reasonably prove the *Book of Mormon* with a quote from the *Book of Mormon* or other Mormon books which depend upon the *Book of Mormon* for their authentication. We must depend on the Bible alone, which says nothing about trusting our feelings. To the contrary, the Bible warns that "there is a way which seemeth right unto a man, but the end thereof are the ways of death" (Proverbs 14:12).

Additionally, in Jeremiah we read, "The heart is deceitful above all things, and desperately wicked: who can know it?" (Jeremiah 17:9).

There is no guarantee from the Bible (or even from our own experiences in life) that our feelings can be trusted. How many times have you *felt* sure that you were right about something, only to find out you were wrong? How often have people *felt* sure that someone really loved them, and then found out they were deceiving themselves without even knowing it? If we can be this easily deceived in human relationships, why trust our immortal souls on such emotional, unreliable methods?

The whole problem of impulse shopping is based on the premise that advertising and marketing can make someone *feel* as if they absolutely *have* to have something, even though they entered the store without any such notion. With all of this evidence to the contrary, why should anyone think that they can trust their heart when it comes to God and His truth?

The human capacity for self-deception is enormous. Attend an Alcoholics Anonymous meeting and find out how many people there used to say, "I don't have a problem with drinking," while they were falling down drunk.

We should not be praying about whether some man is truly a prophet of God; we should be testing him and his utterances to see if they meet biblical tests already given to us for that purpose. The Bible gives several objective tests for measuring spiritual truth and those who claim to be prophets.

1. The utterance must agree with what is already written in the Bible:
   > "To the law and to the testimony: if they speak not according to this word, it is because there is no light in them" (Isaiah 8:20).

Joseph Smith's teachings and prophecies and much of the material in the *Book of Mormon* are in contradiction to the Bible, as we have shown throughout this book.

2. The prophet cannot be leading anyone after other gods. (Obviously, Joseph Smith does lead his people to other gods!)
   > If there arise among you a prophet, or a dreamer of dreams, and giveth thee a sign or a wonder, and the sign or the wonder come to pass, whereof he spake unto thee, saying, Let us go after other gods, which thou hast not known, and let us serve them; thou shalt not hearken

121

unto the words of that prophet, or that dreamer of dreams: for the LORD your God proveth you, to know whether ye love the LORD your God with all your heart and with all your soul (Deuteronomy 13:1-3).

3. The prophet's prophecies must *all* come true. (Joseph Smith's prophecies were mostly false. That makes him a false prophet.)
    But the prophet, which shall presume to speak a word in my name, which I have not commanded him to speak, or that shall speak in the name of other gods, even that prophet shall die. And if thou say in thine heart, How shall we know the word which the LORD hath not spoken? When a prophet speaketh in the name of the LORD, if the thing follow not, nor come to pass, that is the thing which the LORD hath not spoken, but the prophet hath spoken it presumptuously: thou shalt not be afraid of him (Deuteronomy 18:20-22).

These are three objective ways of determining biblical truth. We must trust in them, rather than in our hearts, which can easily be deceived.

CALLING AND ELECTION MADE SURE

The LDS Position

Ironically enough, there is one way that Mormons can have a blessed assurance of their eternal destiny (they think!). This is by having their "calling and election made sure." Bruce R. McConkie explains it in this fashion:

> Those members of the Church who devote themselves wholly to righteousness, living by every word that proceedeth forth from the mouth of God, make their calling and election sure. That is, they receive the more sure word of prophecy, which means that the Lord seals their exaltation upon them while they are yet in this life (*Doctrine*, pp. 109-10).

Of course, few Mormons actually attain this sublime state. Neither is it clear exactly what a Mormon must do to achieve it. LDS founder Joseph Smith taught:

> After a person has faith in Christ, repents of his sins, and is baptized for the remission of his sins and receives the Holy Ghost (by the laying on of hands), which is the first Comforter, then let him continue to humble himself before God, hungering and thirsting after righteousness, and living by every word of God, and the Lord will soon say unto him, Son, thou shalt be exalted. When the Lord has thoroughly proved him, and finds that the man is determined to serve him at all hazards, then the

man will find his calling and election made sure, then it will be his privilege to receive the other Comforter (*Teachings*, pp. 149-51, our emphasis).

In practice, to receive "the other Comforter" is to have Christ appear to the Mormon and to see visions of eternity. This is also called "the more sure word of prophecy" and is dealt with in greater detail in *Doctrine and Covenants*: "The more sure word of prophecy means a man's knowing that he is sealed up unto eternal life, by revelation and the spirit of prophecy, through the power of the Holy Priesthood" (*Doctrine and Covenants* 131:5).

These fortunate Mormons are promised that: "Ye shall come forth in the first resurrection; and shall inherit thrones, kingdoms, principalities, and powers, dominions, all heights and depths" (*Doctrine and Covenants* 132:19).

Additionally, they supposedly receive a kind of "immunity from prosecution" from the commission of virtually all sins except murder and blasphemy against the Holy Spirit (see also *Blasphemy Against the Holy Ghost*). Though they "shall commit any sin or transgression of the new and everlasting covenant whatever, and all manner of blasphemies, and if they commit no murder wherein they shed innocent blood, yet they shall come forth in the first resurrection, and enter into their exaltation" (*Doctrine and Covenants* 132:26).

This means that such people become living gods who walk upon the earth. Naturally, Joseph Smith received a revelation from the Lord that he had attained this status and was sealed for all eternity for thrones and kingdoms (*Doctrine and Covenants* 132:49).

Although Mormons must go through the temple and receive their endowments (see also *Endowments*) and be sealed in celestial marriage (see also *New and Everlasting Covenant*), these by no means assure them of having their calling and election made sure. They merely qualify the Mormon for these higher honors.

It should be clearly understood that these high blessings are not part of celestial marriage. "Blessings pronounced upon couples in connection with celestial marriage are conditioned upon the subsequent faithfulness of the participating parties" (*Doctrines of Salvation*, vol. 2, pp. 46-47).

This can be seen by examining the actual words of the temple rituals, which if examined carefully reveal that all the blessings of the temple given to the Mormon as he takes out his endowment are conditional. For example, the anointing which the temple patron receives before beginning the endowment contains these words: "Brother _____, having authority, I pour this holy anointing oil upon your head and anoint you preparatory to your becoming a King and Priest unto the Most High God, hereafter to rule and reign in the House of Israel forever" (Sackett, p. 19).

Note that the patron is not anointed as a king and priest, but only in preparation to becoming one. Later on in the "Creation Room" teaching of the temple endowment, the very conditional nature of these blessings is driven home still further: "Brethren and sisters, if you are true and faithful, the day will come when you will be chosen, called up and anointed Kings and Queens, Priests and Priestesses, whereas you are now anointed only to become such. The realization of these blessings depends on your faithfulness" (Sackett, p. 21).

Thus, like everything else in Mormonism, temple blessings are entirely conditional upon good works. Now, since only about 25 to 30 percent of Mormons ever make it through the temple, and only about 25 to 30 percent of them are current and regular temple attendees, this means that substantially less than 10 percent qualify for this second blessing.

How is it received? This aspect is, naturally, shrouded in the deepest secrecy. However, through the research of people like Chuck Sackett and his late wife, Dolly, some important information has come to the fore about what Mormons call the "second anointing" (contact Chuck Sackett at Sword of the Shepherd ministries, P.O. Box 4707, Thousand Oaks, CA 91359, for more information on this subject). This seems to be the ritual by which one's calling and election are made sure.

As near as can be determined, it can only be done in the Salt Lake City temple. Unlike regular sealings in the temple, which are presided over by a high priest who has been given special "sealing keys" by the prophet of the church (see also *Sealing Power*), this second anointing can only be presided over by the prophet or one of the First Presidency.

Apparently, if an otherwise worthy Mormon believes that he has had a vision of the Lord or of eternity, he comes and has this vision affirmed by divine revelation from the prophet or one of his counselors. Though details are sketchy because of the secrecy and comparative infrequency of this second anointing, the following seems to be what happens.

The candidate and his wife are brought to the Salt Lake temple and led into a special sealing room not normally seen or used by temple patrons. It may even be the so-called "Holy of Holies" room which opens off the celestial room of the Salt Lake temple. Into this room only the prophet and extremely high level LDS leaders (apostles, etc.) are normally ever permitted. It is there the candidate for the second anointing is brought, along with his wife.

Apparently, the anointings given the couple in their original temple initiatory work as described above are given them again, but this time without the conditional phrasing. They *are* anointed to be a king and queen, a priest and priestess, and to rule and reign in the House of Israel forever. Reports are that either before or after these anointings the wife washes her husband's feet. They are each given a new "new name" (see also *New Name*) and evidently some changes are made to the temple garment which each must wear. Other distinctive marks (none too obtrusive) are added to the design of the garment. They may be also taught new "tokens" (i.e., handshakes and signs) by which they might recognize and be recognized.

Then the couple is sent on their way—although some accounts indicate that they are given the privilege of sleeping in the temple that night and are supposed to experience further visionary experiences. At this point they have "made it" in the fullest sense as Mormons. They are evidently not permitted to discuss their new status with anyone except other "living gods," and probably thousands of Mormons live their entire lives without even knowing that such an exalted status can be attained in this life.

There are no clear estimates of how many have received this second anointing. Certainly all the prophets and apostles of the church down through the years may have had it, as well as some other general authorities and a few of the leading international pillars of the Mormon community, who may not be part of the highest hierarchy but who have still distinguished themselves with lives of faithful service. There is no question but that it represents only the tiniest fraction of one percent of church membership.

That is sad, especially when you consider that all Bible-believing Christians have their calling and election made sure the moment they are saved (2 Peter 1:10,19; see *Born Again*). They have available to them the assurance that only a statistically minute number of Mormons have—plus their assurance is in a true and risen Lord, not in a Mormon counterfeit.

CANCELLATION OF SEALINGS

The LDS practice of canceling sealings of celestial marriages made in the temple (supposedly performed for time and all eternity) is one of the surest testimonies that the LDS church is not all it is supposed to be. LDS author Bruce R. McConkie tells us:

> Properly speaking there is no such thing as a temple divorce; divorces in this day are civil matters handled by the courts of the land. But following a civil divorce of persons who have been married for eternity in the temples, if the circumstances are sufficiently serious to warrant it, the President of the Church has power to cancel the sealings involved. He holds the keys and power both to bind and loose on earth and in heaven (Matt. 16:19; *Doctrine and Covenants* 132:46; *Doctrines of Salvation*, vol. 2, p. 84) (*Doctrine*, pp. 110-11).

Only the prophet himself has the power to grant these cancellations. Though the church will not call temple marriages which have been dissolved by the prophet "temple divorces," the end result is the same. Mormons claim that their doctrines produce happy families and that "families are forever." Certainly all Christian churches suffer from divorce within their ranks, but *not* all Christian churches tie marriage so intimately to salvation as do the Mormons.

Thus, it is significant that the church feels it has to provide mechanisms to undo so sacred and eternal an ordinance as they believe celestial marriage to be. Understand that a Mormon seeking a cancellation of sealing has begun to play Russian roulette with his or her eternal destiny. This is especially true for the LDS wife.

Without a celestial marriage, the highest blessings of Mormonism are not available. Thus, a divorced (and "canceled") Mormon has lost a sure ticket to glory. Of course, they can (and often do) get married again, but there is a chance that they will not find another spouse. In spite of all the church's efforts to the contrary, single or divorced Mormons remain second-class citizens.

Thus, for a Mormon to seek a cancellation of sealing is an admission of spectacular failure. Many Mormons simply get legal divorces and leave their celestial marriage intact, rather than seek their spouse's permission to get a cancellation of a temple marriage. This is especially true for husbands. They can have more than one celestial wife. Thus, he might legally divorce wife number one and later marry wife number two in the temple. Spiritually, he would be a polygamist, even if legally he was not. It is a way of hedging your bets. Some spouses feel that the problems which the marriage entailed on earth might be able to be worked out in the eternities, without all the hassles of this earth complicating matters.

In a church which has idolized marriage and the family, this ability to cancel temple marriages stands as an odd anomaly—a testimony to the fact that there are some things even the Mormon priesthood cannot force to work right.

CELESTIAL GLORY/KINGDOM

(See also *Degrees of Glory*)

The LDS Position

The highest kingdom or degree of glory for the resurrected person is the celestial glory or celestial kingdom. The celestial kingdom is reserved for those Mormons who have lived lives of purity and obedience to all the laws and ordinances of the LDS "gospel" throughout his or her lifetime.

There are three levels of glory within the celestial kingdom. There are some general theories as to how they are divided and peopled, but the official doctrine is this:

In the Celestial glory there are three heavens or degrees; and in order to obtain the highest, a man must enter into this order of the priesthood [meaning the new and everlasting covenant of marriage (LDS note—not author's)]; and if he does not, he cannot obtain it. He may enter into the other, but that is the end of his kingdom; he cannot have an increase (*Doctrine and Covenants* 131:1-4).

In simpler language, only a man (or woman, by default or implied inclusion) who has been married in the temple for time and all eternity, can enter the highest level of the celestial kingdom. This may be done either in the person's lifetime or by a proxy temple ritual after death. Unmarried single people (male, female, or any child under the age of eight who died in that state and did not have proxy work performed for them) will become citizens of one of the two lower levels of heaven in the celestial kingdom.

The key to meriting the highest degree of glory within the celestial grouping is the ability to procreate. In each case, it will be one man and as many wives as possible to advance the massive numbers of offspring necessary to people that new man/god's future world, over which he will be the god. Obviously, he will be very busy raising up his "increase." Remember that while each woman must be just as pure and worthy as each man, the power and authority and rights of godhood rest with the man, not the woman.

One point that might help clarify the situation is that, even today, many single LDS women are sealed to LDS leaders to be their wives in the next stage of eternal progression. Many of them do this in order not to be a servant (unmarried) in the celestial kingdom. It must be a real hardship to have done everything else so perfectly to be awarded a place in the celestial glory, yet fail in that one major area of marriage and have to sit out eternity on the sidelines.

Generally speaking, a Mormon on the road to celestial glory is an active member, attends all required meetings, has taken out his/her endowments, been married in the temple, holds an active temple recommend, and attends regularly. He/she would have to be actively involved in doing genealogical work and submitting names for vicarious baptism and temple work. Paying a full tithe is a must (in fact, just a starter) for a celestial glory candidate. Welfare, building funds, missionary support, and other financial giving will take another 10 to 15 percent of the candidate's income.

Ironically, even if a member fulfills all the above and more but forgets any of the secret grips, passwords, or tokens learned while going through the endowment ceremony or forgets his/her secret "new name," he/she will not be able to get past the sentinels guarding entrance to the celestial kingdom.

Going on a full-term mission for the member/spouse and children is another commandment which must be fulfilled if the candidate is to qualify. If a couple lives to an old age, it helps to serve a

129

late-in-life mission as a couple, as well as to serve as temple workers, assisting in the rituals in various functions.

The *Doctrine and Covenants* lists six basic requirements for celestial glory and the resurrection of the just.

1. They are they who received the testimony of Jesus and

2. believed on his name and were baptized after the manner of his burial, being buried in the water in his name, and this according to the commandment which he has given,

3. that by keeping the commandments they might be washed and cleansed from all their sins,

4. and receive the Holy Spirit by the laying on of hands of him who is ordained and sealed unto this power;

5. and who overcome by faith

6. and are sealed by the Holy Spirit of promise, which the Father sheds forth upon all those who are just and true (*Doctrine and Covenants* 76:50-53).

The promise for those who make the team is pretty exciting:

They are they who are the church of the Firstborn. They are they into whose hands the Father has given all things. They are they who are priests and kings, who have received of his fulness and of his glory; and are priests of the Most High, after the order of Melchizedek, which was after the order of Enoch, which was after the order of the Only Begotten Son. Wherefore, as it is written, they are gods, even the sons of God. Wherefore all things are theirs, whether life or death, or things present, or things to come, all are theirs and they are Christ's and Christ is God's. And they shall overcome all things (*Doctrine and Covenants* 76:54-60).

The Biblical View

The real tragedy is that the shed blood of Jesus has been removed as a covering from the Mormon people, replaced by their own works and purity as the reason and hope of their resurrection and salvation. All have sinned and fall short of the glory of God, and He sees our own works as filthy rags. What hope is there for even the purest Mormon alive? The Scriptures tell us that only Jesus led a sinless life.

Item 3 above requires Mormons to keep the commandments, that they might be washed clean of their sins. The Christian is already washed clean by the blood of the lamb. We are told that "you, that were sometime alienated and enemies in your mind by wicked works, yet now hath he reconciled in the body of his flesh through death, to present you holy and unblameable and unreproveable in his sight" (Colossians 1:21,22). What a promise of blessed assurance!

And what a tragedy that Mormons must stand before God's throne in fig-leaf apron coverings made by their own hands and lift up their own frail works as their only offering of righteousness before a holy God.

CHASTENING AND CHASTISEMENT

LDS doctrine links chastening to the process of Mormon salvation (one is hardly ever really saved in the Mormon church—see *Born Again*). Here is the Mormon perspective:

> By a process of chastening the Lord helps prepare his saints for salvation. It is one of his ways of turning erring souls to paths of righteousness. As varying situations require, chastening may include rebukes for misconduct or subjection to trials and afflictions. It may even take the form of chastisement, meaning corporal punishment.
>
> Men are chastened for their sins (*Doctrine and Covenants* 58:60; 61:8; 64:8; 75:7; 93:50; 97:6; 103:4; 105:6; 1 Nephi 16:25), to bring them to repentance (*Doctrine and Covenants* 1:27; 98:21), because the Lord loves them (*Doctrine and Covenants* 95:1-2; Helaman 15:3; Revelation 3:19). Chastening is designed to try the faith and patience of the saints (Mosiah 23:21), and those who endure it well gain eternal life (*Doctrine*, pp. 122-23).

Mormons believe that "all those who will not endure chastening, but deny me [the Lord] cannot be sanctified" (*Doctrine and Covenants* 101:5). Thus, this chastening is essential to the Mormon's ascension to the higher degrees of glory.

An important (and disturbing) distinction exists in Mormonism between chastening and chastisement. The latter is felt to be actual corporeal punishment, and it must also be endured in order to be worthy of salvation (see *Doctrine and Covenants* 136:31). A key distinction needs to be drawn here. Obviously, there is nothing wrong with either chastening or chastisement, as long as it is God who is doing it. However, there are strange subcultural elements within Mormonism that seldom allow such tasks to be left entirely to the Lord.

Within Mormonism there has been a strong history of violence being meted out against those perceived to be out of the will of the church leaders (see also *Blood Atonement Doctrine*, and *Buffetings of Satan*). Even in contemporary Mormondom, some very strange things are done under the cover of "chastisement."

Deep in Mormon country (Utah, Idaho, etc.), wives who are perceived as not submitting properly to their husbands are sometimes treated to church-directed correction. Of course, there is also the simple but tragic specter of plain old wife abuse. Some Mormon husbands feel that this doctrine of chastening, and especially chastisement, gives them the right to strike or beat their wife if she doesn't respect the "patriarchal order."

To their credit, LDS leaders have recently begun speaking out against wife and child abuse from General Conference pulpits; but these practices are deeply ingrained in the very warp and woof of Mormon culture. Anytime any man (or woman) thinks that he or she can begin meting out the judgment of God upon other human beings, there is serious trouble afoot!

The Biblical View

The Bible does speak of the Lord chastening those He cares for (i.e., His saved, born-again children). But the Bible claims the Lord simply uses chastisement to perfect those saints who are already in His kingdom.

> And ye have forgotten the exhortation which speaketh unto you as unto children, My son, despise not thou the chastening of the Lord, nor faint when thou art rebuked of him: for whom the Lord loveth he chasteneth, and scourgeth every son whom he receiveth. If ye endure chastening, God dealeth with you as with sons; for what son is he whom the father chasteneth not? (Hebrews 12:5-7).

Even in the church itself we see that principle applied. Paul told the elder men to instruct the young men and the young men to submit to them. Surely in dealing with the young men of the church there was godly correction and chastening! "Likewise, ye younger, submit yourselves unto the elder. Yea, all of you be subject one to another, and be clothed with humility: for God resisteth the proud, and giveth grace to the humble" (1 Peter 5:5).

If I were to give a brief summary of the difference between the chastisement of cults like the LDS church and real Christianity, it would be simply this: It is the difference between judgmental law and loving grace.

CHRISTIANITY: The LDS Perspective

Mormonism makes no effort to hide its teaching that true Christianity lies only within its own gates and that the Christianity of the rest of mankind is the work of the enemy. Bruce R. McConkie, probably writing something he thought would be used only by the LDS faithful, said this:

> Christianity is the religion of the Christians. Hence, true and acceptable Christianity is found among the saints who have the fulness of the gospel, and a perverted Christianity holds sway among the so-called Christians of apostate Christendom. In these circles it is believed and taught that Christianity had its beginning with the mortal ministry of our Lord. Actually, of course, Adam was the first Christian, for both he and the saints of all ages have rejoiced in the very doctrines of salvation restored to earth by our Lord in his ministry (*Doctrine*, p. 132).

You must remember that the whole reason for the existence of a Mormon church is that all of Christendom was apostate. Joseph Smith claimed that during his sacred grove visitation, the Lord Himself revealed this truth to him:

> My object in going to inquire of the Lord was to know which of all the sects was right, that I might know which to join. No sooner, therefore, did I get possession of myself, so as to be able to speak, than I asked the Personages who stood above me in the light, which of all the sects was right (for at this time it had never entered into my heart that all were wrong)—and which I should join.

> I was answered that I must join none of them, for they were all wrong; and the Personage who addressed me said that all their creeds were an abomination in his sight; that those professors were all corrupt; that: "they draw near to me with their lips, but their hearts are far from me, they teach for doctrines the commandments of men, having a form of godliness, but they deny the power thereof" (*Pearl of Great Price*, Joseph Smith 2:18,19).

In the *Book of Mormon*, there is another extremely clear delineation of Mormonism and any other group calling itself Christian:

> And it came to pass that he said unto me: Look, and behold that great and abominable church, which is the mother of abominations, whose founder is the devil.
> And he said unto me Behold there are save two churches only; the one is the church of the Lamb of God, and the other is the church of the devil; wherefore, whoso belongeth not to the church of the Lamb of God belongeth to that great church which is the mother of abominations; and she is the whore of all the earth (*Book of Mormon*, 1 Nephi 14:9,10).

Seeing the scathing definition of Christianity in the standard works of Mormonism, one has to wonder why the Mormons are so eager these days to become part of the ecumenical body of Christianity.

No LDS leader has repented of the original reasons that Mormons were told to separate from those other apostate Christians. Early Mormon apostle and writer Orson Pratt put the true Mormon position boldly in his book *The Seer*:

> Both Catholics and Protestants are nothing less than the "Whore of Babylon" [his emphasis] whom the Lord denounces by the mouth of John the Revelator as having corrupted all the earth with their fornications and wickedness. And any person who shall be so wicked as to receive a holy ordinance of the gospel from the ministers of any of these apostate churches will be sent down to hell with them, unless they repent of the unholy and impious act (p. 255).

In the latter part of 1991 the Associated Press ran an article titled "Mormons forge links with other faiths." In it the efforts of Mormons to become accepted as part of Christianity were stressed.

The article, knowingly or not, promulgated several falsehoods about the LDS church.

It stated, "Like other Christians, Mormons regard the Bible as holy Scripture and honor Christ as God's son." The article did not recognize the following additional facts:

1. Mormons are not "like other Christians" because that implies that they are Christians themselves, and that cannot be taken for granted;

2. They regard the Bible as defective, needing the *Book of Mormon* and "living prophets" to correct and interpret it;

3. Though they think Christ is God's son, they also think that he was conceived by sexual relations between God and Mary. They also believe that we are *all* God's sons or daughters!

This effort is part and parcel of the way the "new" 1990s model LDS church wishes to be perceived. There was a time in the not-too-distant past when Mormons would have shunned any such ecumenical cooperation. Christendom in general was whoredom. Today they welcome it. Why the difference?

In its race to look more like general Christianity, Mormonism has gone through some cataclysmic changes in the past two decades—probably more changes than at any other time in its 160-year history. Recent years have seen blacks being given rights to the priesthood; the excommunication of many of those who maintain more fundamental positions in the church; and finally, drastic changes in the Temple ceremony itself, the core of the Mormon faith. Simultaneously, many smaller adjustments can be perceived, all designed to "Christianize" the church's image. Missionary presentations have been rewritten to downplay anything strange or different about the church.

The Temple Square presentations have been overhauled. Beginning with the disappearance of the "Adam and Eve with vegetables" and the "Masonic Moroni" statues, the church has removed item after item which might raise eyebrows on Christian tourists. Gone is the "Sacred Grove" display and almost all references to Joseph Smith. Even the celebrated statue of the "Restoration of the Aaronic Priesthood" has been moved to an out-of-the-way corner of the square. Temple Square officials admit it is because they are

135

getting many more missionary referrals since removing the displays of the "Restoration of the Gospel."

Conference talks have been stripped of virtually anything which would set off alarm bells in the minds of the typical Christian listener. The same tabernacle which echoed a hundred years ago to Brigham Young's cries of "Kill the apostates!" is now filled with cozy bromides about families and Jesus. And the whole thing is broadcast via television to much of the world twice a year. As we watch all this take place, two simple questions must be asked:

1. Which LDS church is the "true" LDS church: the arrogant "all creeds are an abomination" pre-1980 model, or the new 1990s model which purrs like a kitten?

2. If the LDS church is truly God's church, how come He needs to make so many mid-course corrections?

An old saying goes, "If it ain't broke, don't fix it." An awful lot of things are being "fixed" lately in Mormonism. Does that mean they were broken? If it is the "Lord's true church," divinely guided in everything by living prophets, how could it have been broken?

Although the "new and improved" Mormon church now de-emphasizes its unique claims as the only true church, those claims still exist. They have not been abrogated. The LDS scriptures we quoted are still in the canon of LDS standard works. Both of these passages make it clear that there are only two spiritual alternatives: the Mormon church or the "church of the devil."

Thus, when a pastor sits down in "ecumenical fellowship" with Mormons, he is sitting with people who really believe he is a hireling of the "church of the devil." These same pastors are being invited to film showings of LDS videos in wards and invited to bring their congregations along. How many wolves actually invite shepherds to bring their sheep onto the killing fields?

This is the real danger today. Mormonism has totally retooled its spiritual war machines. Since the blizzard of "anti-Mormon" material in the 1970s and 1980s, the LDS church has realized that all of its sins and lies have been laid out on the table for any to see who care to pick up a book or watch a videotape. Mormonism has made tremendous changes in its superficial appearance. The danger is that people will be deceived into thinking that those changes reflect deep theological evolution.

Even though they will try not to admit it, Mormons still believe in the "law of eternal progression"—that God was once a man and that men can become gods. They still believe that Jesus is Lucifer's brother. They still believe that no clergy on the face of the Earth has the authority to baptize or preach the gospel except the LDS priesthood. They still believe that the temple rites are essential for anyone to come into the presence of God, while excluding virtually 75 percent of their own membership from ever receiving those rites.

The Mormon move toward orthodoxy is more apparent than real. Easily 95 percent of its key doctrines taught in the 1960s are still in place. Christians must realize this and not be deceived by the new emphasis. Its missionaries have simply exchanged their old "sheep's clothing" for a newer style. They are still wolves.

The spiritual havoc that Mormonism wreaks in its claim to be the pure holder of true Christianity cannot be overestimated. Day after day the "one true church" grinds up countless people in the monstrous gears of its theology—spitting out wretched, frightened human beings who have all but given up on God, any God. Mormonism's past cannot be forgotten because it is still very much alive underneath the pancake makeup and stage paint of its new "kinder, gentler" image.

Mormonism is still ravaging souls and sending people to hell by the millions. Christians need to wake up! Mormons themselves are the victims, and they need to be snatched like "brands from the burning." We must never mistake the heresy for its victims. We must realize that LDS people are only believing what they have been told. They are trusting sheep following a false shepherd.

Yet we must also bear in mind what God's Word says concerning the adulterous woman, often a biblical symbol of false churches: "Such is the way of an adulterous woman; she eateth, and wipeth her mouth, and saith, I have done no wickedness" (Proverbs 30:20).

The Mormon church has tried to clean itself off and say that it has done no wickedness, all the while still leading souls to hell. True Christianity must stand apart from this counterfeit. Mormons have taken the truth of God, the gospel given to us once and for all, and turned it into a fable for their own purposes. They had better beware the judgment of a righteous God:

For the wrath of God is revealed from heaven against all ungodliness and unrighteousness of men, who hold the truth in unrighteousness; because that which may be known of God is manifest in them; for God hath shewed it unto them. For the invisible things of him from the creation of the world are clearly seen, being understood by the things that are made, even his eternal power and Godhead; so that they are without excuse: because that, when they knew God, they glorified him not as God, neither were thankful; but became vain in their imaginations, and their foolish heart was darkened. Professing themselves to be wise, they became fools, and changed the glory of the uncorruptible God into an image made like to corruptible man, and to birds, and fourfooted beasts, and creeping things. Wherefore God also gave them up to uncleanness through the lusts of their own hearts, to dishonour their own bodies between themselves: who changed the truth of God into a lie, and worshipped and served the creature more than the Creator, who is blessed for ever. Amen (Romans 1:18-25).

CHURCH OF THE DEVIL

The phrase "the Church of the devil," is used several times in LDS scripture and is tied to another phrase—"the great and abominable church"—which is used a number of times in the *Book of Mormon* and just once in *Doctrine and Covenants*. It's not a big issue, but it is an important issue. It shows the real LDS attitude toward other faiths, especially those who are part of real Christianity.

In the *Book of Mormon* we are told that there are only two churches on the earth. One is the church of the Lamb of God, which we can assume is Mormonism. The other is the church of the devil, which includes every other body of believers from the Baptists to the Buddhists. Early Mormonism was clearly a "come out from among them," black or white, right or wrong kind of organization.

Today's Mormonism is trying energetically to hide that deep-down LDS truth as it strives to step into ecumenical circles. It is not something church leaders want to put behind them or purge from their theology. It *is* something they wish to keep hidden.

This is what the *Book of Mormon* says:

And it came to pass that he said unto me: Look, and behold that great and abominable church, which is the mother of abominations, whose founder is the devil.

And he said unto me Behold there are save two churches only; the one is the church of the Lamb of God, and the other is the church of the devil; wherefore, whoso belongeth not to the church of the Lamb of God belongeth to that great church which is the mother of abominations; and she is the whore of all the earth (1 Nephi 14:9,10).

In *Doctrine and Covenants*, section 18, verse 20, we read: "Contend against no church, save it be the church of the devil."

To whom do Mormons believe these scriptures refer? Early Mormon apostle and theologian Orson Pratt, wrote:

All other churches are entirely destitute of all authority from God; and any person who receives Baptism or the Lord's supper from their hands will highly offend God; for he looks upon them as the most corrupt of all people. Both Catholics and Protestants are nothing less than the "Whore of Babylon" whom the Lord denounces by the mouth of John the Revelator as having corrupted all the earth with their fornications and wickedness. And any person who shall be so wicked as to receive a holy ordinance of the gospel from the ministers of any of these apostate churches will be sent down to hell with them, unless they repent of the unholy and impious act (*The Seer*, p. 255).

The next time you hear a Mormon leader saying, "there are truths in all churches" as he attempts to bring the LDS church one step closer into the fellowship of orthodoxy, remember what is behind that smile.

CHURCH ORGANIZATION

Let me deal with two things here. First, there is the organization of the church—the act of or process of organizing the church. Second, there is the structure of the entity that is the church.

The Foundation of the Church

Joseph Smith and Oliver Cowdery received priesthood

139

ordination and baptism under the direction of heavenly messengers in 1829. They then baptized others. This cluster of believers gathered on April 6, 1830 for the formal organization of the church, with Joseph Smith as First Elder and Oliver Cowdery as Second Elder. . . . During the first two years of the church, Deacons, Teachers, Priests and Elders constituted the local ministry. . . . A revelation in 1831 instituted the office of Bishop. . . . The office of High Priest was instituted in 1831, with Joseph Smith as the Presiding High Priest over the church (*Encyclopedia*, vol. 3, pp. 1035-37).

On the following few pages, the LDS encyclopedia goes on to describe the institution of stakes in 1834, to be led by stake presidents and two counselors supported in their duties by a 12-man stake high council. The next year, in 1835, the Quorum of the Twelve Apostles and the Quorum of the Seventy were called.

Originally, the stake high councils were responsible under the stake presidencies to manage the day-to-day affairs of the church within the boundaries of the first few stakes, and the Quorum of the Twelve (Apostles) were called to operate the proselytizing efforts outside the stakes of the church, with the help of the Quorum of the Seventy, who in turn were under a seven-man presidency called the First Council of the Seventy (p. 1037).

In 1835 the church officially set up the two priesthood orders (Aaronic and Melchizedek) and their hierarchy, under stake priesthood quorums, each with its own presidency and two counselors (except the priests who reported directly to their bishop).

The church printed the *Book of Mormon* in 1830, the *Book of Commandments* in 1833, and the first edition of *The Doctrine and Covenants* (which replaced the *Book of Commandments*) in 1835.

In 1856, the long-emerging office of the presiding bishopric, with the presiding bishop and his two counselors, was fully in place to handle the temporal affairs of the church, including the church welfare programs. Among its many duties, it was given the responsibility for the Aaronic priesthood quorums. Another Second Quorum of the Seventy was called and additional general authorities, called the Assistants to the Twelve (apostles), eventually took office beginning in the 1940s to take on some of the ever-growing duties assigned to the Quorum of the Twelve.

The office of church patriarch, which was an administrative calling, was eventually limited to giving patriarchal blessings and was discontinued in 1979 (p. 1038). Today, patriarchs operate their office at the stake level.

The formal organization of the LDS church is designed to operate under a theocratic rule, governed at the top by the church president, who is said to be the literal mouthpiece for God to the Mormons. He is called the prophet, seer, and revelator and is the head of the dispensation. When he speaks, it is as from the throne of God to the believer. Upon the death of the church president, the president of the Quorum of the Twelve is the next in line for the office.

Once called to the office of president and prophet, the office is for life. This has been more than a small problem to the Mormons, since the ranking general authorities have been quite advanced in years. Recent presidents, Spencer W. Kimball and Ezra Taft Benson, have been so infirm while in office that they have been unable to function in their calling, leaving the day-to-day management of the church to the First Presidency counselors.

To lay out the detailed infrastructure of the LDS church would require a book in itself. Remember, the key to the control and growth of the church is rooted strongly in the use of laity. The church has no "professional clergy." All its leaders are called from the general membership, including the general authorities of the church, those in the first three tiers of office. Although the general authorities are paid some amount commensurate with the income they have given up to accept the call, the rest of the organization operates without pay.

The actual "people level" of the organization is at the ward or branch level. The ward is the local unit of the church, with about 200 to 800 members, and operates under the bishopric which reports geographically through the stakes of the church, each stake representing up to about ten wards or about 2000 to 7000 members. Church branches are smaller ward-type units that operate in areas where church membership is very low. They report within districts (similar in function to stakes) to the missions arms of the church (see *Encyclopedia*, vol. 3, pp. 1044-49).

On the next page is a simple breakdown of the organizational structure.

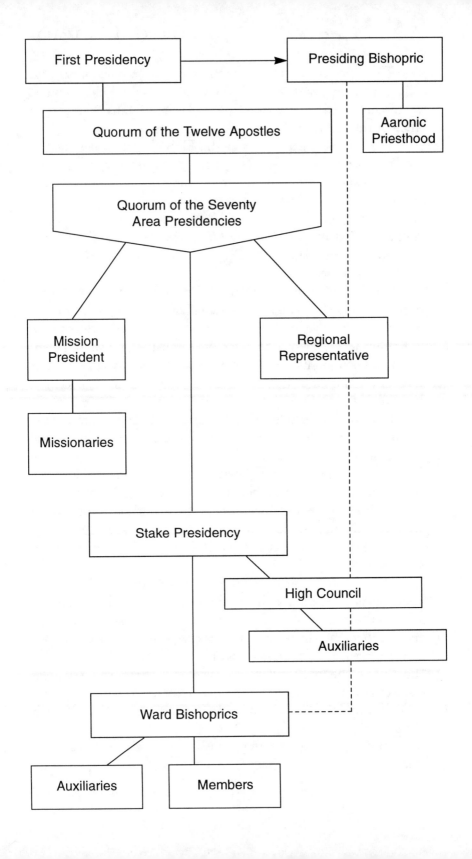

CLERGY

CLERGY

Mormons make a big issue out of the differences between their priesthood and the clergy of other churches. Bruce R. McConkie brags,

> In the sectarian world, the clergy is the whole body of so-called ordained ministers; those ordained to the ministry (as they suppose) are called clergymen. The ministry involved differs so radically from the Lord's true ministry that the terms clergy and clergymen are not ordinarily applied by the true Church to its own ministers (*Doctrine*, p. 147).

Of course the term *clergy* is not found in the Bible. What the LDS church objects to more than the term is the idea of a paid, professional clergy. This, they claim, is not found in the Bible. Mormons assert that they have virtually no paid "clergy"—and to a large extent, that is true.

All the local offices analogous to pastor or elders are filled by entirely volunteer labor—men from within the ward who work secular jobs to support their families and additionally spend many hours a week as bishops, elders, quorum presidents, or ward clerks. These men (the positions are open only to men) hold these positions for a time, then are released from their calling to go back to being simple Melchizedek priesthood holders. Thus, it is claimed, there is no special clerical class within the church.

This, of course, fails to take into account the upper-level church leaders (called general authorities). Though these men are often comfortably off, or even independently wealthy, they are paid traveling and housing allowances just like any other clergy. Additionally, on the upper levels, many of them sit ex officio as officers or even chief executive officers of major church-owned corporations, and they draw hefty salaries from that. Though no one knows for certain how much the prophet and his counselors make, inflation-adjusted figures from the 1950s and 1960s make it certain that they are probably the highest-paid religious leaders in the world, with the possible exception of the Roman Catholic pontiff.

All of this, however, ignores the larger question of whether a "paid clergy" is unscriptural. Actually, the apostle Paul—surely an authority—teaches that an *unpaid* clergy is unscriptural:

Who goeth a warfare any time at his own charges? who planteth a vineyard, and eateth not of the fruit thereof? or who feedeth a flock, and eateth not of the milk of the flock?

Say I these things as a man? or saith not the law the same also? For it is written in the law of Moses, Thou shalt not muzzle the mouth of the ox that treadeth out the corn. Doth God take care for oxen? Or saith he it altogether for our sakes? For our sakes, no doubt, this is written: that he that ploweth should plow in hope; and that he that thresheth in hope should be partaker of his hope. If we have sown unto you spiritual things, is it a great thing if we shall reap your carnal things? If others be partakers of this power over you, are not we rather? Nevertheless we have not used this power; but suffer all things, lest we should hinder the gospel of Christ.

Do ye not know that they which minister about holy things live of the things of the temple? and they which wait at the altar are partakers with the altar?

Even so hath the Lord ordained that they which preach the gospel should live of the gospel (1 Corinthians 9:7-14).

This seems crystal-clear, especially in the light of other verses such as 2 Timothy 2:4-6; Matthew 10:10; Luke 10:7 ("for the labourer is worthy of his hire"); and 1 Timothy 5:18. Obviously, no minister should be in it *only* for the money, nor should any minister become rich at the expense of his flock. Yet the clear teaching of Scripture seems to indicate that the Mormon church is out of order by insisting on an unpaid clergy.

This is especially true when considering the vast wealth of the church and its tightly-held corporate assets, to say little of the corporate benefits afforded its highest officials at the expense of countless thousands of diligent bishops, stake presidents, elders, and quorum presidents who labor long and difficult hours for no (Bible-commanded) monetary reward.

But should the clergy be professionally trained? That is not clear from the Bible. Certainly Paul, the greatest Christian of the New Testament, had a vast education in the Jewish religion. Some modern expositors speculate that he had the equivalent of two earned doctoral degrees—all of which he used to great effect. On the other hand, virtually none of the original 12 whom the Lord chose had any formal education at all (other than spending three years studying under the greatest Teacher who ever walked the earth).

Certainly some case could be made that the more "education" a minister has, the more his faith seems to diminish. That sadly occurs in many instances. Yet some of the mightiest preachers of the past centuries were also highly trained Bible scholars. It seems more to depend on what the minister does with the education he has and how broken and surrendered his life is to the promptings of the Holy Spirit of God.

In any event, the Bible gives no support to the Mormons' chest-thumping about their lack of a professional clergy, either from the financial end or from the standpoint of specialized training.

CONCEIVED IN SIN

Mormons deny the historic Christian doctrine of original sin. LDS apostle Bruce R. McConkie tries in vain to tap-dance around the plain message of Psalm 51:

> From the entire context it should be clear that David is not teaching that he came into this world burdened with the sin of Adam, so that without the cleansing of infant baptism his soul would be lost, but rather that he had been born into a world of sin and temptation that was greater than he could bear, and hence he seemed to think that the Lord should act leniently toward him (*Doctrine*, p. 153).

It may be clear to McConkie, but it is hardly clear to anyone else reading the passage. Reading just before that verse, we see that David is not trying to blame his environment (being born into a world of sin and temptation) for placing overwhelming pressures on him to sin. Quite the contrary, unlike many modern men he is squarely shouldering the burden for his own depravity.

No, McConkie will search in vain in that psalm for any "context" to soften the blow of verse 5. He probably knew that, because he kept meandering on—trying to draw further support from other LDS scriptures:

> Perhaps when David wrote the expression, "conceived in sin," he was familiar with a more ancient scripture which used the same words. In any event, the expression is found in scriptures that date back to Adam's day—found, however, in a context that makes the whole doctrine involved stand out clearly.

"And our father Adam spake unto the Lord, and said: Why is it that men must repent and be baptized in water? And the Lord said unto Adam: Behold I have forgiven thee thy transgression in the Garden of Eden. Hence came the saying abroad among the people, That the Son of God hath atoned for original guilt, wherein the sins of the parents cannot be answered upon the heads of the children, for they are whole from the foundation of the world.

"And the Lord spake unto Adam, saying: Inasmuch as thy children are conceived in sin, even so when they begin to grow up, sin conceiveth in their hearts, and they taste the bitter, that they may know to prize the good. And it is given unto them to know good from evil; wherefore they are agents unto themselves, and I have given unto you another law and commandment. Wherefore teach it unto your children, that all men, everywhere must repent, or they can in nowise inherit the kingdom of God" (Moses 6:53-57) (*Doctrine*, pp. 153-54).

Here again we have this peculiar, Gnostic doctrine of Mormonism that men must experience evil in order to prize the good. It is also a tortured use of the English language to say that "conceived in sin" means that "sin conceiveth in their hearts." Even this demonstrably fake scriptural passage cannot save McConkie from the curse of original sin.

The Biblical View

In holding to this doctrine, the Mormons fly in the face of numerous Scriptures—beginning with the one from which our article heading is drawn:

For I acknowledge my transgressions: and my sin is ever before me. Against thee, thee only, have I sinned, and done this evil in thy sight: that thou mightest be justified when thou speakest, and be clear when thou judgest. Behold, I was shapen in iniquity; and in sin did my mother conceive me (Psalm 51:3-5).

Most Bible scholars agree that David is writing this psalm in response to his grievous sin of adultery and murder with Bathsheba and her husband, Uriah the Hittite (2 Samuel 11). If so, then McConkie's exegesis is almost laughable. What extraordinary pressures was David under at that time? He was blessed of God to be the king of Israel. He had an anointing upon him to write poetry of worship and praise as probably no other man in history. He was enjoying substantial military success and was married to several beautiful women.

It is not as if David were some lonely, forlorn wretch who stepped out on a balcony and chanced to see another man's pretty wife bathing. As the parable told by the prophet Nathan in the next chapter reveals (2 Samuel 12:1-7), David was a man who had everything. He had the Spirit of God, he had wealth, he had many beautiful wives. Yet in spite of having everything going for him, he still chose to lust after another man's wife.

The fifty-first psalm shows that David knows he blew it, and he was making no excuses. He knew excuses were worthless before a holy God who could see into the very depths of his being and expose the rottenness and sin contained therein. In that sense it is probably the most beautiful and perfect penitential prayer in all the Bible. When David says he was "born in sin," he means that he entered this world as a sinner.

Moving beyond Psalm 51, we find many other Scriptures from both Testaments which clearly teach that men are born into sin. Here are but a few of them:

Yet man is born unto trouble, as the sparks fly upward (Job 5:7).

Verily every man at his best state is altogether vanity (Psalm 39:5).

Everyone of them is gone back: they are altogether become filthy; there is none that doeth good, no, not one (Psalm 53:3).

There is a way which seemeth right unto a man, but the end thereof are the ways of death (Proverbs 14:12).

Who can say, I have made my heart clean, I am pure from my sin? (Proverbs 20:9)

But we are all as an unclean thing, and all our righteousnesses are as filthy rags (Isaiah 64:6).

The heart is deceitful above all things, and desperately wicked: who can know it? (Jeremiah 17:9)

As it is written, There is none righteous, no, not one (Romans 3:10).

All have sinned, and come short of the glory of God (Romans 3:23).

There are probably few doctrines which make Mormons more uncomfortable than this doctrine. Yet there are so many Bible verses which teach that men and women are born with a sin nature. Indeed, more than one parent has commented that if you do not believe in original sin, all you need to do is spend an hour or two with an awake two-year-old and you will see the sin nature of that child run rampant, with virtually no environmental influences to cause it. Sadly, Mormons are living in a fool's paradise if they think they can wish original sin out of existence.

CONSECRATION, LAW OF

This "law" is the final one of five "laws" or "covenants" to which temple Mormons swear solemn allegiance in the endowment ceremony (see also *Endowments*). The others are, in order of appearance in the rite:

1. The Law of Obedience
2. The Law of Sacrifice
3. The Law of the Gospel
4. The Law of Chastity

This law is given during the second part of the "terrestrial world" sequence of the endowment rite. This is when the men and women are asked to stand and raise their right arm "to the square" (a Masonic term; see *Endowments, Similarity to Masonry and Occultism*) and covenant and promise to keep:

You and each of you covenant before God, angels, and these witnesses at this altar that you will observe and keep the Law of Consecration as contained in this, the book of Doctrine and Covenants. It is that you do consecrate yourselves, your time, talents, and everything with which the Lord has blessed you, or with which he may bless you, to the Church of Jesus Christ of Latter-day Saints, for the building up of the Kingdom of God on the earth and for the establishment of Zion (Sackett, p. 44).

Each person in the temple session then bows his head and says "yes" to the request to vow to keep this law.

Like the other laws, this sounds reasonably innocent until the terms are defined. The phrase "building up of the Kingdom of God on the earth and for the establishment of Zion" is a code phrase which is actually referring to a *political* kingdom, not a spiritual one. Serious Mormons who take this oath are technically made into the citizens of two countries: first as U.S. (or whatever land in which they reside) citizens, and then subjects of the theocratic kingdom of God, which is the political arm of the LDS church.

Unlike most Christian churches, the Mormons believe that they have a destiny to build a physical, political kingdom on the earth. This means that, in practice, a great deal more might be required to fulfill this oath than the person taking it might originally imagine.

Mormons are occasionally asked to place their jobs, their professional ethics, and even their real estate at the disposal of the "brethren" to do with as they see fit. The best-known example of this is the high level of penetration of Mormons into the FBI. As a result of the large numbers of faithful Mormons in the FBI, the LDS church has access to considerable amounts of information which no other ecclesiastical institution in this country could dream of acquiring.

LDS agents of the bureau have been known to acquire sensitive information for the church, and there have been rumors of "special assignments" being handled for the LDS leaders by faithful FBI agents. These agents can be rewarded upon retirement from the agency with well-paying jobs in the church's "private army," the LDS Church Security.

Professional ethical codes or even national laws can be set aside by doctors, lawyers, or psychiatrists who are asked to do "a little something" to further the cause of the kingdom of God. Because there is no effort to distinguish between the LDS church's private goals and agenda and the kingdom of God, this can mean that any Mormon who was in the right place could be asked at a time of crisis to do just about anything to anyone in the name of the church and be bound to it by their vow to obey the Law of Consecration.

Though Mormons naturally believe in obeying the laws of the land (and indeed usually do), they also believe that their prophet

149

and his counselors represent a higher law to which they must always defer. This is why Mormons in high positions of government and the military can be worrisome. This oath they have taken in their minds supersedes the oath they took to protect and defend the Constitution. Such people bear careful watching in spite of their every good intention.

This Law of Consecration can perhaps be equated to the true Christian's commitment to place obedience to the will of the Lord in first priority, far above self or government (see Acts 4:19), except for one major difference: Here the Mormons have the brethren interpreting the will of the Lord for them. This is particularly dangerous, considering the LDS view of its end-times theocratic calling.

CONSTITUTION OF THE U.S.A.

The Mormons look at the U.S. Constitution as something ordained of God. Joseph Smith said,

> We say that God is true; that the Constitution of the United States is true; that the Bible is true; that the Book of Mormon is true; that the Book of Covenants is true; that Christ is true; that the ministering angels sent forth from God are true, and that we know that we have a house not made with hands eternal in the heavens, whose builder and maker is God (*Teachings*, pp. 147-48).

Bruce R. McConkie explains the spiritual reasons for the existence of the Constitution. There is a purpose beyond the present governmental needs:

> In the providences of the Almighty, the constitution of the United States was established to serve an even greater purpose than that of setting up a stable government under which freedom would prevail. It was designed to do far more than guarantee the preservation of natural and inalienable rights to the American people. The constitution came forth to prepare the way for the restoration of the gospel, the fulfilling of the covenants God made with ancient Israel, and the organization of the Church and kingdom of God on earth in the last days (*Doctrine*, p. 160).

During a Fourth of July celebration in the Tabernacle at Salt Lake City in 1854, Brigham Young told his audience:

> Will the Constitution be destroyed? No: it will be held inviolate by this people; and as Joseph Smith said, "The time will come when the destiny of the nation will hang upon a single thread. At that critical juncture, this people will step forth and save it from the threatened destruction." It will be so (*Journal of Discourses*, vol. 7, p. 15).

Brigham Young referred to this saving of the U.S. Constitution again on February 18, 1855, when he said,

> Brethren and sisters, our friends wish to know our feelings towards the Government. I will answer, they are first rate, and we will prove it too, as you will see if you only live long enough, for that we shall live to prove it is certain; and when the Constitution of the United States hangs, as it were, upon a single thread, they will have to call for the "Mormon" Elders to save it from utter destruction; and they will step forth and do it (*Journal of Discourses*, vol. 2, p. 182).

Mormons believe the day will come when both the ecclesiastic and political head of government will become the same. Of course, something severe will have to take place to bring that to pass. It is generally thought by the LDS church that the Constitution hanging by a thread will precipitate it.

CONTENTION

The LDS Position

Mormons today are taught that it is not godly to be "contentious" in discussing their gospel with others—especially if engaging in dialogue with Bible-believing Christians: "Disputation, debates, dissensions, arguments, controversies, quarrels, and strife or contention of any sort have no part in the gospel; they are of the devil" (*Doctrine*, p. 160).

It is for this reason that many times Mormons will back down in a doctrinal discussion where they seem to be losing ground fast. If the Christian is getting the upper hand, they will withdraw from the field, saying that they are forbidden from engaging in contention.

Oddly enough, this is contrary to a clear commandment from the LDS "prophet" Joseph Smith, who allegedly gave a revelation from the Lord. In *Doctrine and Covenants* 71:7-10, Latter-day Saints are commanded:

> Wherefore, confound your enemies; *call upon them to meet you both in public and in private*; and inasmuch as ye are faithful their shame shall be made manifest. Wherefore, *let them bring forth their strong reasons against the Lord.*
>
> Verily, thus saith the Lord unto you—there is no weapon that is formed against you shall prosper; And if any man lift up his voice against you, he shall be confounded in mine own due time.

This would certainly seem to be a mandate for the Mormon to get into debates with opponents of the church. This is revealed scripture to a Mormon, and yet modern LDS people are being forbidden from obeying it.

The Biblical View

On top of that, the Bible itself commands "that ye should earnestly contend [the root word for *contentious*] for the faith which was once delivered unto the saints" (Jude 3). Beyond that, there are many examples in the Bible of the Lord's representatives being "contentious" in defending the faith including Elijah (1 Kings 18), John the Baptist (Matthew 3:7ff), Paul (Acts 13:38ff), Stephen (Acts 7:51-54), and even Jesus Christ Himself (Matthew 23; John 2:15).

It is evident from these examples that there is nothing wrong with contending for the faith, as long as it is done with the idea of the salvation of the person's soul. The Mormons have simply been using this idea of contention being evil as a way of escaping from any serious discussions with well-informed Christians.

CREEDS

The creeds of Mormonism are summed up in the *Articles of Faith* section of this work. The word *creeds* isn't used by Mormons in identifying their own statement of faith because of what Joseph Smith reported in his first vision account concerning the Lord's opinion of the creeds of Christianity.

Smith said that when God and Christ appeared to him in the first vision, he asked them:

> which of all the sects was right and which I should join. I was answered that I must join none of them, for they were all wrong; and the Personage who addressed me said that all their creeds were an abomination in his sight; that those professors were all cor-rupt; that: "they draw near to me with their lips, but their hearts are far from me, they teach for doctrines the commandments of men, having a form of godliness, but they deny the power thereof" (*Pearl of Great Price*, Joseph Smith—History 1:18,19).

This supposed answer is enough for most Mormons to shun even the first drop of knowledge regarding the Christian creeds. They remain, on the average, frightfully ignorant regarding the standard creeds of the Christian faith.

A fairly successful witnessing tool in speaking to a Mormon who has brought up the abominable creeds story is to read one of the standards, such as the Nicene or Apostles' Creed, and ask them to identify those portions that are filthy in the eyes of God. Even the boldest of LDS apologists will walk carefully around that one.

The Orthodox View

What are the creeds of Christianity and why are they impor-tant to us? We can hardly comprehend today the vital role of the creeds in the establishment and defense of Christian orthodoxy. With Bibles of every size and translation neatly tucked away in virtually every home, church pew, library, hospital, airplane, and hotel room, it would appear that we have more Bibles than people. For those of us who don't like reading, we even have 24-hour Christian television and radio networks and audio cassettes of every kind and style.

Try to imagine a very different world, the one in which the early church survived—a world where the Bible was guarded in sacred trust and which few believers were able to read.

This was the world in which the Christian often gave up his very life for professing faith in the Lord Jesus Christ. Suddenly, what you believed and why you believed it became of vital importance. They understood firsthand what Jesus meant when He said, "Whosoever shall confess me before men, him shall the Son of man also confess before the angels of God" (Luke 12:8).

In trying to understand the historical background of the Christian creeds, we need to understand that many of the central doctrines of the Christian faith did not become explicitly defined until heretical teachings began to erode the simplicity of the faith.

Yet, from the very first statements of faith by the first Christians to the confession of the simple doxology today, we see a uniformity of purpose and doctrine which we must define as Christian orthodoxy. To step outside the general theology of these confessions must be viewed as heresy.

A Simple View

In a simple view, the Bible is the Word of God to man; the creed is man's answer to God. The Bible is to be believed and obeyed; the creed is to be professed and taught. Actually, the first creed dealt with the fundamental Old Testament doctrine of monotheism. The Israelite creed was distinctly the doctrine of a one and only one God. These are the beginning words of the *Shema*, which you still hear today at the Western Wall of the Temple in Jerusalem: "Hear O Israel, Yahweh our Elohim, Yahweh is One..." (Deuteronomy 6:4).

The Confession of Nathanael

"Nathanael answered and saith unto him, Rabbi, thou art the Son of God; thou art the King of Israel [the Messiah]" (John 1:49).

Confession of Peter

"And Simon Peter answered and said, Thou art the Christ [Messiah], the Son of the living God" (Matthew 16:16).

Confession of Thomas

"Thomas answered and said unto him, My Lord and my God" (John 20:28).

The First Trinitarian Creed: The Baptismal Formula

"Go ye therefore, and teach all nations, baptizing them in the name of the Father, and of the Son, and of the Holy Ghost" (Matthew 28:19).

Confession of Paul

"For I delivered unto you first of all that which I also received, how that Christ died for our sins according to the scriptures; and that he was buried, and that he rose again the third day according to the scriptures" (1 Corinthians 15:3,4).

Confession of Ignatius of Antioch, A.D. 107

"Be deaf, therefore, when any would speak to you apart from (at variance with) Jesus Christ, the Son of God, who was descended from the family of David, born of Mary, who was truly born both of God and of the Virgin I truly took a body; for the Word became flesh and dwelt among us without sin, ate and drank truly, truly suffered persecution under Pontius Pilate, was truly, and not in appearance, crucified and died, who was truly raised from the dead, and rose after three days, his Father raising him up, and after having spent forty days with the Apostles, was received up to the Father, and sits on his right hand, waiting till his enemies are put under his feet."

Confession of Irenaeus, A.D. 180

"The Church, though scattered through the whole world to the ends of the earth, has received from the Apostles and their disciples the faith in one God, the Father Almighty, who made the heavens and the earth, and the seas, and all that in them is; and in one Jesus Christ, the Son of God, who became flesh for our salvation; and in the Holy Ghost, who through the prophets preached the dispensations and the Advent, and his birth of the Virgin, and the passion, and the resurrection from the dead, and the bodily assumption into heaven of the beloved Christ Jesus, our Lord, and his appearing from heaven in the glory of the Father, to comprehend all things under one head, and to raise up all flesh of all mankind, that, according to the pleasure of the Father invisible, every knee of those that are in heaven and on the earth and under the earth should bow before Christ Jesus, our Lord and God and Saviour and King, and that every tongue should confess to him, and that he may execute righteous judgment over all: sending into eternal fire the spiritual powers of wickedness, and the angels who transgressed and apostatized, and the godless and unrighteous and lawless and blasphemous among men, and granting life and immortality and eternal glory to the righteous and holy, who have both kept the commandments and continued in his love, some from the beginning, some after their conversion."

He later added, "The Church, having received this preaching and this faith, as said before, though scattered throughout the whole world, zealously preserves it as one household . . . and unanimously preaches and teaches the same, and hands it down as by one mouth; for although there are different dialects in the world, the power of the tradition is one and the same."

Confession of Tertullian, A.D. 200

"The Rule of Faith is altogether one, sole, immovable, and irreformable—namely, to believe in one God Almighty, the Maker of the world; and his Son, Jesus Christ, born of the Virgin Mary, crucified under Pontius Pilate, on the third day raised again from the dead, received in the heavens, sitting now at the right hand of the Father, coming to judge the quick and the dead, also through the resurrection of the flesh."

The Apostles' Creed, A.D. 340

"I believe in God the Father Almighty, Maker of heaven and earth, and in Jesus Christ, His only Son, our Lord; who was conceived by the Holy Ghost, born of the Virgin Mary; suffered under Pontius Pilate, was crucified, dead and buried; He descended into hell; the third day He rose again from the dead; He ascended into heaven and sitteth on the right hand of God, the Father Almighty; from thence He shall come to judge the quick and the dead.

"I believe in the Holy Ghost; the Holy Christian Church; the communion of saints; the forgiveness of sins; the resurrection of the body; and the life everlasting. Amen."

The Nicene Creed, A.D. 381

"I believe in one God, the Father Almighty, Maker of heaven and earth and of all things visible and invisible.

"And in one Lord Jesus Christ, the only-begotten Son of God, begotten of His Father before all worlds, God of God, Light of Light, Very God of Very God, Begotten, not made, being of one substance with the Father, by whom all things were made;

"Who for us men and our salvation came down from heaven and was incarnate by the Holy Ghost of the Virgin Mary and was made man; and was crucified also for us under Pontius Pilate. He suffered and was buried; and the third day He rose again according to the Scriptures; and ascended into heaven, and sitteth on the right hand of the Father; and He shall come again with glory to judge both the quick and the dead; whose kingdom shall have no end.

"And I believe in the Holy Ghost, the Lord and Giver of Life, who proceedeth from the Father and the Son, who with the Father and the Son together is worshipped and glorified, who spake by the prophets. And I believe in one holy Christian and Apostolic Church. I acknowledge one Baptism unto the remission of sins, and I look for the resurrection of the dead, and the life of the world to come. Amen."

The Mormon church has taken the beauty and worship away from the confessions of faith of Christians from the time of Christ to the present day. They have turned their faces from the altar of the living God and raised up a god to fit their heretical doctrine. They had better beware the judgment of a jealous God whose holy Word warns them:

> That we henceforth be no more children, tossed to and fro, and carried about with every wind of doctrine, by the sleight of men, and cunning craftiness, whereby they lie in wait to deceive; but speaking the truth in love, may grow up into him in all things, which is the head, even Christ (Ephesians 4:14,15).
>
> For there shall arise false Christs and false prophets, and shall shew great signs and wonders; insomuch that, if it were possible, they shall deceive the very elect. Behold, I have told you before. Wherefore if they shall say unto you, Behold, he is in the desert; go not forth: behold, he is in the secret chambers; believe it not (Matthew 24:24-26).

The gospel of Jesus Christ has not left the earth since it "was once and for all delivered." It is the very same today as it was the day Christ died for your sins and mine . . . on the cross of Calvary, where He became our sin offering and put the gospel He preached into reality.

CRYSTAL BALLS

Crystal balls (see also *Peep Stones*) are an ancient method of fortune-telling referred to as "crystalomancy" or "scrying." It was believed by medieval sorcerers from Europe and the Middle East that spirits such as djinn or gnomes resided within certain forms of rock or rock-crystal. If found, these rocks could be polished and used to produce hidden (i.e., occult) knowledge.

Crystal balls were among the most highly prized form of stones used in scrying, because they were more rare and expensive to machine and polish to a high, transparent finish. It was believed by practitioners that the spirits within the rocks could cause visions of distant places, hidden objects, or even the future to appear within the globe of the crystal, if the person using it had developed a rapport with the spirit.

This rapport was achieved through various magical rites, including placing a drop of one's own blood on the stone or crystal. Oftentimes a "pact" would be made with the guardian djinn (or "genius") of the stone, in which the soul of the person would be given into the spirit's care for as long as it wished, in exchange for the spirit sharing with the person the ability to see through the stone into distant places or the future.

Mormon founder Joseph Smith is known to have used a primitive form of crystal ball called a "peep stone" or "show stone" (see also *Peep Stones*) both to allegedly help translate the *Book of Mormon* and to find buried treasure for neighbors. Smith seems to have been raised in a family where his father and brothers (and even his mother) were deeply involved in various forms of magic and divination such as dowsing and even drawing magic circles.

The Biblical View

From a biblical perspective, if these crystal balls or peep stones worked at all, it was through demonic agency. Fortune-telling in all its forms is forbidden by the Bible—both in the Old and New Testament. Any sort of soothsaying or divination is a deep sin in the sight of God (see Leviticus 19:26-28, 31; 20:6; Deuteronomy 18:9-14; Isaiah 2:6; 8:19; Micah 5:12; Zechariah 10:2).

Thus, the fact that Joseph Smith practiced scrying even after assuming the leadership of the "Lord's true church" disqualifies him for any spiritual role in the eyes of serious Bible students.

CULTS

The doctrines and practices of Mormonism place it firmly within the kingdom of the cults, as the late Dr. Walter Martin called it. Unfortunately, the word *cult* sounds dark and sinister, and it is hard for an active Mormon to visualize being part of something that reeks of evil. Remember that Mormonism is something of a soft-core cult, with a happy facade. Defining the boundaries of cultic doctrine and behavior can often be a stumbling block to an inquiring Mormon.

It is practical, therefore, when pressed to define a cult, to do so not by what anti-Mormons might say but by what some reasonably distant authority has to say. In that light, here is how Billy Graham defines a cult. It appeared in one of his syndicated newspaper columns in the early 1980s:

> In general, I would say a cult is a group which follows religious ideas (usually taught by a strong leader) which are not in accordance with the Bible. Sometimes cults will have certain writings for which they claim supernatural authority in addition to the Bible. Often the leader of the cult will demand total, blind obedience to his word and may even separate children from parents.
>
> While cults differ greatly with each other, they have in common one thing: they reject Jesus Christ and the Bible as their authorities and therefore reject faith in Jesus Christ as God's way of salvation. Often, they attempt to disguise this by talking a great deal about Jesus. But frequently, the test of a cult is found in their answer to this question: How can I be saved? If the answer is anything other than trusting Jesus Christ, then the group may be a cult. This is particularly true if they say they alone have the truth and salvation is found by joining their group.
>
> I believe the growth of cults is an indication of a deep spiritual hunger on the part of many people today. Many people

have discovered that material things do not satisfy the deepest longings of the human heart. Young people, especially are searching for meaning and purpose in life. Unfortunately, many of them have never really heard the Gospel of Jesus Christ and they are vulnerable to any false doctrine that comes along.

In God's Word, we have all we need to know about God. When a person comes to Christ, he no longer has any reason to be attracted to false religions.

Mormonism surely fits such a definition. It has added to the Word of God with the *Book of Mormon*, *The Doctrine and Covenants*, and *The Pearl of Great Price*. It has belittled the Bible's authority with its "holy priesthood" and its doctrine that God must have a prophet in place to direct His church. Additionally, Mormonism claims that full salvation is found only in it.

The reader might do well to stop here and write down a few of the cult signals described by Billy Graham and look them up under the appropriate heading in this work. A very clear picture of the cultic nature of Mormonism will quickly emerge.

Again, we need to exercise caution here. Witnessing to a Mormon with a judgmental expression of truth will drive a wedge between you just as surely as if you cursed him for his faith.

I know that the urgency of our concerns might drive us to be impetuous in our confrontation with spiritual darkness, but I must tell you that it is a very rare Mormon who knows he is in a cultic group. The 99 out of 100 love God with all their hearts, seek to serve him with all their beings, and back those feelings up with more action than most Christians.

The problem is that they have been deceived and are buried in lies from their leaders. They really believe they can be justified through works. You need to bring gentle truth, love, prayer, and godly persuasion to your encounters. And then perhaps God will be pleased to flood their soul with light.

THE DEAD SEA SCROLLS

It is important to understand what exactly the scrolls are—and what they are not. They consist of some 800 scrolls, including virtually the entire Old Testament (with the exception of the Book of Esther) and seem to date from the third century B.C. to the first century A.D. The scrolls bear witness to the remarkable preservation of the Old Testament Scriptures as contained in today's Masoretic text.

Many of the Dead Sea scrolls contain religious writings and texts from a mystical religious community which lived in Qumran, close to the caves where the scrolls were uncovered. This group taught a number of doctrines that differed from mainstream Judaism at the time of Jesus. It is to this eccentric community and its sectarian writings that many pro-Mormon writers appeal in an attempt to gain legitimacy for their belief systems. For example, just as the Mormons believe today, those people believed that the fulness of the gospel was to be found only with them. They reviewed their adherents annually to determine levels of worthiness, and *only* those who were deemed worthy qualified for a special baptism ritual that was not available to the general membership.

Yet there are also some areas where the Qumran group taught doctrines diametrically opposed to LDS teachings. For example, many members of the community—perhaps all—believed in celibacy. They would not marry. On the other hand, of course, Mormons *must* marry and beget children. If the Mormons are to be consistent in their claim that they are as the primitive Qumran community was, they would have to do away with doctrinal elements at the core of their theology, such as the doctrine of eternal marriage.

For further study in this area, I recommend the works of Dr. William Sanford LaSor, professor of Old Testament, Fuller Theological Seminary. His books and writings are the best.

An overview of his studies on the Dead Sea scrolls and the Qumran community is found in *The Expositor's Bible Commentary* (Grand Rapids, MI: Regency Library—Zondervan, 1979), vol. 1, pp. 395-405.

DEGREES OF GLORY

(See also *Celestial Glory, Terrestrial Glory, Telestial Glory, Sons of Perdition.*)

The LDS Position

Mormonism teaches that when this life is over and final judgment is meted out, all resurrected persons (except sons of perdition) will be sent to one of three degrees of glory or kingdoms of glory. These kingdoms are named (from the highest to the lowest) the celestial, terrestrial, and the telestial degrees of glory. Mormons are told that the beauty and glory of even the lowest, where "liars, and sorcerers, and adulterers, and whoremongers" (*Doctrine and Covenants* 76:103) are sent, is far above and beyond human comprehension.

The kingdoms are described as follows: "And the glory of the celestial is one, even as the glory of the sun is one. And the glory of the terrestrial is one, even as the glory of the moon is one. And the glory of the telestial is one, even as the glory of the stars is one; for as one star differs from another star in glory, even so differs one from another in glory in the telestial world" (*Doctrine and Covenants* 76:96-98).

The LDS position is that all placement and rewards in the hereafter operate on a sliding scale in direct response to our efforts during our lifetime. Even our intelligence and knowledge is to be graded.

Whatever principle of intelligence we attain in this life, it will rise with us in the resurrection. And if a person gains more knowledge and intelligence in this life through his diligence and obedience than another, he will have so much the advantage in the world to come. There is a law, irrevocably decreed in heaven before the foundations of this world, upon which all blessings are predicated and when we obtain any blessing from God, it is by obedience to that law upon which it is predicated (*Doctrine and Covenants* 130:18-21).

Each kingdom seems to have its own grades of glory and it seems probable that one can improve upon one's own lot within a kingdom.

LDS theologian James Talmage stated this about the subject:

It is reasonable to believe, in the absence of direct revelation by which alone absolute knowledge of the matter could be acquired, that, in accordance with God's plan of eternal progression, advancement within each of the three specified kingdoms will be provided for; though as to possible progress from one kingdom to another the scriptures make no positive affirmation. Eternal advancement along different lines is conceivable. We may conclude that degrees and grades will ever characterize the kingdoms of our God. Eternity is progressive; perfection is relative; the essential feature of God's living purpose is its associated power of eternal increase (*Articles of Faith*, Talmage, p. 409).

The Biblical View

It is obvious that the biblical penalty for sin has been removed from Mormon theology; Mormons are taught that they can choose their level of obedience. Yet the Bible says that "*all* have sinned, and come short of the glory of God" (Romans 3:23). While Mormons are promised that in the celestial glory they shall become "gods, even the sons of gods . . . and he [God, the Father] makes them equal in power and in might and in dominion" (*Doctrine and Covenants* 76:58,95), the Bible tells us that there is only one God . . . just one . . . forever.

Does all mankind, sinners and saints alike, achieve some wonderful degree of glory? The Bible denies it: "As by one man sin entered into the world, and death by sin; and so death passed upon all men, for that all have sinned" (Romans 5:12). And in Romans 6 we are told that the "wages of sin is death; but the gift of God is eternal life through Jesus Christ our Lord" (Romans 6:23).

While the Mormons would have us believe that God's gift of eternal life is placement in one or another degree of glory based upon obedience to the laws and ordinances of the [LDS] gospel (*Articles of Faith*, #3), the biblical record says the opposite:

> And you, being dead in your sins and the uncircumcision of your flesh, hath he quickened together with him, having forgiven you all trespasses; blotting out the handwriting of ordinances that was against us, which was contrary to us, and took it out of the way, nailing it to his cross (Colossians 2:13,14).

The LDS church cites Paul's comments on the comparison of earthly things to heavenly things as the biblical proof of this doctrine of the three degrees of glory.

> All flesh is not the same flesh: but there is one kind of flesh of men, another flesh of beasts, another of fishes, and another of birds. There are also celestial bodies, and bodies terrestrial: but the glory of the celestial is one, and the glory of the terrestrial is another. There is one glory of the sun, and another glory of the moon, and another glory of the stars: for one star differeth from another star in glory. So also is the resurrection of the dead. It is sown in corruption; it is raised in incorruption (1 Corinthians 15:39-42).

It is a long jump in logic to take what Paul said and land on the complex Mormon doctrine of degrees of glory. We need to take the statements of Paul in context. Paul was preaching on the mystery and hope of the resurrection, not on degrees of glory. It was perhaps the most difficult doctrine of the New Testament church for many people to understand. It was at his mention of the resurrection of the dead that he was mocked during his preaching on the Areopagus in Athens (see Acts 17:22-34).

The next few verses of his sermon to the Corinthians bear out the context of the message.

> It [the resurrection of the dead] is sown in dishonour; it is raised in glory: it is sown in weakness; it is raised in power: it is sown a natural body; it is raised a spiritual body. There is a natural

body, and there is a spiritual body. And so it is written, The first
man Adam was made a living soul; the last Adam was made a
quickening spirit. Howbeit that was not first which is spiritual,
but that which was natural; and afterward that which is spiritual
(1 Corinthians 15:43-46).

Paul was trying to explain the difference between our earthly
state and our hoped-for resurrected state. Nowhere does he imply
any such three degrees of earned glory as is taught so emphatically
in Mormonism.

One last point. The biblical passage used here by the Mormons
actually destroys the LDS doctrine that underlies the church's
teaching of degrees of glory. The Law of Eternal Progression proclaims that we preexisted with God at Kolob as spirit beings, and
that we came here to gain bodies, be tested, judged, and given our
places in one of these degrees of glory. Yet Paul clearly states in verse
46 that *first* there is the natural or physical body and *afterward* the
spiritual. Mormonism has it reversed!

DEMONS

There is not a great deal of difference between the views of the
LDS church and those of historic Christianity on the subject of
demons. Both agree that demons are evil spiritual beings which
serve the devil and seek to harm human beings through various
forms of attack, obsession, and infestation. LDS author Bruce R.
McConkie writes,

> Devils are demons, the spirit beings cast out of heaven for
> rebellion (Revelation 12:7-9). "We are surrounded by demons,"
> the wicked Nephites cried, "yea, we are encircled about by the
> angels of him who hath sought to destroy our souls" (Helaman
> 13:37). Demonism is belief in demons; a demoniac is one thought
> to be possessed of an evil spirit (*Doctrine*, p. 190).

There is no clear agreement, even among Christians, about
the origin of demons. Some believe that they are the spirits of the
"giants in the earth" or *Nephilim* mentioned in Genesis 6 who
escaped after their bodies were slain in the flood.

Some believe that they are fallen angels. This seems to be the
Mormon position. What we call demons are the spirits which sided

with Lucifer against the plan of Jesus in the Council of the Gods. As such, they will be forever denied bodies of flesh.

Mormons say demons wish to possess people because they desperately desire physical bodies—bodies to which they know they are not entitled.

Of course, Mormons also believe that they alone—through the power of the Melchizedek priesthood—have the authority to command evil spirits to depart. This, of course, is not the case, as any visit to a foreign mission field with real, Bible-believing Christian missionaries would reveal. In fact, LDS missionaries, when confronted with a genuine demoniac, have a great deal of trouble achieving any success in setting the person free.

DESTROYER, DESTROYING ANGEL

Destroyer is a term drawn from Revelation 9:11: "And they had a king over them, which is the angel of the bottomless pit, whose name in the Hebrew tongue is Abaddon, but in the Greek tongue hath his name Apollyon" (Greek "Destroyer").

McConkie provides the LDS interpretation of this term:

> This name for Satan signifies that his great labor is to destroy the souls of men. Incident thereto he rejoices in bringing to pass temporal, spiritual, and mental ruin and waste of all degrees. William W. Phelps, in daylight vision, saw the destroyer riding in power upon the face of the Missouri River; and thereupon the Lord revealed to the Prophet the perils to be wrought upon the waters in the last days by the destroyer (*Doctrine and Covenants* 61) (*Doctrine*, p. 192).

This is the spiritual interpretation of the term *Destroyer*. There is not much in it to be quarreled with, other than the useless and inaccurate nature of Joseph Smith's "prophecies" (see also *Smith, Joseph: a False Prophet?*).

On the other hand, the term *Destroying Angel*, though drawn from this scriptural source, has a much more chilling meaning in LDS history. It was the nickname for William Hickman, a leader of the Danites (or "Avenging Angels") under Brigham Young. Hickman, who was quite a gunslinger and an outlaw, was one of the

leaders of Brigham's enforcers. He was known as "Brigham's Destroying Angel." (See Bill Hickman, *Brigham's Destroying Angel*
[Salt Lake City: Shepard Publishing, 1904]).

Along with Orrin Porter Rockwell and John D. Lee, two other
feared Avenging Angels, Hickman's reputation as a heartless gun-
fighter did much to strike fear into the hearts of those who thought
of opposing Brigham's reign of terror over the territory of Utah.

DOCTRINE AND COVENANTS, CHANGES IN

The *Doctrine and Covenants* (D&C) is regarded by devout
Mormons as sacred revelation from God (see *Encyclopedia*, 1:405).
They consider it the very word of God through (primarily) the LDS
prophet Joseph Smith.

There are 138 sections and two declarations to the *Doctrine
and Covenants*. All but seven were received through Joseph Smith.
The others are said to have been received through Oliver Cowdery
(Sections 102 and 134), John Taylor (Section 135), Brigham Young
(Section 136), Joseph F. Smith (Section 138), Wilford Woodruff
(Official Declaration 1), and Spencer W. Kimball (Official Decla-
ration 2). All of these but Cowdery were prophets of the church.
The *Doctrine and Covenants* is one of the four standard works of the
LDS church, and the one felt to be most applicable to this genera-
tion (ibid., 1:407).

The *Doctrine and Covenants* was first printed in 1833 as a *Book
of Commandments for the Government of the Church* (ibid., 1:406).
Thus, it has been around only for a century and a half. The Holy
Bible, by contrast, was written over a period of about 1300 years and
has been preserved intact for another 2000 years. If the *Doctrine
and Covenants* really came via divine revelation, one might therefore expect that it would contain no errors and be subject to no
changes. Yet that is not the case.

Many sections of *Doctrine and Covenants* have been edited,
censored, or dated in a false manner without any attempt to inform
the Latter-day Saint that this has been done. In places, huge
amounts of textual material—supposedly divinely transmitted—
have been removed. There are no footnotes noting the changes.
Why? Because many of the changes have been made either to
conceal failed prophecies of Joseph Smith or to hush up doctrinal

changes in the LDS church about which church leaders do not wish Mormons to hear.

While by no means exhaustive, the following is a summation of some of the key changes to the *Doctrine and Covenants*.

Significant Deletions

1. The 1835 edition of *Doctrine and Covenants* contained a section some 68 pages long with more than 20,000 words. This was called the "Lectures on Faith." Its official title was "Theology: Lecture First on the Doctrine of the Church of the Latter Day Saints [sic] of Faith." There are actually seven lectures or sections within this larger section. This entire section of the *Doctrine and Covenants* is now missing.

Probable reason for its omission: It taught a doctrine of God which is today regarded as heresy by LDS leaders. In the Fifth Lecture (1835 edition, pp. 52-53) Joseph Smith teaches this:

> There are two personages who constitute the great, matchless, governing and supreme power over all things. . . . They are the Father and the Son: The Father being a personage of spirit, glory and power: possessing all perfection and fulness: The Son, who was in the bosom of the Father, a personage of tabernacle, made or fashioned like unto man, or being in the form and likeness of man.

On the same and following page, Smith proceeded to teach this about the Holy Spirit:

> And he [Jesus] being the only-begotten of the Father . . . possessing the same mind with the Father, which mind is the Holy Spirit, that bears record of the Father and the Son, and these three are one . . . [Jesus] being filled with the fulness of the Mind of the Father, or, in other words, the Spirit of the Father: which Spirit is shed forth upon all who believe on his name and keep his commandments . . . being one in him, even as the Father, Son and Holy Spirit are one.

In these teachings, Joseph Smith landed much closer to Christian orthodoxy than he did later in his life, although his concepts are quite muddled and unclear. Today, Mormon leaders teach that

God the Father is a "Person of Tabernacle"—i.e., He has a physical body (*Encyclopedia*, 2:548-49). This is a direct contradiction of the paragraph above, which teaches that the Father is a Spirit. Thus, since the "Lectures on Faith" were canonized as scripture, we again find the common Mormon phenomenon of one set of "sacred scripture" badly contradicting another set of "sacred scripture."

Additionally, Mormons deny the Christian doctrine of the Trinity (ibid., 2:553—see also *Trinity*) and teach that the Holy Ghost is a separate God (ibid., 2:552). Yet the second paragraph quoted above seems to teach the trinitarian doctrine that the three Persons of the Godhead are one. It also seems to deny that the Holy Ghost is a separate and unique Person; rather, he is only the "mind" of the Father. To have their prophet teach one doctrine in 1835 and a different doctrine a few years later evidently was more than the LDS leaders could stand. Thus, the "Lectures on Faith" vanished out of the *Doctrine and Covenants* with no explanation.

2. From this 1835 edition of *Doctrine and Covenants*, another significant section is also missing. It is "Section CI" (1835 edition, pp. 251-52) and was titled "Marriage."

The fourth verse (or paragraph) of the article has this to say:

> All legal contracts of marriage made before a person is baptized into this church, should be held sacred and fulfilled. Inasmuch as this church of Christ has been reproached with [accused of] the crime of fornication, and polygamy: we declare that we believe, that one man should have one wife; and one woman but one husband, except in case of death, when either is at liberty to marry again.

This is a significant statement, since all evidence points to the fact that Joseph Smith was indeed practicing polygamy at or about the time that this "revelation" was given. As early as 1832, Joseph Smith was linked romantically to a Nancy Marinda Johnson; and in 1835, he became involved with a 17-year-old orphan girl, Fanny Alger (LDS author Fawn Brodie, *No Man Knows My History*, p. 181).

The fact that the paragraph asserts that the Mormons had been accused of "the crime of fornication, and polygamy" indicates that stories were evidently already in circulation about Joseph's "celestial liaisons." Indeed, Brodie asserts in her book that there was an unpublished "revelation" foreshadowing the doctrine of plural marriage as early as 1831. Then church historian (later church president) Joseph F. Smith informed her of this himself (ibid., p. 184, note). Thus this "revelation" was obviously intended as a cover-up of what was going on, at least in Smith's household (see also *New and Everlasting Covenant*).

3. In 1976, Section 137 of the *Doctrine and Covenants* was submitted to the General Conference of the Church of Jesus Christ of Latter-day Saints for a vote to be "sustained" as scripture. The section is a narrative of a vision supposedly seen by Joseph Smith in Kirtland, Ohio, in 1836.

What the members who voted on this new addition to scripture were not told by LDS leaders is that whole paragraphs (216 words) of the actual revelation as recorded in *The History of the Church* had been conveniently left out of the version to be included in the *Doctrine and Covenants*. The reason for these omissions? Four obviously false prophecies were contained in the censored part of the revelation. These four prophecies were so obviously false that even the average LDS reader would pick them up.

What was in these missing parts? The official history of the LDS church still records the missing prophecies (*History*, 2:380-81). Here is what is not in the new *Doctrine and Covenants* 137:

> [Joseph Smith writing:] I saw the Twelve Apostles of the Lamb, who are now upon the earth, who hold the keys of this last ministry, in foreign lands, standing together in a circle, much fatigued, with their clothes tattered and their feet swollen, with their eyes cast downward, and Jesus standing in their midst, and they did not behold him. The Saviour looked upon them and wept.
>
> I also beheld Elder McLellin in the south standing upon a hill, surrounded by a vast multitude, preaching to them, and a lame man standing before him supported by his crutches; he threw them down at his word and leaped as a hart, by the mighty power of God.
>
> Also, I saw Elder Brigham Young standing in a strange land, in the far south and west, in a desert place, upon a rock in the midst of about a dozen men of color, who appeared hostile. He was preaching to them in their own tongue, and the angel of God standing above his head with a drawn sword in his hand, protecting him, but he did not see it.

And I finally saw the Twelve in the celestial kingdom of God. I also beheld the redemption of Zion and many things which the tongue of man cannot describe in full. . . .

A quick look at the official history of the church reveals the four false prophecies contained in these passages.

- A list of Joseph Smith's original apostles can easily be found (*History*, 2:187). Smith claimed to see his (original LDS) 12 apostles all in the celestial kingdom.

This is difficult to imagine, since there was already division between Smith and the majority of the "apostles," beginning with discord in Kirtland, Ohio. The first portion of the "missing words" shows his less-than-subtle rebuke of their resistance to his will: ". . . fatigued . . . tattered . . . eyes cast downward. . . . The Saviour looked upon them and wept." Smith was calling them to get into line and submit themselves to his full authority. That's the carrot offered in the last portion: "I finally saw the Twelve in the celestial kingdom of God."

Yet his "thus saith the Lord" must have had little effect on them, since at least 7 of the 12 under discussion were soon excommunicated or apostatized from the church: John F. Boynton and Luke S. Johnson in 1837 (ibid., 2:528); Lyman Johnson in 1838 (ibid., 3:20); William E. McLellin sometime in 1838 (ibid., 3:31-32); Thomas B. Marsh and Orson Hyde in 1838 (ibid., 3:166-67); and finally Joseph Smith's own brother, William Smith, in 1845 (ibid., 7:483).

How could these men ever have attained the celestial kingdom under those conditions? Not only were they "accursed" by their apostasy and subsequent excommunication, but they fell victim to the LDS church's own scriptural denunciation. *Doctrine and Covenants* 84:40-41 clearly states:

Therefore, all those who receive the priesthood, receive this oath and covenant of my father, which he cannot break, neither can it be moved. But whoso breaketh this covenant after he hath received it, and altogether turneth therefrom, shall not have forgiveness of sins in this world nor in the world to come.

171

Although a few of these men later returned to the church, none of them were remotely close to the standards the Mormon church says is necessary for attainment of the highest degree of glory. And the majority remained estranged for life. Therefore, the "prophetic" utterance, "I finally saw the Twelve in the celestial kingdom of God," was obviously false. It would have been false even if only one "apostle" remained outside the fold.

- The vision of McLellin preaching and working miracles in the south never came true. He apostatized from the church without ever doing any such thing!

- Although Brigham Young did bring the Mormons west and was a successful colonizer and orator, the vision of Young preaching to "men of color" in their own language in some strange and faraway place in the southwest never took place— or at least there is no trace of it in any of the very detailed records and diaries concerning his reign as "prophet."

- "Zion" (i.e., Independence, Missouri) was never "redeemed" and has never been redeemed in the 150-plus years since the prophecy was made (see also *Zion*). Is it any wonder that the brethren chose to remove whole chunks of this "inspired" revelation?

4. *Doctrine and Covenants* Section 2—a revelation supposedly given some ten years before the publication of the *Book of Commandments* in 1823 is not included in the 1833 edition.

5. *Doctrine and Covenants* Section 5 (IV in the 1833 edition) has substantial and significant changes in it. In the modern edition, verse 4 (supposedly the Lord speaking to Joseph Smith) reads:

And you have a gift to translate the [*Book of Mormon*] *plates; and this is the first gift that I bestowed upon you;* and I have commanded that you should pretend to no other gift *until my purpose is fulfilled in this:* for I will grant unto you no other gift *until it is finished.*

The italicized words are not in the original. The 1833 edition (p. 10) reads quite differently and it is almost difficult to tell it is the same passage: "and he [Joseph] has a gift to translate the book, and I have commanded him that he shall pretend to no other gift, for I will grant him no other gift."

This is significant, because the original revelation makes it clear that Joseph Smith was never to have any other gift than the ability to translate the *Book of Mormon*. Obviously, history shows us that Joseph wanted—and subsequently pretended to acquire—many other "gifts," including the Melchizedek priesthood, the ability to partially retranslate the Bible, to officiate over temple rites and marriages with the sealing power, and the gift to bring forth the Book of Abraham. His ambitions grew with time, and the "divine revelation" restricting his gift to translating "the book" had to grow with those ambitions.

The new version states that Smith could not have any other gift until he finished the translation process. God apparently changed His mind, contrary to Malachi 3:6 and Numbers 23:19.

This problem is further compounded in the fact that a verse has been completely added—verse 17: "And you [Joseph] must wait yet a little while, for ye are not ordained." It is evident from this and other historical evidence that the whole idea of a priesthood was not yet in Joseph Smith's mind by 1833, and thus it had to be added later—making for cut-and-paste history and revelation. Once Joseph decided he wanted more power and prestige, he had to scissor up his original "revelation"!

6. In the same revelation on p. 11 (1833 edition), two substantial paragraphs (numbered 5 and 6) of more than 100 words have been completely excised and replaced—partially, it would seem, because of a false prophecy in the sixth paragraph:

> And now if this generation [March 1829] do harden their hearts against my word, behold I will deliver them up unto Satan, for he reigneth and hath much power at this time, for he hath got great hold upon the hearts of the people of this generation: and not far from the iniquities of Sodom and Gomorrah, do they come at this time: and behold the sword of justice hangeth over their heads, and if they persist in the hardness of their hearts, the time cometh that it must fall upon them. Behold, I tell you these things even as I also told the people of the destruction of Jerusalem, and my word shall be verified at this time as it hath hitherto been verified.

173

Yet nothing of the sort happened to the generation alive at the time of this statement, even though they "hardened their hearts" by and large against Mormonism. Notice, too, that the examples the LDS god gives are of concrete physical destruction. Sodom was destroyed by fire from heaven; Jerusalem was leveled by Titus. Yet nothing like these cataclysms happened to the generation in question. No wonder the Mormons felt they needed to remove this!

7. *Doctrine and Covenants* Section 7 (VI in the 1833 edition, p. 18) has almost nearly doubled in size, from a paltry 143 words in the original to 252 words in the modern editions since 1876. This "revelation" concerned whether the apostle John had "tarried on earth." This entire segment has been added:

> But my beloved [John] has desired that he might do more, or a great work yet among men than what he has before done. 6) Yea, he has undertaken a greater work; therefore I will make him as flaming fire and a ministering angel; he shall minister for those who shall be heirs of salvation who dwell upon the earth. 7) And I will make thee to minister for him and for thy brother James; and unto you three I will give this power and the keys of this ministry until I come.

This addition is significant because it reflects the mutating theology of Joseph Smith and his desire to bolster his story that Peter, James, and John came to bestow upon him the "power and the keys" of the Melchizedek priesthood. This addition is all the more odd because the notes to Section 7 tell us that this was actually "translated from parchment, written and hid up by himself" [i.e., John] (1833 edition, p. 18).

Thus, we are asked to believe that not only was the revelation changed, but that somehow this ancient parchment to which Joseph supposedly had access through the spiritual power of the Urim and Thummim also was rewritten.

8. Another entire section was added to the *Doctrine and Covenants* in 1876, *Doctrine and Covenants* Section 13. This addition (at so late a date) is important because the section refers to the alleged ordination of Joseph Smith and Oliver Cowdery to the Aaronic Priesthood (see also *Aaronic Priesthood*) way back on May 15, 1829, by John the Baptist. This allegedly gives us the very words of the ordination.

It is strange that so momentous an event as the restoration of the priesthood to the earth after 1700 years should somehow be left out of a divine document published only four years after the event supposedly occurred—unless, of course, the entire event was made up after 1833.

9. *Doctrine and Covenants* Section 20 in the modern editions was added after the original 1833 edition, even though it was evidently a very lengthy and important "revelation" about "Church Organization and Government" and was supposedly given in April of 1830—three years before the publication of the *Book of Commandments.*

Part of the reason for the late addition is that priesthood offices and functions are discussed, which were not even imagined at the time of the original edition—even though the priesthood was allegedly restored to the earth in 1829!

10. Another large chunk of text was added to Section 27 of the modern *Doctrine and Covenants* (XXVIII in the 1833 edition). About 12 verses were joined to a revelation which originally had but seven verses (1833 edition, p. 60). Hundreds of words were added and then back-dated to make it seem as if they formed part of the original revelation, allegedly given on September 4, 1830. The reason for the addition is quite obvious.

The original was simply a short revelation on how to partake of the sacrament. The new version has significant additions in verses 8,12,13:

> 8) Which John [the Baptist] I have sent unto you, my servants, Joseph Smith, Jun., and Oliver Cowdery, to ordain you unto the first priesthood which you have received, that you might be called and ordained even as Aaron. . . .

> 12) And also with Peter, and James and John, whom I have sent unto you, by whom I have ordained you and confirmed you to be apostles, and especial witnesses of my name, and bear the keys of your ministry and of the same things which I revealed unto them;

> 13) Unto whom I have committed the keys of my kingdom and a dispensation of the gospel for the last times; and for the fulness of times, in the which I will gather together in one all things, both which are in heaven and which are on earth. . . .

These hundreds of words were added to the 1835 edition and the revelation was renumbered "Section L" (1835 edition, pp. 179-80). Interestingly enough, the original 1833 version is dated September 4, 1830; the 1835 edition is dated simply September 1830; and the modern version is dated August 1830. This is an additional source of confusion.

It seems as though Joseph Smith wanted to add this Melchizedek priesthood element to his church and found it necessary to go back and make up a history to go along with it. The addition of this priesthood concept would be the major reason for such a large expansion of the revelation between 1833 and 1835. Yet we must ask, How can you edit or add to a revelation supposedly from the Lord?

ENDOWMENT: Similarity to Masonry and Occultism

The LDS temple ceremony's central feature is the endowment (see also *Endowments*). It is an elaborate ritual drama which begins with the creation of the world as recounted in Genesis (and embellished by the Book of Abraham and Book of Moses from LDS literature). It is designed to lead the participants through a series of ritual experiences representing the progression (a uniquely LDS view) of man from the Garden of Eden into his current state today.

It is important to understand that, despite recent changes in the temple rituals (see also *Temples, Changes to the Ritual*), the endowment still remains as one of the most sacrosanct elements in all of LDS culture. Other than the *Book of Mormon*, the temple and its rituals are considered the central and most unspeakably holy icon of Mormonism. No doubt this is partially because of the effort that is made to keep the rituals secret (more or less) and because those rituals are essential to the fullest form of Mormon salvation.

Rather than deal with the actual content of the endowment ritual, we need to compare it with the much larger and older body of knowledge known as occultism and one subdivision, Freemasonry.

The temple rites fit into a broad and ancient genre of religious events characteristic of mystery religions. These religions are pagan in origin and usually venerate the powers of either human, animal, or vegetative reproduction.

Though the pagan, fertility connotations of the LDS temple rites are well-concealed, virtually all of the distinctive characteristics of such ancient ceremonies as the rites of Eleusis or the rites of

Demeter remain intact in the LDS endowment. The resemblances are manifold, and they can be listed in this fashion:

- Stripping the candidates of all profane (worldly) clothing.
- Ceremonial washing and anointing of the candidates.
- The giving of a new name to be known only within the ritual chamber.
- The giving of special, magical garments designed to protect the wearer from harm.
- The use of special handshakes, pressure points, and secret words to ascertain the worthiness of the candidate.
- The impartation of an ultimate "secret word" or phrase by being whispered in the ear of the candidate.
- The admittance of the candidate into a special, sacred place representing the dwelling place of the gods.
- The participation by the candidate in the *hierosgamos*, or sacred marriage.

Thus we see that even in the broadest sense there are more than seven basic similarities between the LDS temple rites and the ancient pagan mystery and fertility cults.

Most students of LDS history understand that Joseph Smith and his brother Hyrum were Freemasons (see *Smith: Was Joseph a Mason?*). This makes it comparatively easy to explain why there are so many resemblances between the Masonic lodge rituals and the endowment. They include:

1. Both take place in a three-tiered temple with three progressive levels of attainment: LDS: Telestial Room, Terrestrial Room, Celestial Room. Masonry: Lower Chamber of King Solomon's Temple, Middle Chamber of King Solomon's Temple, Sanctum Sanctorum or Holy of Holies of King Solomon's Temple.

2. Both divest their candidates of profane clothing. (Masons also remove all metal.)

3. Both receive sacred aprons as part of their ritual regalia.

4. First ritual handshake (first token of the Aaronic priesthood) absolutely identical in both.

5. Second ritual handshake (second token of the Aaronic priesthood) absolutely identical in both.

6. Signs and penalties (pre-1990 temple rite). Absolutely identical for both in first and second tokens of the Aaronic priesthood.

7. Fourth ritual handshake (second token of Melchizedek priesthood and Master Mason grip) virtually identical.

8. Embrace on Five Points of Fellowship to receive "Sacred Name" (pre-1990 temple rite). Absolutely identical.

9. Use of three Masonic images—the square, the compass and the rule—upon the sacred temple garment and the veil. Absolutely identical.

10. Masonic grand hailing sign of distress ritual gesture and "pay lay ale" gesture (pre-1990 temple rite). Absolutely identical.

11. Use of identical iconography in Freemasonry and early LDS temple architecture: all-seeing eye, inverted pentagrams, handshakes, beehive, sun symbols, hexagrams, etc.

Because of the extreme cross-pollination between nineteenth-century witches, magicians, and Freemasons, it will be noted that there are also many resemblances between the temple rituals and modern white witchcraft or "Wicca." Whether these resemblances are because Masons (or Mormons) borrowed them from witches or that witches borrowed them from Masons cannot be established for certain. However, the resemblances are manifold. These include use of many of the same symbols (pentagrams) and the following:

1. Both strip the candidate of all profane clothing.

2. Both dress the candidate in a shield-like garment preparatory to being anointed.

3. Both anoint similar parts of the candidate's body, including bodily orifices.

4. Both give the candidate a new secret name.

5. Both teach the candidate the wearing of talismanic garments.

6. Both ceremonially veil the priestesses (pre-1990 ritual).

7. Both embrace on the five points of fellowship (pre-1990 ritual).

8. Both bestow upon the candidate a magical apron.

9. Both give secret tokens or handshakes to identify levels of attainment.

10. Both perform marriages for time and eternity.

11. Both have the attainment of godhood or goddesshood as their ultimate goal.

All of these resemblances underscore the heavily Gnostic underpinnings of the LDS faith (see also *Gnosticism*). Mormons, and temple Mormons especially, believe they are saved not by faith nor by grace but by secret, esoteric knowledge acquired in highly occult rituals.

This should not surprise us when we consider the high level of occult involvement on the part of the founder of Mormonism, Joseph Smith, and the rest of his family. Smith was steeped in the culture of the occult from a very early age, and was thus much more familiar with what LDS historian D. Michael Quinn calls the "Magic World View" than the Judeo-Christian worldview.

When Smith became a Mason, he simply added that new level of deception to an already-towering Babel-like edifice of occultic theological intricacy. The current LDS temple rites still reflect Smith's highly eclectic and completely occult religious upbringing. They are mortally dangerous, though most Latter-day Saints believe them to be the highest and most holy thing which they can perform in this life.

ENDOWMENTS

Endowments is a term uniquely used in the Mormon church to apply to special, sacred ceremonies which can be performed only in an LDS temple. These rituals are closed to non-Mormons, and indeed most Mormons are not "worthy" to participate in them. The term *endowment* means "gift." Supposedly the temple endowment is a heavenly gift of wisdom, power, and blessing. Mormons are taught that the endowment, along with other LDS rituals, are the most holy and sacred things which can be performed on this planet. Thus, the temple and its rituals are invested with an awesome amount of emotional and religious freight.

Bruce R. McConkie explains it this way:

> Certain special, spiritual blessings given worthy and faithful saints in the temples are called endowments, because in and through them the recipients *are endowed with power from on high*. They receive an education relative to the Lord's purposes and plans in the creation and peopling of the earth and are taught the things that must be done by man in order to gain exaltation in the world to come. They place themselves in a position to receive the sanctifying and cleansing power of the Holy Ghost, thus becoming clean and spotless before the Lord. *So sacred and holy* are the administrations performed that in every age when they have been revealed, *the Lord has withheld them from the knowledge of the world and disclosed them only to the faithful saints* in houses and places dedicated and selected for that purpose (*Doctrine*, pp. 226-27, emphasis added).

In point of fact, a Mormon cannot be saved in the truest sense of the word without receiving his endowments, and then being married in the bonds of celestial marriage (see also *New and Everlasting Covenant*).

Stripped of all its high-sounding verbiage, the endowment is a mystery play. It is part of a larger cycle of initiatory events which must take place in the temple in each Mormon's life in order for him or her to fully partake of the blessings which they believe can be theirs. Before we examine the endowment itself, let us present in outline form the entire panoply of what goes on within a Mormon temple.

This is what would happen to you, assuming that you had received your coveted temple recommend and you were going through the temple for yourself with your spouse for the first time. (Most temple patrons have already gone through and "taken out their endowments" for themselves, and thus they are now acting on behalf of various dead people whose names they have been given for vicarious proxy work.) Here is what you would expect:

I. Introductory lecture by a temple worker (actually explains very little)

II. Initiatory work

A. Disrobe and place clothes in locker. Put on "shield."

B. Go to initiatory cubicle.

   1. You are washed and anointed with oil preparatory to becoming a king and priest (or queen and priestess).

   2. You are clothed in your temple garment for the first time and instructed to wear it always.

   3. You are given your "new name" which you must never reveal.

III. The Endowment Itself

   A. Return to locker and dress in temple "whites." Take packet of temple robes and ascend to upper level.

   B. Enter Creation room (or theater) and hear Creation room narrative.

      1. Jehovah (Jesus) and Michael (preexistent Adam) go through six days of Creation.

      2. Michael (Adam) is put to sleep by Jehovah and Elohim (Heavenly Father) and awakens not remembering his pre-existence.

   C. The Garden of Eden scene

      1. Lucifer tempts Adam and fails.

      2. Lucifer tempts Eve successfully.

      3. Adam and Eve's eyes are opened and they recognize Lucifer.

      4. Elohim and Jehovah return to Garden and Adam and Eve adopt fig-leaf aprons at Lucifer's suggestion.

      5. Temple patrons are made to put on their green aprons.

      6. Elohim curses Lucifer and he departs.

   D. The Law of Obedience—Jehovah makes Eve swear to obey her husband and she obeys the Lord; then makes Adam swear to obey the commands of God. All temple patrons are made to covenant to Law of Obedience.

   E. The Law of Sacrifice—all temple patrons are made to covenant to it. The First Token of the Aaronic priesthood is taught to them.

   F. "The Lone and Dreary World"—represents our fallen world in its present condition. Jehovah sends Peter, James, and John down to challenge Lucifer and teach Adam and Eve further signs and tokens.

G. The Law of the Gospel—Peter, James, and John lead the patrons in covenanting to obey it.

H. The robes of the holy priesthood are now given to the patrons to wear with the robe hanging on the left shoulder.

I. The second token of the Aaronic priesthood is taught to patrons.

J. The terrestrial world and the Law of Chastity—patrons are made to covenant to obey it. Priesthood robes are changed to be worn hanging on the right shoulder.

K. First token of the Melchizedek priesthood—the sign of the nail.

L. The Law of Consecration—patrons made to covenant to obey it.

M. Second token of the Melchizedek priesthood—the sure sign of the nail is taught to patrons.

N. Lecture before "the veil."

O. The prayer circle—patrons are taught the "true order of prayer."

P. Communication of the final name of the second token of the Melchizedek priesthood through the veil. Patrons are passed through the veil by "the Lord" into His presence in the Celestial Room.

IV. The Sealing Room—temple marriage for time and all eternity— "the new and everlasting covenant of marriage."

This is the broad pattern that is followed in all temples the world over for a first-time patron. The procedure is quite involved, and this brief outline in no way does it justice. The usual length for a first-time endowment is about three and a half hours, followed by the sealing, which might take a half hour.

The endowment itself—which used to be performed entirely with live actors and with the entire audience of patrons moving from a Telestial Room to a Terrestrial Room through the veil to the Celestial Room—is now being done in 90 percent of the temples on film in one room. Only when the veil is brought forward and the patrons go through it do they leave that one theater-type room and enter the Celestial Room. The films allow for greater speed in processing work for the dead (see also *Endowments for the Dead*), plus they are more vivid and interesting than watching a roomful of paintings on walls.

It is this ritual to which all Mormons aspire and which some Mormons do actually experience. Yet many find it surprisingly humdrum and mundane. Some (especially women) find the initiatory parts—where their nearly nude bodies are washed and anointed in intimate places—quite offensive. After the first few times, quite a few in the endowment theater just fall asleep in the middle of the long creation account.

In the 1980s when the church still publicly admitted such things, it was revealed that more than half the people who go to the temple for their own endowments never return. A strange commentary indeed on something which is supposed to be the peak spiritual experience of a Mormon's lifetime!

In this light, it is ironic to read these words of LDS apostle James E. Talmage in his classic work on the LDS temple:

> The ordinances of the endowment embody certain obligations on the part of the individual, such as covenant and promise to observe the law of strict virtue and chastity, to be charitable, benevolent, tolerant and pure; to devote both talent and material means to the spread of truth and the uplifting of the race; to maintain devotion to the cause of truth; and to seek in every way to contribute to the great preparation that the earth may be made ready to receive her King, the Lord Jesus. With the taking of each covenant and the assuming of each obligation a promised blessing is pronounced, contingent upon the faithful observance of the conditions.
>
> No jot, iota, or tittle of the temple rites is otherwise than uplifting and sanctifying. In every detail the endowment ceremony contributes to covenants of morality of life, consecration of person to high ideals, devotion to truth, patriotism to nation, and allegiance to God. The blessings of the House of the Lord are restricted to no privileged class; every member of the Church may have admission to the temple with the right to participate in the ordinances thereof, if he comes duly accredited as of worthy life and conduct (*The House of the Lord*, pp. 100-01).

Notwithstanding these lofty words, many devout people who attend the temple find its oaths bloody and vindictive, its language and treatment of women extremely oppressive and sexist, and its use of eccentric and occult costumes and symbolism deeply disturbing. Many Christian apologists to the Mormon people have raised an outcry about the oaths, the occultism, the thinly disguised Masonry, and the dastardly way in which Protestant preachers were exposed to ridicule in the older temple rites.

Thus in April 1990, without a whisper of explanation, these supposedly ancient and unchangeable rituals were substantially altered (see also *Temples, Changes to the Ritual*). As important as that event was for Christian apologists, it is a hollow victory as long as precious Mormon people continue to trust more in their temple than they do in the true and living God, Jesus Christ.

ENDOWMENTS FOR THE DEAD

(See also *Baptism for the Dead.*)

Perhaps 80 percent of the work that goes on within LDS temples is vicarious work performed for the dead. Every faithful Latter-day Saint is required to "redeem their dead." This means, in practice, gathering all the necessary genealogical information on all their own ancestors for at least four generations back.

That genealogical work may take years, but it is regarded as a sacred obligation by serious Mormons. Once the data is gathered, it is submitted to the church where, after processing, the names of those dead people are ready for "temple work." Members come to the temple and (same sex to same sex) vicariously stand in for their departed relatives as they are baptized and confirmed members of the church.

If the deceased was a male, they are given a priesthood ordination by proxy and then (for both sexes) they are given the initiatory work (see also *Endowments*). All of the work described in the section on the endowment is done for the deceased, with the words "For and on behalf of _____, who is dead" inserted at appropriate places. Because no teaching is needed, the endowment takes perhaps 15 to 20 percent less time. Otherwise, the endowment is the same.

Once you have finished with your own family, the Mormon is given random names from the huge wellspring of genealogical research which church workers are doing the world over. The church believes that ultimately it must do the work for every dead person from the time of Adam to the present.

Ironically, at the moment the church is not even keeping up with the present rate of death. More people are dying every minute in the world than the Mormons are able to do proxy work for. This is partially because the endowment rite itself is a logistical limitation. It takes about an hour and a half at least, thus one person working full-time can do only about four or five a day. It is a tragic waste of time and money, since all of this ritual work does the dead absolutely no good (see Hebrews 9:27). It does, however, keep the Mormons too busy to sit back and reflect on the reality of how they are spending their lives.

ESCHATOLOGY

Eschatology is the biblical study of the "end times" or the last days—the events surrounding the Second Advent of the Lord Jesus Christ. Even among Christian circles it is a controversial subject. Actually, the LDS doctrines on this subject, while strange, are by no means totally outlandish.

Mormons are basically believers in premillennialism (that the Second Coming of Jesus will occur before the millennium). They also would probably believe in a post-tribulation rapture, although Mormons would never use the term *Rapture*.

They believe they will go through the period known as the Great Tribulation, awaiting the coming of their Savior. This is partially why Mormons are noted for having food and water storage to last several years. Many of them also have fuel storage, home generators, and a substantial amount of firearms. They believe in an essentially literalist interpretation of the events of Revelation, thus they are expecting famines, plagues, and earthquakes. They hope, with the help of guidance from their church (which has extensive systems in place to send out relief to its people in areas of disaster) and their own storage and firearms, to ride out the famines and earthquakes until Jesus comes.

Probably the oddest element in their eschatology is their belief in their church's unique place in the end times. Mormons are taught that the U.S. Constitution is an inspired document (see also *Constitution of the U.S.A.*) and that America is an especially chosen and favored nation. They also believe that the time will come when the Constitution will be under attack to such a degree that it will "hang by a thread" and that the "elders of Israel" (i.e., Mormon leaders) will have to intervene to save the day.

They believe it is their destiny to seize the reins of power in America and turn it into a theocracy, a religious dictatorship, led by a prophet-king who would be the supreme earthly head of the Melchizedek priesthood. Since Mormons tend to be right-wing in their political beliefs and conservative in their moral stands (pro-family, pro-life, anti-homosexual, etc.), many Christians have felt comfortable in joining forces with them to try and revive morality in this nation. Mormons are, in turn, using this alliance to build legitimacy within the evangelical and fundamentalist Christian community.

Should the Mormons ever succeed in creating their church-state, it would be a country very much like Utah under Brigham Young. That is to say, it will have very little social or religious freedom. Mormons might criminalize abortion, pornography, and homosexuality, but they might also criminalize soul-winning efforts by Bible-believing Christians.

Thus Mormons, like Kingdom-Now theologians and Christian Reconstructionists, believe that they can bring in a kingdom of political righteousness here on earth and offer it to Jesus when He comes to reign. As noble as some of their goals might be, the fruits of their control—as seen in nineteenth- and twentieth-century Utah—are frightening indeed.

Mormons don't realize that their goals were tried before and that the results of trying to bring in a theocracy without the *right* Jesus Christ reigning personally on the earth were tragic.

ETERNAL DAMNATION

The LDS Position

Talk about eternal damnation in the LDS sense quickly slides into a semantic thicket. McConkie attempts to divide the Mormon doctrine of eternal damnation into three distinct senses in which the phrase is used:

1. Eternal damnation is the opposite of eternal life, and all those who do not gain eternal life, or exaltation in the highest

heaven within the celestial kingdom, are partakers of eternal damnation. Their eternal condemnation is to have limitations imposed upon them so that they cannot progress to the state of godhood and gain a fulness of all things. . . .

2. Eternal damnation is also used to specify the punishment of those who come forth in the resurrection of damnation, meaning those who are destined to inherit the telestial kingdom and those who will be cast out to reign with the devil and his angels as sons of perdition. . . .

3. Eternal damnation is used further to specify the torment and anguish to which the spirits of the wicked are heir in the spirit prison as they await the day of their resurrection. This type of eternal damnation ceases when the offender has finally come forth in the resurrection. In this sense, eternal damnation is the type, kind, and quality of torment, punishment, or damnation involved rather than the duration of that damnation. In other words, eternal is the name of the kind of punishment involved, just as it is the name of the kind of life referred to in the expression eternal life. Eternal punishment is, thus, the kind of punishment imposed by God who is Eternal, and those subject to it may suffer therefrom for either a short or a long period. After their buffetings and trials cause them to repent, they are freed from this type of eternal damnation (*Doctrine*, pp. 234-36).

Mormons, like many other "home-grown religions" that sprang up in nineteenth-century America, refuse to accept the idea of an eternal hell (see also *Hell*). They end up trying to explain it away in one odd fashion or another. The Mormon attempt is an excellent example.

The first sense in which Mormons wish to use the term *eternal damnation* is that of a person who has forfeited eternal life (i.e., godhood and eternal increase of seed; see *Eternal Life*) and who therefore will be eternally *prevented* from progressing. The limitations imposed will prevent such a person from attaining godhood. One LDS teacher was fond of saying that such people were eternally "dammed" in the sense that a river was dammed, when it was blocked from flowing to its proper destination.

The second sense applies to those who come forth in the resurrection of damnation. Elsewhere in the article, McConkie attempts to elaborate:

Abinadi [a *Book of Mormon* prophet] uses the term end-less damnation similarly, to refer to the resurrected state of all the rebellious, those who come forth in the resurrection of the unjust, those who refused to repent when the gospel was offered to them but who chose to go their own carnal ways, receiving eventually an inheritance in the telestial kingdom. Though they attain a kingdom of glory, yet to all eternity they are damned, cannot go where God and Christ are (*Doctrine and Covenants* 76:112), and are never completely free from the lingering remorse that always follows the loss of opportunity (ibid., p. 235).

Here, damnation means being unable to go where Christ and God are. While that is correct in a limited sense, the Mormons are still trying to pussyfoot around the terrible truth about hell.

In the third sense, total semantic chaos rears its ugly head. We are told "eternal" punishment has nothing to do with duration. It is only eternal because it is punishment from God, who is eternal. This, of course, is nonsense. Mormons would like to believe that everyone eventually gets to crawl out of the outer darkness and get a kingdom of glory, however feeble and telestial it might be.

The Biblical View

Mormons would do well to heed the words of Jesus Christ, whose precious name graces the doors of their churches and temples. Jesus preached about an eternal hell more than any other single subject. Here is one of His most gripping descriptions:

And if thy hand offend thee, cut it off: it is better for thee to enter into life maimed, than having two hands to go into hell, into the fire that never shall be quenched: where their worm dieth not, and the fire is not quenched (Mark 9:43,44).

ETERNAL LIFE

The LDS Position

"Eternal life" in LDS doctrine is something beyond and above immortality. In comparing the two, the late prophet and LDS president Joseph Fielding Smith said,

Immortality and Eternal Life are two separate things, one distinct from the other. Every man shall receive immortality, whether he be good, bad, or indifferent, for the resurrection from the dead shall come to all. Eternal life is something in addition. None shall receive eternal life save it be those who keep the commandments of the Lord and are entitled thus to enter into his presence. . . . That is eternal life, to dwell in the presence of the Father and receive exaltation from him. . . . Very gladly would the Lord give to everyone eternal life, but since that blessing can come only on merit—through the faithful performance of duty— only those who are worthy shall receive it (Joseph Fielding Smith, *Doctrines of Salvation*, vol. 2, pp. 4,5).

Modern-day theologian and late apostle of the LDS church Bruce R. McConkie carefully defined *eternal life* as that state of permanent exaltation of those who step beyond the general salvation which is given to all mankind, and through good works and total obedience achieve or earn their own personal salvation. (The Christian reader would do well to see also *Eternal Damnation* and read what happens to the one who doubts this is real LDS doctrine.)

In his encyclopedic work *Mormon Doctrine*, McConkie wrote:

Salvation in its true and full sense is synonymous with exaltation or eternal life and consists in gaining an inheritance in the highest of the three heavens within the celestial kingdom. With few exceptions, this is the salvation of which the scriptures speak. It is the salvation which the saints seek. . . . This full salvation is obtained in and through the continuation of the family unit in eternity, and those who obtain it are gods (p. 670).

That's as plain as day: Eternal life = Godhood = Exaltation. Mormons believe that they can become gods. It is not some isolated, obtuse piece of theology. It is an inherent part of the law of eternal progression that is buried within the bosom of every Mormon believer.

Doctrine and Covenants 14:7 puts a stiff price tag on eternal life, however: "And if you keep my commandments and endure to the end you shall have eternal life, which gift is the greatest of all the gifts of God."

Yet, McConkie seems to do a sidestep with contradictory LDS scripture. In *Mormon Doctrine*, McConkie states,

But only those who obey the fulness of the gospel law will inherit eternal life (*Doctrine and Covenants* 29:43,44). . . . It is the kind, status, type and quality of life that God himself enjoys. Thus those who gain eternal life receive exaltation. . . . They overcome all things, have all power, and receive the fulness of the father. They are gods (*Doctrine*, p. 237).

While this seems to go along with the context of the doctrine, McConkie quoted *Doctrine and Covenants* 29:43-44, which reads:

And thus did I, the Lord God, appoint unto man the days of his probation—that by his natural death he might be raised in immortality unto eternal life, even as many as would believe; and they that believe not unto eternal damnation; for they cannot be redeemed from their spiritual fall, because they repent not.

Here, the LDS scripture clearly states that eternal life is given to those who would believe. Yet there are hundreds of thousands of Mormons who surely *believe* "Mormonism" with every fiber of their being, but who could never hope to inherit the Mormon version of eternal life for a hundred different reasons (perhaps they failed to pay a full tithe or didn't take out their endowments or simply broke the word of wisdom).

The Biblical View

What does the Bible, God's true Word, say about eternal life?

That whosoever believeth in him should not perish, but have eternal life. For God so loved the world, that he gave his only begotten Son, that whosoever believeth in him should not perish, but have everlasting life. For God sent not his Son into the world to condemn the world; but that the world through him might be saved (John 3:15-17).

Romans 6:23 states, "For the wages of sin is death; but the gift of God is eternal life through Jesus Christ our Lord."

It is interesting that we often slide by a very powerful truth in quoting the bedrock Scripture in John 3:16. It is prefaced with several verses rarely quoted:

If I have told you earthly things, and ye believe not, how shall ye believe, if I tell you of heavenly things? And no man hath ascended up to heaven, but he that came down from heaven, even the Son of man which is in heaven (John 3:12,13).

Jesus was about to share heavenly things—things of heaven itself: that we believers will have eternal, forever lives in the presence of Christ Himself. This is glorious news!

Paul said to be absent from the body is to be with Christ. There is no sting of death awaiting the Christian. There is only eternal life.

ETERNAL LIVES

The Mormon doctrine of eternal lives is the teaching that those who attain eternal life [LDS godhood] will have eternal increase in their exaltation. Simply put, LDS "gods" expect to have "goddess wives" who will bear them children throughout their eternities of godhood.

This doctrine depends on the law of eternal progression. Remember that Mormons teach the LDS god was once as we are now and resides near the great star, Kolob, where he continues to sire spirit children with his many wives. These bodiless children are being brought down to this earth to gain bodies [we are some of those children], be tested and judged. Those who earn eternal life will go forward in the married state to start the process all over in some distant galaxy or star system, begetting spirit children for some other Earth. McConkie states:

> Those who gain eternal life (exaltation) also gain eternal lives, meaning that in the resurrection they will have "eternal increase," a "continuation of the seeds," a "continuation of the lives." Their spirit progeny will "continue as innumerable as the stars; or if ye were to count the sand upon the seashore ye could not number them" (*Doctrine*, pp. 237-38).

The Biblical View

It is pretty hard to come up with a biblical view to this doctrine because it is entirely unbiblical—except that it falls into the category of vain imaginations as mentioned in Romans chapter 1. Otherwise, there isn't even a Scripture Mormons can mangle into supporting this doctrine of delusion.

Because that, when they knew God, they glorified him not as God, neither were thankful; but became vain in their imaginations, and their foolish heart was darkened. Professing themselves to be wise, they became fools, and changed the glory of the uncorruptible God into an image made like to corruptible man, and to birds, and fourfooted beasts, and creeping things. Wherefore God also gave them up to uncleanness through the lusts of their own hearts, to dishonour their own bodies between themselves: who changed the truth of God into a lie, and worshipped and served the creature more than the Creator, who is blessed for ever. Amen (Romans 1:21-25).

It is God's solemn word that those who have given themselves over to such doctrines are lost. The Scripture above says that God also gave them up. Instead of eternal lives as gods, they will only find eternal damnation.

EVERLASTING BURNINGS

The LDS Position

There are many strange statements in LDS scripture and in the writings of its prophet Joseph Smith that have long been a puzzle. Separately, many of them do not seem so ominous. But when you start putting them together—their teaching on the angel of light and the phrase *pay lay ale*, for example—one must begin to wonder if there isn't an answer just under the surface of the words.

Smith had an odd understanding about the presence of God. In his recently canonized vision of the celestial kingdom, Joseph Smith wrote this:

The heavens were opened upon us, and I beheld the celestial kingdom of God, and the glory thereof, whether in the body or out I cannot tell. I saw the transcendent beauty of the *gate through which the heirs of that kingdom will enter, which was like unto circling flames of fire; also the blazing throne of God, whereon was seated the Father and the Son* (Doctrine and Covenants 137:1-3, emphasis added).

Joseph Smith was here offering godhood to the pure and elect of his followers. In speaking about man's assent to that degree of glory, he commented:

Here then, is eternal life—to know the only wise and true God, and you have got to learn how to be Gods yourselves, and to be kings and priests to God, the same as all Gods have done before you, namely, by going from one small degree to another, and from a small capacity to a great one; from grace to grace, from exaltation to exaltation, until you attain to the resurrection of the dead, *and are able to dwell in everlasting burnings, and to sit in glory, as do those who sit enthroned in everlasting power* [emphasis added].

He went on to say:

These are the first principles of consolation. How consoling to the mourners when they are called to part with a husband, wife, father, mother, child, or dear relative, to know that, *although the earthly tabernacle is laid down and dissolved they shall rise again to dwell in everlasting burnings in immortal glory*, not to sorrow, suffer, or die any more; but they shall be heirs of God and joint heirs with Jesus Christ. What is it? to inherit the same power, the same glory and the same exaltation, until you arrive at the station of a God, and ascend the throne of eternal power, the same as those who have gone before (*Teachings*, pp. 346-47, emphasis added).

Yet, even Mormons must realize that the everlasting burnings Smith described fit more with the devil than with God. Here is what the *Book of Mormon* says about it:

For, said he, I have repented of my sins, and have been redeemed of the Lord; behold I am born of the Spirit.

And the Lord said unto me: Marvel not that all mankind, yea, men and women, all nations, kindreds, tongues and people, must be born again; yea, born of God, changed from their carnal and fallen state, to a state of righteousness, being redeemed of God, becoming his sons and daughters; and thus they become new creatures; and unless they do this, they can in nowise inherit the kingdom of God. I say unto you, unless this be the case, they must be cast off; and this I know, because I was like to be cast off. Nevertheless, after wading through much tribulation, repenting nigh unto death, *the Lord in mercy hath seen fit to snatch me out of an everlasting burning, and I am born of God* (Mosiah 27:24-28, emphasis added).

Mosiah is speaking about a redeemed person being snatched away from the terrible fate of an everlasting burning. It was hardly a place of glory!

The Biblical View

Jesus Himself gave us an understanding of this fate of the wicked when He said:

> And before him shall be gathered all nations: and he shall separate them one from another, as a shepherd divideth his sheep from the goats: and he shall set the sheep on his right hand, but the goats on the left. . . . Then shall he say also unto them on the left hand, Depart from me, ye cursed, into everlasting fire, prepared for the devil and his angels (Matthew 25:32,33,41).

I have really struggled through this section. For years, I have had a terrible vision of hardworking, dedicated temple Mormons walking into the throne room of their god, as he sits amid the flames of a burning hell. They stand there, watching, as the beautiful face of the god they have imagined melts away to reveal the terrible secret: The god of their everlasting burnings is really Lucifer. He is laughing, crying out, "I told you from the beginning who I was. You have no excuse." It is no laughing matter to the millions of Mormons who stand to meet such an end.

The tragedy of Mormonism is that mixed amongst the sweets are these little doses of darkness, revealing the true nature of the thing that lies just beneath the surface.

Mormonism is like a photo negative of the truth: black where white should be, and difficult to see unless held up to strong light.

EVIL SPIRITS

Evil spirits are substantially the same for Mormons as they are for Bible-believing Christians. They are believed to be the source of much of the wickedness in the world. Evil spirits are the one-third of the spirits who followed Lucifer in his rebellion, and they now do his bidding. They seduce men and women to sin and "to do those things which are carnal, sensual, and devilish" (*Doctrine*, p. 246).

It is interesting that Mormons do admit that "revelations come to men just as easily from devils as they do from holy sources" (ibid.). Yet concerning the operations of evil spirits, there are some important differences between LDS belief and Christian theology:

> Evil spirits control much of the so-called religious worship in the world; for instance, the great creeds of Christendom were formulated so as to conform to their whispered promptings. They have played a substantial part in the formulation of the philosophies of the world; so-called scientific theories have been influenced by them. By hearkening to their promptings, leaders of nations have led their peoples into wars and every sort of evil (ibid.).

Here again, despite the appealing public relations campaign the Mormon church is sponsoring, we see Mormons are taught to believe that the historic creeds of Christendom—the Athanasian, the Nicene, and the Apostles' creeds—are the work of evil spirits (see also *Creeds*). They are taught that the religious worship carried on in Christian churches around the world is inspired by evil spirits.

Ever since Joseph Smith threw down the gauntlet in *The Pearl of Great Price* (Joseph Smith—History 1:19) and said all other churches were abominable in the sight of God and their professors were all corrupt, he drew a line in the sand. There can be no middle ground. Either the historic Christian position which has endured for 2000 years is demon-inspired nonsense and Mormonism is the one true church it claims to be, *or* Joseph Smith and his claims are absolutely false and originate in the pits of hell. The positions are mutually exclusive.

The deceptive response which many LDS missionaries give to questions about other churches is that, "We believe all churches to have some truth." What the missionaries are careful not to say is that they are taught that all churches—Lutheran, Methodist, Baptist, etc.—have all the important things wrong and that not a single person in them can be born again because they have not been baptized by a proper authority (i.e., an LDS missionary). They won't tell you that they believe your pastor is teaching doctrines of devils from his pulpit or that when your church sings "Amazing Grace," they are singing a lie!

This is the difference between the LDS teaching on evil spirits and the Christian teaching. Mormons believe that Christian doctrine is demonically inspired, while Christians believe that LDS theology is demonically inspired.

EVOLUTION

The LDS Position

Like most evangelical and fundamentalist Christians, Mormons are taught that the doctrine of evolution is a scientific heresy of sorts (*Doctrine*, p. 247ff.). Since they believe in a literal (more or less) interpretation of the Genesis account, they believe that the Earth was once better than it is now and that it "devolved" due to the effects of Adam's "transgression."

From the outset of the evolutionary theory, LDS leaders have attacked it, and rightly so. Neither are Mormons allowed to believe in so-called theistic evolution. Their official doctrine is that the six-day creation account is to be taken literally, and that mankind did indeed have only two original human parents, Adam and Eve. Bruce R. McConkie writes, "The period during which birth, and life, and death have been occurring on this earth is less than 6,000 years" (ibid., p. 255).

Oddly enough, though Mormons soundly reject the idea of biological evolution, their key doctrine, the law of eternal progression, teaches a kind of spiritual evolution (see also *Law of Eternal Progression*). Mormons believe that the purpose of man here on earth is to "evolve" into a divine being. The famous couplet of LDS leader Lorenzo Snow is to the point: "As man is, God once was. As God is, man may become."

Thus, while LDS apologists rightly point out the thermodynamic problems with the theory of evolution, they try to work out a system whereby a finite being (man) can somehow evolve into an infinite being. That is a bigger leap than a chimpanzee turning into a college professor.

Mormons believe that man and God are basically the same "species" and are seen now merely at different stages of their evolution—like seeing a caterpillar and a butterfly at the same time. The ignorant observer would find it hard to believe that one came out of the other.

The Biblical View

The LDS attempt to leap the chasm between God and humans is short-circuited by the Bible, which declares that "God is not a man, that he should lie; neither the son of man, that he should repent" (Numbers 23:19).

God and man are not the same species. A devout LDS male cannot evolve into a god any more than a house cat can evolve into a lion.

EXALTATION

The LDS Position

Exaltation is the LDS term for the ultimate spiritual goal of devout Mormons. Bruce R. McConkie defines the term briefly:

> Exaltation consists in the continuation of the family unit in eternity. Exaltation is eternal life, the kind of life which God lives. Those who obtain it gain an inheritance in the highest of three heavens within the celestial kingdom (*Doctrine and Covenants* 131:1-4 in *Doctrine*, p. 257).

An essential component of exaltation is the idea of the continuation of the family (wife and children) beyond death. Only LDS who attain exaltation will be allowed to procreate beyond the veil. This means that in addition to children begotten unto them on Earth, they also will have spirit children in the resurrection and will inherit, in due course, the fullness of the glory of the Father, meaning that they have all power in heaven and on earth (*Doctrine and Covenants* 76:50-60; 93:1-40).

Also notice that McConkie equates exaltation with eternal life. Thus, it is a kind of salvation beyond what is available to those outside the LDS church (and even that which is available to non-temple Latter-day Saints within the church). In order to begin qualifying for exaltation, Mormons must have gone to the temple and received their endowments. Ideally, they must also be married for time and all eternity. Anything less is essentially damnation (*Doctrine and Covenants* 132:4).

This means that even though most Mormons think of themselves as saved and will say as much to Christians, their salvation is incomplete without temple work, an entire life of virtually sinless perfection, and extremely dedicated service in church callings (see also *Salvation*).

The Biblical View

In contrast to the LDS doctrine of exaltation, which is conditional upon doing certain ordinances and works, the biblical understanding of eternal life is that it is an entirely free gift (Romans 6:23). Indeed, one of the central points of Paul's epistle to the Romans is that a gift which must be earned is not really a gift at all (Romans 4:3-6).

It is also helpful to consider the way the Bible uses the word *exaltation* or the verb *to exalt*. *Exaltation* is not found in the Bible at all, but the verb form is used 88 times. Of those times, 37 are references to God Himself, usually in worship. Six would seem to be primarily messianic in character (i.e., referring to the coming Christ). Twenty are references in an extremely negative context, and 14 are positive in relation to people.

Two additional and telling references are found in Isaiah 14:13 and Daniel 11:36, where either Satan or the Antichrist are said to be exalting themselves. The Bible says the Lord alone will be exalted (Isaiah 2:11-17) in eternity. Paul even worries about being exalted too much (2 Corinthians 12:7). How is this possible, if exaltation is to be the goal of every worthy Latter-day Saint?

For such a central doctrine of the true gospel never to be mentioned explicitly in the entire Bible except when falling from the lips of Satan and his chief spokesman is astonishing—unless, of course, it is a doctrine of devils (1 Timothy 4:1) added by Joseph Smith to feed his own pride.

FALL OF ADAM

(See also *Law of Eternal Progression.*)

The LDS Position

The LDS doctrine of the fall of Adam (or original sin) is skewed by its doctrine of the law of eternal progression, which says that man is essentially a god in embryo sent here to earth to gain a physical body necessary in his path to godhood.

LDS doctrine teaches that because of Adam and Eve's innocence, there was no way for them to bear children without disobeying God's instruction not to touch the tree of the knowledge of good and evil. Therefore, the Mormon looks upon the fall of Adam as a *blessing*, not a sin. In effect, Adam fell upwards, not actually sinning, but "transgressing" a lesser law to obey a greater one.

The LDS second Article of Faith removes the burden of the doctrine of original sin from its adherents: "We believe that men will be punished for their own sins and not for Adam's transgression."

The late LDS president, Joseph Fielding Smith, authored and edited a three-volume series titled *Doctrines of Salvation* which defined Mormonism's tenets of faith. President Smith discussed the eternally significant circumstances of Adam's fall in vol. 1, pp. 113-15. In that section, headlined "Fall of Adam a Blessing," Smith claimed there could be no immortality or eternal life without the fall.

When Adam was driven out of the Garden of Eden, the

Lord passed a sentence on him. Some people have looked upon that sentence as being a dreadful thing. It was not; it was a blessing. I do not know that it can truthfully be considered even as a punishment in disguise. In order for mankind to obtain salvation and exaltation it is necessary for them to obtain bodies in this world, and pass through the experiences and schooling that are found only in mortality.

Because of Adam's transgression we are here in mortal life. . . . The fall of man came as a blessing in disguise and was the means of furthering the purposes of the Lord in the progress of man, rather than a means of hindering them.

Claiming that "Adam and Eve rejoiced in falls," Smith stated, "Before partaking of the fruit Adam could have lived forever. . . . When he ate, he became subject to death. . . . It was a transgression of the law, but not a sin in the strict sense, for it was something that Adam and Eve had to do."

Smith went on to quote the joyous comments of both Adam and Eve after they "transgressed," as recorded in the Book of Moses in *The Pearl of Great Price*.

Adam said, "Blessed be the name of God, for because of my transgression my eyes are opened, and in this life I shall have joy, and again in the flesh I shall see God."

Eve said, "Were it not for our transgression we should never have seed and never should have known good and evil, and the joy of our redemption, and the eternal life which God giveth unto all the obedient" (Moses 5:10,11).

The Biblical View

The reader needs to go back to the Scriptures and review the events that took place in the Garden of Eden. To accept the LDS position that man's fall was really what God wanted all along and was one of the greatest blessings of God, one would have to acknowledge Lucifer as the bearer of truth instead of deception!

Yet it is obvious that Lucifer was working under a veil of deception and not truth when he called into doubt the perfection of God's Word: "Yea, hath God said?" (Genesis 3: v. 1) In verse 2, Eve compounded the sin by misquoting God (see Genesis 2:16) and leaving out something from the Word of God—the very important word *freely*. She further worsened the sin in verse 3 by adding to the Word of God when she said, "neither shall ye touch it"—words which God never spoke.

Satan's next lie was in verse 4: "Ye shall not surely die," which is obviously a big lie, since people have been dying ever since. And in verse 5, we read, "Then your eyes shall be opened." This was true, but not in the way that Satan implied.

Of course, their eyes were opened (v. 7), but the big question is, To what were they opened? The answer: that they were sinners (another truth the LDS church denies—see *Articles of Faith*, #2). That is why they covered themselves and hid.

Lucifer continued with his lies. In verse 5, he said, "And ye shall be as gods, knowing good and evil." This is the same lie he has been selling down through the centuries to witches, Gnostics, occultists, and now Mormons.

Mormon apologists cross-reference this to Genesis 3:22 to somehow validate this satanic teaching, but does this work? Let's see: "And the LORD God said, Behold, the man is become as one of us, to know good and evil: and now, lest he put forth his hand, and take also of the tree of life, and eat, and live for ever . . . (Genesis 3:22).

It says that "the man is become as one of us." What did God mean by that? It is clear that God could not mean that Adam had become a god. Why?

If Adam and Eve at that moment became god and goddess, then the LDS law of eternal progression becomes irrelevant. If they were gods then, at the nadir of their transgression and long before they brought forth their first offspring, then why should Mormons have to go through all the years of works and obedience to achieve what Adam and Eve gained at the moment of their fall?

Since we are all children of Adam, we would all be gods at birth without ever having to lift a finger—unless something else is meant in the passage. It is!

Notice that the text says "the man is become as one of us." The man had somehow become *similar* to God. Follow this thought very carefully. If the law of eternal progression doctrine is true, then Adam and Eve at birth already were similar to God—they were His spirit babies, right? If God was a daddy God who had already fathered these two in the preexistence, then his kids should be infant gods. Isn't that the law of eternal progression put into simple terms?

Yet this text says that after Adam and Eve ate of the fruit, some essential change took place. They became more like gods—by sinning. Does it make sense that we can become more godlike by breaking God's commandment?

If the LDS interpretation of these events is true, then man became as God by eating of the fruit. But then the concept of us being spirit babies of God cannot be true, can it?

Beyond that, we need to ask, *How* did the man become as "one of us"? In what fashion did he come to resemble God? The verse tells us plainly: "The man is become as one of us, *to know good and evil.*" The way in which man began to resemble God is to know good and evil. Adam and Eve, through their experience with the fruit, came to know good and evil because the tree was the tree of the knowledge of good and evil.

Mankind has been knowing good and evil ever since that day in the Garden, and ever since that day man has had to choose between the two. The one brings eternal life; the other, eternal death. Far more have gone the way of the latter than have chosen the former. That is the way of man. And that's where redemption through Christ enters the picture.

To establish a doctrine that Adam and Eve could not bring children into the world and fill the earth without knowing evil is to say that the act of procreation is evil to God. Yet the animals in the garden were already bearing young, and there was no evil; the fall had yet to take place. Why would it be evil for Adam and Eve? It flies in the face of logic.

It is obvious that God's perfect plan for man was that we be in an Eden, without sin, without evil. Adam and Eve were never meant to know evil, never meant to be banished. Had they been obedient to God's word, life would have been a joy instead of a trial. For the LDS church and its scriptures to proclaim that Adam and Eve were happy with what happened is to defy the very Word of God:

> Unto the woman he said, I will greatly multiply thy sorrow and thy conception, in sorrow thou shalt bring forth children; and thy desire shall be to thy husband, and he shall rule over thee.
>
> And unto Adam he said, Because thou has hearkened unto the voice of thy wife, and hast eaten of the tree, of which I commanded thee, saying, Thou shalt not eat of it: cursed is the

ground for thy sake; in sorrow shalt thou eat of it all the days of thy life; thorns also and thistles shall it bring forth to thee; and thou shalt eat the herb of the field; in the sweat of thy face shalt thou eat bread, till thou return unto the ground; for out of it wast thou taken: for dust thou art, and unto dust shalt thou return (Genesis 3:16-19).

FAMILIES

The LDS Position

There are not many differences in the way Mormons and Christians look at family life, except in the eternal or eschatological (last days) sense. Both Latter-day Saints and Christians revere and respect the family as a God-ordained institution, and both believe in chastity before marriage and fidelity within marriage.

The one notable exception to fidelity is the Mormon doctrine of plural marriage, which is not now officially practiced, although there are thousands of polygamous marriages in Utah. The average Mormon sees plural marriage in eternity as the plan of God. Mormons believe that God Himself is polygamous and expect that same status if and when they become gods themselves.

Mormons are instructed to hold weekly family home evenings, where they work at being good families. Many of the converts to the LDS church point to the strong family-centered priorities of the church as the most compelling aspect of their conversion.

Both Mormons and Christians regard children as blessings from God and stand firmly against abortion. Mormons also oppose all forms of artificial birth control under most conditions, which is less commonly taught among evangelicals.

The Biblical View

In the biblical sense, Joseph Smith violated his marriage vows by consummating "celestial marriages" with many women (some of them in their early teens) and by "marrying" other men's wives. Mormons, of course, believe this was ordained of God, but God does not bless fornication or adultery.

A huge difference between Mormons and Christians is that Mormons believe in eternal marriage, and that if they are worthy they will continue to be married and have children throughout eternity. This is contrary to the clear teaching of Jesus: "For in the resurrection they neither marry, nor are given in marriage, but are as the angels of God in heaven" (Matthew 22:30). Also, eternal marriage is a subtle form of idolatry, since it virtually replaces God with the family as the centerpiece of heaven.

In the book of Revelation, the Bible gives a clear picture of life in the heavenly kingdom. It consists of worshiping God and praising Him throughout eternity (Revelation 4:8-11; 5:6-14; 7:9-17; 11:15-18; 15:2-4; 19:1-9). You will search the Bible from cover to cover and not find anything which indicates that we will be married or raising families in heaven. That argument from silence, combined with Matthew 22:30, is pretty compelling.

FAST AND TESTIMONY MEETINGS

In modern LDS practice, the first Sunday of each month has been designated as a "fast and testimony meeting." Mormons believe, as do Christians, that fasting is an important spiritual discipline. They are taught that fasting sharpens one's spirituality and (if done with a proper heart) can bring one closer to God.

In addition to whatever fasting may be done by the individual Mormon as he feels led, this once-a-month fast meeting is mandated—except of course for the ill, for small children, or for pregnant women. Mormons are supposed to go without at least two meals. Some choose to skip Saturday dinner and Sunday breakfast; others skip Sunday breakfast and Sunday lunch.

Unlike most LDS practices, the severity of the fast is left up to individual practice. Some especially devout Mormons will not even brush their teeth while fasting. Others simply abstain from solid food and drink water (or possibly some juice). Then the money which would have been spent on food for the family is supposed to be applied to a "fast offering" which is to be brought in on this Sunday. The monies from this are over and above the tithe which Mormons are expected to pay, and they go into the church welfare fund to help needy families in the ward. It is actually a nice idea, except for the fact that it is part of a "works-righteousness" system of salvation (Ephesians 2:8,9). Mormons believe that if they do not fast on this day, they are imperiling their standing in the kingdom.

It is to the "testimony" part of the meeting to which we now turn our attention. Mormons believe, as do Christians, that bearing their testimony is an act which brings great spiritual victory into their lives (Revelation 12:11). Characteristically, however, the LDS definition of "bearing your testimony" is radically different from the Christian/biblical definition.

Christian testimonies are usually thought of as an account of how men and women were brought to salvation and who Jesus Christ is to them. As is true of most cults, however, Mormons remove the focus of attention from Jesus Christ and turn it on themselves. Usually Jesus is just a tiny part of "bearing your testimony," if He is mentioned at all. Additionally, a Mormon's testimony is usually *not* extemporaneous. It is virtually a memorized, rote litany of statements about the Mormon church. It does not vary much—at least in the beginning. Here is a typical testimony:

> I want to solemnly bear you *my* testimony that God lives, that Jesus is the Christ, that this is God's true church on the earth today, that Joseph Smith is a true prophet of God, that Howard W. Hunter (or whomever is the current "prophet") is a prophet of God, that the *Book of Mormon* is true, etc.

At this point, the testimony can begin to mutate into heartfelt statements about how much the person loves his wife, his family, his bishop (if a missionary, his companion missionary), his ward, etc. It is frequently delivered with teary eyes, even at the beginning, and with sincere emotional content.

Occasionally, especially at fast and testimony meetings, testimonies have been known to "get off course" and to wander into statements about UFOs, relief society recipes, or ancient American airfields in Central America. This is because the fast and testimony meeting is the closest thing a Mormon gets to spontaneity.

The other three Sundays of the month, prepared talks are given by members of the ward—often by teens or even little children. These are often read from articles in church magazines and are delivered with little or no oratorical panache. These topics are pre-chosen by the ward bishopric and must not be deviated from in the tiniest detail. It is believed that the topics and the person giving the talk are chosen by divine revelation.

But on fast and testimony Sunday, all bets are off! Once the bishop makes an opening remark, the ward "has the floor." Anyone who wishes can come up and bear their testimony. They can say virtually anything they want, as long as they begin with the standard paragraph. It is considered ideal if little children (even toddlers) get up and mumble something into the microphone, like "I bear you my testimony that Joseph Smith is a prophet—in Jesus' name. Amen." It is considered even better if women (or even men) get up and begin to openly weep as they share their testimony.

Since the first part of the testimony is always the same, sitting through these things year after year 12 times a year begins to create an almost hypnotic effect on the devout Mormon. A typical fast and testimony meeting might have up to a dozen people getting up and saying, "I bear you testimony that . . ." and, at that point, the eyes begin to glaze over, even as they begin to brim with tears. This is especially true because lifelong Mormons have been encouraged to get up and bear their testimony since they were knee-high to a seagull. They are also encouraged to bear it in any religious discussion they might be having, especially with an investigator of the church—again with as much weeping and heartfelt emotion as can possibly be generated.

The net result of years of this is a mind-control phenomenon—an autohypnotic trance state which the sincere Mormon generates without even realizing it anytime he starts to bear his testimony. The next time you are with a Mormon and he begins to bear you his testimony, watch his eyes carefully. Often his pupils will begin to dilate, even as he begins to drone, "I want to solemnly bear you *my* testimony that God lives," etc. He will frequently drop into a state of clinical autohypnosis. You can almost watch the tape recorder running behind his forehead, playing the message for you.

In LDS etiquette, you are never to interrupt a person giving his testimony. This is why so many fast meetings end up with old men standing up there rambling on for half an hour about their food storage of 5000 cans of stewed tomatoes. There is no way the bishop—or anyone else—can get the mike away from the person until they hear the words "in Jesus' name. Amen."

Because of this cultural expectation, it is often instructive to gently but firmly interrupt when a Mormon is bearing his testimony. When he begins to tell you that he *knows* that Joseph Smith is a prophet of God, stop and ask him *how* he knows it. Watch the eyes of the Mormon at this point. You can almost see the "Tilt" signs going off. Nothing in his entire life has prepared him for having his testimony derailed in mid-recitation. Some recover quickly, but others actually reel back, their eyes glazed over like marbles, trying to get reoriented. This is because you have prematurely called them out of a hypnotic state.

No one has ever asked them *how* they know these things to be true. Probably they have never even dared ask themselves this question. Yet it is an important and challenging question. It can be a good opening for a very worthwhile discussion between the Christian and the Mormon.

FREEMASONRY

Freemasonry—also known as Masonry or the Ancient, Free and Accepted Masons—is a relatively modern evolution of medieval stone mason guilds. As it is currently constituted, it has little or nothing to do with the actual craft trades of the stone masons.

Modern Masonry is a secret society and is divided (at least in America) into three major segments: the first three degrees of the Blue Lodge—the foundational initiations upon which all Freemasonry rests. These degrees are named after the ancient stone-mason guilds' ranks: Entered Apprentice, Fellow Craft, and Master Mason. These are the most ancient parts of Masonry.

In the last couple of centuries, two branches grew out of the original Blue Lodge degrees: the York Rite and the Scottish Rite. The Master Mason, once he becomes proficient in his "craft," is allowed to pursue either or both branches which go past the third degree. The York Rite consists of seven degrees and culminates in a so-called "Christian" degree called the Knights Templar. The Scottish Rite has 29 degrees and culminates in the thirty-second degree, "Sublime Prince of the Royal Secret."

Additionally, there are a dozen or so "Auxiliary Masonic Bodies" which are available to Masons and their relatives. These include the Shrine (only for thirty-second degree Masons and Knights Templar), the Order of the Eastern Star (for Masons and their female relations), and Job's Daughters, Rainbow Girls, and DeMolay (respectively, for adolescent girls and boys related to Masons).

The philosophical and ritual influence of Freemasonry upon Joseph Smith and his brother Hyrum was profound. Both Smith brothers were Masons (see also *Smith: Was Joseph a Mason?*), and indeed, many of the early church leaders like Brigham Young were also Masons. The influence of Masonry upon the development of the temple endowment ritual is unarguable (see also *Endowment, Similarity to Masonry and Occultism*).

Additionally and somewhat curiously, strong Masonic (actually *anti*-Masonic) elements can be found in the *Book of Mormon*. At the time Joseph Smith was "translating" the *Book of Mormon* (c. 1826-30), a strong anti-Masonic sentiment was sweeping the United States because of the murder of a Captain William Morgan— a Mason who had dared to write a book revealing the secrets of the Lodge. Rumors circulated at the time that there were marauding bands of Masons roving the country, killing and terrorizing the population. For the most part, these rumors were unfounded.

Smith worked the concept of a satanic, secret society which murdered, pillaged, and robbed throughout the land into his *Book of Mormon* material and into other of his "scriptures," most notably the so-called Book of Moses (see also *Master Mahan*). This he does in the form of the "secret combinations" of "the Gadianton robbers," introduced here:

> For there was one *Gadianton*, who was exceedingly expert in many words, and *also in his craft*, to carry on *the secret work of murder and of robbery*; therefore he became the leader of the band of Kishkumen.
>
> Therefore he did flatter them, and also Kishkumen, that if they would place him in the judgment-seat he would grant unto those who belonged to his band that they should be placed in power and authority among the people; therefore Kishkumen sought to destroy Helaman.
>
> And it came to pass as he went forth towards the judgment-seat to destroy Helaman, behold one of the servants of Helaman, having been out by night, and having obtained, through disguise, a knowledge of those plans which had been laid by this band to destroy Helaman . . .
>
> And it came to pass that he met Kishkumen, and *he gave unto him a sign*; therefore Kishkumen made known unto him the object of his desire, desiring that he would conduct him to the judgment-seat that he might murder Helaman.

> And when the servant of Helaman had known all the heart of Kishkumen, and how that it was his object to murder, and *also that it was the object of all those who belonged to his band to murder, and to rob, and to gain power (and this was their secret plan, and their combination),* the servant of Helaman said unto Kishkumen: Let us go forth unto the judgment-seat (*Book of Mormon*, Helaman 2:4-8, emphasis added).

Just as in Masonry *and in temple Mormonism*, these "Gadianton robbers" knew each other by secret signs and bound themselves to each other by murderous blood oaths. Thus, there is an odd dissonance in Mormonism on the subject of secret societies.

On the one hand, the temple rituals were (up until 1990) full of dire blood oaths and penal signs depicting various ways people could be killed, disemboweled, etc. To this day, they contain many other elements of Masonry presented in a positive way, including the wearing of a ceremonial apron (see also *Aprons, Temple*).

On the other hand, these Gadianton bands of robbers (with their secret oaths and signs) are presented as a major evil in the *Book of Mormon*. Either Joseph Smith could not seem to figure out exactly how he felt about the Masonic Lodge, or this paradox was intentionally designed for some occult purpose.

Beyond its connections to Mormonism, Freemasonry is a sinister, anti-Christian institution. Thus, its being woven so integrally into Mormonism is highly problematic. Masonry claims to go back to the building of Solomon's temple, although there is no biblical proof for that. It claims to go back even further, by referring to the biblical character "Tubalcain" as a Freemason, and using his name as the password for the third degree. He is regarded as the first Mason, and yet a careful reading of Genesis 4:16-26 shows that Tubalcain was of the cursed lineage of Cain—not a very auspicious beginning, considering both Freemasonry's and Mormonism's early attitudes toward those of African-American lineage.

Masonry also asserts that it comes from the Egyptians, who were indeed great city builders. But the Egyptians were pagans and their priests, sorcerers.

Actually, there is no evidence for any of this historic lineage. The earliest historic link we have is with the aforementioned stone-mason guilds of the high Middle Ages. History does show that these masons ultimately began admitting non-stonemasons (called "speculative Masons") to their membership in the eighteenth century because of the decline of cathedral building.

The first documented reference in English to Masonry as a society is nearly 100 years older than that—and *it is directly tied to occultism and magic.* It occurs in Anderson's poem "Muses Threnody" from 1638: "For we be brethren of the Rosey Cross/We have the Mason Word and second sight."

Rosicrucians (Brethren of the Rosey Cross) are occultists and their society exists to this day. Its most notable branch is called AMORC (Ancient and Mystical Order of the Rosey Cross) and is headquartered in San Jose, California. The "second sight" is the witchcraft power of clairvoyance—being able to see the future or faraway events by psychic power. Thus we see that from its very beginning in modern times, Masonry was linked to sorcery.

The first Grand Lodge of modern Masonry was formed in a tavern in England in 1717. It is from this source that all English Freemasonry comes. From its beginning, it has been filled with the anti-Christian philosophies of deism, naturalism, and universalism; and it is contrary to the true gospel of Jesus Christ.

GENEALOGY

Whenever the world speaks of Mormonism, the subject of genealogy is soon to come up. The genealogical activities of the church operate under the Genealogical Society of Utah. Its massive Family History Library in Salt Lake City has over 1000 library branches throughout the world.

Between the library files in downtown Salt Lake City and a vault buried deep in a nearby mountain, the Mormons maintain some 1,500,000 rolls of microfilm and 200,000 microfiche for over 1,500,000,000 deceased people. Detailed records of millions of people in some 90 countries go back to the early 1500s. Everything is indexed through extensive computer systems. Millions of new records are added every year (LDS *Encyclopedia of Mormonism*, vol. 2, pages 537-38).

While millions of genealogists use these extensive files and are able to trace family lines through numerous generations, the LDS church has an interest that is unique to itself.

Mormonism's concern for its roots goes deeper than an interest in family trees. To Mormons, the family is eternally linked, both forward and in reverse. The church teaches that each Mormon has the responsibility to see that all the temple ordinances (see *Baptism for the Dead*) performed by the living must also be performed, by proxy, on behalf of the dead. This finding, identifying, and doing temple work for the dead goes beyond suggestion. It is one of the key principles of the LDS faith.

In volume 2 (pages 146-47) of his work *Doctrines of Salvation,*
Joseph Fielding Smith puts this in eternal perspective. First, he
quotes Joseph Smith:

> "The preaching of the [LDS] gospel to the nations of the
> earth . . . *is the greatest responsibility of the church"* [his emphasis].
> He goes on to say, *"It is our duty as individuals to seek after our
> immediate dead*—those of our own line" [his emphasis].

He continues with another quote of Joseph Smith's:

> *The greatest responsibility in this world that God has laid
> upon us is to seek after our dead.* The reason, J.F. Smith states, is
> that all the dead must be redeemed from their sins through obe-
> dience to the [LDS] gospel just as the living are. It is required of us
> to perform this labor on their behalf.
> . . . *Our salvation and progression depends on the salvation of
> our worthy dead with whom we must be joined in family ties* [his
> emphasis]. This can only be accomplished in our temples.

The *Doctrine and Covenants* confirms that a person's very
salvation is tied to it:

> And now my dearly beloved brethren and sisters, let me
> assure you that these are principles in relation to the dead and the
> living that cannot be lightly passed over, as pertaining to our
> salvation.
> For their salvation is necessary and essential to our salva-
> tion, as Paul says concerning the fathers—that they without us
> cannot be made perfect [a reference to Hebrews 11:40]—neither
> can we without our dead be made perfect (*Doctrine and Covenants*
> 128:15).

Therein is the entire motivation behind all the genealogy
work. Every member of the LDS church, and especially the convert, is expected to fulfill this mighty role of "savior to the family
dead," back through as many generations as possible.

The Biblical View

The Mormons strain at finding any biblical evidence of such a
thing. They go to Scriptures that talk about captives being set free,

or hearts of the children turned to the fathers, or releasing those who are bound, and so on, using the latter-day "revelation" to guide them.

Again, I refer the reader to the section on *Baptism for the Dead*, where the biblical view is almost identical to what I would say here. There are several other points, however, we need to look at from the broader perspective.

Mormons teach that those people who have not heard and renounced the Mormon gospel are being taught it in a place called spirit prison, where they await the resurrection. LDS missionaries come from a place called spirit paradise, where righteous LDS people await the resurrection.

Those people who receive the teachings and convert to that gospel known on Earth as Mormonism need to be baptized and have their temple work done so they can go on and eventually earn godhood and all the other benefits of the faith.

In other words, to the Mormon there is a second chance for almost all of mankind; it is through their genealogical efforts that thousands will be brought vicariously into the fold.

Unfortunately for the Mormon and the supposed converts in the spirit world, the Bible does not teach this doctrine, nor has the orthodox Christian church ever taught it in the almost 2000 years since Christ began His ministry.

The Bible says: "And as it is appointed unto men once to die, but after this the judgment" (Hebrews 9:27).

In fact, even the *Book of Mormon* teaches the very opposite of this doctrine of a second chance:

And now, as I said unto you before, as ye have had so many witnesses, therefore, I beseech of you that ye do not procrastinate the day of your repentance until the end; for after this day of life, which is given us to prepare for eternity, behold, if we do not improve our time while in this life, then cometh the night of darkness wherein there can be no labor performed.

Ye cannot say, when ye are brought to that awful crisis, that I will repent, that I will return to my God. Nay, ye cannot say this; for that same spirit which doth possess your bodies at the time that ye go out of this life, that same spirit will have power to possess your body in that eternal world.

For behold, if ye have procrastinated the day of your repentance even until death, behold, ye have become subjected to the spirit of the devil, and he doth seal you his; therefore, the Spirit of the Lord hath withdrawn from you, and hath no place in you, and the devil hath all power over you; and this is the final state of the wicked (Alma 34:33-35).

GLASS LOOKING

(See also *Peep Stones.*)

This is an old-fashioned term for the occult practice called crystal gazing or more technically, "scrying." This is the belief that a person can look into some sort of solid object (sometimes reflective, but not necessarily so) and see either unseen objects (clairvoyance) or else foretell future events (precognition).

Though the best-known form of this practice is the use of the crystal ball, oftentimes people thought to be gifted in this area would use mirrors, water glasses filled with ink, watch glasses, or even special stones. In the folk culture of the nineteenth-century eastern United States, the "gift" of glass looking was frequently used to hunt for buried treasure.

Founding LDS prophet Joseph Smith, "the glass looker," was convicted of this occult practice on March 20, 1826, and charged $2.68 by Justice Albert Neely to cover the sheriff's cost for bringing Smith in. This was nearly six years after Smith's alleged vision of God the Father and God the Son (History 1:5). It would have been toward the end of the series of yearly visits Joseph claimed to have received from the Angel Moroni in 1823-27 (ibid., pp. 9-18).

Smith claimed to be able to find buried treasure with a seer stone or peep stone he had in his possession. He would place the stone in his hat and then place his face in the hat. He claimed that he could see in the stone the place where buried treasure lay. It is amazing that in the middle of these supposedly earthshaking visitations from God, Jesus, and angels, that Joseph would be willing not only to dabble in highly occult practices, but also actually use those practices for illegal gain.

What is even more dismaying is the fact that later Smith apparently used the same rock in the same (or similar) hat to allegedly "translate" the *Book of Mormon.*

GNOSTICISM

Gnosticism is the name of an ancient heresy which was a serious challenge to the early Christian church. The term itself is derived from the Greek word *gnosis*, which means "knowledge."

Gnosticism refers to a complex belief system that essentially claimed one was saved through knowledge, not grace. Many Greco-Roman mystery religions brought an initiate in from the "profane" world into ever-increasing realms of secret information, often derived from abstruse interpretations of the Bible and of pseudepigraphal (false Scripture) writings like the Gospel of Thomas or the Pistis Sophia.

Most forms of this heresy were radically dualistic; they believed that matter was evil and spirit was good. They taught that the material universe was created by a lesser being called the Demiurge, a rival to the true, higher, and unknowable deity which dwelt in the Pleroma (fullness). Separating the Pleroma from the evil material world was first of all, the Logos (Word) and secondarily, a complex hierarchy of spiritual beings called Aeons and Archons.

This dualism prompted forms of Gnosticism to take the story of Jesus Christ and distort it into their own image. Key errors included the introduction of a complicated system of angelic or aeonic hierarchies which intervened between Jesus and humanity, thus making Christ more distant and inaccessible; the already-mentioned denial of grace in favor of salvation by esoteric knowledge; and (by some) the denial of the physical incarnation of Jesus as the *logos* and denial of His physical suffering, death, and resurrection.

Originally, LDS leaders like Bruce R. McConkie condemned Gnosticism not only as a heresy, but also as a chief source of the false concept of God as Spirit taught in historic Christianity (*Doctrine*, p. 316). As the dialogue between Mormonism and Christian orthodoxy continues to heat up, however, many LDS apologists have sought confirmation of the truth of LDS doctrines from Gnostic sources.

Often, LDS apologists will cite the Nag Hammadi scrolls as proof that there are lost scriptures around the world just waiting to be unearthed—evidently without comprehending that the Nag Hammadi community was far from Christianity. They were Gnostics!

Additionally, these defenders of Mormonism will cite many other similarities between LDS doctrine and Gnosticism:

1. The belief that there is no real qualitative difference between man and God (see Elaine Pagels, *The Gnostic Gospels*, p. 144).

2. A denial of the truly sinful nature of Adam's fall; with the serpent "playing the role of initiator into hidden knowledge" (Kurt Rudolph, *Gnosis*, p. 97)—as he does in the LDS temple endowment.

3. An overvaluing of knowledge in contradistinction to faith (Harold O.J. Brown, *Heresies*, p. 39).

4. The use of elaborate rituals, including washings, anointings, secret handshakes, sacred marriages, and sacred garments to attain ever higher and higher heavens (Rudolph, *ibid.*, pp. 228, 188, 226).

5. The practice of baptism for the dead (*ibid.*, p. 301).

With resemblances like these, it is no wonder that LDS defenders are seeking to foist these ancient pseudepigrapha on their people. Yet somehow they don't understand that it does their cause no good to compare their church to an ancient heresy.

The Biblical View

Many Christian commentators agree that more than a few of the New Testament writers were striving against fledgling forms of Gnosticism. It is important to remember that the Gnostics found the simplicity of the gospel message (1 Corinthians 15:1-5) entirely too unsophisticated for their minds, which were steeped in Hellenic thought, and especially Neoplatonism. Thus, much of the dialogue back and forth involves the conflict between complicated esotericism and the plain truth of Jesus.

Some of the key biblical passages which assault Gnosticism also work well against Mormonism, which is in many ways a modern form of the ancient heresy. At least two of Paul's epistles condemn proto-Gnostic ideas:

Beware lest any man spoil you through philosophy and vain deceit, after the tradition of men, after the rudiments of the world, and not after Christ (Colossians 2:8).

Wherefore if ye be dead with Christ from the rudiments of the world, why, as though living in the world, are ye subject to ordinances, (touch not; taste not; handle not; which all are to perish with the using;) after the commandments and doctrines of men? Which things have indeed a shew of wisdom in will worship, and humility, and neglecting of the body; not in any honour to the satisfying of the flesh (Colossians 2:20-23).

There is also his charge in 1 Timothy: "O Timothy, keep that which is committed to thy trust, avoiding profane and vain babblings, and oppositions of science [Greek *gnoseos*] falsely so called" (6:20).

The later writings of John reflect this dialectic even more strongly:

But unto you I say, and unto the rest in Thyatira, as many as have not this doctrine, and which have not known the depths of Satan, as they speak; I will put upon you none other burden (Revelation 2:24).

That which was from the beginning, which we have heard, which we have seen with our eyes, which we have looked upon, and our hands have handled, of the Word of life (1 John 1:1). [Handling the Word—*logos*—would have been unthinkable to a Gnostic!]

They went out from us, but they were not of us; for if they had been of us, they would no doubt have continued with us: but they went out, that they might be made manifest that they were not all of us. But ye have an unction from the Holy One, and ye know all things (1 John 2:19,20).

And the Word was made flesh, and dwelt among us, (and we beheld his glory, the glory as of the only begotten of the Father,) full of grace and truth (John 1:14).

But the Comforter, which is the Holy Ghost, whom the Father will send in my name, he shall teach you all things, and bring all things to your remembrance, whatsoever I have said unto you (John 14:26).

These passages clearly refute both the Gnostic denial of the physical, fleshly reality of the Word, and the need for "further revelation." Thus, we see striking similarities between ancient Gnosticism and modern Mormonism—similarities which Mormons themselves seem ready to cultivate, in spite of the clear reproach of the Bible.

GOSPEL

The LDS Position

The word *gospel* has a special meaning to the Mormon. It is the generic word for Mormonism. Throughout the writings of all the LDS prophets and leaders, the word is in common use. When a Mormon missionary says that he is called to preach "the gospel of Jesus Christ," he is not attempting to mislead you. He really means that he is called to preach the *Mormon* gospel of Jesus Christ, as interpreted by LDS prophets. It is not the biblical gospel of Jesus Christ, even though the actual words are the same.

Confusing? "The gospel" to a Mormon includes every single doctrine of Mormonism. Often a Mormon leader will be even more specific and call it "the fullness of the gospel" or "the fullness of the everlasting gospel."

Joseph Smith said that the new and exciting doctrines he was revealing to the Latter-day Saints came directly from Jesus Christ and were the true doctrines of Christ:

> We, Joseph Smith, Jun., and Sidney Rigdon, being in the Spirit on the sixteenth day of February, in the year of our Lord one thousand eight hundred and thirty-two—By the power of the Spirit our eyes were opened and our understandings were enlightened, so as to see and understand the things of God—Even those things which were from the beginning before the world was, which were ordained of the Father, through his Only Begotten Son, who was in the bosom of the Father, even from the beginning; of whom we bear record; and the record which we bear is the fulness of the gospel of Jesus Christ, who is the Son, whom we saw and with whom we conversed in the heavenly vision (*Doctrine and Covenants* 76:11-14).

Bruce R. McConkie defined "the gospel" this way:

The fulness of the gospel consists in those laws, doctrines, ordinances, powers, and authorities needed to enable men to gain the fulness of salvation. Those who have the gospel fulness do not necessarily enjoy the fulness of gospel knowledge or understand all of the doctrines of the plan of salvation. But they do have the fulness of the priesthood and sealing power by which men can be sealed up unto eternal life. The fulness of the gospel grows out of the fulness of the sealing power and not out of the fulness of gospel knowledge (*Doctrine*, p. 333).

McConkie claims on that same page that the *Book of Mormon* contains the fullness of the gospel:

And gave unto him [Joseph Smith] commandments which inspired him; and gave him power from on high, by the means which were before prepared, to translate the Book of Mormon; which contains a record of a fallen people, and the fulness of the gospel of Jesus Christ to the Gentiles and to the Jews also (*Doctrine and Covenants* 20:7-9).

In the eulogy given in honor of Joseph Smith at his death and published as Section 135 of the *Doctrine and Covenants*, we again read:

Joseph Smith, the Prophet and Seer of the Lord, has done more, save Jesus only, for the salvation of men in this world, than any other man that ever lived in it. In the short space of twenty years, he has brought forth the Book of Mormon, which he translated by the gift and power of God, and has been the means of publishing it on two continents; has sent the fulness of the everlasting gospel, which it contained, to the four quarters of the earth (v. 3).

The Biblical View

What does the Bible say about "the gospel"? Paul, writing to the Galatians, said:

I marvel that ye are so soon removed from him that called you into the grace of Christ unto another gospel: which is not another; but there be some that trouble you, and would pervert the gospel of Christ. But though we, or an angel from heaven,

preach any other gospel unto you than that which we have
preached unto you, let him be accursed. As we said before, so say I
now again, If any man preach any other gospel unto you than that
ye have received, let him be accursed.

For do I now persuade men, or God? or do I seek to please
men? for if I yet pleased men, I should not be the servant of
Christ. But I certify you, brethren, that the gospel which was
preached of me is not after man. For I neither received it of man,
neither was I taught it, but by the revelation of Jesus Christ
(Galatians 1:6-12).

Paul strongly warned about this again when dealing with the
Corinthians. It would seem that Paul had people like Joseph Smith
and the Mormons in mind when he said:

For I am jealous over you with godly jealousy: for I have
espoused you to one husband, that I may present you as a chaste
virgin to Christ. But I fear, lest by any means, as the serpent
beguiled Eve through his subtilty, so your minds should be corrupted from the simplicity that is in Christ. For if he that cometh
preacheth another Jesus, whom we have not preached, or if ye
receive another spirit, which ye have not received, or another
gospel, which ye have not accepted, ye might well bear with
[him]. . . .

For such are false apostles, deceitful workers, transforming themselves into the apostles of Christ. And no marvel; for
Satan himself is transformed into an angel of light. Therefore it is
no great thing if his ministers also be transformed as the ministers
of righteousness; whose end shall be according to their works
(2 Corinthians 11:2-4,13-15).

What was the gospel Paul preached? Let us hear once more
from the apostle:

Moreover, brethren, I declare unto you the gospel which
I preached unto you, which also ye have received, and wherein ye
stand; By which also ye are saved, if ye keep in memory what I
preached unto you, unless ye have believed in vain. For I delivered unto you first of all that which I also received, how that
Christ died for our sins according to the scriptures; and that he
was buried, and that he rose again the third day according to the
scriptures: and that he was seen of Cephas, then of the twelve:

after that, he was seen of above five hundred brethren at once; of whom the greater part remain unto this present, but some are fallen asleep. After that, he was seen of James; then of all the apostles. And last of all he was seen of me also, as of one born out of due time (1 Corinthians 15:1-8).

A simple gospel—but certainly *not* the gospel as presented by the prophet Joseph Smith, his successors, nor his church. Here is a primer to use in distinguishing the real gospel from the false.

The Real Gospel

Believe God's Word when He says:

There is only one true God (Deuteronomy 6:4; Isaiah 43:10,11; 1 Corinthians 8:4).

God is a Spirit who fills the heavens and the earth (Jeremiah 23:24; John 4:24).

God is not a man (Numbers 23:19; Job 9:32; Hosea 11:9).

Jesus is Almighty God manifest in the flesh (John 1:1-3, 14,18; Colossians 1:15-17; 1 Timothy 3:16).

Jesus preexisted in heaven; man didn't (John 8:23; 1 Corinthians 15:46-49; Genesis 2:7; Zechariah 12:1).

We become children of God only by adoption (Romans 8:14-16; Galatians 4:5,6; Ephesians 1:5).

The gospel (good news) by which we are saved is that Jesus provided forgiveness of sins, resurrection, and eternal life through His finished work (1 Corinthians 15:1-4; Hebrews 1:3; John 19:30; Colossians 1:20-22).

We're saved by grace through faith unto good works as God's workmanship (Ephesians 2:8-10).

He makes us new creatures as the author and finisher of our faith (2 Corinthians 5:17-21; Hebrews 12:2).

So what must one do to be saved?

1. Confess your sins to God and turn from them (Romans 3:23; 1 John 1:8,9).

2. Confess with your mouth the Lord Jesus and believe with your heart that God raised Him from the dead (Romans 10:9).

3. Ask Jesus to come into your life and make you what He wants you to be (Philippians 2:13; 3:9; Romans 12:1-3).

GOSPEL HOBBIES

"Gospel hobbies" is a term in Mormonism used to describe what are considered to be unhealthy or out-of-balance religious emphases. Bruce R. McConkie explains gospel hobbies as

> specializing and centering on some chosen field as though that field were the gospel. . . . [They are] dangerous signs of spiritual instability; they lead to fanaticism and sometimes even to apostasy and the consequent loss of eternal life (*Doctrine*, p. 334).

Joseph F. Smith warns that "hobbies" "give undue prominence to certain principles or ideas to the detriment and dwarfing of others just as important, just as binding, just as saving as the favored doctrines or commandments" (*Gospel Doctrine*, fifth edition, p. 116).

The gospel hobby is of significance because that term has been applied in a critically important direction by McConkie, by all accounts the leading theologian of the LDS church in his generation (1915-85). On March 2, 1982, as an LDS apostle, he gave a devotional at Brigham Young University in which he asserted that he was "express[ing] the views of the Brethren, of the prophets and apostles of old, and of all those who understand the scriptures and are in tune with the Holy Spirit" (devotional transcript, p. 1).

In this devotional, he first condemned the "many false and vain and foolish things [which] are being taught in the sectarian world and even among us about our need to gain a special relationship with the Lord Jesus" (ibid., p. 2).

He then went on to declare that the creeds of historic Christianity illustrate perfectly "what Lucifer wants so-called Christian people to believe about Deity into order to be damned" (ibid., p. 3). He described the doctrine of the Trinity as the "most grievous and evil heresy ever imposed on an erring and wayward Christianity" (ibid.).

He went on to caution his listeners not to worship Jesus Christ but only Heavenly Father; and that our relationship with Jesus should be one of brother and sister (ibid., pp. 5, 17). He then proceeds to teach that laboring to gain a "special, personal relationship with Christ [is] both improper and perilous" (ibid., p. 19). He states that this course of action "particularly in the lives of some who are spiritually immature, is a gospel hobby which creates an unwholesome holier-than-thou attitude" (ibid.).

Thus, McConkie defines the core experience of orthodox Christianity—the personal, saving, and regenerating relationship with Jesus Christ—as a "perilous gospel hobby." He assures his listeners that "You have never heard one of the First Presidency or the Twelve, who hold the keys to the kingdom . . . advocate this excessive zeal that calls for gaining a so-called special and personal relationship with Christ" (ibid., p. 21).

He speculates if this relationship is

> much different from the feelings of fanatical sectarians [born-again Christians—ed.] who with glassy eyes and fiery tongues assure us they have been saved by grace and are assured of a place with the Lord in a heavenly abode, when in fact they have never even received the fulness of the gospel [ibid].

This again illustrates how far from true Christianity Mormonism has wandered, when it mocks the message of salvation by grace as a "gospel hobby."

HEAVENLY FATHER

Heavenly Father is a name of God. It is the common or familiar name used by the average member of the LDS church when either addressing him: "Heavenly Father, I come to you with this prayer," or mentioning him: "Heavenly Father would want us to behave." One observer of this unusual usage commented, "It is almost as if God has a first and last name."

McConkie states:

> The designation Father is to be taken literally; it signifies that the Supreme Being is the literal Parent or Father of the spirits of all men (Hebrews 12:9). All men, Christ included, were born as his children in pre-existence. (*Doctrine and Covenants* 93:21-23; Moses 1–4; Abraham 3:22-28.)

> It is only by understanding the real and literal sense in which God is our Father that we are able to understand what is meant by the Fatherhood of God and the Brotherhood of Man. In addition to the fact that all men are brothers in the sense that all have descended from Adam, they are also brothers in that they have the same personal Father who begat them in the spirit (*Doctrine*, p. 278).

Remember, Mormons look at God as a literal father who was their physical, actual father in the preexistence. They look upon this man/god with love and respect. The term is perhaps the most common name of God used by the LDS people.

Joseph Smith regularly used the term as his familiar name for God. His usage instilled in his followers a belief in a special physical relationship with God.

HEAVENLY MOTHER

The LDS Position

Although it is not a doctrine which Mormons advertise frequently, they do believe that their God, Heavenly Father, has at least one goddess wife in the celestial kingdom—possibly more. This allegedly exalted personage is commonly known as Heavenly Mother or our Mother in heaven.

> An exalted and glorified Man of Holiness could not be a Father unless a Woman of like glory, perfection and holiness was associated with him as a Mother. The begetting of children makes a man a father and a woman a mother, whether we are dealing with man in his mortal or immortal state (*Doctrine*, p. 516).

This makes clear the implicit LDS belief that all people were first conceived by some sort of marital act in the celestial kingdom between a father and mother god. So central is the concept of a Heavenly Mother to LDS theology that premier LDS hymnologist Eliza Snow wrote a hymn which is well-beloved today by devout Mormons, and which contains the following verses:

In the heavens are parents single?
No; the thought makes reason stare!
Truth is reason, truth eternal,
Tells me I've a Mother there.

When I leave this frail existence,
When I lay this mortal by,
Father, Mother, may I meet you
In your royal courts on high?

Though "Mother" is not often mentioned, partially because of disturbing investigators who may be in sacrament meeting, she is obviously firmly ensconced as an essential feature of the law of eternal progression. There can be no "spirit babies" from God without a "Mrs. God."

The Biblical View

What does the Bible say about this extraordinary "revelation"? First, there is no biblical evidence for God the Father creating human beings as spirit children in celestial glory through sexual intercourse (see also *Preexistence*).

Second, although the Bible does speak about a mother in heaven, it is not quite what the Mormons have in mind: "The children gather wood, and the fathers kindle the fire, and the women knead their dough, to make cakes to the queen of heaven, and to pour out drink offerings unto other gods, that they may provoke me to anger" (Jeremiah 7:18).

Jeremiah 44:25-28 also makes clear that God is furious with the Israelites for offering worship to the queen of heaven. Now surely, if this is God's bride, He would not object to a little honor being shown her, would He? Most husbands are delighted when their wives are treated nicely.

God responds the way He does because this "queen of heaven" has no more to do with truth than does Mormonism's "Heavenly Mother." Both are essentially forms of ancient pagan fertility goddesses like Ishtar or Diana of the Ephesians (Acts 19:24-35). All "Heavenly Mother" does is betray Mormonism's pagan roots.

HELL

The LDS Position

As might be expected, there are some resemblances between the LDS doctrine of hell and the authentic biblical teaching. Yet there are also important differences. Mormons are taught that eternal punishment is not eternal (see also *Eternal Damnation*).

Hell will have an end. Viewing future events, John saw that "death and hell delivered up the dead which were in them: and they were judged every man according to their works" (Revelation 20:13).

Jacob taught that this escape from death and hell meant the bringing of the body out of the grave and the spirit out of hell. "And this death of which I have spoken, which is the spiritual death," he said, "shall deliver up its dead; which spiritual death is hell; wherefore, death and hell must deliver up their dead, and hell must deliver up its captive spirits, and the grave must deliver up its captive bodies, and the bodies and the spirits of men will be restored one to the other" (2 Nephi 9:10-12).

It was in keeping with this principle for David to receive the promise: "Thou wilt not leave my soul in hell" (Psalm 16:10; Acts 2:27).

After their resurrection, the great majority of those who have suffered in hell will pass into the telestial kingdom; the balance, cursed as sons of perdition, will be consigned to partake of endless wo [sic] with the devil and his angels. Speaking of the telestial kingdom the Lord says: "These are they who are thrust down to hell. These are they who shall not be redeemed from the devil until the last resurrection, until the Lord, even Christ the Lamb, shall have finished his work. . . . These are they who are cast down to hell and suffer the wrath of Almighty God, until the fulness of times" (*Doctrine and Covenants* 76:84-85,106).

As to the sons of perdition, the revelation says that after their resurrection, "they shall return again to their own place" (*Doctrine and Covenants* 88:32,102), that is, they shall go back to dwell in the lake of fire with Perdition and his other sons. Thus those in hell "are the rest of the dead; and they live not again until the thousand years are ended, neither again, until the end of the earth" (*Doctrine and Covenants* 88:101).

Statements about an everlasting and endless hell (Helaman 6:28; Moroni 8:13), are to be interpreted in the same sense as those about eternal and endless punishment (*Doctrine and Covenants* 19:4-12; 76:44,105 in *Doctrine*, pp. 349-50).

As noted in the section on eternal damnation, the term *eternal* is believed by Mormons to reflect as much a *quality of punishment* as a *time of punishment*. Since the punishment of damnation is God's punishment, it is an eternal punishment, because God is eternal (even though He wasn't eternally *God* in LDS theology; see *Law of Eternal Progression*).

Strongly influencing the LDS doctrine of hell is its doctrine of a three-tiered heaven. Unlike the afterlife of the Bible, which is simply divided up into heaven and hell, the LDS afterlife is divided up into the celestial kingdom (the highest), the terrestrial kingdom, and the telestial kingdom (the lowest) and another, farther place for those sons of perdition, the outer darkness (see also *Degrees of Glory*). With so many choices, it is the LDS belief that almost all of those who would normally be consigned to hell in the Bible will ultimately end up in the telestial kingdom:

> Who will go to hell? This query is abundantly answered in the scriptures. Since those going to a telestial kingdom travel to their destination through the depths of hell and as a result of obedience to telestial law, it follows that all those who live a telestial law will go to hell. Included among these are the carnal, sensual, and devilish—those who live after the manner of the world. Among them are the sorcerers, adulterers, whoremongers (*Doctrine and Covenants* 76:103), false swearers, "those that oppress the hireling in his wages," the proud, "and all that do wickedly" (Malachi 3; 4; 2 Nephi 9:27-39; 26:10).
>
> Several specific groups of wicked persons are singled out to receive the prophetic curse that their destination is the fires of hell. . . . *Sex sin* is rewarded with the torments of hell (2 Nephi 9:36; Proverbs 7:6-27). "Wo unto all those that discomfort my people, and drive, and murder, and testify against them, saith the Lord of Hosts; a generation of vipers shall not escape the damnation of hell" (*Doctrine and Covenants* 121:23). Such also is the fate of *liars* (2 Nephi 9:34), *of "all those who preach false doctrines"* (2 Nephi 28:15), of those who believe the damnable doctrine of infant baptism (Moroni 8:14,21), of the rich who will not help the poor (*Doctrine and Covenants* 104:18; Luke 16:19-31), and of those who heap cursings on their fellow men (Matthew 5:22; 3 Nephi 12:22). *"The sectarian world are going to hell by hundreds, by thousands and by millions,"* the Prophet said [emphasis added] (*History of the Church*, vol. 5, p. 554) (*Doctrine*, pp. 350-51).

It is important and ironic to note that by the standards mentioned in this last paragraph, the members of historic Christian churches ("the sectarian world") are said to be going to hell in vast numbers. This is certainly not the friendly, ecumenical picture painted by the Mormon church today in its attempts to woo Christian ministers and congregations into thinking that Mormons are just another Christian church.

Even more ironic is the fact that by the standards of that paragraph, LDS founding prophet Joseph Smith would be consigned to hell. He certainly committed adultery multiple times, one of the most serious "sex sins" in LDS doctrine (see also *New and Everlasting Covenant*). Today the LDS church admits to at least 27 "plural wives" of Smith.

Additionally, he "married" the wives of other men, and sometimes wives and daughters both. By both biblical standards (1 Timothy 3:2; Matthew 19:6; Mark 10:8) and (more importantly for the Mormon) *Book of Mormon* standards (see especially Jacob 2:21-34; 3:5-10), Smith was guilty of gross sexual immorality.

Smith also lied about his various sexual liaisons, during his life denying vehemently his polygamous practices which the church now admits (see *Smith, Joseph: Are We Too Hard on Him?*). Finally, as much of this volume is intended to demonstrate, Smith taught a substantial amount of false doctrine. Thus, by their own standards, he is three times condemned to the LDS hell.

Mormons believe that all but the most fiendish of humans will end up being let out of hell and admitted to the telestial kingdom. Those who are not admitted to the telestial realm are known as sons of perdition:

> After death and hell have delivered up the bodies and captive spirits which were in them, then, as John foresaw, "death and hell were cast into the lake of fire" (Revelation 20:14). This lake of fire, a figure symbolical of eternal anguish and wo, is also called hell, but is a hell reserved exclusively for the devil and his angels which includes the sons of perdition (*Doctrine and Covenants* 29:38; 88:113; 2 Peter 2:4).

> Thus, for those who are heirs of some salvation, which includes all except the sons of perdition (*Doctrine and Covenants* 76:44), hell has an end, but for those who have wholly given themselves over to satanic purposes there is no redemption from the consuming fires and torment of conscience. They go on forever in the hell that is prepared for them (*Doctrine*, p. 351).

Sons of perdition are generally defined as those who have received all the "light" and truth of the LDS gospel and have willfully spurned it. This includes all those who have been devout temple Mormons and have left the LDS church for the sake of the true Jesus Christ.

The Biblical View

Biblical verses which clearly teach eternal punishment for all those who reject the Lord Jesus—not just for a handful of extreme reprobates like Hitler and Nero—are quite numerous:

He that believeth and is baptized shall be saved; but he that believeth not shall be damned (Mark 16:16).

He that believeth on him is not condemned: but he that believeth not is condemned already, because he hath not believed in the name of the only begotten Son of God (John 3:18).

He that believeth on the Son hath everlasting life: and he that believeth not the Son shall not see life; but the wrath of God abideth on him (John 3:36).

Note that in the above verses, the cause of condemnation to eternal flame is not being evil, or a sexual monster, liar, or false teacher—but simply *not believing* in Jesus. This makes it obvious that more than just a few utterly evil people are going to be in hell. Now, as to the "eternal" part of the issue:

The sinners in Zion are afraid; fearfulness hath surprised the hypocrites. Who among us shall dwell with the devouring fire? who among us shall dwell with everlasting burnings? (Isaiah 33:14).

And they shall go forth, and look upon the carcases of the men that have transgressed against me: for their worm shall not die, neither shall their fire be quenched; and they shall be an abhorring unto all flesh (Isaiah 66:24).

Whose fan is in his hand, and he will thoroughly purge his floor, and gather his wheat into the garner; but he will burn up the chaff with unquenchable fire (Matthew 3:12).

Wherefore if thy hand or thy foot offend thee, cut them off, and cast them from thee: it is better for thee to enter into life halt or maimed, rather than having two hands or two feet to be cast into everlasting fire (Matthew 18:8).

Then shall he say also unto them on the left hand, Depart from me, ye cursed, into everlasting fire, prepared for the devil and his angels (Matthew 25:41).

> And these shall go away into everlasting punishment: but the righteous into life eternal (Matthew 25:46).
>
> And if thy hand offend thee, cut it off: it is better for thee to enter into life maimed, than having two hands to go into hell, into the fire that never shall be quenched: where their worm dieth not, and the fire is not quenched (Mark 9:43,44).
>
> Whose fan is in his hand, and he will thoroughly purge his floor, and will gather the wheat into his garner; but the chaff he will burn with fire unquenchable (Luke 3:17).
>
> And the smoke of their torment ascendeth up for ever and ever: and they have no rest day nor night, who worship the beast and his image, and whosoever receiveth the mark of his name (Revelation 14:11).
>
> And the devil that deceived them was cast into the lake of fire and brimstone, where the beast and the false prophet are, and shall be tormented day and night for ever and ever (Revelation 20:10).
>
> But the fearful, and unbelieving, and the abominable, and murderers, and whoremongers, and sorcerers, and idolaters, and all liars, shall have their part in the lake which burneth with fire and brimstone: which is the second death (Revelation 21:8).

These verses all show conclusively that the torments of damnation will last *forever*. It is true, as Bruce R. McConkie says, that hell will be thrown into the lake of fire; however, so will all those who are in hell (see Revelation 20:11-15). Boiling in a lake of fire for all eternity scarcely seems an improvement over hell.

One final bit of spiritual irony in regard to the first Scripture above, Isaiah 33:14, which speaks of hell as "everlasting burnings" (see also *Everlasting Burnings*). Joseph Smith himself taught that worthy Mormons who attained their exaltations would sit enthroned in such a place, and that, indeed, the Mormon god sits in a place of everlasting burnings:

> Here then, is eternal life: to know the only wise and true God, and you have got to learn how to be Gods yourselves, and to be kings and priests to God, the same as all Gods have done before you, namely, by going from one small degree to another, and from a small capacity to a great one; from grace to grace, from exaltation to exaltation, until you attain to the resurrection of the

dead, *and are able to dwell in everlasting burnings, and to sit in glory,* as do those who sit enthroned in everlasting power (*Teachings,* pp. 346-47).

Quite a commentary on the nature of the god of Mormonism and the sad destiny of those who serve him!

HENOTHEISM

Henotheism is defined in the dictionary as "belief in one god, without denying the existence of others" (*Webster's New World Dictionary,* College edition, 1966, p. 677). It is a kind of subdivision of the larger theological view called polytheism—the belief in many gods. LDS apostle Bruce R. McConkie, however, puts a slightly different spin on the definition:

> Henotheism is the belief in and worship of one God without at the same time denying that others can with equal truth worship different gods. It is falsely taught in the sectarian world that Abraham, for instance, was a henotheist, that is, he worshipped the Almighty, but that at the same time he considered that other nations could worship their own gods with equally beneficial results. This apostate view is erroneously considered to be one step advanced from polytheism and one step behind the final type of monotheism that was in the process of evolving (*Doctrine,* pp. 351-52).

McConkie rejects the notion that Abraham was a henotheist. Whether or not we can safely infer from this that he would deny that Mormons are henotheists is not clear. However, elsewhere he does firmly declare that "saints [i.e., Mormons] are not polytheists" (ibid., p. 579).

This extraordinary statement is astonishing in the light of the central doctrines of the LDS church. *Doctrine and Covenants* 76:55-58 teaches:

> They [those saints who rise in the resurrection of the just] are they into whose hands the Father has given all things—They are they who are priests and kings, who have received of his fulness and his glory; and they are priests of the Most High, after the order of Melchizedek, which was after the order of Enoch,

which was after the order of the Only Begotten Son. Wherefore, as it is written, they are gods, even the sons of God.

Doctrine and Covenants 121:32 speaks of "the Council of the Eternal God of all other gods before this world was." McConkie himself, in his same work, writes under the entry "Plurality of Gods" that "It is evident... that a plurality of gods exists."

Now, if LDS doctrine teaches that there are other gods, then Mormons must be at least henotheists, if not polytheists. The book which Mormons believe that Abraham wrote, the Book of Abraham, contains an account of the creation of the world in chapter 4. This chapter contains multiple references, beginning with verse 3, to "the Gods" who created the heavens and the earth (see also verses 5-31, where virtually every verse begins with "And the Gods..." did such and such). In fact, it might safely be said that the Book of Abraham is the most blatantly polytheistic book in the standard works of the church.

Now, presumably these "Gods" are not false gods. Even the fact that the Mormons believe that the Godhead is composed of three separate Gods makes them polytheists (*Doctrine*, p. 576). Now, if those other "Gods" are true gods—perhaps some of them are gods of other worlds somewhere—then henotheism truly is a foundational belief of the LDS church.

Presumably Mormons would not object to people on other planets worshiping "their gods" which they believe would be the true gods for their worlds. Then how can they, when challenged about their plurality of gods, say: "We worship only the God of this world"? That is a quintessentially henotheistic statement! It is also an excellent opportunity to point out to the Mormon 2 Corinthians 4:4 and its warning about the "god of this world": "In whom the god of this world hath blinded the minds of them which believe not, lest the light of the glorious gospel of Christ, who is the image of God, should shine unto them."

THE HOLY GHOST

Joseph Smith supposedly revealed the specific nature of the Holy Ghost in his writing on the matter found in Section 130 of *Doctrine and Covenants:*

The Father has a body of flesh and bones as tangible as man's; the Son also; but the Holy Ghost has not a body of flesh and bones, but is a personage of Spirit. Were it not so, the Holy Ghost could not dwell in us.

A man may receive the Holy Ghost, and it may descend upon him and not tarry with him (vv. 22,23).

Brigham Young taught this about the Holy Ghost:

The Holy Ghost, we believe, is one of the characters that form the Trinity, or the Godhead. Not one person in three, nor three persons in one; but the Father, Son, and Holy Ghost are one in essence, as the hearts of three men who are united in all things. He is one of the three characters we believe in, whose office it is to administer to those of the human family who love the truth. I have stated that they are one, as the hearts of three men might be one. Lest you should mistake me, I will say that I do not wish you to understand that the Holy Ghost is a personage having a tabernacle, like the Father and the Son; but he is God's messenger that diffuses his influence through all the works of the Almighty (*Journal of Discourses* 6:95).

Bruce R. McConkie identified him in this manner:

The Holy Ghost is the third member of the Godhead. He is a Personage of Spirit, a Spirit Person, a Spirit Man, a Spirit Entity. He can be in only one place at one time, and he does not and cannot transform himself into any other form or image than that of the Man whom he is, though his power and influence can be manifest at one and the same time through all immensity (*Doctrine*, pp. 358-59).

The Mormons don't quite know what to make of the Holy Ghost. He apparently became a god in the preexistence. In doing so, he bypassed the first, second and third estates—stepping-stones that even Jesus was required to follow. He is somehow a physical person without a body and is therefore severely limited by space and time. The many LDS and Christian scriptures that talk about the omnipresence of the Holy Spirit somehow do not fit this man/god/spirit existing in an almost fleshly form. The Mormons' Holy Spirit poses serious contradictions for them. For example, McConkie wrote:

Three separate and distinct meanings of the title, Spirit of the Lord, are found in the revelations: 1. It has reference to the spirit body of Christ . . . the body which he had from the time of his birth as the Firstborn of the Father until he was born of Mary in mortality; 2. It is used to mean the Spirit of Jesus Christ or light of truth, or light of Christ—the Spirit which is impersonal and fills the immensity of space, the Spirit which is the agency by means of which God governs and controls all things and 3. It is also a synonym for the Holy Ghost, that Spirit entity or personage of spirit who is a member of the godhead (*Doctrine* p. 752).

LDS president Joseph F. Smith had this to say about the difficulties in understanding the nature of the two:

The question is often asked, is there any difference between the Spirit of the Lord and the Holy Ghost? The terms are frequently used synonymously. We often say the Spirit of God when we mean the Holy Ghost; we likewise say the Holy Ghost when we mean the Spirit of God. The Holy Ghost is a personage in the Godhead, and is not that which lighteth every man that comes into the world. It is the Spirit of God which proceeds through Christ to the world, that enlightens every man that comes into the world, and that strives with the children of men, and will continue to strive with them, until it brings them to a knowledge of the truth and the possession of the greater light and testimony of the Holy Ghost. If, however, he receive that greater light, and then sin against it, the Spirit of God will cease to strive with him, and the Holy Ghost will wholly depart from him. Then will he persecute the truth; then will he seek the blood of the innocent; then will he not scruple at the commission of any crime; except so far as he may fear the penalties of the law, in consequence of the crime, upon himself (*Improvement Era*, vol. 11, pp. 380-82).

If this sounds a bit confusing, remember that in Mormonism neither God the Father nor the Holy Ghost can be in more than one place at one time; therefore LDS teachers need to come up with this nebulous "Spirit of the Lord" as a sort of fudge factor to explain how a finite "God" can function in so many different ways at once.

Adding to the confusion, Mormons have taught since the time of Joseph Smith that in order to become a god you had to be born, acquire a physical body, keep the commandments, go to the temple, die, and be resurrected into a glorified body. Satan and the fallen angels' greatest punishment is that they are forever denied physical bodies. Yet they teach the Holy Ghost is "God" without having a physical body. How can that be? Both the Father and Jesus have physical bodies, but the Holy Ghost does not. And none of them can be in more than one place at one time.

This is why Mormons pray in their sacrament meetings for "a portion of thy Spirit to be present here today, O Heavenly Father." Surely they don't imagine that God is up there slicing off chunks of the Holy Ghost and giving this ward one chunk and that ward another? Of course they never bother to think it out in quite that way. But how else can they explain that in the thousands of sacrament meetings going on just in one time zone of the U.S., the Holy Ghost has to somehow be in all of them?

The Biblical View

In one sense, LDS doctrine represents the Holy Ghost in almost biblical terms. He, the Holy Ghost, is a personage. Yet they do not see Him as a member of the Trinity.

The word *trinity* is not (as our friends in the cults love to remind us) used in the Bible. However, there are two consistent and central themes which run through the very warp and woof of both the Old and New Testaments about the nature of God. The first theme is that God is one (Deuteronomy 6:4; Isaiah 43:10; etc.). The second theme is that Jesus Christ is fully, utterly, and completely God, yet somehow distinct from God the Father (John 1:1,14; Colossians 1:12-19).

This leaves us with two pieces of data which are apparently in contradiction: 1. There is only one God, and 2. The Father is God and Jesus is God. A corollary to this is that the Bible also tells us the Holy Ghost is God (Acts 5:3,4). Let's look at this text in Acts carefully. "But Peter said, Ananias, why hath Satan filled thine heart to lie to the Holy Ghost, and to keep back part of the price of the land? Whiles it remained, was it not thine own? and after it was sold, was it not in thine own power? why hast thou conceived this thing in thine heart? thou hast not lied unto men, but unto God." In one verse, Peter states that Ananias lied to the Holy Ghost; and in the next verse, Peter states that God was the one lied to. Peter evidently saw the Holy Ghost as equal to God.

This brings up the second part of the Mormon dilemma. Is the Holy Ghost a power or a force of God, or is He a Person? The Bible is clear that the Holy Ghost is a Person. In the above text, for example, He is lied to. You can't lie to a force or a power; only a person with a personality can be lied to. Similarly, elsewhere in the New Testament the Holy Ghost is shown to have other attributes of personality:

1. "As they ministered to the Lord, and fasted, the Holy Ghost said, Separate me Barnabas and Saul for the work whereunto I have called them" (Acts 13:2). The Spirit here speaks, and refers to Himself as "me" and says that "I have called them." Impersonal powers do not call themselves by first-person pronouns. These are characteristics of personalities.

2. "So they, being sent forth by the Holy Ghost . . ." (Acts 13:4). Again, sending requires a person to send.

3. "For it seemed good to the Holy Ghost, and to us, to lay upon you no greater burden than these necessary things" (Acts 15:28). Here the Spirit has an opinion. Something cannot "seem good" to nuclear energy.

4. "Now when they had gone throughout Phrygia and the region of Galatia, and were forbidden of the Holy Ghost to preach the word in Asia" (Acts 16:6). Something impersonal can hardly forbid.

5. "Save that the Holy Ghost witnesseth in every city, saying that bonds and afflictions abide me" (Acts 20:23). The Bible clearly teaches that the Holy Ghost is a Person, and that He is God.

Lest we emphasize only the New Testament, a couple of Old Testament passages have the same kind of message. They also clearly teach the Trinity, the Three-in-One God. In Isaiah we find a rather lengthy passage, which we quote in full to get the impact:

Hearken unto me, O Jacob and Israel, my called; I am he; I am the first, I am also the last [this is obviously God speaking—there can be no other "first and last"]. Mine hand also hath laid the foundation of the earth, and my right hand hath spanned the heavens: when I call unto them, they stand up together. All ye, assemble yourselves, and hear; which among them hath declared

240

these things? The LORD hath loved him: he will do his pleasure on Babylon, and his arm shall be on the Chaldeans. I, even I, have spoken; yea, I have called him: I have brought him, and he shall make his way prosperous. Come ye near unto me, hear ye this; I have not spoken in secret from the beginning; from the time that it was, there am I: and now the Lord GOD, and his Spirit, hath sent me (Isaiah 48:12-16).

Notice that all three members of the Trinity appear here in the space of a few short verses—and this from the supposedly "anti-Trinitarian" Old Testament! Also, note that both the Lord GOD [i.e., the Father] and His Spirit "hath sent me" [i.e., the Son]. Here again is the Spirit sending—an action only a person can do.

With this in mind, we see that the Mormon concept of the Godhead and the Holy Ghost's position and function within it is fractured by the LDS misconception of the very nature of God and of man's relationship to God.

Mormonism doesn't need a nudge of correction in its understanding of the nature and being of the Holy Ghost; the LDS church needs to throw their concept out in its entirety.

IDOLATRY

The LDS Position

Official LDS doctrine condemns idolatry, both in its official sense (of worshiping statues, graven images, etc.) and in its broader sense of putting anything before God (money, power, sex, worldly learning, etc.). Bruce R. McConkie writes:

> Idol worship prevails among nearly all uncivilized, pagan peoples and also to a degree and *in a sense among portions of those who are supposedly enlightened by Christianity and modern civilization.* Pagans and others frequently worship graven images, or idols of wood, stone, or metal.
>
> However sincere men may be in their views, they cannot gain salvation by worshipping idols, images, or false gods of any kind. Eternal life is attained through a knowledge of "the only true God, and Jesus Christ whom" he hath sent (John 17:3) (*Doctrine*, pp. 373-74, emphasis added).

This sounds essentially biblical, except for the backhanded slap at "Christian idolatry." While we are seeing a "softer" Mormonism today, the more haughty, hard-line Mormons are not afraid to say that all the historic Christian creeds are idolatrous in nature and that the conventional Christian image of God and Jesus is also idolatrous.

The Biblical View

The problem with this is that, by the biblical definition,

Mormonism is, in itself, idol worship. Though Jesus clearly taught that God is Spirit (John 4:24), Mormons insist that God the Father is a glorified, resurrected man with a body of parts and passions. This makes the LDS deity much more akin to the many pagan idols from all over the world than it does to the God of Christianity.

Indeed, the Mormons have unwittingly fulfilled the very definition of paganism and idolatry given by Paul in Romans 1:21-25:

> Because that, when they knew God, they glorified him not as God, neither were thankful; but became vain in their imaginations, and their foolish heart was darkened. Professing themselves to be wise, they became fools, and changed the glory of the uncorruptible God into an image made like to corruptible man, and to birds, and fourfooted beasts, and creeping things. Wherefore God also gave them up to uncleanness through the lusts of their own hearts, to dishonour their own bodies between themselves: who changed the truth of God into a lie, and worshipped and served the creature more than the Creator, who is blessed for ever. Amen.

Additionally, the Mormons have "another gospel" (Galatians 1:6) which is of works, not of grace; and they have "another Jesus" (2 Corinthians 11:4) who is not truly Almighty God, but only a god. They deny the doctrine of the Trinity (1 John 5:7) and the virgin birth. This means that as much as they might fulminate against idolatry, that very sin crouches at their own door (see also *Baal*).

This is why there can be no essential compromise between Mormonism and biblical Christianity. Their differences are not negotiable. If one is true, the other must be false. The LDS and Christian views of God, Jesus, the atonement, and Scripture are so radically different that they cannot be mixed. They cannot logically coexist in the same theological base. This is why the ecumenical overtures of the Mormon church must be looked upon with grave suspicion.

INDEPENDENCE, MISSOURI, TEMPLE PROPHECY

Independence, Missouri, is a critical place in both Mormon history and doctrine. Many of Joseph Smith's more spectacular teachings and "revelations" concerned this community and its surroundings. The one in view here is the prophecy made about the building of a temple in Independence.

These prophecies provide swift, solid, empirical evidence for either the truth or falsity of Smith's prophetic utterances. Some prophecies are vague, but his prediction of a temple is pretty concrete (if the reader will excuse the pun). Since Deuteronomy 18:20-22 states that *one* false prophecy disqualifies a "prophet" from consideration forever as a true prophet, we can test Joseph Smith rather quickly.

First, in *Doctrine and Covenants* 84 we read the following prophecy, given in 1832:

> ²Yea, *the word of the Lord concerning his church,* established in the last days for the restoration of his people, as he has spoken by the mouth of his prophets, and for the gathering of his saints to stand upon Mount Zion, which shall be the city of New Jerusalem.

> ³Which city shall be built, *beginning at the temple lot,* which appointed by the finger of the Lord, *in the western boundaries of the State of Missouri, and dedicated by the hand of Joseph Smith, Jun.,* and others with whom the Lord was well pleased.

> ⁴Verily this is the word of the Lord, that the city New Jerusalem shall be built by the gathering of the saints, *beginning at this place, even the place of the temple, which temple shall be reared in this generation.*

> ⁵*For verily this generation shall not all pass away until an house shall be built unto the Lord,* and a cloud shall rest upon it, which cloud shall be even the glory of the Lord, which shall fill the house. . . .

> ³¹Therefore, as I said concerning the sons of Moses . . . for the sons of Moses and also the sons of Aaron shall offer an acceptable offering and sacrifice in the house of the Lord, *which house shall be built unto the Lord in this generation, upon the consecrated spot as I have appointed* [emphasis added].

The place referred to is a lot which Smith and others specifically consecrated and dedicated to building a temple. There are two specific conditions of the prophecy: 1. that the temple be built on that site; and 2. that the temple be built within that generation.

Neither of those conditions is yet to be met. The generation alive in 1832 was all dead by 1940, and although the church had built many temples all over the nation (and even some in other lands by then), there were none built in Missouri or anywhere near Independence.

Strangely, in just the past couple of years, a temple *was* built in Independence—but not by the LDS church. Rather, it was built by the largest rival to the Utah church, the Reorganized Church of Jesus Christ of Latter-day Saints (RLDS), which has its world headquarters in Independence (see also *Reorganized Church of Jesus Christ of Latter-day Saints*).

Yet even that church could not build the temple on the "right" spot because the temple site is owned by a *third* rival to the Utah church, the "Temple Lot" Church, which is a tiny splinter group which claims it is the one, true church succeeding Joseph Smith's original foundational church.

Naturally, the Mormon church (LDS church headquartered in Utah) asserts that these churches are both false cults and declares that *it* is the only true successor of Joseph Smith's work. Thus, the RLDS temple cannot be a fulfillment of the prophecy. It is built on the wrong place, by the wrong church, and is almost a century late. This clearly establishes Smith as a false prophet.

JEHOVAH

The LDS Position

The name *Jehovah* carries a considerably different meaning in Mormonism than it does in biblical Christianity. Mormons are taught that Jehovah is the name of the second person of the Godhead, who came to earth as Jesus Christ. Bruce R. McConkie states that "Christ is Jehovah, they are one and the same Person" (*Doctrine*, p. 392).

God the Father is *not* called Jehovah in Mormonism; that is because his name is Elohim (ibid., p. 224). Nowhere is this belief more clearly shown than in the ceremonies of the LDS temple endowment, which feature lengthy conversations between characters called "Elohim" and "Jehovah" concerning the creation of the world (Chuck Sackett, *What's Going On in There?* pp. 22-26). They are clearly depicted as separate persons.

The Biblical View

This disparity between the names of the two "gods" is telling since Mormonism denies the absolute oneness of the true God. The Bible teaches that the true name of God is represented by the Hebrew letters YHWH—in English sometimes rendered *Yahweh*, "I AM" (Exodus 3:14). The problem with the way Mormons use the name *Elohim* is that in the Bible it is just another name for the Lord.

The name YHWH is so sacred that Jewish scribes for thousands of years have read aloud the Hebrew word *Adonai* ("Lord") whenever they come to the name YHWH in their manuscripts.

In the King James version of the Bible (and most other modern translations) the places where the Hebrew text reads YHWH are rendered "LORD," and the places where the Hebrew term *Elohim* appears are rendered "God." Thus, the common biblical phrase, "the LORD God" reflects the use of both names to refer to the same Being: God.

Beginning with Genesis 2:4, this phrase, "the LORD God" (in Hebrew, *Yahweh Elohim*) is used 518 times in the Old Testament—to refer to the same Person. This makes the LDS concept of two distinct personages with two different names manifestly impossible.

JESUS

The Jesus of biblical Christianity and the Jesus of Mormonism are quite obviously very different persons.

The Jesus of Mormonism is our elder brother from our first estate, from our life during the preexistence, where we lived with our Heavenly Father, Elohim, and our Heavenly Mothers, near that great star, Kolob. He is not God without beginning or end, who was within the bosom of God from before time began, as the Bible insists.

There is no better place to see this enormous difference than in the *Book of Mormon*, which Mormons advertise as "Another Testament of Jesus Christ." This claim is even stamped in print on the cover of the book's recent editions. But is it true?

The word *another* on the *Book of Mormon* cover implies an additional testament. The dictionary defines *another* as "different" or "changed." As you read this section, you determine which definition fits the *Book of Mormon* and the Mormon Jesus.

What happened when Jesus went to Calvary in the Bible and in the *Book of Mormon?* If the Jesus of the *Book of Mormon* is truly the same, the "Testament" should be the same.

The Jesus of the *Book of Mormon*

In the *Book of Mormon*, Jesus brought death and destruction with him to the cross. Third Nephi, chapters 8 and 9, details the events testifying of Christ's crucifixion. It describes the desolation of the great city of Zarahemla by fire, and the city of Moroni...

> did sink into the sea and the inhabitants thereof were drowned. ... The earth was carried up upon the city of Mornihah.... There was great and terrible destruction in the land southward ... terrible destruction in the land northward... the highways were broken up... many great and noble cities were sunk and many burned and many shaken till the buildings thereof had fallen to the earth.... All these great and terrible things were done in the space of three hours.

Third Nephi chapter 9 tells of further wrath as the cities and inhabitants of Gigal, Onihah, Mocum, Jerusalem, Gadiandi, Gadiomnah, Jacob, Gimgimmo, Jacobugath, Laman, Josh, Gad, and Kishkumen are annihilated—a total of 16 major cities.

Who did all this killing to testify of our Lord's atonement on Calvary? Third Nephi 9:15 reveals the murderer of approximately two million innocent inhabitants of the *Book of Mormon* lands: "Behold, I am Jesus Christ the son of God. I created the heavens and the earth and all things that in them are." He adds in verse 21, "Behold, I have come unto the world to bring redemption unto the world to save the world from sin."

It appears that the easiest way for the *Book of Mormon* Jesus to "bring redemption" was to kill millions of human beings, a vast proportion of his "other sheep." The *Book of Mormon* Jesus wipes out millions of people who knew nothing of Calvary. Is that what we see in the Bible, or do we see two different Jesuses here?

The Jesus of the Bible

Contrary to the Mormon Jesus, the biblical Jesus cried out to His Father on behalf of those who nailed Him to a cross with cruel spikes. "Father," He said, "forgive them, for they do not know what they are doing."

> Jesus, when he had cried again with a loud voice, yielded up the ghost. And, behold, the veil of the temple was rent in twain from the top to the bottom; and the earth did quake, and the rocks rent; and the graves were opened; and many bodies of the saints which slept arose, and came out of the graves after his

resurrection, and went into the holy city, and appeared unto many. Now when the centurion, and they that were with him, watching Jesus, saw the earthquake, and those things that were done, they feared greatly, saying, Truly this was the Son of God (Matthew 27:50-54).

And Jesus cried with a loud voice, and gave up the ghost. And the veil of the temple was rent in twain from the top to the bottom. And when the centurion, which stood over against him, saw that he so cried out, and gave up the ghost, he said, Truly this man was the Son of God (Mark 15:37).

And it was about the sixth hour, and there was a darkness over all the earth until the ninth hour. And the sun was darkened, and the veil of the temple was rent in the midst. And when Jesus had cried with a loud voice, he said, Father, into thy hands I commend my spirit: and having said thus, he gave up the ghost. Now when the centurion saw what was done, he glorified God, saying, Certainly this was a righteous man (Luke 23:44-47).

When Jesus therefore had received the vinegar, he said, It is finished: and he bowed his head, and gave up the ghost (John 19:30).

The word *earthquake* is used here to state that the earth shook. It could not have been terribly severe; John doesn't even mention it. Luke indicates that people stood by as the earth shook and the sun went into eclipse for three hours. Note one thing in all of this: No one died. In fact, at His resurrection on the third day, graves were opened and some saints were *resurrected* to walk into the city.

In the end of the sabbath, as it began to dawn toward the first day of the week, came Mary Magdalene and the other Mary to see the sepulchre. And, behold, there was a great earthquake: for the angel of the Lord descended from heaven, and came and rolled back the stone from the door, and sat upon it. His counte-nance was like lightning, and his raiment white as snow: and for fear of him the keepers did shake, and became as dead men. And the angel answered and said unto the women, Fear not ye: for I know that ye seek Jesus, which was crucified. He is not here: for he is risen, as he said. Come, see the place where the Lord lay (Matthew 28:1-6).

Again, this earthquake was not destructive. The earth shook and the stone rolled away from the door, but people were not killed.

"The Vapor of Darkness"

Another comparison we can make between the Bible's Jesus and the Jesus of Mormonism centers around astronomical occurrences at the death of Jesus.

Luke's gospel says that there was a darkness over all the earth (23:44,45). Matthew 27:45 says, "Now from the sixth hour there was darkness over all the land unto the ninth hour," and Mark 15:33 concurs almost exactly. Yet it seems clear from the Bible that there is nothing unusual about the darkness itself. Jesus' disciples and the Romans around the cross were able to see the Lord die. John, an eyewitness, even makes a special point of saying that he saw Jesus pierced (John 19:34,35).

On the other hand, the darkness in the *Book of Mormon* seems to have started at the time the biblical darkness ended (3 Nephi 8:19):

> And it came to pass that there was thick darkness upon all the face of the land, insomuch that the inhabitants thereof . . . could feel the vapor of darkness; and there could be no light, because of the darkness, neither candles, neither torches; neither could there be fire kindled . . . so that there could not be any light at all; and there was not any light seen . . . neither the sun nor the moon nor the stars, for so great were the mists of darkness upon the face of the land. And it came to pass that it did last for the space of three days that there was no light seen (3 Nephi 8:20-23).

Now that's quite a different type of darkness! It seemed to be a tangible thing which allowed no light at all. Not only that, but it lasted for three days instead of three hours. This is utterly different from the Bible. While the Bible says gloom covered the land during the crucifixion, the *Book of Mormon* teaches that some mysterious "vapor of darkness" started right after the crucifixion and lasted for three days.

This is some way for the *Book of Mormon* Jesus to celebrate the first Easter—by wiping out a couple of million people and then smothering the survivors in impossible darkness! The question must be asked, Why would Jesus inflict so horrifying a punishment upon

His "other sheep" when the very people who nailed Him to the cross only got a tremor and a gloomy afternoon?

The LDS Jesus also does another rather unbiblical thing. After descending to Earth following his crucifixion, he orders the surviving Nephites to: "thrust your hands into my side . . . [and] feel the prints of the nails in my hands and my feet" (3 Nephi 11:14).

Then, what most LDS experts estimate to be about a half-million people marched forward and drove their hands into his wounds! Figuring 30 seconds per person, it would have taken almost *three days* for the LDS Jesus to stand there and let people do this.

Now remember, these are the Nephite "true believers"—the ones who were counted worthy enough to escape having their cities fall on them. These were the cream of the crop!

Does the biblical Jesus ever do anything like this? Well, of course there is Thomas. But Thomas is not presented as any kind of paragon. Jesus told him: "Because thou hast seen me, thou hast believed: blessed are they that have not seen, and yet have believed" (John 20:29).

The biblical Jesus valued faith and gave a special blessing to those who did not need flashy demonstrations. And Thomas never did actually touch Him.

Earlier, in John 20:17, Jesus discouraged Mary Magdalene from touching Him at all. Yet, we are asked to believe that this same Jesus instructed a "multitude" to spend days doing it. Can this be the Jesus of the Bible?

Another Jesus?

All this LDS baggage imposed upon the Savior makes it little wonder that Mormons do not consider Jesus to be the third Person of the Trinity. They have a hard time accepting John's testimony of Him:

> And the Word was made flesh, and dwelt among us, (and we beheld his glory, the glory as of the only begotten of the Father,) full of grace and truth. John bare witness of him, and cried, saying, This was he of whom I spake, He that cometh after me is preferred before me: for he was before me. And of his fulness have all we received, and grace for grace. For the law was given by Moses, but grace and truth came by Jesus Christ. No man hath

seen God at any time; the only begotten Son, which is in the bosom of the Father, he hath declared him (John 1:14-18).

Mormonism also has a hard time dealing with the grace of Christ. The Scripture clearly states that the law was given through Moses while Christ brought truth *and* grace . . . and a release from the law. Yet, the Jesus of Mormonism has to abide by the law of eternal progression—the base doctrine of Mormonism that binds every Mormon to the task of earning personal salvation, outside the gift of Christ's shed blood at Calvary.

This is a crucial matter, for until the LDS people can see that salvation is something impossible to earn or pay for with our own works of righteousness, they will never be drawn to surrender their lives to Jesus Christ, accept His one-time sin offering for us, and stand covered by the blood of Calvary.

In Mormonism, like any cult, Jesus must be no more than a pointer, an example. Without the individual working and earning and being tested for worthiness by cult leaders, there can be no control, no bondage. The peace, joy, and personal knowledge of salvation that so fully comes upon everyone who is truly born again would release those in spiritual darkness from the power of the cults. So the Jesus of Mormonism must be less than God come in the flesh.

The Christ of Mormonism is not the Christ of the Bible. Second Corinthians 11:3,4 tells us that there will be those who would teach a different Christ. Paul says of them, "For such men are false apostles, deceitful workmen, masquerading as apostles of Christ" (2 Corinthians 11:13 NIV).

The Mormons have a terrible time understanding what actually happened at Calvary. In their pamphlet *What the Mormons Think of Christ*, we see the problem. In the section, "The Blood of Christ" (p. 22 in the 1976 edition), we read:

> Christians speak often of the blood of Christ and its cleansing power. Much that is believed and taught on this subject, however, is such utter nonsense and so palpably false that to believe it is to lose one's salvation. For instance, many believe or pretend to believe that if we confess Christ with our lips and avow that we accept him as our personal savior, we are thereby saved. They say that his blood, without any other act than mere belief, makes us clean.

What is the true doctrine of the blood of Christ? Salvation comes because of the atonement, and the atonement was wrought through the shedding of the blood of Christ. In Gethsemane Christ sweat great drops of blood from every pore when he conditionally took upon himself the sins of the world, and then the shedding of his blood was completed upon the cross.

This is not the biblical account of the atonement. Jesus went to Gethsemane to pray and prepare; the atonement was accomplished only at the cross. In the garden the sin offering (Jesus) was sanctified to be given *once for all* at the cross.

The LDS church teaches in Article of Faith #3, "We believe that through the atonement of Christ, all mankind may be saved, *by obedience to the laws and ordinances of the gospel* [the laws and ordinances of the *Mormon* gospel]."

These Mormon laws and ordinances have been placed in the way of the cross, blocking the LDS people from it and its cleansing power. The Bible clearly teaches a different Christ and another gospel. In Colossians 2:13-15 Paul writes:

And you, being dead in your sins and the uncircumcision of your flesh, hath he quickened together with him, having forgiven you all trespasses; blotting out the handwriting of ordinances that was against us, which was contrary to us, and took it out of the way, nailing it to his cross; and having spoiled principalities and powers, he made a shew of them openly, triumphing over them in it.

And in Ephesians 2:13-17:

But now in Christ Jesus ye who sometimes were far off are made nigh by the blood of Christ. For he is our peace, who hath made both one, and hath broken down the middle wall of partition between us; having abolished in his flesh the enmity, even the law of commandments contained in ordinances; for to make in himself of twain one new man, so making peace; and that he might reconcile both unto God in one body by the cross, having slain the enmity thereby: and came and preached peace to you which were afar off, and to them that were nigh.

The Mormon Jesus has been stripped of his unique deity and his sacrifice on the cross has been robbed of its power. Theirs is a tragically bloodless Christ, whose death brought only immortality, not eternal life. Their Jesus forces us under laws, ordinances, and an all-too-human priesthood. This is not the "good news" of the Bible.

> But Christ being come an high priest of good things to come, by a greater and more perfect tabernacle, not made with hands, that is to say, not of this building; neither by the blood of goats and calves, but by his own blood he entered in once into the holy place, having obtained eternal redemption for us. For if the blood of bulls and of goats, and the ashes of an heifer sprinkling the unclean, sanctifieth to the purifying of the flesh: how much more shall the blood of Christ, who through the eternal Spirit offered himself without spot to God, purge your conscience from dead works to serve the living God? And for this cause he is the mediator of the new testament, that by means of death, for the redemption of the transgressions that were under the first testament, they which are called might receive the promise of eternal inheritance. . . . Nor yet that he should offer himself often, as the high priest entereth into the holy place every year with blood of others; for then must he often have suffered since the foundation of the world: but now once in the end of the world hath he appeared to put away sin by the sacrifice of himself (Hebrews 9:11-15,25,26).

> He that despised Moses' law died without mercy under two or three witnesses: of how much sorer punishment, suppose ye, shall he be thought worthy, who hath trodden under foot the Son of God, and hath counted the blood of the covenant, wherewith he was sanctified, an unholy thing, and hath done despite unto the Spirit of grace? (Hebrews 10:28,29).

A more orthodox Christ was preached in the early LDS church. But when Joseph Smith began to teach the strange doctrines of his false Christ—one without redemptive powers—the church could no longer deal with the reality of the blood of Calvary and its full redemptive work. That was when the church removed the red wine from the communion table and substituted water. This act washed away the reality of the blood from its basically Christian converts.

The same holds true today. The Jesus of the cross who shed His redemptive blood has become a stranger to the Latter-day Saints. The Jesus of Mormonism is no Jesus at all.

JESUS: THE HOLLYWOOD VERSION

Do you remember the outrage across Christendom when Universal Pictures released a film called *The Last Temptation of Christ?* Our ministries were energetically implored to get involved in fighting an all-out battle to stop the showing of that film. We agreed it was filth—nothing but religious pornography.

We had already called the office of Mr. Sidney Sheinberg, president of MCA, Inc., the owners of Universal Studios, and told them that if the film were distributed, we were planning to work with churches and visit all the theaters that would be showing the film. We were as personally offended as anyone.

Yet we were also a bit confused. We had been trying to get churches and ministries outraged about that same Jesus for years. That Universal Pictures "Jesus" exactly matched the description of the Mormon Jesus. He was the "other Jesus" about whom we had been trying to warn everyone.

Listen to the movie script:

> Jesus says to Judas: "No, I don't have any pride. I don't go to Synagogue. I disobey the commandments. I work on the Sabbath." Judas: "And who will pay for your sins?" Jesus: "I don't know. I'm struggling."

Listen to the Mormon Jesus:

> His [Jesus'] trials were continuous. Perhaps his brother, Lucifer, had heard him say when he was still but a lad of 12, "Whist ye not that I be about my Father's business?" (Luke 2:49).

> Then came the time when Satan thought to trip him. Their encounter in the previous world had been on more equal terms, but now Jesus was young and Satan was experienced (*Ensign*, December 1980, pp. 3-5, "Jesus of Nazareth," Spencer W. Kimball, First Presidency message).

> As far as this life is concerned it appears that he had to start just as all other children do and gain his knowledge line upon line. Without doubt, Jesus came into the world subject to the same condition as was required of each of us—he forgot everything and he had to grow from grace to grace (Joseph Fielding Smith, *Doctrines of Salvation*, vol. 1, "Christ Worked Out His Own Salvation," pp. 32, 33).

Note it please, the Lord Jesus worked out his own salvation while in this mortal probation . . . ("Our Relationship with the Lord," an address at Brigham Young University, March 2, 1982, Bruce R. McConkie, p. 9).

Listen to the script:

Jesus says to Mary Magdalene: "I've done a lot of wrong things. I'm going to the desert to be cleansed. The worst things are to you. Forgive me."

According to the AFA *Journal*,

The story has Jesus marrying Mary Magdalene and allowing his guardian angel to watch while Jesus and Magdalene engage in sex. In other dialogue, Jesus tells Mary Magdalene. "Now I know: A woman is God's greatest work. And I worship you. God sleeps between your legs." After Magdalene dies, Jesus moves in with Mary and Martha, the sisters of Lazarus, and has children by them.

Listen to the Mormon Jesus:

Jesus was the bridegroom at the marriage of Cana of Galilee. . . . We say it was Jesus Christ who was married, to be brought into relationship whereby he could see his seed (Apostle Orson Hyde, *Journal of Discourses* 2:82).

There was a marriage in Cana of Galilee; and on a careful reading of that transaction, it will be discovered that no less a person than Jesus Christ was married on that occasion. If he was never married, his intimacy with Mary and Martha and the other Mary also whom Jesus loved, must have been highly unbecoming and improper to say the best of it (Apostle Orson Hyde, *Journal of Discourses* 4:259).

In Church councils, it was spoken of: "Joseph F. Smith . . . He spoke upon the marriage in Cana of Galilee. He thought Jesus was the bridegroom and Mary and Martha the brides" (*Journal of* [Apostle] *Wilford Woodruff*, July 22, 1883).

The grand reason of the burst of public sentiment in anathemas upon Christ and his disciples, causing his crucifixion, was evidently based upon polygamy, according to the testimony of the philosophers who rose in that age. A belief in the doctrine of a plurality of wives caused the persecution of Jesus and his followers. We might almost think they were Mormons (Apostle Jedediah Grant, *Journal of Discourses* 1:346).

One thing is certain, that there were several holy women that greatly loved Jesus, such as Mary and Martha her sister, and Mary Magdalene; and Jesus greatly loved them and associated with them much; and when he arose from the dead, instead of first showing himself to his chosen witnesses, the Apostles, He appeared first to these women, or at least to one of them—namely, Mary Magdalene. Now, it would be very natural for a husband in the resurrection to appear first to his own dear wives, and afterwards show himself to his other friends. If all the acts of Jesus were written, we no doubt should learn that these beloved women were his wives (Orson Pratt, *The Seer*, p. 159).

I discover that some of the eastern papers represent me as a great blasphemer, because I said, in my lecture on marriage, at our last conference, that Jesus Christ was married at Cana of Galilee, that Mary, Martha, and others were his wives, *and that he begat children*. All that I have to say in reply to that charge is this—they worship a Saviour that is too pure and holy to fulfill the commands of his Father. I worship one *that is just pure enough* "to fulfill all righteousness;" not only the righteous law of baptism, but the still more righteous and important law *"to multiply and replenish the earth."* Startle not at this, for even the Father himself honored that law by coming down to Mary, without a natural body, and begetting a son; and if Jesus begat children, he only did that which he had seen his Father do (Orson Hyde, *Journal of Discourses* 2:210).

Ogden Kraut, Mormon polygamist writer, writing about the "holy order of polygamy," quoted Luke: "There followed him a great company of people, and of women, which also bewailed and lamented him. But Jesus turning unto them and said, Daughters of Jerusalem, weep not for me, but weep for yourselves, *and for your children*" (Luke 23:27,28).

Kraut adds the Mormon twist to the biblical story:

These women were wives and mothers who "bewailed and lamented" because Jesus was going to the cross. . . . Jesus

knew the sorrows that would continue for those women and children because the persecutors would not stop at the death of Jesus.
They would continue to destroy his children, his relatives and his
disciples (Ogden Kraut, *Jesus Was Married*, p. 84).

Finally, in a March 17, 1963, letter to President Joseph Fielding
Smith, Mr. J.R. Smith asked the then-living prophet the direct
question:

> In a discussion recently, the question arose, "Was Christ
> Married?" The quote of Isaiah 53:10 was given which reads, "Yet it
> pleased the Lord to bruise him; he hath put Him to grief: when
> thou shalt make his soul an offering for sin, he shall see His seed,
> he shall prolong His days, and the pleasure of the Lord shall
> prosper in his hand."
> What is meant by "he shall see his seed?" Does this mean
> that Christ had Children?
> In the Temple ceremony we are told that only through
> Temple marriage can we receive the highest degree of exaltation
> and dwell in the presence of our Heavenly Father and Jesus Christ.
> Christ came here to set us the example and therefore, we believe
> that he must have been married. Are we right? (Copy of letter on
> file.)

President Smith answered in his own hand on the page, mark-
ing the word *seed* in the first paragraph and noted "Mosiah 15:10-12.
Please read your Book of Mormon!" He marked the word *married* in
the last paragraph and noted, "YES! But do not preach it! The Lord
advised us not to cast pearls before Swine!"

The LDS Jesus is a polygamist who fathered many children. He
was imperfect and had to work out his own salvation through works
of the law. Even worse, the LDS theology teaches that God the
Father came to earth and physically had sexual intercourse with the
virgin Mary to beget Jesus in the flesh.

Since Mormonism teaches that we all are born first in Kolob
by God and one of his goddess wives, he was committing incest
when he slept with Mary, one of his own children.

The Tip of the Iceberg

The facts are these: *The Last Temptation of Christ* was a blasphemous, evil work purposely written and filmed to defame and

dishonor our Lord and Savior, Jesus Christ. We must stand against filth like this with all our might!

Yet the church needs to know that the Jesus of Mormonism is every bit as blasphemous. The vilest portrayal of Jesus that Hollywood can create is in basic agreement with LDS theology.

KING FOLLETT DISCOURSE

During the April 1844 conference of the LDS church, Joseph Smith preached a funeral sermon for a member of the church named King Follett who died in a well-digging accident. Not much is known about Follett, but the sermon was a milestone in LDS history, laying out before approximately 20,000 Saints a "revelation" of the nature and character of God and man. It was Smith's last great sermon. He died three months later.

To any good student of Mormonism, the sermon is well worth reading in its entirety and can be found in the book *The Teachings of the Prophet, Joseph Smith* on pages 342-62. The sermon stands as the best source document of many of the more esoteric doctrines of Mormonism.

The speech laid out the LDS doctrine on the character of God for all to hear. Smith said:

> I will go back to the beginning before the world was, to show what kind of being God is. What sort of a being was God in the beginning? Open your ears and hear, all ye ends of the earth, for I am going to prove it to you by the Bible, and to tell you the designs of God in relation to the human race and why He interferes with the affairs of man.
>
> God himself was once as we are now, *and is an exalted man* [emphasis added], and sits enthroned in yonder heavens! That is the great secret. If the veil were rent today, and the great God who holds this world in its orbit, and who upholds all worlds and all

things by his power, was to make himself visible—I say, if you were to see him today, you would see him like a man in form—like yourselves in all the person, image, and very form as a man; for Adam was created in the very fashion, image and likeness of God, and received instruction from, and walked, talked and conversed with him, as one man talks and communes with another (p. 345).

Here then, is eternal life—to know the only wise and true God, and you have got to learn how to be Gods yourselves, and to be kings and priests to God, *the same as all Gods have done before you* [our emphasis], namely, by going from one small degree to another, and from a small capacity to a great one; from grace to grace, from exaltation to exaltation, until you attain to the resurrection of the dead, and are able to dwell in everlasting burnings, and to sit in glory, as do those who sit enthroned in everlasting power. And I want you to know that God, in the last days, while certain individuals are proclaiming His name, is not trifling with you or me (pp. 345-46).

Smith told them that this whole plan was designed by a council of the gods. There was a plurality of gods to deal with:

In the beginning, the head of the Gods called a council of the Gods; and *they came together and concocted a plan to create the world and people it* [emphasis added]. When we begin to learn this way, we begin to learn the only true God, and what kind of a being we have got to worship. Having a knowledge of God, we begin to know how to approach him, and how to ask so as to receive an answer. When we understand the character of God, and know how to come to him, he begins to unfold the heavens to us, and to tell us all about it. When we are ready to come to him, he is ready to come to us (pp. 349-50).

You would think that the whole body of the church in attendance at that service would have bolted out of the chairs and fled for the hills. But they didn't; they were deeply under the influence of this new "prophet" of God.

Unfortunately, they did not compare what Joseph Smith said to the Word of God. Even if every prophecy out of the mouth of this man was coming to pass before their eyes, Smith was failing one of the most basic biblical tests of a prophet. And their doom was being sealed, right along with his:

If there arise among you a prophet, or a dreamer of dreams, and giveth thee a sign or a wonder, and the sign or the wonder come to pass, whereof he spake unto thee, saying, Let us go after other gods, which thou hast not known, and let us serve them; thou shalt not hearken unto the words of that prophet, or that dreamer of dreams: for the LORD your God proveth you, to know whether ye love the LORD your God with all your heart and with all your soul. Ye shall walk after the LORD your God, and fear him, and keep his commandments, and obey his voice, and ye shall serve him, and cleave unto him. And that prophet, or that dreamer of dreams, shall be put to death; because he hath spoken to turn you away from the LORD your God, which brought you out of the land of Egypt, and redeemed you out of the house of bondage, to thrust thee out of the way which the LORD thy God commanded thee to walk in. So shalt thou put the evil away from the midst of thee (Deuteronomy 13:1-5).

KOLOB

The LDS Position

Kolob is supposedly the great star nearest to the throne of God. In *The Pearl of Great Price*, the Book of Abraham 3:2-4, the Lord tells Abraham:

I saw the stars, that they were great and that one of them was nearest unto the throne of God; and there were many great ones which were near unto it; and the Lord said unto me: these are the governing ones; and the name of the great one is Kolob, because it is near unto me for I am the Lord thy God; I have set this one to govern all those which belong to the same order as that upon which thou standest.

Kolob supposedly is the sun or star around which rotates the planet upon which resides the LDS god. The next few verses explain that one day on Kolob is equal to a thousand years on Earth. Somehow, Kolob and its planets control or govern all the other celestial orbs such as Earth. One could say, it is the core of creation. Bruce R. McConkie calls it the "First Creation" (*Doctrine*, p. 428).

The LDS god rarely leaves his planet. In the Garden of Eden section of the LDS temple ritual, the Mormon God wonders how

Adam and Eve are doing on Earth and dispatches Jesus and Michael to go down and check it out, apparently unable to know the answer without hearing the report of their findings.

The Biblical View

Of course, it's difficult to respond to something like this in kind. Orthodoxy clearly does not teach that God is an exalted man living on some planet in the center of the galaxies. The orthodox God is everywhere present.

To put God physically on a certain planet orbiting a certain star with a given time relationship to the other planets, is to quantify God, giving Him measurement, scope, and range. The true God has no measurement, range, or physical limitation. Then why do it? The LDS church needs those limitations in order to bring their god down to a level to which its adherents can aspire.

LAMANITES

The word *Lamanite* comes from the *Book of Mormon*, which claims that a small group of Hebrews arrived in the New World centuries before Christ. From the lineage of Lehi, their prophet, supposedly came two basic lines of people.

Those descended from Nephi (the good son) came to be called Nephites and were referred to in the *Book of Mormon* as "white and delightsome" until quite recently, when the Mormon church revised their scriptures to say "*pure* and delightsome": "And then shall they rejoice; for they shall know that it is a blessing unto them from the hand of God; and their scales of darkness shall begin to fall from their eyes; and many generations shall not pass away among them, save they shall be a pure and delightsome people" (Nephi 30:6).

Those descended from the bad, rebellious son, Laman, came to be known as "Lamanites." These Lamanites, Mormons believe, were cursed with a darker skin because they practiced wickedness and idolatry. Mormon scripture says this: "For this people shall be scattered, and shall become a dark, a filthy, and a loathsome people, beyond the description of that which ever hath been amongst us, yea even that which hath been among the Lamanites, and this because of their unbelief and idolatry" (Mormon 5:15).

Mormons believe that dark skin is the sign of a curse from God for their wickedness:

Wherefore, the word of the Lord was fulfilled which he spake unto me, saying that: Inasmuch as they will not hearken unto thy words they shall be cut off from the presence of the Lord. And behold, they were cut off from his presence.

And he had caused the cursing to come upon them, yea, even a sore cursing, because of their iniquity. For behold, they had hardened their hearts against him, that they had become like unto a flint; wherefore, as they were white, and exceedingly fair and delightsome, that they might not be enticing unto my people, the Lord God did cause a skin of blackness to come upon them.

And thus saith the Lord God: I will cause that they shall be loathsome unto thy people, save they shall repent of their iniquities. And cursed shall be the seed of him that mixeth with their seed; for they shall be cursed even with the same cursing. And the Lord spake it, and it was done.

And because of their cursing which was upon them they did become an idle people, full of mischief and subtlety, and did seek in the wilderness for beasts of prey (2 Nephi 5:20-25).

The official *Book of Mormon* concordance says this about "Lamanites":

The people who, in connection with their kindred, the Nephites, occupied the American continent from 590 B.C. to 385 A.D. in which latter year they [the Lamanites] destroyed the Nephites and remained possessors of the entire land. The American Indians are their degraded descendants. These people were of Hebrew origin and are called Lamanites (p. 395).

Mormons believe that the native people in both South and North America are the physical descendants of these degraded *Book of Mormon* sinners. They believe that their darkened skin is the result of God's curse. Thus, since in appearance there is little difference between native Americans and many Hispanics, most Mormons consider all Hispanics "Lamanites."

Naturally, Mormons have concocted an even worse story to explain the origin of those with black skin, the Negro race. We recommend you review the sections on the Lamanites and Negroes.

LAW OF ETERNAL PROGRESSION: BECOMING GODS?

The Mormon principle of eternal progression is the bedrock doctrine of Mormonism. In it are placed all the Mormon's hopes and expectations of personal glory. It is summed up in the aphorism, "As man is, God once was, and as God is, man may become." This axiom is generally attributed to Lorenzo Snow, but was hardly a new concept with him.

Perhaps the most public exposure of this heretofore hidden core of Mormon heresy came forward with the release of the film *The God Makers*. In the movie, the filmmakers summed up the law of eternal progression in a short, animated presentation. Here is the transcript from that portion of the film:

> Mormonism teaches that trillions of planets scattered throughout the cosmos are ruled by countless gods who once were human like us.
>
> They say that long ago, on one of these planets, to an unidentified god and one of his goddess wives, a spirit child named Elohim was conceived. This spirit child was later born to human parents who gave him a physical body.
>
> Through obedience to Mormon teaching, death and resurrection, he proved himself worthy and was elevated to godhood as his father before him.
>
> Mormons believe that Elohim is their Heavenly Father and that he lives with his many wives on a planet near a mysterious star called Kolob. Here the god of Mormonism and his wives, through endless Celestial sex, produced billions of spirit children.
>
> To decide their destiny, the head of the Mormon gods called a great heavenly council meeting. Both of Elohim's eldest sons were there, Lucifer and his brother Jesus.
>
> A plan was presented to build planet earth where the spirit children would be sent to take on mortal bodies and learn good from evil. Lucifer stood and made his bid for becoming Savior of this new world. Wanting the glory for himself, he planned to force everyone to become gods. Opposing the idea, the Mormon Jesus suggested giving man his freedom of choice as on other planets. The vote that followed approved the proposal of the Mormon Jesus who would become Savior of the planet earth.
>
> Enraged, Lucifer cunningly convinced one-third of the spirits destined for earth to fight with him and revolt. Thus, Lucifer became the devil and his followers the demons. Sent to this world, they would forever be denied bodies of flesh and bone.
>
> Those who remained neutral in the battle were cursed to be born with black skin. This is the Mormon explanation for the Negro race. The spirits that fought most valiantly against Lucifer

would be born into Mormon families on planet earth. These would be the lighter skinned people, or white and delightsome, as the Book of Mormon describes them.

Early Mormon prophets taught that Elohim and one of his goddess wives came to the earth as Adam and Eve to start the human race. Thousands of years later, Elohim in human form once again journeyed to earth from the star base Kolob, this time to have physical relations with the Virgin Mary in order to provide Jesus with a physical body.

Mormon Apostle Orson Hyde taught that after Jesus Christ grew to manhood, he took at least three wives, Mary, Martha and Mary Magdalene. Through these wives, the Mormon Jesus supposedly fathered a number of children before he was crucified. Mormon founder, Joseph Smith, is supposedly one of his descendants.

According to the Book of Mormon, after his resurrection, Jesus came to the Americas to preach to the Indians whom the Mormons believe are really Israelites. Thus, the Jesus of Mormonism established his church in the Americas as he had in Palestine. By the year 421 A.D., the dark skinned Israelites, known as the Lamanites, had destroyed all of the white skinned Nephites in a number of great battles. The Nephites' records were supposedly written on golden plates buried by Moroni, the last living Nephite, in the Hill Cumorah.

400 years later, a young treasure seeker named Joseph Smith, who was known for his tall tales, claimed to have uncovered the same gold plates near his home in upstate New York. He is now honored by Mormons as a prophet because he claimed to have had visions from the spirit world in which he was commanded to organize the Mormon Church because all Christian creeds were an abomination. It was Joseph Smith who originated most of these peculiar doctrines which millions today believe to be true.

By maintaining a rigid code of financial and moral requirements, and through performing secret temple rituals for themselves and the dead, the Latter-day Saints hope to prove their worthiness and thus become gods. The Mormons teach that everyone must stand at the final judgment before Joseph Smith, the Mormon Jesus, and Elohim.

Those Mormons who were sealed in the eternal marriage ceremony expect to become polygamous gods in the Celestial Kingdom, rule over other planets, and spawn new families throughout eternity. The Mormons thank God for Joseph Smith, who claimed that he had done more for us than any other man, including Jesus Christ. The Mormons claim that he died as a martyr, shed his blood for us, so that we, too, may become Gods.

During the years just after the film was released, almost every Mormon who saw the film was jolted by this little animation sequence. The general response was to strongly deny that any part of it could truly be LDS doctrine. When pushed to name even a single error, they failed to do so; and when any particular doctrine was mentioned, they would readily agree that the LDS position was accurately represented.

I concluded that while every Mormon really did believe the truth of each of these segments of the law of eternal progression, they had never been confronted with them all strung together. Even for a Mormon believer, the foolishness of the full picture was staggering.

The LDS Position

The creators of *The God Makers* did not have to invent this business of gods having been men and men becoming gods. Joseph Smith was the first to teach it publicly in a sermon he delivered before approximately 20,000 Saints at the funeral of an elder named King Follett. It was on April 7, 1844, when he said:

> God himself was once as we are now, and is an exalted man . . . that is the great secret. . . . I say, if you were to see him today, you would see him like a man in form—like yourselves in all the person, image and very form as a man. . . . He was once a man like us; yea, that God himself, the Father of us all, dwelt on an earth.

Smith then claimed, "Here then is eternal life—to know the only wise and true God; and you have got to learn how to be Gods yourselves, and to be kings and priests to God, the same as all gods have done before you. . . . To inherit the same power, the same glory and the same exaltation, until you arrive at the station of god" (*History*, vol. 6, pp. 305-06).

As if that isn't clear enough, modern theologian and late apostle of the LDS church, Bruce R. McConkie, carefully defined "eternal life" in *Mormon Doctrine*:

269

Salvation in its true and full sense is synonymous with exaltation or eternal life and consists in gaining an inheritance in the highest of the three heavens within the celestial kingdom. With few exceptions, this is the salvation of which the scriptures speak. It is the salvation which the saints seek. . . . This full salvation is obtained in and through the continuation of the family unit in eternity, and those who obtain it are gods (p. 670).

That's as plain as day! "Eternal life = Godhood = Exaltation." Mormons believe that they can become gods. It is not some isolated, obtuse piece of theology. *Doctrine and Covenants* 132:20 speaks of those who abide in the new and everlasting covenant of [plural] marriage: "Then they shall be gods, because they have no end; therefore shall they be from everlasting to everlasting, because they continue; then shall they be above all, because all things are subject unto them. Then shall they be gods, because they have all power, and the angels are subject unto them."

The Biblical View

It is shocking for an orthodox Christian to come face-to-face with such an arrogantly stated, self-serving bit of LDS "scripture." It is our holy God who is everlasting to everlasting, not man!

Before the mountains were brought forth, or ever thou hadst formed the earth and the world, even from everlasting to everlasting, thou art God (Psalm 90:2).

But the mercy of the LORD is from everlasting to everlasting upon them that fear him, and his righteousness unto children's children (Psalm 103:17).

Blessed be the LORD God of Israel from everlasting to everlasting: and let all the people say, Amen. Praise ye the LORD (Psalm 106:48).

Was God once a man? Can we become gods? Jesus Christ was a man, but He was not a man who became God; He is God who became man. There is a world of difference between the two. Read Philippians 2:6,7 and see that Jesus did just the opposite of what Mormons hope to do: "[He] being in the form of God, thought it not robbery to be equal with God: but made himself of no reputation and took upon him the form of a servant, and was made in the likeness of men."

This, coupled with John 1:1-14, makes it clear that Jesus was God before He came to Earth and was born of the virgin.

This is *not* the case with us! Romans 8:17 does not teach that we will become gods, because godhood is not something we can inherit. Jesus always had godhood (John 1:1) and God was *always* God (Psalm 90:2). Therefore it cannot be something one can inherit. Such a teaching would be in violation of Isaiah 43:10, Deuteronomy 6:4, and a dozen other Scriptures which teach that God is unique; and God cannot contradict Himself.

Hebrews 1:1,2 says, "God, who at sundry times and in divers manners spake in time past unto the fathers by the prophets, hath in these last days spoken unto us by his Son, whom he hath appointed heir of all things."

It is true that those who suffer with Christ will be joint heirs with Him and will inherit all things. But godhood is not one of the things Christ inherits, for the simple reason that He is already God.

Suppose a man with a fortune died, leaving one son and one cat. He liked the cat as much as his son, and upon his death willed half his money to the son and the other half to the cat. That makes the cat a joint heir with the son. The fact that the cat is a joint heir with the son does not make the cat a human being. In the same way, the fact that Christians who suffer with Christ are joint heirs with the only-begotten Son does not make them gods.

LAYING ON OF HANDS

The LDS Position

The Mormon practice of laying one's hands upon the head of another is believed to be the only efficacious way of transmitting blessings, ordinations, etc.—*if* the person doing the "laying on" is a "legal administrator":

> Special blessings, anointings, sealing of anointings, confirmations, ordinations, callings, healings, offices, and graces *are conferred by the laying on of hands by the Lord's legal administrators.* As with all of the Lord's prescribed procedural requisites, the

proffered blessings come *only when the designated formalities are observed* (*Teachings*, pp. 198-99, emphasis added).

Following baptism in water, the bestowal of the Holy Ghost takes place by the laying on of hands of the elders. Those who receive this conferral, in a very real sense, have the hand of the Lord laid upon them. For instance, to Edward Partridge the Lord said: "I will lay my hand upon you by the hand of my servant Sidney Rigdon, and you shall receive my Spirit, the Holy Ghost, even the Comforter, which shall teach you the peaceable things of the kingdom" (*Doctrine and Covenants* 36:1-2).

"According to the order of God," ordination to offices in the priesthood is performed by the laying on of hands (Alma 6:1; Acts 6:5,6; 1 Timothy 5:22). Setting apart to positions of presidency, administration, or special responsibility comes in the same way (Fifth Article of Faith; Numbers 27:18-23; Deuteronomy 34:9). Formal blessings are conferred by the laying on of hands (*Doctrine and Covenants* 20:70; Matthew 19:13-15; Acts 9:17), and the healing of the sick and the casting out of devils are oftentime accomplished in accord with this same formality (*Doctrine and Covenants* 42:44; 66:9; Mark 5:23; 6:5; 16:18; Luke 4:40,41; 13:11-13; Acts 28:8; James 5:14-16) (*Doctrine*, p. 438).

The Biblical View

The Mormon insistence upon the laying on of hands is not biblically supported, either in cases of reception of the Holy Spirit or investiture with priesthood offices. Nowhere in the passages on priestly ordination in the Old Testament were hands laid on Aaron or his sons. Additionally, one can search in vain in the New Testament for Jesus laying His hands upon anyone to ordain them to any office of any church. While there certainly are instances where laying on of hands was done after the Lord's ascension, it never seems to be a rigid rule. It is not wise on our own to try and restrict the Lord in the way He does things.

For example, Cornelius and his household (in Acts 10:44) received the Holy Spirit without anyone so much as laying a finger on them or being water baptized. What happened in Acts 10 is totally out of the LDS formula for "the designated formalities." Beyond that, the apostles and the 120 in the upper room received the Holy Spirit without anyone touching them (Acts 2). And the Holy Spirit fell upon them like flames of fire!

Of course, the question of being a "legal administrator" ties in with the strange LDS doctrine of restoration and supposed priesthood succession (see also *Aaron*), which is utterly without biblical support. The LDS men who claim the Aaronic priesthood and/or Melchizedek priesthood have no biblical right to either. The entire LDS doctrine of laying on of hands is biblically unwarranted. In fact, as experience has shown, it can be quite dangerous.

Many former Mormons have noted that when they used to go into the bishop's office for counseling and/or a blessing, the experience seems to have increased their level of distress. Since the LDS priesthood is a false priesthood, the blessings it transmits must be, at best, placebo-like in effect. At worst, these blessings may be demonically empowered. Whatever else may be said, it is certain that the true Holy Spirit is not involved.

Then there is the enormous impact of the patriarchal blessing, which also involves the laying on of hands (see also *Patriarchal Blessings*). Additionally, temple Mormons have hands laid on them multiple times in the initiatory work (see also *Endowments*). Those who do multiple proxy work for the dead could have hands laid on them many times in one day.

If each time this is done evil energy is transmitted from the blesser to the blessee, then the level of spiritual oppression of many active Mormons must truly be appalling in scope. This is indeed the testimony of many former Mormons emerging from the bondage of their church. Many who minister to Mormons and former Mormons have found it very liberating and helpful to have the new Christian ex-Mormon formally renounce—in prayer before the Lord—all priesthood blessings, covenants, and their confirmation into the church (and temple vows, if applicable) and ask Jesus' forgiveness for having participated in such things. In James 5:16, we find this helpful instruction: "Confess your faults one to another, and pray one for another, that ye may be healed. The effectual fervent prayer of a righteous man availeth much."

This destroys the power of Satan's counterfeit through the administration of the genuine article from a born-again Christian. It also provides an excellent basis for psychological "closure" by shutting the door on the old, false beliefs and embracing the new, Bible-based beliefs in a formal, prayerful fashion.

LUCIFER

Lucifer is a Latin name meaning "light bringer." It is the name of the devil or Satan in Mormonism, especially applied to him before his rebellion against God. Of course, it is also the name of Satan in orthodox Christianity (Isaiah 14:12). However, this initial similarity conceals some important doctrinal differences between the two faiths.

Lucifer is actually the Latin form of the Hebrew word *Hayelel* in the Isaiah passage (*Strong's Concordance* #1966). Technically, the name *Satan* is not the devil's name, but only a title that describes his function (*ha satan* in Hebrew). It means "the adversary" or "he who opposes" (*Smith's Bible Dictionary*, p. 75). This distinction is held in both Mormonism and Christianity (*Doctrine*, p. 677). Both faiths believe Lucifer to be some sort of fallen angel, the tempter, and an opponent of both man and God.

The LDS Position

The differences between Christianity and Mormonism are quite significant. Mormons believe Lucifer to be a "son of God" in the same way that Jesus is a "son of God"—indeed, in the same way that we are all sons or daughters of Heavenly Father (see also *Law of Eternal Progression*). This means that the Mormon Lucifer, like all of us, was born to the LDS god and one of his goddess wives on that planet near the great star, Kolob. Thus, there is no essential difference between Jesus and Lucifer. There is only an accidental difference: Lucifer went wrong.

McConkie explains Satan's initial sin in this way:

> When the plan of salvation was presented [to the Council of the Gods] and when the need for a Redeemer was explained, Satan offered to come into the world as the Son of God and be the Redeemer. "Behold, here am I, send me," he said. "I will be thy son." But then, as always, he was in opposition to the full plan of the Father, and so he sought to amend and change the terms of salvation; he sought to deny men their agency [free will] and to dethrone God. "I will redeem all mankind, that one soul shall not be lost, and surely I will do it; wherefore give me thine honor," he continued (Moses 4:1-4 in *Doctrine*, p. 193).

When Lucifer's plan was voted down by the council, he rebelled and managed to convince a third of the heavenly host—preexistent spirit children of Heavenly Father—to rebel. Lucifer and his spirit partisans were cast out of the presence of the gods and forever denied physical bodies. Thus Satan was and always will be "only" a spirit being.

In Mormonism this contrasts to Heavenly Father, who has a glorified physical body of parts and passions. The LDS church believes it is an error of the apostate church to teach that God is a purely spiritual being. Thus, it can truthfully be said (as Brigham Young observed) that there seems to be a great deal of resemblance between the Christian God and the LDS version of Satan:

> Their [Christian] belief reminds me that brother Joseph P. Nobles once told a Methodist priest [sic] after hearing him describe his god, that the god they worshipped was the "Mormons" Devil—a being without a body, whereas our God has a body, parts, and passions. The Devil was cursed and sent down from heaven. He has no body of his own (*Journal of Discourses* 5:331, October 7, 1857).

Additionally, Lucifer is presented in the secret temple endowment ceremony almost as a teacher and conveyer of important wisdom. The LDS theology of the fall of man denies that Adam sinned (see *Fall of Adam*). Thus, Lucifer's part in the eating of the tree is oddly positive, especially as portrayed in the temple rite. At first, he teaches LDS doctrine to Adam and Eve, and then after the fall he teaches Christian orthodoxy through his preacher lackey— at least until the temple rites were changed (see *Temples, Changes to the Ritual*).

Thus there is a strange ambivalence in Mormonism about Satan. On one hand he is the rebel and the tempter, but on the other hand he is the one who helped Eve understand the gospel plan. He also instructs the temple patrons in the wearing of the apron which is the symbol of his "power and priesthoods" (Chuck Sackett, *What's Going On in There?* pp. 28-29)—aprons which temple Mormons wear in the temple for the rest of their lives. They are even buried in that apron!

Satan is presented to faithful Latter-day Saints in the *Book of Mormon* as a wily deceiver who "cheateth their souls, and leadeth them away carefully down to hell. And behold, others he flattereth away and telleth them there is no hell—even a lake of fire and brimstone, which is endless torment" (2 Nephi 28:21-23).

Yet he is also the only person in the Bible who taught (through the serpent) the LDS law of eternal progression, that "ye shall be as gods" (Genesis 3:5). It is even more strange because LDS doctrine teaches the very same thing Lucifer is credited with teaching in 2 Nephi 28:23—that there is no eternal hell (*Doctrine*, pp. 349-50).

Is it any wonder that many Mormons do not know precisely what to make of Lucifer?

The Biblical View

First, it is clear from all the related sections herein that the LDS concept of God, Christ, the Holy Ghost, salvation, the fall, and other key doctrinal issues is 180 degrees away from biblical truth. It should not be surprising that they have Lucifer caught up in the same whirlwind of confusion.

The Bible is clear about Lucifer. In the Garden of Eden he is the arch deceiver, the liar who whispered that man can be as God. We still live in the consequence of that deception. It is the same lie that the Mormons have believed and it still brings the curse of death with it.

Lucifer was once a beautiful angel. But he believed his own lie and it brought him the same swift justice it later brought Adam and Eve:

> How art thou fallen from heaven, O Lucifer, son of the morning! how art thou cut down to the ground, which didst weaken the nations! For thou hast said in thine heart, I will ascend into heaven, I will exalt my throne above the stars of God: I will sit also upon the mount of the congregation, in the sides of the north: I will ascend above the heights of the clouds; I will be like the most High. Yet thou shalt be brought down to hell, to the sides of the pit (Isaiah 14:12-15).

To say that Lucifer was a son of God in the same manner as is Jesus is once more only the prattling of arrogant liars who instruct their followers in their own ignorance of Scripture.

> God, who at sundry times and in divers manners spake in time past unto the fathers by the prophets, hath in these last days

spoken unto us by his Son, whom he hath appointed heir of all things, by whom also he made the worlds; who being the brightness of his glory, and the express image of his person, and upholding all things by the word of his power, when he had by himself purged our sins, sat down on the right hand of the Majesty on high; being made so much better than the angels, as he hath by inheritance obtained a more excellent name than they. For unto which of the angels said he at any time, Thou art my Son, this day have I begotten thee? And again, I will be to him a Father, and he shall be to me a Son? (Hebrews 1:1-5).

MASTER MAHAN

This strange term is found in *The Pearl of Great Price*, one of the standard works of the LDS church, in the Book of Moses. Chapter 5 retells the story of Cain and Abel from Genesis 4, with an entire account inserted between the time of Cain's rejected offering and the time of the first murder.

In the Mormon version, Cain goes off and pouts and the Lord places a curse upon him even before he kills Abel (Moses 5:23-25). Cain refuses to listen to God anymore (v. 26) and his parents mourn over his disobedience. Cain marries one of his sisters and "they loved Satan more than God" (v. 28). It is at this point that Satan actively enters the picture:

> And Satan said unto Cain: *Swear unto me by thy throat, and if thou tell it thou shalt die*; and swear thy brethren by their heads, and by the living God, that they tell it not; for if they tell it, they shall surely die; and this that thy father may not know it; for this day I will deliver thy brother Abel into thy hands. And Satan sware unto Cain that he would do according to his commands. And all these things were done in secret. And Cain said: *Truly I am Mahan*, the master of this great secret, that I may murder and get gain. Wherefore Cain was called *Master Mahan*, and he gloried in his wickedness (vv. 29-31).

This is followed by the murder of Abel. This passage is a reflection of a strong trend in the standard works of Mormonism to attack secret societies which feature murderous blood oaths. This comes forth primarily in the *Book of Mormon* under condemnations of things like "Gadianton robbers" (Helaman 3:23) and "secret combinations of murder" (2 Nephi 9:9).

Many historians feel that these references are a reflection of the anti-Masonic furor which followed the murder of Captain William Morgan by Masons contemporary to Joseph Smith and the "bringing forth" of the *Book of Mormon* (see also *Freemasonry*). The strong public sentiment against secret societies in general and the Masons in particular might well have influenced Joseph Smith to add it as a subplot in his opus.

The very term *Master Mahan* is a not-too-well disguised form of "Master Mason"; and, of course, the first degree oath of a Mason involves "swearing by your throat." The odd twist in this bit of history is the fact that Joseph's brother Hyrum seems to have been a Mason and that Joseph himself joined the Lodge a few years later (*History*, 4:552).

In fact, Joseph Smith became a "Master Mahan," and almost immediately incorporated the throat-cutting oaths into the secret temple endowment (ibid., 5:1-2), where they remained until April 1990 (see also *Temples, Changes to the Ritual*). Thus, faithful LDS temple patrons have been "swearing by their throats" for almost 150 years.

This strange kind of ambivalence is found throughout Mormonism. For example, the priesthood apron which Lucifer wears in the temple rite is full of Masonic emblems. Yet the very same Masonic symbolism ends up on the "sacred" temple garments (see also *Temple Garments*) and on the "sacred" veil of the temple itself (see also *Endowments*).

Whether Joseph Smith changed his mind about Masonry or simply joined it for political expediency is not clear. But it is abundantly clear that Masonry has made a profound mark not only on LDS scripture but also upon the LDS temple ceremonies.

MELCHIZEDEK PRIESTHOOD

The LDS Position

The higher of the two priesthoods in the Mormon church is called the Melchizedek priesthood. Joseph Smith explained its great power this way:

> "What was the power of Melchizedek?" It was not the Priesthood of Aaron which administers in outward ordinances, and the offering of sacrifices. Those holding the fulness of the Melchizedek Priesthood are kings and priests of the Most High God, holding the keys of power and blessings. In fact, that Priesthood is a perfect law of theocracy, and stands as God to give laws to the people, administering endless life to the sons and daughters of Adam (*Teachings*, p. 322).

The real power of the office is supposedly found in the words "that Priesthood is a perfect theocracy, and stands as God." Mormonism claims to be the theocratic government of God for earth and this higher priesthood is the power by which it controls its kingdom of God on earth. Smith taught that God has always conducted the affairs of man through this priesthood. He stated, "All the prophets had the Melchizedek Priesthood and were ordained by God himself" (*Teachings*, p. 181).

The offices of the Melchizedek priesthood include elder, seventy, and high priest. Ordination to offices in this "higher priesthood" are the direct responsibility of the stake president. Bishops are responsible to recommend to the stake presidency worthy young men and prospective elders (usually from the new converts to the church) to receive the Melchizedek priesthood. To be recommended, young men must be either called on a mission, getting married in the temple, going in the service, or be at least 18 years of age.

No male member can receive a temple recommend without being at least an elder. In order to be called to the office of bishop or patriarch, a man must be a high priest. The three separate groups of the order function separately within each ward. Each has its own quorum, presidency, and meetings. The quorum presidents report separately to the stake president through an appointed representative member of the stake high council.

At the organization of the church in 1830, this priesthood of Melchizedek did not exist (although the term *Elder* was in regular use, Oliver Cowdery being called the second elder). It did not appear until a conference at the city of Kirtland, held June 3 to 6, 1831. On June 6, Joseph revealed that the "Holy Melchizedek priesthood" had been restored to Earth. He ordained several of the brethren present to the office of high priest. This new priesthood was above that which had been restored by John the Baptist (*History of the Church*, vol. 1, p. 176).

While conference attendees were not given the details of when this restoration supposedly took place, the general consensus in the church is that it occurred about a month following the arrival of John the Baptist and the Aaronic priesthood. Bruce R. McConkie states,

> In June, 1829, by divine appointment, Peter, James and John came to Joseph Smith and Oliver Cowdery and conferred upon them the Melchizedek Priesthood (*Doctrine and Covenants* 27:12-13). By the hands of Elijah and others of the prophets, also, an additional revelation of the priesthood was given, meaning that these ancient prophets came with keys and powers which authorized the use of the priesthood for additional purposes (*Doctrine and Covenants* 110:11-16; 128:17-21; *Pearl of Great Price*, Joseph Smith 2:38). This priesthood—with all its powers, parts, keys, orders, and ramifications—is now fully operative among men (*Doctrine*, p. 478).

The Biblical View

The Mormon claim to the Melchizedek priesthood fails to meet the test of both Scripture and logic. In Mormonism, no man can hold the Melchizedek priesthood without first holding the Aaronic priesthood. This was true even of Joseph Smith and Oliver Cowdery.

Yet it is certain that those great apostles of the Lord, Peter, James, and John, were clearly *not* Levites. Everything they did as recorded in the Word of God places them totally outside that dead priesthood.

Also, the true Melchizedek priesthood was always a priesthood of *one*. It existed before the law was given (Genesis 14:18) and after the law was ended (Hebrews 7:11-17). It sprang forth with the offering of the bread and wine. It reappeared only when that final offering of the broken body of Christ and His shed blood ended the penalty of the law as He became our sin offering by the sacrifice of Himself (Hebrews 9:12-14).

The final test of reason is this: Are these alleged actions of heavenly visitors consistent with biblical doctrine? Do the dead saints of old return in bodily form to pass on their authority elsewhere in the Scriptures? The answer is an unequivocal no. On that basis, the whole structure of a Mormon Melchizedek priesthood collapses.

MINISTERING ANGELS

As in so many other areas, the LDS doctrine on angels and their ministrations is partially in line with orthodoxy. Yet in many places it is seriously askew. In fact, the LDS view of the angelic nature strikes to the very core of one of the central heresies of the Mormon church, the law of eternal progression (see also *Law of Eternal Progression*).

The LDS Position

Mormons believe that angels exist and that there are good and bad angels. The good angels exist to serve God and His people, and bad angels are in rebellion against God and in league with Lucifer. In Mormonism, angels are usually invisible spirit beings who can, if needed, appear in human form in order to help people or communicate messages to them from the Lord. This is where the resemblance between LDS angelology and that of the Bible ends.

In Mormon thought, angels are on a kind of spiritual continuum between manhood and godhood. Upon their deaths, certain righteous men become angels. Later, presumably, they become gods. Mormons like to say that a man or woman is a "baby-god" or a god-in-embryo; an angel is an adolescent god; and an "adult god" is a full-fledged deity like the LDS god, Elohim.

A well-known example of this is the supposed prophet/general Moroni in the *Book of Mormon*. He was said to be a righteous, mortal man who died at the end of the *Book of Mormon* civilization (c. A.D. 421). Today it is *very* common for Mormons to refer to him as the "Angel Moroni." He allegedly appeared in angelic form to the young Joseph Smith and ultimately led him to the gold plates of the *Book of Mormon*. It is for this reason that the "Angel Moroni" is one of the most popular figures in LDS iconography. Indeed, gold-plated statues of him adorn the top spires of most LDS temples.

This same Moroni is said (by Mormons) to be the angel described in the Book of Revelation: "And I saw another angel fly in the midst of heaven, having the everlasting gospel to preach unto them that dwell on the earth, and to every nation, and kindred, and tongue, and people" (Revelation 14:6).

Naturally, this "everlasting gospel" is said to be the gospel of Mormonism, even though it is never recorded in LDS literature that Moroni "flew" anywhere or preached a gospel to anyone on the earth except Joseph Smith.

The problem here for Mormonism is that in LDS thought, to be an angel is to be part of a lesser kingdom than that to which a good Mormon aspires (see also *Degrees of Glory*). Bruce R. McConkie writes: "The practice of the ministering of angels is not limited to mortality. In eternity those in the terrestrial kingdom will be ministered to by those of the celestial, and those in the telestial by angels sent to them from the terrestrial world" (*Doctrine and Covenants* 76:86-88) (*Doctrine*, p. 504).

Therefore, to be a "ministering angel" is actually to fail in one's attempt to achieve the eternal increase of seed in the glory of the celestial kingdom. It is therefore odd that so mighty a religious leader as Moroni should still be a mere angel after being dead for more than 1000 years. If *he* could not make it to godhood, what hope is there for the typical Mormon?

Mormons also believe that they can command angels to come and minister unto them. They believe this is not only their privilege (through the power of the priesthood), but it is even a litmus test for the truth of the LDS gospel. McConkie mentions this:

> Indeed, from Adam to the present moment, whenever men have had sufficient faith, angels have ministered unto them. So invarying [sic] is this principle that it stands forth as the conclusive test of the divinity of any organization on earth. If angels minister to a people, they are the Lord's people, and his kingdom is with them. If angels do not minister unto them, they are not the Lord's people, and his kingdom is not with them (Moroni 7:27-38).

> Judged by this standard it is not difficult to find which of all the churches is right and which one men should join if they have a truth-inspired desire to gain eternal salvation. As is well known, angels have and do minister to faithful members of The Church of Jesus Christ of Latter-day Saints [*Doctrine*, pp. 503-04].

Stories abound in popular LDS literature and folklore of angelic visitations and assistance. There are tales of LDS people getting help with flat tires from one of the "Three Nephites" (see

3 Nephi 28:5-9), three supposed disciples of Christ in the New World mentioned in the *Book of Mormon* who are said to remain on the earth as translated beings until Jesus comes again. There are other accounts of angels helping people find genealogical data so that their ancestral work can get done. We do not suggest that the people who tell such stories are lying. They may very well be describing genuine experiences they have had with the spirit realm— but not with heaven's representatives.

The Biblical View

All this mystical lore fails to heed the Bible's warning that Satan can appear as an angel of light (see also *Angel of Light*) to deceive those who do not know the truth of God's Word or measure all things by it (see 2 Corinthians 11:13-15). The presence of alleged angelic ministrations in a church says nothing about that church's truth—unless its doctrine lines up with the Word of God. Indeed, the numerous incongruities which exist within the angelology of Mormonism serve only to expose the falsity of its belief system.

The Bible clearly presents angels as created beings, not human. They are beneath Jesus Christ and are an entirely different species from the Godhead (Hebrews 1:4-8,14). In Colossians 1, for example, we read:

> In whom [Jesus] we have redemption through his blood, even the forgiveness of sins: who is the image of the invisible God, the firstborn of every creature: For by him were all things created, that are in heaven, and that are in earth, visible and invisible, whether they be thrones, or dominions, or principalities, or powers: all things were created by him, and for him: And he is before all things, and by him all things consist (Colossians 1:14-17).

Angels are real. They heralded the birth of Christ, they ministered to Him in the desert and in the Garden of Gethsemane. They came to Abraham in human form and ministered to Daniel and to Elijah, and in the New Testament to Paul and Peter.

But as it has done to every other facet of orthodox theology, Mormonism has skewed its understanding of ministering angels. It has "changed the truth of God into a lie, and worshipped and served the creature more than the Creator, who is blessed for ever. Amen" (Romans 1:25).

MONEY DIGGING

(See also *Peep Stones.*)

The phrase *money digging* as used here is a reference to a late eighteenth- and early nineteenth-century practice of seeking buried treasure through some sort of occult power. The period during and following the American Revolution was a time filled with tales of truth and (more frequently) imagination about pirates and hidden treasures. Historically, the heyday of the pirates was just coming to an end.

There were many stories—some which persist to this day—about famous and fabulously wealthy pirates who came ashore on the eastern seaboard of the American colonies to bury huge hoards of gold. It was thought that the area where Joseph Smith was raised was exceptionally rich in buried treasure.

Smith was born into a family obsessed with the occult, even to the point of drawing magic circles (D. Michael Quinn, *Early Mormonism and the Magic World View* [Salt Lake City: Signature Books, 1987], p. 53). His father, Joseph Smith, Sr., was involved in an occult band of "rodsmen" (men who used divining rods) known as "The Wood Scrape," named after their founder, Nathaniel Wood (ibid., p. 31ff). Essentially they were water witches or dowsers, except they often looked for treasure instead of water.

Young Joseph followed in the footsteps of his father, but with a different occult tool. Instead of a rod, he used a rock—a "peep stone" or "seer stone." He would place his magic stone in his hat to keep out extraneous light. Then he would bury his face in the hat and claim to see images in the rock. The peep stone allegedly would show him where buried treasure was to be found.

Eventually, Smith's reputation grew to the place where gullible people in the community were willing to pay him good money to find buried treasure on their farmland in the hopes of striking it rich.

Proof emerged in the 1970s that Smith's venture into "professional" money digging got him into legal trouble. He was convicted of being a "glass-looker and a disorderly person." A Christian researcher into LDS history, the Reverend Wesley Walters, found documents detailing that conviction in the basement of the old courthouse of Bainbridge County (Wesley P. Walters, sworn affidavit, October 28, 1971).

Joseph Smith used that same method of divination in his supposed prophetic calling. He used a peep stone to help him "translate" the *Book of Mormon*. In fact, there is strong evidence that Smith was indulging in occult practices right up to the time of his death at the Carthage jail (see also *Talisman, Jupiter*).

The Biblical View

The Lord forbids soothsaying or divination, which is what money digging essentially is (see Deuteronomy 18:10; 2 Kings 17:17; 2 Kings 21:6; Isaiah 8:19,20; 47:9; Malachi 3:5; Revelation 18:23; 21:8). The question must be asked, How could someone who was supposedly being groomed by visits from God the Father, God the Son, and other heavenly messengers to restore the pristine gospel of Jesus Christ to the Earth, turn around and commit such serious sins? The Old Testament penalty for what Joseph Smith spent much of his life doing was immediate death by stoning.

This would certainly seem to cast doubt on the truth of Smith's prophetic "calling," especially since the Mormon church today soundly condemns occultism and divination.

NAUVOO HOUSE

The Nauvoo House is of interest because it is the subject of a prophecy in *Doctrine and Covenants*. The prophecy, given in 1841 by Joseph Smith, is unambiguous and straightforward, and provides an easy way of determining whether Smith was a true prophet of God:

> [56]*And now I* [the Lord] *say unto you, as pertaining to my boarding house* which I have commanded you to build for the boarding of strangers, let it be built unto my name, and let my name be named upon it, and *let my servant Joseph and his house have place therein, from generation to generation.*

> [57]For this anointing have I put upon his head, that his blessing shall also be put upon the head of his posterity after him.

> [58]And as I said unto Abraham concerning the kindreds of the earth, even so I say unto my servant Joseph: In thee and in thy seed shall the kindred of the earth be blessed.

> [59]Therefore, *let my servant Joseph and his seed after him have place in that house, from generation to generation, forever and ever, saith the Lord.*

> [60]*And let the name of that house be called Nauvoo House;* and let it be a delightful habitation for man, and a resting-place for the weary traveler, that he may contemplate the glory of Zion, and the glory of this, the corner-stone thereof (*Doctrine and Covenants* 124:56-60, emphasis added).

The problem with this prophecy, of course, is that it missed by the proverbial country mile. Nauvoo House exists today in Nauvoo, Illinois, the city where Joseph Smith made his "last stand" in creating a Mormon utopia before he was murdered.

Nauvoo House did not remain in the Smith family then (in the 1840s) and it is not owned by its descendants today. The prophecy is simply false, as can easily be verified by any fair-minded Mormon.

Of course, the Bible tells us that even one false prophecy spoken by a supposed prophet of God is enough to disqualify that person forever from being considered a true prophet (Deuteronomy 18:20-22), since God does not make mistakes (see also *Smith: Was Joseph a False Prophet?*). Joseph made plenty of mistakes, however, and so cannot possibly be a prophet of God.

NEGROES: Mormons and the Blacks

Blacks were not allowed to hold the LDS priesthood until 1978 because Mormon doctrine claimed that people born with black skins were "less valiant" in their preexistence support of Jesus in a great battle against Lucifer.

The LDS Position

Mormons believe we all existed prior to birth in a preexistent spirit world with our Heavenly Father (and mothers), and that one-third of the spirits there rebelled against God with Lucifer and became demons. Another third of the spirit beings allegedly fought valiantly with Jesus and are rewarded with white skins. The final third, although they sided with Jesus in that great battle, are punished for their lack of zeal by being born with black skin.

Mormons believe that black skin is the mark of the curse of Cain, and therefore it was always taught that blacks were accursed and would never hold the priesthood or be allowed in the temple. Mormon doctrine teaches that the real curse is the denial of the priesthood in this life and the mark of black skin is to "tell them apart" from those without the curse.

The curse was lifted in 1978, even though the official line had been that it wouldn't be lifted until every white person had the Mormon priesthood. It seems to have been lifted primarily because of social pressure and because the LDS church was in danger of losing its Internal Revenue Service nonprofit status due to its racist policies. Of course, the Mormons say the curse was lifted by revelation—even though the decree contradicted earlier "revelations."

About blacks and the war in heaven, LDS prophet and president Joseph Fielding Smith wrote in *Doctrines of Salvation*, vol. 1, pp. 66-67:

> There is a reason why one man is born black and with other disadvantages, while another is born white with great advantages. The reason is that we once had an estate before we came here, and were obedient, more or less, to the laws that were given us there. Those who were faithful in all things there received greater blessings here, and those who were not faithful received less. . . . There were no neutrals in the war in heaven. All took sides either with Christ or with Satan. Every man had his agency there, and men receive rewards here based upon their actions there, just as they will receive rewards hereafter for deeds done in the body. The Negro, evidently, is receiving the reward he merits.

That seems pretty clear. Mormons taught that blacks were being punished for something they did in the preexistence. This teaching is racist doctrine to the core, and the 1978 rescission doesn't change that ugly fact one bit.

In the same *Church News* that heralded the release of the blacks from the curse, there was an article warning the faithful to avoid mixed marriages.

The LDS church seems able to sweep some of the most horrific things under the carpet of "progressive revelation." It acts as though its ungodly doctrine against blacks never existed. When pushed to the wall with an embarrassing quote from one of their leaders, Mormons tend to smile and say, "Well, that's what God had to say in the matter, not us. We love the negro people and always have." Yet, look at what some of the LDS leaders have said under the cover of divine leadership. Joseph Smith said, "Had I anything to do with the negro, I would confine them by strict law to their own species, and put them on a national equalization" (*History*, vol. 5, pp. 218-19).

Brigham Young, the LDS second prophet, said that blacks are: "uncouth, uncomely, disagreeable and low in their habits, wild and seemingly without the blessings of the intelligence that is generally bestowed upon mankind" (Brigham Young, *Journal of Discourses* 7:290).

John Taylor, the third prophet of the LDS church said, "After the flood we are told that the curse that had been pronounced upon Cain was continued through Ham's wife, as he had married a wife of that seed. And why did it pass through the flood? Because it was necessary that the devil should have a representation upon the earth as well as God" (*Journal of Discourses* 23:336).

Finally, let Bruce R. McConkie speak:

> The negroes are not equal with other races where the receipt of certain spiritual blessings are concerned, particularly the priesthood and the temple blessings that flow therefrom, but this inequity is not of man's origin. It is the Lord's doing, based upon His eternal laws of justice, and grows out of the lack of spiritual valiance of those concerned in their first estate (*Doctrine*, original 1966 edition, p. 528).

It is interesting to note that this eternal law of God has apparently been violated and modified in McConkie's latest release. In a recent edition, still showing only the 1966 copyright and no new revision date, all the racist statements have been eliminated. A black investigator reading McConkie's work today would never suspect the vicious, racist things that were once within those pages and in the theocratic beliefs of the LDS people.

The Biblical View

While there are major social and cultural problems to this day over interracial marriage and there are denominations which believe that interracial marriage is not of God, there is little (if any) evidence that the old covenant restrictions on marriage between the races was carried over into the new covenant. And there is absolutely no hint that any one race is any more or less worthy of the gospel than any other. We are all in the same boat—condemned sinners offered the gift of eternal life through faith in the risen Christ.

Christ, in fact, *commanded* the apostles to take the gospel "unto the uttermost part of the earth" (Acts 1:8)—which would certainly include Africa. If we are indeed all part of one body—Jesus' body, which is the fulness of Him that filleth all in all (Ephesians 1:23; Romans 12:5; Colossians 2:19)—then isn't it odd that a black or yellow believer would be forbidden to marry a white believer?

We are no longer under law, but under grace. If you wish to adhere to the old covenant, remember that Paul discouraged us from it. Most Christians do not try to keep the dietary laws of the old covenant; they make no effort to avoid pork and shellfish. They trim the corners of their beards and wear clothing of more than one fiber, and seem to have no problem with growing hybrid plants or crops.

Why? Because all of these things were nailed to the cross with Christ (Colossians 2:14). Therefore, in the absence of any statement to the contrary in the New Testament, we see no reason to think that interracial marriage is any different from all the other old covenant laws which were done away with in the New Testament. The only mixed marriage Paul seems to forbid is between a believer and a nonbeliever (1 Corinthians 7). It is upon grace that we base our theology, and not upon racist Mormon myths.

NEW AND EVERLASTING COVENANT

The new and everlasting covenant also has been referred to as the law of the priesthood, celestial marriage, plural marriage, and polygamy. Today, it is fair to say that, to the average LDS member, the breadth of Mormonism is encompassed by the new and everlasting covenant, relegating celestial or plural marriage to what McConkie calls just one of a number of such covenants within the big one (*Doctrine*, p. 530).

In this section we will look at the new and everlasting covenant from the perspective of the marriage covenant. In the section "Eternal Lives" we discussed the LDS view of continued procreation in the eternal, exalted state, when fully righteous LDS men and women supposedly become gods and goddesses. In that section, we showed the LDS doctrine of eternal increase or continuation of seed for those who obtain the highest degree of glory, celestial exaltation. But there are some conditions that must be met.

In *Doctrine and Covenants* 131, we read:

> In the celestial glory there are three heavens or degrees; and in order to obtain the highest, a man must enter into this order of the priesthood [meaning the new and everlasting covenant of marriage]; and if he does not, he cannot obtain it. He may

enter into the other, but that is the end of his kingdom; he cannot have an increase (vv. 1-4).

In *Doctrine and Covenants* 132, that covenant is not only defined, but serious consequences are attached to disobedience:

> For behold, I reveal unto you a new and an everlasting covenant; and if ye abide not that covenant, then are ye damned; for no one can reject this covenant and be permitted to enter into my glory. For all who will have a blessing at my hands shall abide the law which was appointed for that blessing, and the conditions thereof, as were instituted from before the foundation of the world. And as pertaining to the new and everlasting covenant, it was instituted for the fulness of my glory; and he that receiveth a fulness thereof must and shall abide the law, or he shall be damned, saith the Lord God (vv. 4-6).

This involves some crossover in terms. This order of the priesthood cannot be found anywhere else in LDS standard works in the context given in section 131 [note: it does appear in *Doctrine and Covenants* 94:6 in reference to a building for use in ministry of the presidency], but the reference made in section 131 is to "the new and everlasting covenant of marriage" which is clearly defined on the very next page in section 132. It is linked in a reference to the "law of the Priesthood." Again, severe penalties apply for failure to adhere to this special covenant, and this section is still an active portion of LDS scripture as this book goes to press:

> And again, as pertaining to the law of the priesthood: if any man espouse a virgin, and desire to espouse another, and the first give her consent, and if he espouse the second, and they are virgins, and have vowed to no other man, then is he justified; he cannot commit adultery for they are given unto him; for he cannot commit adultery with that that belongeth unto him and to no one else.
>
> And if he have ten virgins given unto him by this law, he cannot commit adultery, for they belong to him, and they are given unto him; therefore is he justified.
>
> But if one or either of the ten virgins, after she is espoused, shall be with another man, she has committed adultery, and shall be destroyed; for they are given unto him to multiply and replenish the earth, according to my commandment, and to fulfil

the promise which was given by my Father before the foundation of the world, and for their exaltation in the eternal worlds, that they may bear the souls of men; for herein is the work of my Father continued, that he may be glorified (vv. 61-63).

There can be no question but that the new and everlasting covenant [of marriage] pertains to plural wives, or polygamy. This was exactly as it was interpreted and practiced until the *Manifesto* which the president of the church, Wilford Woodruff, brought before the October 6, 1890, General Conference. It canceled polygamy or plural marriage as an official practice of the church.

The church was under pressure from the U.S. government to abandon this practice if Utah was to join with the rest of the nation and attain statehood. The LDS church bowed to the pressure as it became apparent that the issue would not go away. The actual text of the *Manifesto* is as follows:

To Whom It May Concern:

Press dispatches having been sent for political purposes, from Salt Lake City, which have been widely published, to the effect that the Utah Commission, in their recent report to the Secretary of the Interior, allege that plural marriages are still being solemnized and that forty or more such marriages have been contracted in Utah since last June or during the past year, also that in public discourses the leaders of the Church have taught, encouraged and urged the continuance of the practice of polygamy.

I, therefore, as President of the Church of Jesus Christ of Latter-day Saints, do hereby, in the most solemn manner, declare that these charges are false. We are not teaching polygamy or plural marriage, nor permitting any person to enter into its practice, and I deny that either forty or any other number of plural marriages have during that period been solemnized in our Temples or in any other place in the Territory.

One case has been reported, in which the parties allege that the marriage was performed in the Endowment House, in Salt Lake City, in the Spring of 1889, but I have not been able to learn who performed the ceremony; whatever was done in this matter was without my knowledge. In consequence of this alleged occurrence the Endowment House was, by my instructions, taken down without delay.

295

Inasmuch as laws have been enacted by Congress forbidding plural marriages, which laws have been pronounced constitutional by the court of last resort, I hereby declare my intention to submit to those laws, and to use my influence with the members of the Church over which I preside to have them do likewise.

There is nothing in my teachings to the Church or in those of my associates, during the time specified, which can be reasonably construed to inculcate or encourage polygamy; and when any Elder of the Church has used language which appeared to convey any such teaching, he has been promptly reproved. And I now publicly declare that my advice to the Latter-day Saints is to refrain from contracting any marriage forbidden by the law of the land.

Wilford Woodruff
President of the Church of Jesus Christ of Latter-day Saints

President Lorenzo Snow offered the following:

I move that, recognizing Wilford Woodruff as the President of the Church of Jesus Christ of Latter-day Saints, and the only man on the earth at the present time who holds the keys of the sealing ordinances, we consider him fully authorized by virtue of his position to issue the Manifesto which has been read in our hearing, and which is dated September 24th, 1890, and that as a Church in General Conference assembled, we accept his declaration concerning plural marriages as authoritative and binding.

The vote to sustain the foregoing motion was unanimous.

Salt Lake City, Utah, October 6, 1890

Today, orthodox Mormons await their exaltation with the expectation that this divine principle will be the regular order of eternal life. Mormon fundamentalists do not wait for that day, believing that the orthodox Mormon church broke an eternal covenant given by God and is in apostasy. They openly practice "the principle."

LDS apologists often respond to our comments about the lot of LDS plural wives in early Mormondom with the reminder that their Scripture clearly states that for the man to take other wives, "the first [must] give her consent" (*Doctrine and Covenants* 132:61). Yet one must wonder how many plural wives were willing to take the consequences of denial as promised three verses away:

296

And again, verily, verily, I say unto you, if any man have a wife, who holds the keys of this power, and he teaches unto her the law of my priesthood, as pertaining to these things, then shall she believe and administer unto him, or she shall be destroyed, saith the Lord your God; for I will destroy her; for I will magnify my name upon all those who receive and abide in my law (v. 64).

NEW NAME

The phrase *New Name* in Mormonism has a couple of meanings. Of course, the scriptural basis in the Bible for the term is found in Isaiah and Revelation:

And the Gentiles shall see thy righteousness, and all kings thy glory: and thou shalt be called by a new name, which the mouth of the LORD shall name (Isaiah 62:2).

He that hath an ear, let him hear what the Spirit saith unto the churches; To him that overcometh will I give to eat of the hidden manna, and will give him a white stone, and in the stone a new name written, which no man knoweth saving he that receiveth it (Revelation 2:17).

Him that overcometh will I make a pillar in the temple of my God, and he shall go no more out: and I will write upon him the name of my God, and the name of the city of my God, which is new Jerusalem, which cometh down out of heaven from my God: and I will write upon him my new name (Revelation 3:12).

The first verse is the Lord's promise to the people of Israel. This is not a problem for Mormons, of course, because they believe that *they* are the true Israel. The second two verses are more specifically directed to the Christian church, but of course Mormons believe they are the only true Christian church.

Mormons claim that their very title, The Church of Jesus Christ of Latter-day Saints, is the *actual* new name referenced in the Bible texts [*Doctrine*, p. 534]. Obviously, the last part of the name, "Latter-day," could not be used until recent centuries; so this makes it a new name. Previously, they claim, it was simply called the Church of Jesus Christ.

There is, however, a more mysterious and oblique reference to a new name in LDS scripture which bears closer examination. In *Doctrine and Covenants* 130:8-11, we read:

⁸The place where God resides is a great Urim and Thummim.

⁹This earth, in its sanctified and immortal state, will be made like unto crystal and will be a Urim and Thummim to the inhabitants who dwell thereon, whereby all things pertaining to an inferior kingdom, or all kingdoms of a lower order, will be manifest to those who dwell on it; and this earth will be Christ's.

¹⁰Then the white stone mentioned in Revelation 2:17, will become a Urim and Thummim to each individual who receives one, whereby things pertaining to a higher order of kingdoms will be made known;

¹¹*And a white stone is given to each of those who come into the celestial kingdom, whereon is a new name written,* which no man knoweth save he that receiveth it. *The new name is the key word* [emphasis added].

This passage, and especially the last verse, refers to part of the secret temple ritual (see also *Endowments*). At the conclusion of what is called the initiatory work, new temple Mormons are clothed with a temple garment (see *Temple Garments*) and given a secret, new name.

They are instructed *never to reveal this name to anyone, at any time,* except at a certain place within the confines of the temple endowment ritual which would occur later in the day (Sackett, p. 20).

The name is usually some comparatively mundane biblical name like "Joseph" or "Mary." What the person is not told is that everyone of the same gender who took out their own endowment in that temple on that day is given the same name. Thus there are dozens of people emerging from the temple at the end of the day with the same highly secret "new name."

A significant exception to the above-mentioned secrecy is for married women. Their husbands are given their name; they themselves are forbidden to know the name. This is partially because it is believed that on the morning of the first resurrection, the Lord Jesus Christ will call forth all worthy male temple Mormons out of their graves by their new name. Then these temple Mormons will call their wives out of their graves by their new names.

It is widely presumed (but never actually articulated) that if the husband did not do this, *the wife would remain in the grave.* Some LDS husbands will actually jokingly (or not so jokingly) chastise their wives and say, "Honey, if you burn the pot roast one more time, I'm going to leave you in the grave on the morning of the first resurrection." No wonder LDS women feel so spiritually oppressed!

When one understands the heavy occult element of the temple endowment, this bizarre bit of sexism begins to make sense. It is a time-honored occult principle that knowing someone's name gives you power over them. When people are initiated into a mystery cult, both today and in ancient times, they are given a secret name which they must never reveal to anyone. This secrecy protects the initiate's new status and power (Sir James Frazer, *The New Golden Bough*, ed. by Dr. Theodore Gaster, Criterion Books, 1959, p. 87; and *Man, Myth and Magic*, ed. by Richard Cavendish, London, 1972, pp. 1940-41). Thus, the fact that the Mormon husband knows the wife's name but she does not know his gives him a power edge, a "one up" in the marriage relationship.

The final point which needs to be explained about the new name of the temple rite is the statement in *Doctrine and Covenants* 130:11: "The new name is the key word." Once temple Mormons are given their new name, they progress through the labyrinth of the endowment ritual. At one point, they are told that their new name is the name of the "First Token of the Aaronic Priesthood" (Sackett, p. 32). It is a kind of secret password by which they are supposedly permitted to enter into the higher degrees of glory. It is therefore incumbent upon them to remember the name.

Interestingly enough, if they do forget it (after leaving the temple that day), there is an extremely involved process through which they must go to retrieve the new name. They must contact the temple from which they took out their original endowment and then in a set of circumstances worthy of a Tom Clancy novel, the temple Mormon's new name is sent to him in a cipher form which only the highest local officials of the church have the key to decode. All of this, of course, is designed to foster the idea (completely false) that everyone's new name is unique. Actually, there are many thousands of temple Mormons with the same new names.

This entire process certainly does not fit with the biblical picture mentioned above. Revelation 2:17 says that the new name is one "which no man knoweth saving he that receiveth it." This quite evidently cannot be the new name given in the LDS temple, for not only does the temple patron know it, but every temple worker present that day knows it and so does the temple president. A woman's husband also knows it. But the Bible is explicit. "No man" means just that—no human being can know the name which we are to be given. It is given by the Lord, and Him alone.

Whether the new name is something which Christians receive at the moment of their salvation or only later in heaven is something about which Bible students disagree, but the key thing to remember is that the name must be known only to the Christian and to God. This clearly disqualifies the LDS procedure from start to finish. The Mormon rite is simply an occult, initiatory practice and has nothing of the Lord in it.

OATH AND COVENANT OF THE PRIESTHOOD

The LDS Position

The LDS church teaches that every man ordained to the "Holy Melchizedek Priesthood" is raised up with the same oath from God that made the priesthood of Christ an eternal one. "The Lord sware and will not repent, Thou art a priest for ever after the order of Melchizedek" (Hebrews 7:21).

Joseph Smith said, "The power of the Melchizedek Priesthood is to have the power of 'endless lives'; for the everlasting covenant cannot be broken" (*Teachings*, p. 322).

He further claimed that those called to this higher priesthood would not only have the same eternal glory and power as God, but would, in fact, be gods themselves:

> They are they into whose hands the Father has given all things. They are they who are priests and kings, who have received of his fulness, and of his glory; and are priests of the Most High, after the order of Melchizedek, which was after the order of Enoch, which was after the order of the Only Begotten Son. Wherefore, as it is written, they are gods, even the sons of God—Wherefore all things are theirs (*Doctrine and Covenants* 76:55-59).
>
> Therefore, all those who receive the priesthood, receive this oath and covenant of my Father, which he cannot break, neither can it be moved (*Doctrine and Covenants* 84:40).

The Biblical View

One can only wonder where the theologians of Mormonism are hiding. This is the same blatant lie of Satan recorded in the third chapter of Genesis that first put mankind in bondage to sin. It is an encouragement to break one of God's commandments and become as gods. It is the same vain self-glory that hurled Lucifer from the heavens to the pit:

> How art thou fallen from heaven, O Lucifer, son of the morning! how art thou cut down to the ground, which did weaken the nations! For thou hast said in thine heart, I will ascend into heaven, I will exalt my throne above the stars of God: I will sit also upon the mount of the congregation, in the sides of the north: I will ascend above the heights of the clouds; I will be like the most High. Yet thou shalt be brought down to hell, to the sides of the pit (Isaiah 14:12-15).

Mormons claim that the God of the universe has sworn an eternal oath placing hundreds of thousands of Mormon men to an equal position of power and authority with His only-begotten Son. They further claim that this power shall be as God's. This is blasphemy of the first order, as the Bible makes clear.

> And when all things shall be subdued unto him, then shall the Son also himself be subject unto him that put all things under him, that God may be all in all (1 Corinthians 15:28).
>
> And what is the exceeding greatness of his power to usward who believe, according to the working of his mighty power, which he wrought in Christ, when he raised him from the dead, and set him at his own right hand in the heavenly places, far above all principality, and power, and might, and dominion, and every name that is named, not only in this world, but also in that which is to come: and hath put all things under his feet, and gave him to be the head over all things to the church (Ephesians 1:19-22).
>
> That at the name of Jesus every knee should bow, of things in heaven, and things in earth, and things under the earth; and that every tongue should confess that Jesus Christ is Lord, to the glory of God the Father (Philippians 2:10,11).

The oath of God was spoken to One without sin. It was Jesus who is our surety of a better covenant, not the LDS order of

Melchizedek. It is Jesus who is able to save to the uttermost, not the Mormons. It is Jesus who is "holy, harmless, undefiled, separate from sinners and made higher than the heavens" (see Hebrews 7:17-28).

What man who breathes would dare claim that same honor before our holy and mighty God?

OATH OF VENGEANCE

The LDS Position

During the LDS temple ritual, certain oaths and covenants are made before God that are said to be both solemn and eternal. One such oath that was part of the ritual until approximately the early 1930s was called the oath of vengeance, which was sworn against the United States of America in retribution for the deaths of Joseph and Hyrum Smith: "You and each of you do solemnly promise and vow that you will pray, and never cease to importune high heaven to *avenge the blood of the prophets on this nation*, and that you will teach this to your children and your children's children unto the third and fourth generation."

While this oath was removed as Mormonism moved into the mainstream of American society, one must remember that the oath was supposedly an eternally binding one, given in the holiest of places, under the power of their eternal Melchizedek priesthood.

Almost every member of the LDS First Presidency, from Brigham Young to Howard Hunter, has been of an age to have taken that oath when they "took out their own endowments" in the LDS temple. They were bound under those oaths.

Did they officially renounce this oath? Or were they still under its power? If they did *not* renounce it, how could they presume to lead millions of American citizens under Article 12 of the LDS Articles of Faith ("We believe in being subject to kings, presidents, rulers and magistrates, in obeying, honoring and sustaining the law") and still be bound to call upon heaven to curse our nation?

If they did renounce it, how could they justify doing so after having sworn such a bitter, *eternal* oath in their sacred temple before their god? This surely places an untenable burden upon all the LDS people who have gone through the temple and sworn oaths of total obedience to these leaders. What of the Mormons who hold office in our government or serve in the military? There is an obvious conflict of interest between their oaths of office and their higher loyalty to a group of men who are sworn to seek vengeance against this great nation.

Bruce R. McConkie states, "While the oaths of the saints have furthered righteous purposes, similar swearing by the wicked has led to great evil" (*Doctrine*, p. 538).

The Biblical View

It would appear that McConkie has his cables crossed. In the Bible, Jesus Himself said, "Again, ye have heard that it hath been said by them of old time, Thou shalt not forswear thyself, but shalt perform unto the Lord thine oaths: but I say unto you, swear not at all; neither by heaven; for it is God's throne: nor by the earth for it is his footstool" (Matthew 5:33-35).

That should be plain enough, yet in its oath-taking, Mormonism has denied His admonition and reverted to precisely that which He has told us *not* to do.

The biblical gospel also has a different way of dealing with one's enemies. Christ said, "I say unto you which hear, Love your enemies, do good to them which hate you, bless them that curse you and pray for them which despitefully use you" (Luke 6:27,28).

Paul instructed the church to "bless them which persecute you: bless, and curse not" (Romans 12:14).

We need to remember the times during which the oath was instituted. The early Mormons thought the government had been harassing them all along the way. Smith had been killed. The Saints had fled to the Rockies where they hoped to live in their own land of Deseret, outside the control of the U.S. government. Troops had been sent in to break the back of the political power of Brigham Young and his followers. They were a people who were not happy and they blamed much of their misfortunes on the government.

They also never had intended that any of the secret oaths within the temple would ever see the light of day. Of course, the secret oath came out, and in a new and happier political world the Mormons just removed the embarrassing oath from its ritual, just as it has recently changed much of its temple ritual.

The Word of God stands true and unbending. It is the word of pretenders that changes with each breeze.

OBEDIENCE, LAW OF

The "Law of Obedience" is the first of five "laws" or "covenants" to which temple Mormons swear solemn allegiance in the endowment ceremony (see also *Endowments*). This law is given during the Garden of Eden sequence of the endowment rite to the characters of Adam and Eve right after their transgression.

In the ritual, the LDS god Elohim has just cast out Lucifer because he tempted Adam and Eve into eating the forbidden fruit (Sackett, p. 29). The implication is that because the pair were not able to obey the commandment the Lord gave them, he is giving them a different kind of law to obey. Elohim then explains to Adam:

> Inasmuch as Eve was the first to eat of the forbidden fruit, if she will covenant that from this time forth she will obey your law in the Lord, and will harken unto your counsel as you harken unto mine, and if you will covenant that from this time forth you will obey the Law of Obedience and Sacrifice, and we [the Godhead] will provide a Savior for you, whereby you may come back into our presence and with us partake of eternal life and exaltation (Sackett, ibid.).

Eve then promises, "Adam, I now covenant to obey your law as you obey our Father." Adam, in turn, promises, "Elohim, I now covenant with you that from this time forth I will obey your law and keep your commandments."

Then a "witness couple" comes forward from the audience of patrons. They are a man and wife who have been selected to exemplify all the other patrons who remain in their seats but still must stand and take the oaths. This is what the men and women are asked to promise:

Sisters: You and each of you solemnly covenant and promise before God, angels and these witnesses at this altar that you will each observe and keep the law of your husband, and abide by his council in righteousness.
Brethren: You and each of you solemnly covenant and promise before God, angels and these witnesses at this altar that you will obey the law of God and keep His commandments (Sackett, p. 30).

305

As with other laws covenanted to within the temple, the breaking of this covenant places the temple Mormon under the power of Lucifer (Sackett, p. 38). Naturally, since all mankind sins (Romans 3:23), this means that all temple Mormons eventually fall under an extremely legalistic curse. The character of Lucifer actually proclaims just this destiny toward the end of the endowment: "I have a word to say concerning these people [temple patrons]. If they do not walk up to every covenant they make at these altars in this temple this day, they will be in my power" (ibid.).

It is evident that any but the most arrogant of Mormons would feel a bit intimidated by that pronouncement. It thrusts them firmly out from under the umbrella of the biblical God's grace and under a legalistic system worse than that of the Pharisees.

Feminists within and without the Mormon church had voiced serious objections to the way in which the wife's part of this covenant was phrased. Essentially, it made the husband stand in the place of God, and his wife had to swear to obey him as [her] God. This caused a great many minor (and some major) abuses within LDS temple marriages. Because a key point of LDS authority is the "patriarchal order," women are forced to seek access to God solely through male figures, either their husbands (if married) or through priesthood leaders.

Women are not allowed to hold the priesthood, and thus they are not allowed to officiate in any meetings, give blessings, baptize, or distribute the sacrament. In spiritual matters, all they are allowed to do is offer prayers and "bear their testimony" (see *Fast and Testimony Meetings*).

LDS husbands who are of an authoritarian temperament can invoke the patriarchal order and through this Law of Obedience virtually enslave the wife, since he is virtually her only access to the blessings of the priesthood. Cases of wife abuse in Utah are significantly higher than normal, and this grim statistic has not escaped the notice of feminist critics of the church.

It must be noted that, along with numerous other changes which were made (without explanation), the content of the covenant for wives was changed in April 1990. Evidently in response to feminist pressure, the equating of the husband with the Lord was removed from the text and a more lenient text was substituted (see also *Temple, Changes in the Ritual*). Still, entire generations of temple marriages are yet in existence which are bound by the "old"

Law of Obedience—an interesting double standard. It makes for a combination of legalism and sexual oppression which is unhealthy in the emotional realm and damnable in the spiritual realm.

OCCULT

The term *occult* is a broad designation for various practices forbidden by the Lord in the Bible. An older, less polite term for *occultism* is *witchcraft*. The *Random House Dictionary of the English Language* defines the occult thus: "1. of or pertaining to magic, astrology, or any system claiming use or knowledge of secret or supernatural powers or agencies. 2. beyond the range of ordinary knowledge or understanding; mysterious. 3. secret; disclosed or communicated only to the initiate (1983, p. 1339).

Occult practices would include, but not necessarily be limited to:

Forms of divination (fortune telling) such as:

1. *Astrology*: foretelling one's future or personality composition through the position of the stars at birth.
2. *Cheiromancy*: palm-reading.
3. *Clairaudience*: hearing things inaudible to normal hearing.
4. *Clairvoyance*: seeing things far away or invisible to normal sight.
5. *Crystallomancy*: crystal ball gazing.
6. *Dowsing* (water witching): finding things with a divining rod.
7. *Geomancy*: telling the future by dots on paper or particles of earth.
8. *Lithomancy*: telling the future by looking at stones.
9. *Necromancy*: communicating with the spirits of the dead, or with corpses to learn unknown or future events.
10. *Oneiromancy*: telling the future or unknown events by dreams.
11. *Phrenology*: foretelling one's future or personality composition through the position of bumps on the head.
12. *Rhabdomancy*: finding objects or unknown information with a wand or divining rod.
13. *Scrying*: using a crystal or peep stone to see the unknown or future events.

Witchcraft or Magic: the use of spells, incantations, or rites, often within a magic circle and/or accompanied by blood sacrifice, to create changes in the environment or future of the person. It can also include calling out to other gods.

Spiritism: holding seances or other religious services in an attempt to communicate with departed loved ones, either for comfort or to gain information.

Talismanic magick: the investiture of power in certain inanimate objects so that the power can later be tapped. These objects are then worn or carried to give magical virtue, power, or good fortune. They may also be believed to give the bearer occult power over the minds or actions of others. A well-known example would be the rabbit's foot.

Invocation or Evocation: actually a major subdivision of magic. Invocation (also called *Theurgy*) is the calling upon of higher-than-human beings (angels, archangels, or gods) to request them to do your bidding. Evocation is the summoning up of demons or devils to try and force them to do your bidding.

Lycanthropy: also called shape-shifting. This is the supposed magical practice of turning animals into people or people into animals. The best known example is the werewolf.

The astute observer will notice that two out of the three dictionary definitions given above apply to the Mormon church, either historically or currently. This is not to say that official LDS teaching condones the open practice of occultism in any of its forms. Late LDS apostle Bruce R. McConkie writes, "Occultism has reference to the hidden and mysterious powers subject to the control of those who engage in divination, alchemy, astrology, sorcery, and magic. Practice of occultism in any form is contrary to revealed truth and should be avoided" (*Doctrine*, p. 542).

This puts the LDS church in the unenviable position of condemning practices in which many of its founding members, especially Joseph Smith, were engaged.

As has been amply shown by both non-LDS and LDS researchers, Joseph Smith was involved heavily in the following occult practices:

1. *Astrology*—see Quinn, pp. 59-63

2. *Necromancy*—communication with the dead Moroni, for example (ibid., p. 118)

3. *Casting of ceremonial magic circles* complete with blood sacrifice of animals—ibid., p. 53

4. *Scrying or crystallomancy*—Quinn, p. 41; see *Peep Stones; Money Digging*

5. *Talismanic magic*—the use of specially made coins or parchments which supposedly have intrinsic magical virtue for protection or to acquire wealth, love, or power—ibid., pp. 69, 79; see *Talisman, Jupiter*

6. *Demonic conjuration of spirits*—ibid. pp. 122-28

7. *Transformation* (shape-shifting or lycanthropy) and *Theurgy*—using magic to supposedly communicate with divine beings—ibid., p. 133

8. Involvement in the highly occult fraternity, *Freemasonry*—see *Smith: Was Joseph a Mason?*

9. Involvement in *Spiritism*—especially through the attempts to receive communications from dead loved ones and relatives in the LDS temple

10. Joseph Smith, Sr. (the prophet's father) and almost certainly Jr. were involved in dowsing or *Rhabdomancy*—ibid., pp. 31-35; see also the 1933 edition of *Doctrine and Covenants*, which discusses the use of the "rod of nature" or the "rod of Aaron" as a euphemism for a divining rod

11. There is ample evidence of early LDS leaders' endorsement of *Phrenology*—ibid., pp. 218-20

All this pretty fully illustrates the first definition. Even in today's occult-riddled society, you would have to go some distance to find a New Age disciple or witch who had more experience in as many different varieties of occult practice as had Joseph Smith.

Of course, the third *Random House Dictionary* definition of the occult—"secret; disclosed or communicated only to the initiate"—applies perfectly to the practices going on within the LDS temple. The temple rites are carefully guarded secrets, although Mormons will insist the temple is not secret, but sacred. It remains that the most dire oaths prohibit temple Mormons from ever discussing what goes on within the temple with anyone, even another temple Mormon, except within the actual walls of a temple.

Only through "leaks" in the church and through former temple Mormons getting born again and coming out of the church to talk about the temple rites has any information been conveyed about the goings-on within those imposing structures.

Not just any Mormon can be admitted to the temple rituals. There is a highly selective screening process which only admits about 25 to 30 percent of the actual membership (see also *Temple Recommend*). In fact, most Mormons never get to see the inside of a temple unless they go on a tour before one is dedicated. This makes the temple rituals eminently qualified to be called occult, for they are available only to the "initiate" (worthy Mormon) and are secret to the general Mormon population and to the outside world.

This occult influence is far from biblical. Of course, historic Christianity condemns occultism just as soundly as does official Mormonism. The only difference is that Christians practice what they preach. Certainly there is no Christian fellowship which has institutionalized occultism to the degree that Mormonism has.

Even devout Mormons tend to be obsessed with fringe occult practices such as astrology, New Age medicine and healing practices, and even sorcery. The church pays lip service to abstaining from the occult, but its founders and many of its rank-and-file members still practice or at least dabble in it.

Indeed, in October 1991, a story surfaced in the *Salt Lake Tribune* which revealed that a high-level LDS general authority, Bishop Glenn Pace, had conducted an in-house report for the First Presidency and had determined that Satanism and satanic ritual abuse was going on within the LDS membership in north-central Utah in and around Salt Lake. (Satanic ritual abuse is an alleged form of child sexual abuse which features systematic torture of children and the use of anti-Christian rituals, robes, rubrics, and symbolism.)

The Pace report, which leaked to the press, indicated that this horrid abuse was not limited to "Jack Mormons" or fringe Mormon groups. Rather, it allegedly involved church leadership people, and even members of the famed Mormon Tabernacle Choir. Accounts from over 60 survivors of the abuse (Pace states that those were all he had time to interview; there were more victims available than he had time for) also indicated that many of the rituals took place within LDS meetinghouses. Pace estimated that his subjects incriminated more than 800 other LDS members in the greater Wasatch region. Other scattered reports, less well-established, have also indicated or alleged that occult rituals—including orgies and some form of blood sacrifice—were being done in LDS facilities. To date there has been no reported evidence that a single Mormon has been reprimanded or excommunicated for such occult involvement.

This should not surprise biblically knowledgeable Christians. The Bible teaches that the sins of the fathers are visited upon the children, up to four generations (Exodus 20:5). When a church's founder practiced necromancy and ceremonial magic, such as did Joseph Smith, a dreadful satanic momentum is built up. It must be acknowledged and repented of before its power can be broken.

Mormons are not Christians and spurn—even mock—the cleansing power of the blood of Jesus Christ. Without applying that blood, this juggernaut of generational occultism cannot help but snowball. Sin cannot get better of its own accord; it can only get worse. The Bible makes that clear. Thus, if the grandparents and great-grandparents of contemporary LDS leaders were occultists and Freemasons (and many were), then it would be amazing if even more horrible forms of occult and witchcraft practice were not going on in those same families today.

God will not be mocked. The evil seeds of occultism in Mormonism's past may now be spreading their noxious blossoms (Galatians 6:7). Mormons need to repent and turn to Christ. "It is a fearful thing to fall into the hands of the living God" (Hebrews 10:31).

ORACLES

In general, oracles are communications supposed to be from a divine or at least supernatural source. The term could generally be considered to be synonymous with prophecy and prophets.

A key point within the Mormon church is its contention that it is headed up by a "living prophet," as opposed to other churches of Christianity, which have only the "dead prophets" (Isaiah, Jeremiah, etc.) of the Bible on which to depend. This, we are told, makes the LDS church a superior institution to any other church.

Yet the use of prophecy or oracles is actually tightly controlled within the church, just like everything else. Bruce R. McConkie explains: "The First Presidency are appointed 'to receive the oracles for the whole church' (Doctrine and Covenants 124:126). When these revelations or oracles are given to the people, the recipients are under solemn obligation to walk in the light thus manifest" (*Doctrine*, p. 547).

Mormons are held strictly accountable to receive and obey the edicts passed down from "the brethren" at Salt Lake headquarters. This is based on a revelation given (conveniently enough) by founding LDS prophet Joseph Smith, who exhorted his disciples in *Doctrine and Covenants* 90:5: "And all they who receive the oracles of God, let them beware how they hold them lest they are accounted as a light thing, and are brought under condemnation thereby, and stumble and fall when the storms descend, and the winds blow, and the rains descend, and beat upon their house."

Though Mormons will often claim to investigators that they evaluate and "pray over" revelations which come from the brethren, this is practically ignored. Though the LDS church leaders have not issued a formally designated "prophecy" or revelation since 1978, in actual day-to-day practice, everything taught or handed down from church headquarters is regarded with slavish devotion as if it were holy writ.

Sunday school lessons, Relief Society lessons, home-teaching assignments, and church callings (appointments to office) are all regarded as oracles from God. Of course, this leaves little room for originality in the way that LDS functions are carried out. Nor can members demur when called to *one more* church responsibility.

Mormons take great stock in the fact that they have "living oracles":

> Men who receive revelations or oracles for the people are themselves called oracles (2 Samuel 16:23). Members of the First Presidency, Council of the Twelve, and the Patriarch to the Church—because they are appointed and sustained as prophets, seers, and revelators to the Church—are known as the living oracles. All those who preach the gospel have the obligation to do it by revelation so that they themselves, as they teach, are acting as oracles to their hearers. "If any man speak," Peter said, "let him speak as the oracles of God" (1 Peter 4:11) [ibid.].

The problem in the scriptural sense with this is that these supposed "living oracles" have repeatedly failed to receive any practical, prophetic revelation. The most massive and glaring examples are the 50-plus false prophecies of founding prophet Joseph Smith (see also *Smith: Was Joseph a False Prophet?*). Additionally, there is a paucity of empirical evidence for any kind of prophetic insight on the part of Smith's successors. If the succession of "prophets, seers, and revelators" which followed Smith in office were truly hearing from God almost daily, then how does one explain the following anomalies:

1. Joseph Smith (and the church) tried to instigate numerous efforts at social engineering, such as the United Order and the Kirtland Safety Society—all of which failed dismally.

2. The church (contrary to "faith-promoting stories") was actually caught flat-footed by the Great Depression, and had to scramble to institute its celebrated "welfare program."

3. The church leadership gave no warning to devout Mormons in Germany during the rise of the Third Reich. In fact, the vast majority of Mormons in Germany began to persecute Jews (contrary to the Bible, and even LDS teaching) and became enthusiastic supporters of Hitler Youth and the Nazi regime—this, despite the fact that American Mormons vigorously opposed Hitler.

4. "Prophet" Spencer W. Kimball (and his colleagues in the First Presidency and the Twelve) failed to discern they were being defrauded by Mormon Mark Hoffmann out of tens of thousands of dollars (perhaps hundreds of thousands) in his celebrated forgery scam in the late 1980s. Why didn't God warn His oracles that substantial portions of His tithing money were being used to line the pockets of a crook who later on murdered two innocent Mormons with pipe bombs?

The conclusion: LDS "living oracles" function more in theory and fantasy than in practical fact.

ORIGINAL SIN

The LDS Position

Mormons deny the universal sinful state of mankind or the doctrine of original sin (see also *Fall of Adam*). Listen to the late apostle Bruce R. McConkie in *Mormon Doctrine*:

> In contrast to the doctrines of free agency and personal accountability for sin, modern Christendom has the *false* doctrine

of original sin. Although the scriptures abundantly show "that men will be punished for their own sins and not for Adam's transgression" (Second Article of Faith; *Articles of Faith*, pp. 57-73) . . . the common view is that *all men are tainted with sin* because of Adam's fall. . . . One false doctrine begets another (p. 550).

To say that "there is none righteous" is to teach false doctrine by Mormon standards. The second Article of Faith teaches the same denial of original sin: "We believe that men will be punished for their own sins, and not for Adam's transgression."

The Biblical View

Let's look at this carefully, because this is a central point of difference between Christianity and Mormonism. Look at Paul's statement in Romans 3:10-18:

> As it is written, There is none righteous, no, not one: there is none that understandeth, there is none that seeketh after God. They are all gone out of the way, they are together become unprofitable; there is none that doeth good, no, not one. Their throat is an open sepulchre; with their tongues they have used deceit; the poison of asps is under their lips: whose mouth is full of cursing and bitterness: their feet are swift to shed blood: destruction and misery are in their ways: and the way of peace have they not known: there is no fear of God before their eyes (see also Psalm 14:1-3; 53:1-3).

Paul's words are absolutely contrary to LDS theology. Read Psalm 51:5: "Behold, I was shapen in iniquity; and in sin did my mother conceive me." Romans 3:23 says, "All have sinned, and come short of the glory of God." Mormonism does not teach that. Mormons do not believe that men and women are born sinners, even though the Bible clearly teaches this truth.

Therefore, Mormons can have no sense of their own sinfulness, no sense of the enormous depravity of man—or more importantly, of the unimaginable holiness of God. They have tried to bring God down to their level and make Him a man, and then thought they could bridge the gap between man and God and become gods themselves.

This is contrary to the clear teaching of the Bible, as well as to human experience. In Psalm 51:5, David cries out, "I was shapen in iniquity; and in sin did my mother conceive me." Also, Psalm 53:3; Proverbs 20:9; Isaiah 53:6; Isaiah 64:6; Romans 3:23; and 1 John 1:8 all proclaim sin as the universal human experience. Obviously, David in his mother's womb did not sin, nor was he conceived out of wedlock. Therefore, what is taught here is that man emerges from the womb with the taint of Adam's sin.

But is he punished for this? Obviously he is. Ezekiel 18:4b says that the "soul that sinneth, it shall die." James 1:15 tells us, "When lust hath conceived, it bringeth forth sin: and sin, when it is finished, bringeth forth death." What could be clearer?

Yet, there is an answer: "The wages of sin is death; but the gift of God is eternal life through Jesus Christ our Lord" (Romans 6:23).

I have probably said it a dozen times already in this encyclopedic work: It doesn't matter to God how nice Mormonism *appears*. If the LDS understanding of the very basics of the Christian faith is warped, its theology must be as warped—and the Mormons are a lost people.

The concept of original sin is at the very core of Christian theology. Without original sin, there would be no separation from God. Without separation from God, there is no need for reconciliation; without the need for reconciliation, there is no need for Christ to die for our sins, to be our ransom on the cross. As always, we can turn to the Scriptures to see God's truth.

> Wherefore, as by one man sin entered into the world, and death by sin; and so death passed upon all men, for that all have sinned (Romans 5:12).
>
> And, having made peace through the blood of his cross, by him to reconcile all things unto himself; by him, I say, whether they be things in earth, or things in heaven. And you, that were sometime alienated and enemies in your mind by wicked works, yet now hath he reconciled. In the body of his flesh through death, to present you holy and unblameable and unreproveable in his sight (Colossians 1:20-22).

ORTHODOXY

The actual word *orthodox* is a combination of two Greek words: *orthos*, meaning "right or correct," and *doxa*, meaning "praise or worship"; therefore, "right worship." Thus, the LDS definition of orthodoxy and the Christian one could be superficially identical: "In the true sense, orthodoxy consists in believing that which is in harmony with the scriptures" (*Doctrine*, p. 550).

However, McConkie does not stop there:

> Thus gospel orthodoxy requires belief in the truths of salvation as they have been revealed in this dispensation through Joseph Smith, and as they are understood and interpreted by the living oracles who wear the mantle of the Prophet. Orthodoxy is the opposite of heterodoxy or of believing heretical doctrines (ibid.).

Thus, although the "scriptures" are paid lip service, the true test of orthodoxy for a Mormon is whether you accept Joseph Smith, his revelations, and his successors as genuinely from God. If you don't, then you are (by McConkie's own words and the Mormon definition) a heretic.

Contrary to the current warmth with which Christian churches are treated in public dialogues, the official LDS position is that *all* Christian churches are in apostasy and are heretical, to a greater or lesser degree. Conversely, virtually all historic, *orthodox* Christian churches agree that Mormonism is a heretical cult.

So distinct are the essential differences between historic Christianity and Mormonism that it is logically impossible for both theological systems to be true. Either Mormonism must be the yardstick by which we measure orthodoxy, or else biblical Christianity must be. In point of fact, Mormons have:

1. A radically different god than Christians; Mormons are polytheists and Christians are monotheists.

2. A different "plan of salvation"; by works rather than grace.

3. An extremely different view of the Bible; Mormons regard the Bible as imperfect and insufficient in and of itself to bring mankind to salvation.

4. A Jesus with an entirely different nature and origin; Mormons deny the virgin birth and claim Jesus and Lucifer are brothers.

5. A radically different anthropology; Mormons see man as a basically good "God in embryo," and the Bible teaches that men and women are fallen, sinful creatures.

These differences can be clearly demonstrated from the Holy Bible. Additionally, one can search in vain throughout the past three millennia of Judeo-Christian history for any orthodox group, either Christian or Jewish, which held the beliefs now espoused by LDS leaders.

Thus, though Mormons can claim to be orthodox, the Bible (and Christian history) clearly judges them to be otherwise. Claiming orthodoxy does not make one so.

PATRIARCHAL BLESSINGS

The LDS Position

The patriarchal blessing is a specialized type of blessing given only to "worthy" members of the Mormon church. It is distinguished from the usual priesthood blessings given by elders, church leadership, or bishops in that this patriarchal blessing is usually given only once in a lifetime, and it cannot be given by just any priesthood holder (see also *Priestcraft*). It can only be given by a male ordained to the office of patriarch.

Bruce R. McConkie explains that "nearly every member of the Church is a *literal* descendant of Jacob who gave patriarchal blessings to his 12 sons" (*Doctrine*, p. 558). This means that every male member of the church has a right to the patriarchal office and to give what are called "natural" patriarchal blessings. This is different from the blessings given by an ordained patriarch. The natural patriarch is simply a father in the home who happens to be a worthy Mormon holding the Melchizedek priesthood (see *Doctrines of Salvation*, vol. 3, pp. 169-72; *Gospel Kingdom*, p. 146).

Such a man is said to be able to give special blessings to his wife and especially to his children—blessings which might offer allegedly inspired counsel and advice, and even perhaps have some predictive quality concerning the child's destiny. It is his natural right as a father and as a supposed descendent from Jacob, who gave such blessings to his children (cf. Genesis 49).

McConkie quotes the following "official" definition:

The First Presidency . . . in a letter to all stake presidents, dated June 28, 1957, gave the following definition:

"Patriarchal blessings contemplate an inspired declaration of the lineage of the recipient, and also where so moved upon by the Spirit, an inspired and prophetic statement of the life mission of the recipient, together with such blessings, cautions, and admonitions as the patriarch may be prompted to give for the accomplishment of such life's mission, it being always made clear that the realization of all promised blessings is conditioned upon faithfulness to the gospel of our Lord, whose servant the patriarch is. All such blessings are recorded and generally only one such blessing should be adequate for each person's life. The sacred nature of the patriarchal blessing must of necessity urge all patriarchs to most earnest solicitation of divine guidance for their prophetic utterances and superior wisdom for cautions and admonitions" (ibid.).

Here is what actually happens. The Mormon usually waits until late adolescence to receive his or her patriarchal blessing; young men often receive it before they go on their missionary service.

The Mormon is required to be "worthy" (comparatively free of sinful habits or associations) and the inquiries and demands made of him or her are similar to those required of someone wishing to receive a temple recommend (see also *Temple Recommend*).

An appointment is made with the stake patriarch. Usually there is only one such patriarch per stake—a fairly large unit of church membership roughly analogous to a Catholic diocese (see also *Church Organization*). This is a man, usually older, who is regarded as being very saintly and absolutely above reproach. Often he might be a former bishop (head of a ward) or stake president (head of a stake). He is called and ordained as a patriarch by "revelation" from Salt Lake City.

The person receiving the blessing goes to the stake center (where the administrative offices of the stake are; usually, just a large church meetinghouse) and to the office of the patriarch. This is a very special office, some even with a huge baffled door for soundproofing, and soundproof walls as well. This is because the blessing is intended only for the ears of the person receiving it (and his spouse, if any) and a special recording machine which takes down what the patriarch utters. Every word uttered is believed to be a special revelation from God for a person's life.

The patriarch lays his hands upon the person's head and begins to speak the "inspired utterances." Usually these consist of statements covering the following broad areas:

1. the person's genealogy—this is not anything specific, but rather what "tribe of Israel" they are from. Most Mormons are told they are from Ephraim or Manasseh (unless they happen to be the rare Jewish convert with an obvious name like Levi, Levine, or Cohen).

2. certain blessings the person might receive, *always* conditional upon faithfulness to the church.

3. exhortations to be "saviors on Mount Zion" and to do their family genealogy and frequent temple work for the dead.

4. exhortations to be married in the temple and be faithful to their covenants.

5. *very* broad statements about their future.

The blessing is then sealed upon them by the patriarch in the name of Jesus and the tape is transcribed and sent off to Salt Lake City to the famous and voluminous church archives. A typed copy of the blessing is eventually given to the person, who usually keeps it in a journal or book of remembrance (see also *Book of Remembrance*).

The Biblical View

All this is but a pallid shade of the full-blown patriarchal blessing. The problem with the Mormon doctrine from a biblical perspective is that it is like going to a psychic or a channeler. Of course, the Mormon doesn't understand that. He or she thinks that the patriarchal blessing is a godly thing, invoked by the power of the "holy Melchizedek priesthood." Anyone who has read the actual *Instruction Manual for Patriarchs* published by the LDS church would get a rude awakening! As we have shown elsewhere (see also *Melchizedek Priesthood*), this priesthood cannot be coming from God, and that is the problem.

This makes the patriarch a false prophet of sorts, and thus just like a carnival palm reader. The process he often uses involves a kind of trance communication such as has been used by mediums

321

(channelers) for centuries. He is providing access (supposedly) to hidden information—the person's tribal heritage in Zion. He is providing information, however bland and generalized, about the person's future. This is very akin to having a "past-life" reading from a psychic or a fortune-telling session to learn about your future. The general nature of the predictions in no way lessens the sin involved. Frankly, most psychics don't *dare* give detailed predictions, because they know the odds are vast that they will be wrong.

Thus, the poor Mormon brings upon himself the curse of God from visiting a false prophet and seeking divination (see Leviticus 19:31; 20:6; Deuteronomy 18:14; Isaiah 19:3; Jeremiah 27:9; Ezekiel 13:23). Additionally, the works-oriented and LDS-controlled nature of the blessing actually reinforces the Mormon's flawed idea of the plan of salvation. It makes him think that he is saved by what he will do rather than by what Jesus has already done.

So the patriarchal blessing is unfortunately a curse upon the life of the Mormon, even though he or she seeks it for the best of all possible reasons. As the metaphor goes: If you innocently drink arsenic in a bottle of soda, thinking it is soda, it will still kill you.

Because of the highly occult nature of the blessing, it is our recommendation that it be one of several things which a newly saved Mormon ought to renounce and reject in order to get full victory (Philippians 3:13,14). It probably wouldn't hurt to destroy the copy of the blessing either (Acts 19:19).

PECULIAR PEOPLE

Mormons often refer to themselves as a peculiar people, meaning that they are different from the rest of mankind. The expression "a peculiar people" is used often in speeches, articles, and books about the Latter-day Saints, by the Saints. Outsiders might think the words themselves are a bit peculiar, even offensive, to describe a religious people, but the Saints take the name and the meaning to heart.

> For thou art an holy people unto the LORD thy God, and the LORD hath chosen thee to be a peculiar people unto himself, above all the nations that are upon the earth (Deuteronomy 14:2).

But ye are a chosen generation, a royal priesthood, an holy nation, a peculiar people; that ye should shew forth the praises of him who hath called you out of darkness into his marvellous light (1 Peter 2:9).

Brigham Young said, "The Latter-day Saints are a very peculiar people, and they are led in a peculiar way" (*Journal of Discourses* 12:206). And Bruce R. McConkie summed it up best when he said:

In every age the Lord's people are classified by the world as a peculiar people, a designation which the saints accept and in which they rejoice (Exodus 19:6; Deuteronomy 7:6; 14:1; 1 Peter 2:5,9). They are peculiar, distinctive, unusual, not like any other people, because they have overcome the world. Their doctrines, practices, and whole way of life runs counter to the common course of mankind (*Doctrine*, p. 565).

The Mormon people are a peculiar people, but certainly not in the way Peter meant. The sad fact is that they are peculiar in the same sense that they are eccentric or alien in their belief system. There also has to be something peculiar with a people who will believe the many bizarre doctrines of Mormonism without testing any of it by the standards of truth set forth in the Bible.

PEEP STONES

(See also *Occult*.)

The term *peep stone* is an antiquated expression for scrying or crystallomancy (crystal ball gazing). A peep stone is a rustic, folk-magic version of the more elegant crystal ball or magic mirror—a poor man's scrying device. Hence, it is a form of divination or fortune-telling, which is indisputably an occult practice.

The term is relevant to an examination of Mormonism because LDS founder Joseph Smith was an admitted user of a peep stone, both before his involvement in the foundation of the Mormon church and afterward.

Contrary to popular belief, you do not need a crystal ball to do scrying or crystal gazing. It can be done with mirrors, either regular or "black" (a black mirror is actually a small pane of glass with black velvet behind it). It can also be done with clock glasses painted black, or even a small glass filled with water and black ink. Finally, it can be done with special noncrystalline rocks.

These are often small rocks, frequently worn smooth by lying in the bottom of a stream or river. The ones Smith used ranged in size from that of an egg down to the size of a U.S. quarter, and of varying colors and configurations (Quinn, photo plates 9-13). The actual shape or surface of the stone is not important, but rather that it contains some sort of indefinable magical "virtue" which only the scryer can evaluate.

Those holding a magic worldview, as opposed to a biblical worldview (such as Smith), believed that spirits lived in rocks. These spirits, sometimes called gnomes, might be coaxed to produce visions from within the rock (or crystal). Thus, Smith probably wasn't looking at the actual stone's surface but rather at something produced within the stone—either by a spirit (demon) or his own demonstrably fertile imagination.

Smith would put the stone in his hat, which served to keep out extraneous light and distractions. Then he would place his face in the hat and "see" or "peep" things from within the stone. This is how Smith allegedly was able to locate buried treasure in his youth (see also *Money Digging*) and also how he received many of his supposed revelations later in his career. As has been noted elsewhere, occultism and divination are serious sins and forbidden by God in the Bible (see also *Occult*).

It is impossible that a supposed man of God such as Joseph Smith—allegedly chosen by a holy God to bring forth the true church after 18 centuries of apostasy and ecclesiastical darkness—should be practicing crystal gazing. This is particularly true in that Smith practiced it *after* the foundation of the Mormon church. His occultism is one of many character flaws which disprove the truth of Smith's claims.

PREEXISTENCE

The LDS Position

LDS theology teaches that human beings had a premortal existence as spirit children with Heavenly Father. Bruce R. McConkie teaches that this is predicated upon two great truths which must be accepted:

1. that God is a personal being in whose image man is created, an exalted, perfected and glorified Man of Holiness, and NOT a spirit essence that fills the immensity of space.

2. that matter or element is self-existent or eternal in nature, creation being merely the organization of matter that "is not created or made, neither indeed can be" (*Doctrine and Covenants* 93:29) (*Doctrine*, p. 589).

McConkie remarks that "unless God the Father was a personal Being, he could not have created spirits in his image, and if there had been no self-existent spirit element, there would have been no substance from which those spirit bodies could have been organized" (ibid.).

Mormons believe that they were spiritually "born" in heaven of Heavenly Father and Heavenly Mother, although they are a bit vague about the details of just how that occurred. As preexistent spirit beings they had fully mature free will and were subject to the laws and ordinances of Mormonism. Their preexistent state was one of trial and probation and learning.

They also believe that some preexistent spirits were so obedient and outstanding that they became "noble and great" and were thus foreordained by the Lord to perform important missions in this earthly life (Book of Abraham 3:22-28). Christ is felt to be the noblest and mightiest of these spirit children, but Joseph Smith is not far behind Him.

This doctrine was stitched together entirely out of the writings and "revelations" of Joseph Smith. The Mormons strain to use a couple of biblical proof texts to try and support it. Key passages they use are Jeremiah 1:5 and 1 Peter 1:2. They have a great deal of trouble handling the idea of God's foreknowledge. For this reason, they also wrestle with Romans 8:28ff.

One other approach is to cite the passages which refer either explicitly or implicitly to Jesus Christ in the Bible, and then try to apply them to us all.

The Biblical View

Mormons quote from Proverbs 8:23,24, which is a poetic image of "Wisdom" personified. It does not refer to any human being. Most scholars feel it could apply to the pre-incarnate Jesus Christ as the *logos* or Word.

In context, the entire chapter deals with wisdom. Notice that Proverbs 8:12 says: "I, wisdom, dwell with prudence," and then continues in the first person all the way through to verse 36; so it is highly unlikely that any human person is meant. It is important to remember that in the Bible there is a radical discontinuity between Jesus as God and human beings as creatures. Mormonism seeks to erase that discontinuity.

Concerning Romans 8:28-30, Mormons need to understand that God knows all about the future. He knew, from the beginning of creation, which of us would be saved through His Son. This has nothing to do with preexistence, but only with the sovereign foreknowledge of an Almighty God.

It is just like an artist who begins to paint on a canvas. The picture he wishes to create is in his mind, but that doesn't mean that the painting actually exists out there in the "real world." It is only a potential in the artist's mind. Similarly, just because God knows in advance if we are going to reach out to Jesus Christ doesn't mean we existed way back in eternity past.

First Peter 1:2 deals with much the same problem. Again, God's foreknowledge about us does not mean we preexisted, any more than an artist's conception of a painting in his mind means that the painting is already hanging in the gallery. These analogies don't begin to touch the awesome majesty of God and His sovereignty, but they do put it in terms we can understand.

Half the problem with Mormons is that they cannot conceive of a God big enough to be able to do what I have described. We simply need to humble ourselves before Him and realize that His ways are as far above ours as the stars of heaven are above the earth. Jeremiah 1:5 reflects precisely the same principle: "Before I formed thee in the belly I knew thee; and before thou camest forth out of the womb I sanctified thee, and I ordained thee a prophet unto the nations."

Yes, God knew Jeremiah and sanctified him before he came out of the womb. Obviously, a God who knows the future knows each member of His creation centuries in advance. Of course, once Jeremiah is "in the womb," he is no longer preexistent. John the Baptist also seems to have been sanctified in the womb of his mother (Luke 1:41). This says nothing of preexistence before birth.

Though there aren't as many solid passages in the Bible which show the fallacy of the doctrine, there are a few. First Corinthians 15:46 is an answer to preexistence, and so is Genesis 2:7. The Corinthian passage says, "Howbeit that was not first which is spiritual, but that which is natural; and afterward that which is spiritual."

This shows that the creation proceeds in this fashion: first that which is "natural" (i.e., material or fleshly); and afterward the spiritual. This is seconded by the following passage in Genesis: "And the LORD God formed man of the dust of the ground, and breathed into his nostrils the breath of life; and man became a living soul."

It is a general principle of Bible interpretation that the first time something is done, it becomes the normal way things are done from then on. This was how the first man was made, and therefore we can assume that the process is the same within the womb: 1. form the body; 2. bring in the "breath of life," and 3. become a living soul.

Also, there is Zechariah 12:1: "The burden of the word of the LORD for Israel, saith the LORD, which stretcheth forth the heavens, and layeth the foundation of the earth, and formeth the spirit of man within him."

Note again: The spirit is formed where? In the spirit world? No—*within man.* Zechariah merely confirms Genesis and Corinthians, and out of the mouths of two or three witnesses shall all things be established. Psalm 139:16 further confirms it. There is no human being until he or she is formed in the womb.

Beyond the scriptural arguments, there is also a logical fallacy in the LDS cosmology. It is an enormous assumption to suppose that matter or spirit are eternal or self-existent. This is the same error that secular evolutionists make—the assumption that matter just happens to be there with no cause.

It is philosophically untenable for there to be an inanimate, uncaused element. A rock, or dust motes, or star twinkles cannot just *be.* An object, or even energy, must proceed from somewhere. Someone had to make the first rock or dust mote. That someone is the biblical God.

The LDS god, however, is so far down the spiritual food chain from the biblical God that he might as well be a protozoan. Even the pagan philosophers of classical Greece deduced that there must be a God and that He must be what they called an "unmoved Mover" or "Prime Cause."

An intelligent, self-conscious Being can be an "unmoved Mover," but a rock cannot. The biblical God is by definition (both scriptural and philosophical) that unmoved Mover ("I am that I am"—Exodus 3:14).

Another logical fallacy in the doctrine of preexistence: Where did the first man come from if no one can become a god except by evolving into godhood from manhood through the law of eternal progression? It is like the proverbial chicken and the egg.

The biblical answer to the chicken/egg riddle is that God made the first chicken (Genesis 1:20). The biblical answer to the Mormon godhood problem is that God made the first man, and neither that man nor any other will ever be a god.

PRIESTCRAFT

The LDS Position

The term *priestcraft* originally meant simply the training and education which went into the production of a priest in the Roman Catholic church, just as we might talk about a carpenter and his woodcraft (see *Random House Dictionary*, op. cit., p. 1536).

In LDS usage, however, *priestcraft* has a negative connotation which is virtually unique. This is because Mormons frown upon a paid, professional clergy, whether minister or priest. The supposed ancient American prophet leader Nephi taught in the *Book of Mormon* that the Lord "commandeth that there shall be no priestcrafts; for, behold, priestcrafts are that men preach and set themselves up for a light unto the world, that they may get gain and praise of the world; but they seek not the welfare of Zion" (2 Nephi 26:29). LDS apostle McConkie elaborates:

> Priesthood and priestcraft are two opposites; one is of God, the other of the devil. When ministers claim but do not possess the priesthood; when they set themselves up as lights to their congregations, but do not preach the pure and full gospel;

when their interest is in gaining personal popularity and financial gain, rather than in caring for the poor and ministering to the wants and needs of their fellow men . . . they are engaged, in a greater or lesser degree, in the practice of priestcrafts (*Doctrine*, p. 593).

The chief objections which Mormons raise against the clergy of the historic Christian church are these:

1. They constitute an elite, paid, professionally educated (i.e., Bible college or seminary) class unlike anything in the New Testament.

2. They do not teach the "Restored Gospel" (i.e., Mormonism).

3. They are egotistical and prideful, and exploit the poor and gullible.

Sadly, history and recent events within both the Protestant and Catholic churches have done little to dispel at least points 1 and 3. The vast wealth of the Vatican and its effete priesthood caste is now rivaled by a few pastors and "televangelists" who live like kings and who beg and whine over the airwaves for money and the widow's mite.

Happily, these increasingly well-known stereotypes are counterbalanced by the countless clergymen who labor tirelessly among the poor and unfortunate for scarcely any wages. Of course, they do not receive media attention. For every prelate and TV preacher who drives an expensive car and lives in a mansion, there are probably a thousand honest ministers who struggle to feed their children and drive ten-year-old autos kept running through the power of prayer!

The Biblical View

The central problem here is what the clergy or ministerial class is supposed to be. It is true that Paul worked a secular job to support his ministry. However, there is ample biblical evidence from the New Testament that he intended his example to be the exception rather than the rule. It is evident that there were other Christian ministers and elders who received money from their congregations.

Of course, since Christianity was a subversive, underground religion in the time of the New Testament, there were no "megachurches," nor probably any church buildings of any kind. Thus, the lifestyle of the paid clergy of New Testament times could hardly have been princely. Nor is it for most pastors today.

There is nothing in the Bible to indicate that training people for the ministry is wrong, whether this training takes place in a formal academic setting or not. Indeed, there is a command in 2 Timothy 2:15 to study and prepare for the ministry: "*Study* to shew thyself approved unto God, a workman that needeth not to be ashamed, rightly dividing the word of truth."

The formalized fulfillment of that commandment in seminaries and Bible colleges could hardly be considered evil—unless, of course, the education militated against the Christian faith (which does sometimes happen in more liberal schools).

The Mormons have taken a cheap shot at professional clergy here. Indeed, they also have formal training for people, all the way up to the college level in religion, including seminary and institute.

Certainly, there *are* prideful ministers or priests, and they are out of the will of God. Yet some of the most humble clergy are among the best educated. There are also egotistical Mormon priesthood holders. All of us are sinners.

Second, Mormons think that they have the true priesthood and that Christianity's doctrine and clergy are fallen. As has been shown repeatedly in this volume, the Mormon church is seriously out of step with the Bible on virtually every essential doctrinal issue. The "Restored Gospel" of Mormonism is actually the "another gospel" of Galatians 1:8, and it is accursed in the sight of God.

A deeper issue springs from this. Implicitly in their definition of priestcraft, Mormons accuse non-LDS clergy of appropriating a priesthood that is not theirs to have. Yet it is ironic to note that in the light of biblical truth, it is the LDS church which stands guilty of the very priestcraft of which they accuse historic Christianity.

Mormons, of course, assert that they have been given the "holy Melchizedek priesthood" as part of the restoration allegedly bestowed upon Joseph Smith. Most "worthy" LDS men claim to possess that priesthood (see also *Melchizedek Priesthood*). It is clear from Hebrews, however, that Jesus' Melchizedek priesthood was "unchangeable" (i.e., nontransferable) since He could never die (see Hebrews 7:23,24).

The Old Testament norm called for one Levitical high priest at a time. When he died, the office passed to his successor. The author of Hebrews points out that Jesus holds the Melchizedek priesthood (verse 17) and that since He died and is now resurrected and lives forever (something Mormons attest to), His is a priesthood *of one* and it can never be transferred to another. Thus, Joseph Smith could not have received it. You will search the New Testament in vain for any evidence of a Christian "priest" or "high priest" in the church organization, except for Jesus Himself.

This means that the Mormons are the ones committing the sin of priestcraft, because they:

1. have grown enormously wealthy, often at the expense of poor Mormons who are driven to tithe and contribute otherwise to the church financially, often to the near breaking point of their financial stability;

2. have dared to be arrogant and prideful enough to declare that their ministerial class is alone in all the world in its ability to truly preach Jesus Christ;

3. have appropriated the priesthood of Jesus Christ which the Bible says belongs to Him alone;

4. have appropriated the priesthood of Aaron, which the Bible says belongs only to those Jews literally descended from the house and family of Aaron—something virtually no Mormon, and certainly not Joseph Smith, can claim (see also *Patriarchal Blessings*).

It is the Mormons who need to repent of their priestcraft, not the Christian church.

PROTESTANTS

This is an extremely important entry, in light of the current offensive in which the Mormon church is engaging to become accepted as just another Christian church.

LDS leaders (bishops and stake presidents) are frequently seeking to be admitted to local ministerial associations, either as observers or as full-fledged members. Through their strong involvement in Scouting, in the pro-life movement, and in the "religious right,"

Mormons are becoming increasingly accepted as a kind of Protestant church with minor doctrinal differences. Indeed, LDS chaplains are already classified as "Protestant" in the armed services of the United States and regularly take their turns at officiating in Protestant services in the place of Methodist, Baptist, or Lutheran chaplains as the opportunities present themselves.

This is a radically different face of Mormonism than was presented even 15 or 20 years ago. It is true that Mormon writers have many kind things to say about the Protestant Reformers: Luther, Calvin, Knox, etc. They aver that the Protestant Reformation was "inspired of God; it was one of the necessary occurrences which prepared the way for the 'restoration of the gospel'" (*Doctrine*, p. 610).

It is also true that in an external sense the LDS church closely resembles many Protestant churches. It has no incense, candles, or statuary (unless one counts the Moroni statues atop the temples). Its services are austere and very "low church," and there are no clerical robes. Yet it also resembles the Roman Catholic church in its concepts of a hierarchical priesthood, headed up by a pope-like prophet; in its "works for the dead"; in its extra-biblical "scripture" and in its insistence upon being the "only true church." One might say it is both fish and fowl in its appearance.

Of course, appearances can be deceiving. This is the problem. A few years ago, LDS authorities were more open about their relation to the Protestant churches and we need to keep their remarks in mind today:

> *Members of The Church of Jesus Christ of Latter-day Saints are not Protestants, and the Church itself is not a Protestant church.* The true Church is not a dead branch broken from a dead tree; it is a living tree planted again by revelation in the vineyard of the Lord, and it shall grow and flourish long after the vineyard has been burned and each dead branch and vine has been consumed as stubble (ibid., emphasis added).

Today, Mormons would not be so bold. However respectfully they may speak of Martin Luther, the fact remains that they have even baptized *him* (by proxy, centuries after his death) into the LDS church. This shows that they believe Lutheranism and every other Protestant denomination to be in apostasy.

There is simply too radical a difference between the god, the plan of salvation, and the "Jesus" of Mormonism for us to ever consider Mormons as Protestants with just a few quaint and minor doctrinal differences.

If Mormonism is true, then all Protestant churches are false and damnable—and LDS "Scripture" says as much (see *Pearl of Great Price*, Joseph Smith—*History* 1:19). If historical Christianity is true, then Mormonism is false. There cannot logically be any middle ground between those two positions, and Protestant leaders who pray, work, and fellowship with LDS church leaders are in clear violation of 2 Corinthians 6:14,15: "Be ye not unequally yoked together with unbelievers: for what fellowship hath righteousness with unrighteousness? and what communion hath light with darkness? and what concord hath Christ with Belial? or what part hath he that believeth with an infidel?"

REORGANIZED CHURCH OF JESUS CHRIST OF LATTER DAY SAINTS

Key among Mormon doctrines is that upon the death of Christ and His disciples, there came a great apostasy and falling away. It was at this time that all authority to act in the name of God was taken from the earth. It then became necessary that God restore His church and authority in the last days. The Mormon church claims that it is that restored church, brought to earth once more by God, through the prophethood and leadership of Joseph Smith (see also *Restoration of the Gospel*).

One of the other products of this movement, however, is more than 100 separate restorationist groups who also claim that their authority comes from the prophet Joseph Smith. Chief among them is the group calling itself "The Reorganized Church of Jesus Christ of Latter Day Saints" (RLDS), headquartered in Independence, Missouri. Its membership is somewhere around 250,000.

The death of Joseph Smith in June 1844 brought shock and confusion to his followers. The bulk of the LDS power structure was centered in and around Nauvoo, and groups of Saints gathered around various leaders, anticipating that their man would become the new prophet/leader of the church.

Under the leadership of Brigham Young, the Saints began their famous exodus from Nauvoo to the West. By 1846, over 16,000 of the total membership of approximately 20,000 Saints were on the plains, part of the great Salt Lake migration. The census report of 1850 accounted for just over 19,200 Mormons who had followed Brigham Young. The estimates of those who remained at Nauvoo ranged around 1000.

RLDS historians tell the story from a different perspective. It splintered from the LDS group because of its belief that the Lord would raise up the eldest son of Joseph Smith to be the prophet-president of the church. Since Joseph III was only 12 years of age at the time of his father's death, this was obviously impossible to enact.

For a period of time, many of those who shared the RLDS viewpoint continued to worship, conduct meetings, and organize branches of the church in accordance with what they felt was the same spirit, doctrine, and authority as observed when the church was first organized. Some remained strong, while others fragmented. By 1852, the remnant of many of these groups began joining together and in 1860, Joseph Smith III was asked to take his rightful place and become his father's true successor. This body became known as the Reorganized Church of Jesus Christ of Latter Day Saints.

Obviously, both the LDS and RLDS groups claim with great vigor and strong arguments that they alone have the true authority and the other church is an apostate.

We will leave the debate to their respective apologists and historians. The rest of us have to recognize that they both exist, are groups to be reckoned with, and that they all need to understand the vast doctrinal differences between their theology and that of orthodox Christianity.

Basic Doctrines of the RLDS Church

1. There was a complete apostasy in the early Christian church.

2. God and Christ spoke to Joseph Smith and raised him up as the prophet of His final restoration.

3. The Angel Moroni appeared to Joseph Smith and led him to the discovery of the gold plates.

4. The *Book of Mormon* is the true and holy Word of God (as edited by their own group).

5. The *Doctrine and Covenants* are the holy Words of God, containing the continuity of divine revelation through Joseph Smith (and their own individual prophets).

6. The restoration of the Aaronic and Melchizedek priesthood.

7. Baptism for the remission of sins (baptismal regeneration).

8. The return of Jesus Christ to earth (and Independence) for His thousand-year reign of peace.

9. Just recently, the Utah church has formally acknowledged the authenticity of the *Inspired Version of the Bible*, by Joseph Smith, the copyright for which has always been in the possession of the RLDS group.

10. The RLDS church rejects the Utah doctrine of the physical nature of God and man's progression to godhood.

11. In spite of tremendous documentation proving that Joseph Smith was deeply involved in polygamy as early as the days of Kirtland, Ohio, the RLDS reject the doctrine of polygamy and strongly deny that their founder ever practiced or taught it.

12. The RLDS church again rejects the Utah church's teachings with regard to temples and temple ordinances. It does not believe or teach that men can ever become gods, nor does it believe that works done in secret inside a temple will have any effect upon anyone in either this life or in the next.

Basic Doctrinal Errors of the RLDS

While the RLDS church operates from a base of orthodox doctrine regarding the nature of God and man, it has added the doctrines of men to the precious gospel of grace.

Its belief that the work and authority of Christ was lost and required restoration, its continuing requirement for a prophet/revelator, its "restoration" of the Aaronic and Melchizedek priesthoods, and its extra-biblical "scripture" all take away from the finished work of Calvary.

RESTORATION OF THE GOSPEL

LDS apostle LeGrand Richards in his book *A Marvelous Work and a Wonder* set the stage for Joseph Smith's calling by describing the need for the restitution of all things. Chapter 5 deals with the necessity for a restoration of all the truths lost in what the LDS church describes as "the great apostasy." He says:

> It is the pronouncement of The Church of Jesus Christ of Latter-day Saints, that this is the dispensation of the fulness of times, that through the restitution of all things, the Lord has made provision to "gather together in one all things in Christ, both which are in heaven, and which are on earth." This restitution of all things will, however, not be complete until the end of the thousand years of the personal reign of Christ upon the earth when death will be destroyed. . . . There is no other such plan in the world today (p. 35).

Perhaps no clearer statement as to the importance of Joseph Smith and the restoration of the gospel can be made than Richard's final paragraph in this chapter. As you read it, you can understand the power of their "prophet" and their new "scriptures" over their lives, their thoughts, and their faith:

> This [his remarks in the chapter] makes it easy to understand why the everlasting gospel could not be discovered through reading the Bible alone—the old bottles full of wine could not contain the new wine. So glorious was to be the day when the Lord would "proceed to do a marvelous [sic] work and a wonder" that he had to select one free from all exposure to the unsound philosophies of men. That is why our original statement is consistent: that this is the only Christian church in the world that did not have to rely upon the Bible for its organization and government and that if all the Bibles in the world had been destroyed we would still be teaching the same ordinances as introduced and taught by Jesus and the prophets. True, we take the Bible to prove that these principles and ordinances are in accord with divine of all ages, *but if we had no Bible, we would still have all the needed direction and information through the revelations of the Lord to his servants the prophets in these latter days* (p. 40, emphasis added).

LDS apostle James Talmage wrote an entire book on the subject in 1909, the classic titled *The Great Apostasy*. In his preface he states the supposed eternal place of the LDS church:

> The Church of Jesus Christ of Latter-day Saints proclaims the restoration of the Gospel, and the re-establishment of

the Church as of old, in this, the Dispensation of the Fulness of Times.

> The restored Church affirms that a general apostasy developed during and after the apostolic period and the primitive Church lost its power, authority and graces as a divine institution, and degenerated into an earthly organization only.

Talmage made another interesting point. He said, "The significance and importance of the great apostasy, as a condition precedent to the re-establishment of the Church in modern times, is obvious. If the alleged apostasy of the primitive Church was not a reality, The Church of Jesus Christ of Latter-day Saints is not the divine institution its name proclaims."

Other LDS works throughout the years have worked off the theme of the spiritual darkness and the dawn of the restoration of the fullness of the everlasting gospel. The story of that "long night of spiritual darkness" and the young "prophet boy" Joseph Smith's search for truth became actual LDS scripture (Joseph Smith, *Pearl of Great Price*). It is the foundation, the bedrock of Mormonism.

I recall the first time I went through the temple. I was secretly aghast that I was instructed to put my thumb to my throat in what I recognized was a blood oath. A few weeks later, I had a chance to speak to my bishop privately and cautiously approached him on the subject. The bishop strongly suggested that I never speak to anyone again in this regard. He said that it was a divinely restored temple ritual and if Jesus Himself had to do it, then how could any good Latter-day Saint dare refuse? I recall asking if Jesus also had to wear the underwear, and then melting under my bishop's penetrating glare. Yet, parts of that very sacred ritual *have* been drastically changed. How could that be?

The problem with being a restorationist church is that there is no room for modernizing the restored ritual. I can understand the changes in church dress code and building or temple features over the years, but certain things cannot be altered.

Mormons are told about those "plain and precious things" that were taken away from the gospel and how the prophet Joseph Smith restored them in their purity for the work of the true Saints in this last dispensation of time. So what does this "pure" LDS restoration of the gospel look like?

1. God supposedly ordained the temple garment as a one-piece "union suit" going to the wrist and ankle. The "prophet"

described it in detail. Yet today, it is available in several styles, and shortened to the upper leg and arm.

2. A required temple blood oath, cursing this nation for the deaths of Joseph and Hyrum, was dispatched quietly some years ago as the LDS church began to step actively into a more mainstream civic and political arena.

3. The literal gathering of the saints to Zion on the American continent has ceased to be the war cry. Converts are now told to stay where they are.

4. The United Order, the communistic form of LDS government, went the way of the call to Zion. It failed to work in the early church, even though it was a commandment of God.

5. Polygamy, the new and everlasting covenant, without which eternal life was impossible and its detractors damned to hell, disappeared by way of a politically motivated manifesto in an effort to keep LDS leaders out of jail and to pacify a righteously angry nation.

6. The local Quorum of the Seventies became a here-again-gone-again priesthood office when the church established the Seventies (and then recently disbanded them).

7. LDS prophets gave strong reasons and revelations to support them as to why blacks would never hold the priesthood in this lifetime, yet what God set in motion before the Earth was formed was wiped out in another revelation of convenience.

8. The LDS church quietly adjusted its "restored to its purity" temple ritual and wiped out, among other things, a series of blood oaths, the mocking of Christian pastors, the *pay lay ale* chant and the Masonic five points of fellowship at the celestial veil, as well as several items repugnant to LDS women—all in the name of modernizing the ritual.

Yet these are not items open for modernizing. They were given as absolutes, part of the "restoration of the gospel." They were changed not because God made some mistake, but because the LDS church needed to modify its public face as it tried to move into a place of general acceptance. Our many ministries have heightened that pressure, and there will be many more changes to come.

During a Capstone conference, on Sunday morning, July 29, 1990, Hank Hanegraaff and I walked through Temple Square while we had some time before Hank caught a flight back to Los Angeles. As we walked through the North Visitor Center, we were amazed. That building housed the many displays dealing with the "restoration of the gospel." Yet, every single thing that dealt with the restoration story and Joseph Smith had been removed from public view.

The main floor was all about the prophets of the Old Testament. The second floor was all about Jesus, and the lower floor had been converted to theme film viewing theaters, dealing with Jesus Christ, families, and our relationship with God.

There may be some restoration material stored in plain wrappers somewhere under a counter that can be had if you flashed a temple recommend, but not so anyone would know it.

The South Visitor Center displayed some information on the construction of the LDS temple and Solomon's temple, and downstairs you can hear about the *Book of Mormon*—but we found only one mention of Joseph Smith on the main floor. There was a picture of Jesus, under which was a statement from LDS scripture with a heading something like "Jesus Testifies of Joseph Smith."

Another thing also amazed us: All the older men and women guides had been replaced by very young (and very pretty) women.

Conrad Sundholm from Truth in Love Ministries in Oregon asked one older man who looked like a supervisor what had happened to all the restoration displays. The man, thinking he was talking to an upset church member, said that when they featured all the restoration displays, they averaged about 5000 missionary referrals each year (out of how many million visitors?). But now with the "Jesus only" approach, they have surpassed that number monthly!

The weekly *Church News* now runs regular articles about such things as the soup kitchens and the LDS programs to help the homeless or the flood victims or the earthquake survivors or the hurricane victims. It's great and vital to those getting help, but we are convinced the Mormon church is orchestrating this assistance in order to achieve public approval as never before.

The LDS church is spending tens of millions of dollars on ever-slicker ad campaigns, working ever harder to look more Christian than the Christians. Mormons are attempting to join Christian organizations like never before. Local pastors' groups are the hardest hit.

I believe it is the LDS leadership goal of the 1990s to tone down their "restoration of the gospel" story and get into the general orthodox Christian community. Every stone on the roadway is being smoothed out to make that work.

This work is to help prevent that from happening. As many cult ministries have done a good job of pointing out heresies, the

Mormons have just as diligently removed them from view. We who want to reach LDS people for Christ are probably in for the roughest time in 150 years!

REVELATION, FOR TODAY?

The LDS Position

Mormonism claims to receive ongoing prophecies from God through its leadership, and that these "revelations" are binding on the church. Implicit in the LDS argument is the idea that the church collapsed (or apostasized) soon after the death of the apostles. The LDS church cannot even exist without this great apostasy having taken place.

The Biblical View

We have no problem with God speaking to believers today. The New Testament is clear that there *are* prophets in the body of Christ (1 Corinthians 12–14). However, in the New Testament you will not find the idea of a single "prophet" who makes decisions or revelations for the entire church. You will find individual prophets (like Agabus, who seemed to be a relatively minor person) in the body who bring words from the Lord; but none of these are called apostles (Acts 11:27,28; 13:1; 15:32; 21:9). How could the daughters of Philip hold the LDS Melchizedek priesthood, which Mormonism claims is necessary for one to become a prophet?

Additionally, it is evident from the Bible that what a prophet says must be judged by what already has been written in God's Word: "Let the prophets speak two or three, and let the other judge. If any thing be revealed to another that sitteth by, let the first hold his peace. For ye may all prophesy one by one, that all may learn, and all may be comforted. And the spirits of the prophets are subject to the prophets" (1 Corinthians 14:29-32).

Since God cannot change (Malachi 3:6), His Word cannot contradict itself. The Old Testament must judge the New, and the entire Bible must judge any subsequent revelation. Since many of the key doctrines of Mormonism contradict the Bible, they must be dismissed (such as the nature of God being a man, Jesus not being Almighty Eternal God, etc.). Certainly God, in His sovereign will, can bring forth new revelation—but it can never contradict what He has already said.

Second, the Mormon doctrine of a great apostasy contradicts the Bible where Jesus said that He would be "with you alway, even unto the end of the world" (Matthew 28:20) and that "upon this rock I will build my church; and the gates of hell shall not prevail against it" (Matthew 16:18). The divinely inspired Paul also wrote, "Unto him be glory in the church by Christ Jesus throughout all ages, world without end. Amen" (Ephesians 3:21).

Now, if Jesus promised He would be with us always and that the gates of hell could never prevail against His church, then how could there have been such a universal apostasy as Joseph Smith taught? How could Jesus be glorified by His church "throughout all ages" if from A.D. 300–1830 it was drowning in apostasy and all power and authority was removed from the Earth? One only has to read *Foxe's Book of Martyrs* to know that the power of God through his Son, manifest by the Holy Spirit, was alive and well in the worst days of the Dark Ages.

Certainly there have been times when the church was not all it should be, but Jesus was still at its head. In isolated places throughout the world, brave little pockets of Bible-believing Christians existed, worshiped, and won souls. Jesus was with them as He promised, and prevented hell from crushing them. Let's believe Jesus' Word over Joseph Smith's.

Remember, prior revelation (the Bible) must always judge later revelation. The living prophets of Mormonism must be judged by the Bible, since the Bible came long before Joseph Smith (Isaiah 8:19,20). I recommend that you review the section, *Smith: Was Joseph a False Prophet?* and look at him through the eyes of biblical judgment.

SACRIFICE, LAW OF

The Law of Sacrifice is the second of five "laws" or "covenants" to which temple Mormons swear solemn allegiance in the endowment ceremony (see also *Endowments*). It is essential to Mormon salvation. This law is given during the Garden of Eden sequence of the endowment rite to the characters of Adam and Eve right after their transgression and their subsequent acceptance of the covenant of the Law of Obedience (see also *Obedience, Law of*). The LDS god, Elohim, administers the covenant to them.

This law is based, in part, on the eccentric version of the Genesis account given by Joseph Smith in the so-called Book of Moses (found in *The Pearl of Great Price*). In the temple ritual, the patrons are told:

> The Law of Sacrifice was given to Adam in the Garden of Eden, who, when he was driven out of the Garden, built an altar on which he offered sacrifices. And after many days, an angel of the Lord appeared unto Adam, saying: "Why doest thou offer sacrifice unto the Lord?" And Adam said unto him: "I know not, save the Lord commanded me." And then the angel spake, saying: "This thing is a similitude of the Sacrifice of the Only Begotten of the Father, who is full of grace and truth. Wherefore, thou shalt do all that thou doest in the name of the Son, and thou shalt repent and call upon God in the name of the Son forever-more."

The posterity of Adam down to Moses and from Moses to

Jesus Christ offered up the first fruits of the field and firstlings of the flock, which continued until the death of Jesus Christ, which ended sacrifice by the shedding of blood. And as Jesus Christ has laid down his life for the redemption of mankind, so we should covenant to sacrifice all that we possess, even our own lives if necessary, in sustaining and defending the Kingdom of God [Sackett, pp. 30-31].

After this explanation, all the patrons of the temple are made to raise their right arms to the square and agree to this covenant: "You and each of you solemnly covenant and promise before God, angels and these witnesses at this altar that you will each observe and keep the Law of Sacrifice as contained in the Old and New Testaments, as it has been explained to you" (ibid.).

Though much of this sounds quite noble, it is important to provide some "subtitles." The term "kingdom of God" in this teaching actually refers to the Mormon church—a physical entity now on the earth. This is not a reference to the heavenly reign of Jesus.

Thus, Mormons in the temple are being asked to give their all—even up to the taking of their own lives—for the LDS church. In fact, their very salvation depends on it. LDS founder Joseph Smith himself taught:

Those, then, who make the sacrifice, will have the testimony that their course is pleasing in the sight of God; and those who have this testimony will have faith to lay hold on eternal life; and *will be enabled, through faith, to endure unto the end,* and receive the crown that is laid up for them that love the appearing of our Lord Jesus Christ.

But those who do not make the sacrifice cannot enjoy this faith, because *men are dependent upon this sacrifice* in order to obtain this faith: therefore, *they cannot lay hold upon eternal life, because the revelations of God do not guarantee unto them the authority so to do, and without this guarantee faith could not exist* (*Lectures on Faith,* p. 60, emphasis added).

This only serves to illustrate that the Mormon, and especially the temple Mormon, is caught up in a works-righteousness system which is contrary to the New Testament gospel of grace.

SALVATION

The LDS Position

Mormonism has a very distinctive view on salvation. The foundation for its belief is in the LDS third Article of Faith (see also *Articles of Faith*). "We believe that through the Atonement of Christ, all mankind may be saved, by obedience to the laws and ordinances of the Gospel."

The late apostle James Talmage wrote:

> The extent of the atonement is universal, applying alike to all descendants of Adam. Even the unbeliever, the heathen, and the child who dies before reaching the years of discretion, all are redeemed by the Savior's self-sacrifice from the individual consequences of the fall. It is proved by scripture that the resurrection of the body is one of the victories achieved by Christ through His atoning sacrifice (*Articles of Faith*, p. 85).

Talmage says that while the firstfruits of the atonement was a universal resurrection, the result was really twofold.

This twofold effect is implied in the Article of Faith (#3) now under consideration. The first effect is to secure exemption from the penalty of the fall to all mankind, thus providing a way of *general salvation*. The second effect is to open a way for *individual salvation* whereby mankind may secure remission of personal sins. As these sins are the result of individual acts, forgiveness for them should be conditioned on individual compliance with prescribed requirements—"obedience to the laws and ordinances of the Gospel" (ibid., p. 87).

This is where LDS theology takes a sharp turn from orthodoxy. Mormons believe there are various levels of salvation because there are varying degrees of faith and of doing good works (see *Doctrine and Covenants* 76:99-101).

Bruce R. McConkie clarifies the distinction between general and individual salvation:

1. Unconditional or general salvation, that which comes by grace alone without obedience to gospel law, consists in the mere fact of being resurrected. In this sense, salvation is synonymous with immortality. This kind of salvation eventually comes to all mankind, excepting only the sons of perdition.

2. Conditional or individual salvation, that which comes by grace coupled with gospel obedience, consists in receiving an inheritance in the celestial kingdom of God. This kind of salvation follows faith, repentance, baptism, receipt of the Holy Ghost, and continued righteousness to the end of one's mortal probation (*Doctrine and Covenants* 20:29; 2 Nephi 9:23,24). Even those in the celestial kingdom, however, who do not go on to exaltation will have immortality only and not eternal life. Along with those of the telestial and terrestrial worlds they will be "ministering servants, to minister for those who are worthy of a far more, and an exceeding, and an eternal weight of glory." They will live "separately and singly" in an unmarried state "without exaltation, in their saved condition, to all eternity" (*Doctrine and Covenants* 132:16-17).

3. Salvation in its true and full sense is synonymous with exaltation or eternal life and consists in gaining an inheritance in the highest of the three heavens within the celestial kingdom. With few exceptions, this is the salvation of which the scriptures speak. It is the salvation which the saints seek. . . . This full salvation is obtained in and through the continuation of the family unit in eternity, and those who obtain it are gods (*Doctrine*, pp. 669-70).

When Mormons claim to be saved, it only means that they have gained this general resurrection. Beyond this, everything in the LDS "plan of salvation" is by works (*Encyclopedia*, 3:1257).

Thus, to meet a Mormon on his own terms, one must ask the important question, "Do you have eternal life?" Mormons believe that eternal life is exaltation, the highest degree of salvation. Few, if any, Mormons will claim to possess this eternal life.

At this point, a door to evangelism is opened for Christians, since they can rightfully (and biblically) claim that they *do* have eternal life. Mormons believe eternal life must be earned, and thus they can never be assured of its possession.

The Biblical View

Several key Bible passages can be brought to bear to help the Mormon see that he cannot earn eternal life.

"For the wages of sin is death; but the gift of God is eternal life through Jesus Christ our Lord" (Romans 6:23). The Bible insists that eternal life is a gift; and a gift, by definition, is not something one earns, but rather receives free of charge.

Additionally, the Christian can recount to the Mormon the promise of Jesus Christ: "Verily, verily, I say unto you, He that believeth on me hath everlasting life" (John 6:47). The soul-winner can point out that this is in the present tense. If a person believes in the Jesus Christ of the Bible, he or she has (right now) eternal life.

Confirm this wonderful promise with a second scripture: "These things have I written unto you that believe on the name of the Son of God; that ye may know that ye have eternal life, and that ye may believe on the name of the Son of God" (1 John 5:13).

The Christian can lovingly indicate to the Mormon that it is possible to know for certain if one has eternal life. It is wise to distinguish between the LDS version of Jesus and the Bible's Jesus at this point, and reveal to the Mormon that perhaps the reason he does not have this sure knowledge of his eternal destiny is because the object of his fervent faith (the LDS Jesus) has no power to give this precious gift of eternal life.

SAVIOR, JESUS CHRIST AS

(See also *Salvation*.)

The LDS Position

You will often hear Mormons call Jesus "the Savior" or even "my Savior." But while that sounds very Christian, most Mormons define Jesus Christ differently than do Christians. When a Mormon says Jesus is his personal Savior, in most cases, the "Jesus" being mentioned is not Almighty God, but merely the son of God or "a god" (see 1 Timothy 3:16; John 1:1-4). This "Jesus" did not die on the cross for our sins, but only for Adam's transgression. Thus, he cannot really save any of us from our sins.

When most Mormons call Jesus "Savior," or speak of Him as such, they only mean that He saved them from physical death—that He bought our resurrection from the grave by rising Himself. Bruce R. McConkie writes:

The spiritual death of the fall is replaced by the spiritual life of the atonement [of Christ], in that all who believe and obey

349

the gospel law gain spiritual or eternal life—life in the presence of God where those who enjoy it are alive to things of righteousness or things of the Spirit. The temporal death of the fall is replaced by the state of immortality which comes because of the atonement and resurrection of our Lord. The body and spirit which separated, incident to what men call the natural death, are reunited in immortality, in an inseparable connection that never again will permit the mortal body to see corruption. Immortality comes as a free gift by the grace of God alone without works of righteousness. Eternal life is the reward for "obedience to the laws and ordinances of the Gospel" (Third Article of Faith) (*Doctrine*, p. 62).

The second Article of Faith of the LDS church states: "We believe that men will be punished for their own sins, and not for Adam's transgression." Mormons believe that Jesus in His atonement wiped out the effects of Adam's "transgression." (Mormons don't believe that Adam actually sinned in eating from the tree; see *Fall of Adam*).

The Biblical View

The Bible warns us:

> But I fear, lest by any means, as the serpent beguiled Eve through his subtilty, so your minds should be corrupted from the simplicity that is in Christ. For if he that cometh preacheth another Jesus, whom we have not preached, or if ye receive another spirit, which ye have not received, or another gospel, which ye have not accepted, ye might well bear with him (2 Corinthians 11:3,4).

There *is* more than one "Jesus," though only one true Jesus. The definitions of both *Jesus* and *Savior* are vastly different in the Christian biblical view and the LDS view. This difference is critical, for the Bible is clear that Jesus did not just die for Adam's sin but for the individual sins of individual people. For example:

> And she shall bring forth a son, and thou shalt call his name JESUS: for he shall save his people from their sins (Matthew 1:21).

So Christ was once offered to bear the sins of many; and unto them that look for him shall he appear the second time without sin unto salvation (Hebrews 9:28).

Therefore will I divide him a portion with the great, and he shall divide the spoil with the strong; because he hath poured out his soul unto death: and he was numbered with the transgressors; and he bare the sin of many, and made intercession for the transgressors (Isaiah 53:12).

Who his own self bare our sins in his own body on the tree, that we, being dead to sins, should live unto righteousness: by whose stripes ye were healed (1 Peter 2:24).

And ye know that he was manifested to take away our sins; and in him is no sin (1 John 3:5).

If Mormons do not believe that Jesus' blood can save them from their own personal sins, then they obviously are not really saved. An official pamphlet published by the LDS church (1982), *What the Mormons Think of Christ*, has this to say:

Christians [note here how the LDS church tacitly admits that Christians are something other than Mormons] speak often of the blood of Christ and its cleansing power. Much that is believed and taught on this subject, however, is such utter nonsense and so palpably false that to believe it is to lose one's salvation. For instance, many believe or pretend to believe that if we confess Christ with our lips and avow that we accept him as our personal Savior, we are thereby saved. They say that his blood, without any other act than mere belief, makes us clean. . . . Salvation in the kingdom of God is available because of the atoning blood of Christ, but it is received only on condition of faith, repentance, baptism, and enduring to the end by keeping the commandments of God (pp. 19-20).

Mormons deny the Bible's teaching that "the blood of Jesus Christ his Son cleanseth us from all sin" (1 John 1:7) and that "by grace are ye saved through faith; and that not of yourselves: it is the gift of God: not of works, lest any man should boast" (Ephesians 2:8,9). Romans 6:23 makes it very clear that the much-vaunted "eternal life" which Mormons believe can only be earned through obedience is actually a free gift: "For the wages of sin is death; but the gift of God is eternal life through Jesus Christ our Lord."

When Mormons say Jesus is their Savior, they are talking about a different Jesus, and a salvation which really saves them from nothing. It is a salvation which walks carefully around the blood and the cross of Jesus Christ, even though the Bible makes it clear that "without shedding of blood is no remission [of sin]" (Hebrews 9:22).

SCRIPTURES: Plain and Precious Things Missing

Mormonism teaches that the Bible contains only part of the fullness of the gospel, and while Mormons accord it a place of honor and consider it one of their standard works, it is with some reservation. This doctrine causes serious problems for the Christian who hopes to witness to the Mormon through the Bible.

The LDS eighth Article of Faith states: "We believe the Bible to be the word of God as far as it is translated correctly; we also believe the Book of Mormon to be the word of God."

This tenet of faith undermines and destroys the power of biblical truth in the minds of all believing Mormons and sends them to the *Book of Mormon* and the LDS living prophets for the "fulness of the gospel":

> He [Joseph Smith] has brought forth the Book of Mormon . . . has sent the fulness of the everlasting gospel, which it contained, to the four quarters of the earth (*Doctrine and Covenants* 135:3).

> I [Joseph Smith] told the Brethren that the Book of Mormon was the most correct of any book on earth, and the keystone of our religion, and a man would get nearer to God by abiding by its precepts, than by any other book (*History of the Church*, vol. 4, p. 461).

Mormons believe that the Bible is the Word of God as far as it is translated correctly. That is another way of saying that "many plain and precious things" were removed from the Bible by the "great and abominable church."

The *Book of Mormon*, which the LDS people are told contains the fullness of the gospel, tells them to be cautious when using the Bible because it has been badly vandalized:

And the angel of the Lord said unto me: Thou hast beheld that the book [the Bible] proceeded forth from the mouth of a Jew; and when it proceeded forth from the mouth of a Jew it contained the fulness of the gospel of the Lord, of whom the twelve apostles bear record; and they bear record according to the truth which is in the Lamb of God. Wherefore, these things go forth from the Jews in purity unto the Gentiles, according to the truth which is in God.

And after they go forth by the hand of the twelve apostles of the Lamb, from the Jews unto the Gentiles, thou seest the formation of a great and abominable church, which is most abominable above all other churches; for behold, *they have taken away from the gospel of the Lamb many parts which are plain and most precious; and also many covenants of the Lord have they taken away.* And all this have they done that they might pervert the right ways of the Lord, that they might blind the eyes and harden the hearts of the children of men.

Wherefore, thou seest that after the book hath gone forth through the hands of the great and abominable church, that there are many plain and precious things taken away from the book, which is the book of the Lamb of God.

And after these plain and precious things were taken away it goeth forth unto all the nations of the Gentiles; and after it goeth forth unto all the nations of the Gentiles, yea, even across the many waters which thou hast seen with the Gentiles which have gone forth out of captivity, thou seest—because of the many plain and precious things which have been taken out of the book, which were plain unto the understanding of the children of men, according to the plainness which is in the Lamb of God—because of these things which are taken away out of the gospel of the Lamb, an exceedingly great many do stumble, yea, insomuch that Satan hath great power over them (1 Nephi 13:24-29, emphasis added).

Now, after decimating the credibility of the Bible, the *Book of Mormon* promises itself to the believer. Incredibly, it tries to become the proof of itself.

And it came to pass that the angel of the Lord spake unto me, saying: Behold, saith the Lamb of God, after I have visited the remnant of the house of Israel . . . and this remnant of whom I speak is the seed of thy father . . . wherefore, after I have visited them in judgment, and smitten them by the hand of the Gentiles, and after the Gentiles do stumble exceedingly, because of *the most plain and precious parts of the gospel of the Lamb which have been kept back by that abominable church,* which is the mother of harlots, saith the Lamb—I will be merciful unto the Gentiles in that day, insomuch that I will bring forth unto them, in mine own power, much of my gospel, which shall be plain and precious, saith the Lamb (1 Nephi 13:34, emphasis added).

The Mormon therefore "knows" that the *Book of Mormon* is the true Word of God. It did not have many "plain and precious things" removed, as did the Bible. It did not suffer at the hands of many translations, as did the Bible. It contains Christ's full teachings (the ones stolen away from the Bible) to His other sheep.

And now it came to pass that when Jesus had told these things he expounded them unto the multitude; and he did expound *all things* unto them, *both great and small* (3 Nephi 26:1, emphasis added).

And he did expound *all things,* even from the beginning until the time that he should come in his glory—yea, even all things which should come upon the face of the earth, even until ... the heavens and the earth should pass away (3 Nephi 26:3, emphasis added).

The Mormon Jesus proclaims that his church shall be called by his name (3 Nephi 27:6,7) and be built upon his gospel:

But if it be called in my name then it is my church, it be so that they are built upon *my gospel* (3 Nephi 27:8, emphasis added).

Verily I say unto you, that ye are built upon *my gospel;* therefore ye shall call whatsoever things ye do call, in my name; therefore if ye call upon the Father, for the church, if it be in my name the Father will hear you (3 Nephi 27:9, emphasis added).

The LDS Jesus also sets forth a judgment of what He taught. In 3 Nephi 27:10,11, He says that if his church is not built upon his gospel (given in complete detail) and is built upon the works of a man or the devil, it will give: "joy in their works for a season, and by and by the end cometh, and they are hewn down and cast into the fire, from whence there is no return."

In 1 Nephi 13:32-35 the LDS god promises that a day will come when these "plain and precious promises" would be restored, after the "mother of harlots" takes away the "most plain and precious things of the gospel" of the Lamb and causes the Gentiles to stumble. He says he will manifest himself to the seed of Nephi and they shall write many things—all the precious things taken away by the church—and they will bear fruit even after their seed are all gone. These things were to be hidden, then later delivered to the Gentiles. "And in them shall be written my gospel, saith the Lamb, and my rock [the word *rock* refers to "gospel"; see *Doctrine and Covenants* 11:24] and my salvation" (v. 36).

Therefore, according to Mormonism, the "plain and precious things" taken away by the great and abominable church must be restored in the *Book of Mormon*. This claim is verified by latter-day "revelations":

> For in them are all things written concerning the foundation of my church, my gospel, and my rock (*Doctrine and Covenants* 18:4).

> And again, I command thee that thou shalt not covet thine own property, but impart it freely to the printing of the Book of Mormon, which contains the truth and the Word of God (*Doctrine and Covenants* 19:26).

> And gave him power from on high, by the means which were before prepared, to translate the Book of Mormon; which contains a record of a fallen people, and the fulness of the gospel of Jesus Christ to the Gentiles and to the Jews also (*Doctrine and Covenants* 20:8,9).

> And again, the elders, priests and teachers of this church shall teach the principles of my gospel, which are in the Bible and the Book of Mormon, in the which is the fulness of the gospel (*Doctrine and Covenants* 42:12).

So what are the things contained in the "fulness of the gospel," the *Book of Mormon*, which are lost, hidden, and not contained in the Bible? Some of the "restored" doctrines that separate Mormonism from orthodox Christianity are listed here:

- God has a body of flesh and bones.

- God is an exalted man.

- God is a product of eternal progression.

- The plurality of gods.

- God "organized" the world rather than "created" it.

- These is no eternal hell and punishment.

- Men can become gods.

- "Intelligences" are eternal.

- Preexisting spirits of men.

- Marriage for eternity.

- Polygamy is not an abomination in the sight of God.

- Three degrees of glory.

- A "Mother" in heaven.

- A Melchizedek priesthood consisting of the offices of elder, seventy, and high priest.

- An Aaronic priesthood consisting of the offices of deacon, teacher, and priest.

- The functions and offices of evangelist, bishoprics, stake presidencies, assistants to the Twelve, a First Presidency, and a president of the church.

- The *Book of Mormon* is the "stick of Joseph."

Now, the interesting thing is this: Not only can none of these things be found in the *Book of Mormon*, but the *Book of Mormon* is absolutely opposed to some of these LDS doctrines. The *Book of Mormon* actually teaches against these "eternal LDS doctrines." Because of the length of the references, I have listed them here and hope that the interested reader will look them up for the details.

Eternal Progression

Alma 41:8	3 Nephi 24:6
Mormon 9:9,10,19	Moroni 8:18

Salvation

2 Nephi 9:21-23	3 Nephi 11:33
Mosiah 5:7	Mormon 9:23-24
Mosiah 27:24-26	Ether 3:14
Alma 11:40-41	Ether 4:18
Helaman 5:9-11	Moroni 8:23

Baptism for the Dead

Alma 34:32,35

Polygamy

Jacob 1:15	Mosiah 11:2
Jacob 2:22-27	Ether 10:5
Jacob 3:5	

Temples, Oaths

Mormon 8:27	Alma 34:36
2 Nephi 9:9	Alma 37:23,31
2 Nephi 26:22	

God Organized the World, Rather Than Created It

Mormon 9:17

The Nature of God

2 Nephi 11:7	Mosiah 15:1-5
2 Nephi 26:12	Mosiah 16:15
2 Nephi 31:21	Alma 11:26-33,38,39,44
Mosiah 7:27	Alma 34:32,35
Mosiah 13:34	3 Nephi 11:27,40

In a court of law, evidence is based upon the testimony of several witnesses. Any witness for Mormon theology must be supported by both the Bible and the LDS book of scripture, the *Book of Mormon*. Therefore it is strange that the doctrine of the *Book of Mormon* and the doctrine of the Bible both directly contradict official Mormon theology.

While Mormons completely swallow the idea that "the great and abominable church" stole all the LDS doctrine out of the Bible, they never raise so much as a question as to the *Book of Mormon's* bizarre rebuttal of everything Mormon. I have said elsewhere in this work that much of Mormonism is like a film negative of truth. Dark is light and light is dark. I can't think of a better example of spiritual darkness in action.

SEALING POWER

The LDS Position

Sealing power is the supposed ability of the Mormon church to enforce ecclesiastical rituals and contracts not only in "time"—the here and now of life—but also into eternity. Bruce R. McConkie elaborates:

> Whenever the fulness of the gospel is on earth, the Lord has agents to whom he gives power to bind on earth and seal eternally in the heavens (Matthew 16:19; 18:18; Helaman 10:3-10; *Doctrine and Covenants* 132:46-49). This sealing power, restored in this dispensation by Elijah the Prophet (*Doctrine and Covenants* 2:1-3; 110:13-16), is the means whereby "All covenants, contracts, bonds, obligations, oaths, vows, performances, connections, associations, or expectations" attain "efficacy, virtue, or force in and after the resurrection from the dead" (*Doctrine and Covenants* 132:7) (*Doctrine*, p. 683).

Mormons believe that any marriage or filial relationship (between parent and child) that is not sealed by the power of the Melchizedek priesthood is only "for time" and will terminate upon death. However, as part of the LDS concept of progression (see also *Law of Eternal Progression*), Mormons believe that it is everyone's divinely intended destiny to have their marriage and family relationships endure into the eternities. Of course, one must a) become a Mormon, b) go to the temple for endowments (see also *Endowments*) and sealings, and then c) keep all the many commandments of the Mormon church perfectly in order to benefit from these supposed eternal relationships and attain the state of godhood or "exaltation" (see also *Exaltation*).

This sealing power supposedly seals up the children on earth to their fathers who went before, and forms the enduring patriarchal chain that Mormonism claims will exist eternally among exalted beings (see *Doctrines of Salvation*, vol. 2, pp. 115-28). Mormons believe that this can be accomplished only within the confines of an LDS temple.

Certain selected men who hold the office of high priest in the Melchizedek priesthood are personally called by the prophet of the LDS church and have this sealing power given to them. It is taught that only the prophet and, to a lesser degree, the Council of Twelve (Apostles) have this sealing power by right. Since they cannot be in all the temples on any given day, they delegate this sealing power to these various high priests who happen to live near a temple and are considered consummately worthy. Yet it is only theirs temporarily and by delegation.

The high priests who are sealers come into play only in the temple rituals after the endowment is over. When a married couple goes through the temple for the first time, they "take out" their own endowment. After they go through the veil and are admitted to the celestial room, they are ready to be sealed. If they are a newly married couple or if they have no children, they are simply brought into a sealing room. If they are either converts to the church who have already been married and have children or Mormons who have waited until later in their marriage to be sealed, then their children are brought to the sealing room to join them.

The sealing rooms are small enough to be intimate and are beautifully appointed. They vary in size, depending on the size of the wedding party. Many times, a large part of the party— sometimes even the parents of the bride or groom—are not allowed into the sealing room because they are not Mormons or are not worthy enough Mormons to have a temple recommend (see also *Temple Recommend*). They may have to wait in the anterooms of the temple and are allowed to attend only a reception.

The centerpiece of the sealing room is a small, richly upholstered altar, with elegantly padded "kneelers" all the way around. It is upon this altar that the couple will be sealed. Around the altar are chairs enough for the wedding party, and a larger, throne-like chair for the person doing the sealing. Most temple sealing rooms since the days of the Salt Lake temple feature two lengthwise walls covered with mirrors. Since these mirrors face each other, they reflect each other's images. As the couple kneel and face each other across the altar, the mirrors create an illusion of almost infinite reflections. This is intended as a visual metaphor for the "eternal increase" of marriage in the eternities.

The couple joins hands in the "patriarchal grip" (the last of the secret handshakes one learns in the endowment; it is also called the "sure sign of the nail") kneeling across from each other at the altar, and there the sealer claims to seal them for time and all eternity in the "new and everlasting covenant" of marriage.

If the couple has children, the children join them and kneel around the altar together. If they are newlyweds and have been sealed, any children born of the union are automatically sealed and "under the covenant." They do not have to go through this ritual.

It is only this ritual which supposedly enables the Mormon to go on into the celestial kingdom and have "eternal increase of seed" (i.e., continue to have children beyond death). Even then, it is only worthy Mormons who have been sealed who have even a hope of this family unit continuing into eternity. If either spouse errs and commits serious sin and does not repent, then, in death, the other (worthy) spouse and children would be given to another person(s) in celestial glory.

Children who fail to "make the grade" can also shatter the eternal family unit forever. This is because the entire concept is based upon individual, personal worthiness and keeping perfectly an impossibly long list of commandments—even more binding than the Old Testament Mosaic law.

This is one of the core teachings of LDS theology and is absolutely essential for the full salvation Mormons believe can be theirs.

The Biblical View

All this is an utterly vital part of the LDS gospel, yet the Bible says nothing of any of this—except to deny it. The "binding and loosing" power which the Mormons cite out of Matthew 16 says nothing about marriage or family relationships. Even more damaging is the Lord Jesus Christ's clear teaching, which He could well have been proclaiming to Joseph Smith and the LDS leaders: "Ye do err, not knowing the scriptures, nor the power of God. For in the resurrection they neither marry, nor are given in marriage, but are as the angels of God in heaven" (Matthew 22:29,30).

Add to this Paul's teaching about a wife being free to marry after her husband's death (Romans 7:2; 1 Corinthians 7:39), which makes it sound as though the greatest apostle of his day was ignorant of this wonderful sealing power. These two verses alone present a damning case against the entire Mormon doctrine.

SECRET SOCIETIES

(See also *Freemasonry.*)

As a matter of course, Mormons today are discouraged from joining secret societies. This is based upon the many passages in the *Book of Mormon* and other LDS scriptures which speak of secret oaths, secret combinations, and a marauding band of secret vigilantes which terrorized the supposed *Book of Mormon* civilizations 1600 or more years ago in ancient America (see also *Master Mahan*).

This is, of course, rather strange. As has been pointed out elsewhere (see also *Freemasonry*), the LDS temple ritual is a secret ritual, even though it is the most sacred element in Mormon thought (see also *Temple Ordinances*). Temple Mormons, in fact, constitute a kind of secret society in every reasonable sense of the definition. This is true even down to the dire blood oaths and ritual throat-cutting/body-disemboweling gestures which were eliminated from the endowment in 1990 after public exposure by a number of ex-Mormon authors and filmmakers.

Additionally, Joseph Smith and many other early Mormon leaders were Freemasons. This puts the Mormons, once again, in the odd position of discouraging their members from doing something which their founders enthusiastically embraced—an activity which is also regarded as nearly the most sacred thing a Mormon can do on Earth: going to the temple.

SEER STONES

(See also *Peep Stones.*)

The term *seer stone* is a more elegant and biblical-sounding term for the device (or devices) which LDS prophet Joseph Smith used to work various occult operations. *Crystal ball* or *peep stone* would be a more accurate term.

Smith used his seer stones at first to supposedly find buried pirate treasure for neighboring farmers in his hometown of Palmyra, New York. Later, after he allegedly was given the gold plates which were to ultimately constitute the *Book of Mormon*, he supposedly used the same (or similar) stones to aid in translating the text from "Reformed Egyptian" into English.

Yet to use an occult device for supposedly godly purposes is unthinkable in the biblical worldview. Such a practice disproves Joseph Smith's supposed prophetic calling (see also *Occult* and *Oracles*).

SERPENTS

The serpent is something of an ambivalent symbol in both the Bible and the Mormon church. This ambivalence is reflected in the fact that although virtually all the uses of the serpent—either literally or in metaphor—relate to the devil, the serpent is also used as a symbol of Christ in Numbers 21:4-9. Here Moses is commanded by God to make an image of a serpent and lift it up upon a pole so that the children of Israel might look upon it and be saved from a plague of serpents which came into the camp because of their disobedience.

This analogy, puzzling as it is, is impossible to deny. Jesus Himself cites it in John 3:14,15: "And as Moses lifted up the serpent in the wilderness, even so must the Son of man be lifted up: that whosoever believeth in him should not perish, but have eternal life."

Still, in the face of dozens of uses of the serpent as a symbol for Satan, it would be a mistake to build an entire doctrine upon this single passage. Unfortunately, the Mormons try to do exactly this.

In an attempt to bring plausibility to the supposed visit of Jesus to the New World after the resurrection (see 3 Nephi 11–28), they connect this myth to the celebrated legend of the Meso-American feathered serpent god, Quetzalcoatl.

> Moses, by command of the Lord raised a brazen serpent before Israel, in similitude of the fact that Christ would be lifted up on the cross—thus giving foundation to the use of serpents as a good symbol. Among the Lamanite descendants of Lehi, Quetzalcoatl, the feathered serpent, became a symbol for the great

White God who had ministered among their ancestors (*Doctrine*, p. 705).

While it is true that the Aztecs worshiped a "great White God" named Quetzalcoatl, the resemblance between him and Jesus is nonexistent. First, contrary to the "blonde, Aryan-superman" image of Jesus found in paintings in LDS visitors' centers, the biblical Jesus was a Semite. The difference between a Jew living and walking constantly under the hot, Palestinian sun for 33 years, and an Aztec Indian's skin tones, would probably be small indeed!

Additionally, Quetzalcoatl was a bloodthirsty god whose votaries slew innocent victims—often children—and tore out their hearts by the thousands as a form of worship before Cortez came to the New World. Even allowing for a certain amount of corruption over a supposed 1000-year interval, how could the gentle gospel of the Lord be turned into a cultus which disemboweled the innocent? Quetzalcoatl is a pitiful historical argument for the truth of the *Book of Mormon*.

Serpents play an even stronger hand against the authenticity of the *Book of Mormon* in a passage which stretches the credulity of even the most gullible Mormon. It might be called "the Ballad of the Cowboy Serpents" (or at least "Shepherd Serpents"). Here it is in full context:

28And there came prophets in the land again, crying repentance unto them . . . that they must prepare the way of the Lord or there should come a curse upon the face of the land; yea, even there should be a great famine, in which they should be destroyed if they did not repent.

29But the people believed not the words of the prophets, but they cast them out; and some of them they cast into pits and left them to perish. . . .

31*And there came forth poisonous serpents* also upon the face of the land, and did poison many people. And it came to pass *that their flocks began to flee before the poisonous serpents, towards the land southward, which was called by the Nephites Zarahemla.*

32And it came to pass that there were many of them which did perish by the way; nevertheless, there were some which fled into the land southward.

33 And it came to pass that the Lord did cause *the serpents* that they should pursue them no more, *but that they should hedge*

up the way that the people could not pass, that whoso should attempt to pass might fall by the poisonous serpents.

³⁴And it came to pass that the people did follow the course of the beasts, and did devour the carcasses of them which fell by the way, until they had devoured them all. Now when the people saw that they must perish they began to repent of their iniquities and cry unto the Lord (Ether 9:28-34, emphasis added).

If we understand the limited amount of data we have on *Book of Mormon* geography, this herding of flocks by the serpents would have covered hundreds of miles. Can you imagine herds of sheep or cattle being driven hundreds of miles by poisonous snakes? Can you imagine those snakes corralling the flocks—and even people—for an indeterminate period of time? What did the snakes do at night? Did some sleep and some watch the herds?

Now admittedly, the God of the Bible did some pretty spectacular miracles with animals, especially in Exodus. Yet this alleged miracle seems more silly than awe-inspiring. None of the events surrounding the Exodus event tend to bring snickers to people's lips, but "cowboy snakes" certainly do!

SMITH, JOSEPH

Am I Too Hard on Him?

As a critic of the doctrines of Mormonism and of Joseph Smith, I am often asked many important questions and receive a number of valid criticisms. Part of these legitimate inquiries can be answered with a better understanding of LDS history.

For example, we need to understand that Mormons regard Joseph Smith and Brigham Young as more than merely spiritual leaders like Billy Graham. These men are considered "prophets of God." They are not to be challenged. To a Christian, however, what they said or did must be measured by the biblical standard of prophets. Dr. Graham does not claim to actually speak for God, as Joseph Smith did.

The premise that we must follow in this kind of apologetic can easily be placed in syllogistic form:

A. God does not change (Malachi 3:6).

B. A prophet who claims to speak for God cannot change the divine message (Deuteronomy 13:1-4).

C. Joseph and Brigham changed their messages (or the church leaders who succeeded them did), therefore they cannot be prophets of God.

A second syllogism is this:

A. God does not change.

B. All revelation comes from God (2 Timothy 3:16).

C. Therefore, all revelation must be judged by earlier revelation.

A third related syllogism is:

A. God has set very high standards for his prophets (Deuteronomy 13:1-3; 18:20-22).

B. Neither Joseph nor Brigham came close to meeting those standards (lying, adultery, false prophecies, false doctrine, murder).

C. Therefore, neither Joseph nor Brigham can be true prophets.

It is on the basis of these three syllogisms that I pursue the line of reasoning I do. None of the leaders of the Reformation, nor Henry VIII, nor Calvin, nor Roger Williams, claimed to be prophets of God. None of them claimed to have divine fiat for everything they said. *The LDS leaders did and do.*

That was their unique claim to fame. Joseph Smith stood up in an area of upper New York state in the midst of much religious enthusiasm and controversy and claimed to have a brand-new Word from God which would settle all discussions.

All the great Protestant leaders acknowledged they were sinners saved by grace. They knew they were imperfect and that their churches were imperfect attempts to follow the New Testament. The LDS leaders claimed to have a direct pipeline to God which would set aside 1800 years of Christianity. That is a big difference.

Christians should not look to leaders for their perfection; they should look to Jesus alone, proclaiming Jesus alone. Mormons, on the other hand, must trust in their leaders to guide them to their celestial goal. They cannot get there without their leaders. Christianity stands or falls on the character of Jesus—not on the strengths or flaws of Calvin or Luther.

Mormonism, on the other hand, literally demands that we test and measure it not on the basis of Jesus but on the basis of Joseph Smith and the *Book of Mormon*. Even there, we are not allowed to use biblical tests already in place for such things, but to trust in a subjective "burning in the bosom."

Nevertheless, if Joseph Smith fails the biblical test of a prophet (either through immorality or through failed prophecy), then Mormonism fails. This is why Joseph Smith is the linchpin upon which Mormonism stands or falls.

Questionable antecedents, wrong beliefs, and practices don't prevent a person from being transformed and used by God. Yet if those beliefs and practices remain after the alleged regenerative experience (which most LDS believe to be the first vision, in Smith's case), then we must begin to question the fruits we are seeing.

When deep sin like perjury, adultery, and murder is being called "commandments of God" and practiced years after the supposed regeneration, one must question the genuineness of the conversion. Joseph and his cohorts didn't merely commit little sins in their wild and misspent youth. They were indulging in gross sin—sin which, indeed, was getting worse—right up to the time Smith was jailed and murdered. And it was carried on even after his death.

Yes, I am hard on Joseph Smith. But truth is like that.

Was Joseph Smith a Boaster?

Reproduced below is one of the few prophecies Joseph Smith actually got right. In *Doctrine and Covenants* 3 (1828), I find this in verse 4: "For although a man may have many revelations, and have power to do many mighty works, yet if he boasts in his own strength, and sets at naught the counsels of God, and follows after the dictates of his own will and carnal desires, he must fall and incur the vengeance of a just God upon him."

Now bear that prophecy in mind as I move ahead to 1844. In May of that year, Smith proclaimed this:

> I have more to boast of than any man ever had. I am the only man that has ever been able to keep a whole church together since the days of Adam. A large majority of the whole have stood by me. Neither Paul, John, Peter, nor Jesus ever did it. I boast that no man ever did such a work as I. The followers of Jesus ran away from him; but the Latter-day Saints never ran away from me yet (*History of the Church*, vol. 6:408-09).

If that isn't boasting in his own strength, I don't know the meaning of the term. Obviously, God agreed with such an assessment, for just 30 days after making that boast—on June 27, 1844—Joseph Smith was murdered by a mob in Carthage jail (ibid., p. 618).

Was Joseph Smith a Descendant of Jesus?

One of the more obtuse teachings of Mormonism is the doctrine that Joseph Smith and others were the physical descendants of Jesus Himself. This involves another less obtuse teaching that Jesus was married. While I agree that the average Mormon will cry, "We do not believe that!" those in the know fully understand it and keep it quietly reserved for members who are prepared for the "higher truths."

If Joseph Smith didn't believe and teach that he was descended from Christ, then what does *Doctrine and Covenants* 113, verses 1-6 mean? It says:

> Who is the stem of Jesse spoken of in the 1st, 2d, 3d, 4th and 5th verses of the 11th chapter of Isaiah? Verily thus saith the Lord: It is Christ. What is the rod spoken of in the first verse of the 11th chapter of Isaiah, that should come of the stem of Jesse? Behold, thus saith the Lord, it is a servant in the hands of Christ, who is partly a descendant of Jesse, as well as of Ephraim, or of the house of Joseph, on whom is laid much power. What is the root of Jesse spoken of in the 10th verse of the 11th chapter? Behold, thus saith the Lord, it is a descendent of Jesse, as well as of Joseph, unto whom rightly belongs the priesthood and the keys of the kingdom, for an ensign, and for the gathering of my people in the last days.

Now ask the Mormon, "Unto which descendent of Joseph does the priesthood and the keys of the kingdom rightly belong in the last days?" Mormons fully believe it is Joseph Smith. Joseph himself believed and taught that he was descended from Christ, and later he blessed several of his close associates and told them that they were, as well.

Was Joseph Smith a False Prophet?

The LDS Position

Mormon missionaries will tell you that you can know Joseph Smith is a true prophet by reading the *Book of Mormon* and by praying about it. They talk about a "burning in the bosom" that will confirm their claim.

Yet the trouble with subjective, inner feelings is that they can be deceptive. This fact is proved by the fact that there are many religions with millions of members, all of whom feel they are in the right religion. Jehovah's Witnesses have assuredly prayed about it and feel that their church is right. How can Mormons argue with that, when they too are trusting in a feeling?

The Biblical View

It is because people make such claims that the Bible gives concrete, solid ways to identify a true prophet. The Bible gives explicit instructions on how to identify a true prophet—and praying about it is not mentioned.

The Bible tells us that "The heart is deceitful above all things, and desperately wicked: who can know it?" (Jeremiah 17:9). It also says, "There is a way which seemeth right unto a man, but the end thereof are the ways of death" (Proverbs 14:12). How can we trust our feelings?

The Bible says that there are two tests of a prophet. One is found in Deuteronomy 13:1-5.

> If there arise among you a prophet, or a dreamer of dreams, and giveth thee a sign or a wonder, and the sign or the wonder come to pass, whereof he spake unto thee, saying, Let us go after other gods, which thou hast not known, and let us serve them; thou shalt not hearken unto the words of that prophet, or

that dreamer of dreams: for the LORD your God proveth you, to know whether ye love the LORD your God with all your heart and with all your soul.

Ye shall walk after the LORD your God, and fear him, and keep his commandments, and obey his voice, and ye shall serve him, and cleave unto him. And that prophet, or that dreamer of dreams, shall be put to death; because he hath spoken to turn you away from the LORD your God, which brought you out of the land of Egypt, and redeemed you out of the house of bondage, to thrust thee out of the way which the LORD thy God commanded thee to walk in. So shalt thou put the evil away from the midst of thee.

The passage makes it clear that even though a prophet's predictions come to pass, that is not enough. If the prophet tells you to follow another god than the one of the Bible, then that prophet is false. The penalty for violating this was death.

Now the question becomes, Did Joseph Smith teach men to follow a god other than the one in the Bible? As far as the identity of the Mormon god, it is obvious that their god is:

1. an exalted, resurrected man, in possession of a physical, but glorified body.

2. evolved from a normal human male.

3. limited in both power and knowledge.

4. subject to gods above him.

5. unable to create something out of nothing.

Most Mormon missionaries will admit to most of these doctrines, and they can all be found in the standard writings of LDS prophets. On the other hand, the biblical God

1. is a Spirit (John 4:24).

2. is not a man, nor the son of a man (Numbers 23:19).

3. is all powerful (Habakkuk 3:6; Matthew 19:26) and all-knowing (Psalm 147:5; Hebrews 4:13; 1 John 3:20).

4. says there are no other gods before Himself (Isaiah 43:10; 44:6-8).

5. made the entire universe from nothing (Genesis 1:1,2; Hebrews 11:3).

It is clear that in these five key areas the Mormon god and the God of the Bible are exact opposites; they cannot possibly be the same being. This means that Joseph Smith preached a false god, and that makes him a false prophet. It is that simple.

Yet there is a second test, given in Deuteronomy 18:20-22. Here is how it reads in verses 21,22: "How shall we know the word which the LORD hath not spoken? When the prophet speaketh in the name of the LORD, if the thing follow not, nor come to pass, that is the thing which the LORD hath not spoken, but the prophet hath spoken it presumptuously: thou shalt not be afraid of him."

Verse 20 calls for the death of such a prophet! Now we must ask, Did Smith make any false prophecies? See *Nauvoo House* and *Doctrine and Covenants, Changes in* for a detailed look at some of his prophecies.

Only one false step is necessary. This is a man who claimed to be a spokesman for Almighty God, a person who claimed to hold the spiritual keys to this entire dispensation. It only takes one false prophecy to make a false prophet, just as it only takes one murder to make a man a murderer. Yet Joseph Smith made literally dozens of false prophecies.

An easy one for Mormons to check out is found in *Doctrine and Covenants* 84:3,5,31. Here Smith prophesied in 1832 that the temple (house of the Lord) would be built in Independence, Missouri, during *that* generation. After 155 years, there is still no temple in Independence, and Bible scholars agree that a generation is never more than 70 years.

It is evident from Mormon speeches in the nineteenth century that they believed the temple would be built in their own time. They were genuinely bewildered when the twentieth century arrived and there was not even a sign of the temple being built. By the standards of Deuteronomy 13 and 18, that makes Joseph Smith a false prophet.

There is no need to pray about it. The simple tests above easily prove that Smith was a false prophet.

Was Joseph Smith a Glass-looker?

Glass-looking is an old-fashioned term for the magical practice of scrying or crystal gazing. We have all certainly seen pictures of witches or gypsies staring into crystal balls (Stewart Farrar, *What Witches Do*, Phoenix Pub., 1983, pp. 94-96, 183).

Since crystal balls used to be rather expensive and hard to come by, often in rural nineteenth-century America a substitute was found. Some folk used a mirror painted black (mirrors used to be called "glasses" or "looking glasses").

Others used small bowls or cups filled with water with a little ink to darken it. And still others put lampblack on the outside of watch glasses (crystals). Joseph Smith seems primarily to have used some sort of smooth, egg-shaped stone as a "seer stone," but the concept is the same and is still generically referred to as glass-looking.

One of Joseph Smith's right-hand people, David Whitmer, reported that he also allegedly translated the *Book of Mormon* using his rock or crystal ball, placing it in his hat and then putting his face in the hat and gazing into the hat. Supposedly the stone would glow and the words for translating the gold plates would appear therein and Joseph would then dictate them to a scribe (David Whitmer, *An Address to All Believers in Christ*, p. 12).

This was borne out also by Joseph's wife Emma, who was present during parts of the process (*The Saints' Herald*, May 19, 1888, p. 310).

Was Joseph Smith a Mason?

In the official *History of the Church*, vol. 4, pp. 551-52, Joseph Smith writes that, "In the evening I received the first degree in Free Masonry in the Nauvoo Lodge" (March 15, 1842), and on the next page he writes that "Wednesday, March 16 . . . I was in the Masonic lodge and rose to the sublime degree" [Master Mason].

Freemasonry is basically a religion. Its Lodge rooms feature an altar and a Bible where members kneel and pray and take oaths that in some cases are, word for word, the very oaths Mormons have taken for 150 years at LDS temples.

The question is, Why did Joseph Smith join a competing religion when he was the prophet of the LDS church? Especially when Joseph claimed that:

> I was commanded to join none of them [religions], for they were all wrong; and the Personage that addressed me said that all their creeds were an abomination in his sight; that those

professors were all corrupt; that they draw near to me with their
lips, but their hearts are far from me, they teach for doctrines the
commandments of men, having a form of godliness but they deny
the power thereof (*Pearl of Great Price*, Joseph Smith—History
1:19).

This means that by joining the Masonic Lodge, Smith broke
his god's commandments. This is not even to address the issue of
the many close resemblances between the temple endowment rite
(which came after his Masonic initiation—*History of the Church*,
vol. 5, pp. 1-2) and Masonic ritual (William Schnoebelen, *Mormonism's Temple of Doom*, Triple J, 1987, pp. 36-43).

Was Joseph Smith a Money Digger?

When the movie *The God Makers* first informed the world
that Joseph Smith was a treasure seeker or a "teller of tall tales," was
that an unfair or unhistorical characterization?

First and most important, there is the legal fact that Joseph
Smith was convicted of being a "disorderly person and an impostor"
on March 20, 1826. The complaint against Smith accused him of
having

a certain stone which he had occasionally looked at to determine
where hidden treasures in the bowels of the earth were; that he
professed to tell in this manner where gold mines were a distance
underground, and had looked for Mr. Stowell several times and
informed him where he could find these treasures, and Mr. Stowell had been engaged in digging for them . . . (*Fraser's Magazine*,
1873).

This report was confirmed in 1971 through the discovery by
Wesley Walters of the actual bill for the trial of Smith (sworn
affidavit by Rev. Wesley P. Walters, October 28, 1971; see also
Leonard Arrington and David Britton, *The Mormon Experience*,
pp. 10-11).

For more on this element (and there is a great deal more), I
would recommend Mormon D. Michael Quinn's *Early Mormonism
and the Magic World View* (Salt Lake City: Signature Books, 1987).

As for his tall tales, Smith's own mother, Lucy Mack Smith,
wrote that he liked to tell tall tales in her now-censored (by the LDS

church) account of her son's life (*History of Joseph Smith by His Mother*, Lucy Mack Smith, Salt Lake City, 1945).

Was Joseph Smith our Judge?

The LDS Position

That Joseph Smith will one day be our judge is clearly LDS doctrine. We can quote many different authorities. Brigham Young taught that:

> No man or women in this dispensation will ever enter into the celestial kingdom of God without the consent of Joseph Smith. From the day that the priesthood was taken from the earth to winding-up scene of all things, every man and woman must have the certificate of Joseph Smith as a passport to their entrance into the mansion above where God and Christ are . . . I with you and you with me. I cannot go there without his consent (*Journal of Discourses*, 7:289).

LDS prophet Joseph Fielding Smith taught: "[There is] no salvation without accepting Joseph Smith. . . . No man can reject that testimony without incurring the most dreadful consequences, for he cannot enter the kingdom of God" (Joseph Fielding Smith, *Doctrines of Salvation*, 1:189-90).

There you have it: The Mormons believe that Joseph Smith will have the say-so on who makes it into the celestial kingdom and who does not. Even today, in the official *Melchizedek Priesthood Manual*, we are told: "If we get out salvation, we shall have to pass by him [Joseph Smith]; if we enter into our glory, it will be through the authority that he has received. We cannot get around him" (1984 *Melchizedek Priesthood Manual*, p. 133).

The Biblical View

The Bible says much about judges and judging. In fact, a quick count reveals it is mentioned about 200 times in both the Old and the New Testament. As one glances through the verses, however, it becomes clear that God has appointed some to sit as judges in temporal matters.

The New Testament clearly instructs us to stay away from judging motives:

Judge not, that ye be not judged. For with what judgment
ye judge, ye shall be judged: and with what measure ye mete, it
shall be measured to you again (Matthew 7:1,2).

Judge not, and ye shall not be judged: condemn not, and
ye shall not be condemned: forgive, and ye shall be forgiven
(Luke 6:37).

The Mormons tell us that Joseph Smith shall be our judge. We
need to tell them that we don't want him, nor do we need him.
There already is a Judge and the Bible identifies him for us: "Because he hath appointed a day, in the which he will judge the world
in righteousness by that man [Jesus] whom he hath ordained;
whereof he hath given assurance unto all men, in that he hath
raised him from the dead (Acts 17:31).

Clearly that man is not Joseph Smith, for Smith surely died
and he surely remained dead, just like all the other false saviors of
the world. Jesus died for our sins, was buried, and rose from the dead
to sit at the right hand of the Father. He will judge the world in His
righteousness.

SON OF GOD

The LDS Position

There is much confusion regarding the phrase "Son of God" in
Mormon doctrine. Mormons believe that Jesus is actually twice the
literal son of God. First, he was conceived by Elohim and one of his
goddess wives in the preexistence (see also *Preexistence; Law of
Eternal Progression*), born there as a spirit child, and raised in a
family unit until it was his time to come to earth and fulfill his
calling here. He was then physically conceived again by Elohim and
Mary (see *Virgin Birth*), born, and raised the second time. Mormonism teaches that we shared this natural manner of conception
and birth in our preexistent state and this made Jesus (even Lucifer,
too) our elder brother(s). Because we, too, were natural offspring,
sexually conceived there, we are also the literal sons of God.

Bruce R. McConkie clearly moves the nature of the Mormon
Christ outside the realm of biblical orthodoxy:

God the Father is a perfected, glorified, holy Man, an
immortal Personage. And Christ was born into the world as the

374

literal Son of this Holy Being; he was born in the same personal, real, and literal sense that any mortal son is born to a mortal father. There is nothing figurative about his paternity; he was begotten, conceived and born in the normal and natural course of events, for he is the Son of God, and that designation means what it says (1 Nephi 11).

Father Adam, the first man, is also a son of God (Luke 3:38; Moses 6:22,59), a fact that does not change the great truth that Christ is the Only Begotten in the flesh, for Adam's entrance into this world was in immortality. He came here before death had its beginning, with its consequent mortal or flesh-status of existence (*Doctrine*, pp. 741-42).

Regarding men being called the sons of God, McConkie also teaches the unique, unorthodox theological position of Mormonism. On page 745 of his book *Mormon Doctrine*, he states:

Those who receive the gospel and join The Church of Jesus Christ of Latter-day Saints have power given them to become the sons of God (*Doctrine and Covenants* 11:30; 35:2; 39:1-6; 45:8; John 1:12). Sonship does not come from church membership alone, but admission into the Church opens the door to such high status, if it is followed by continued faith and devotion (Romans 8:14-18; Galatians 3:26-29; 4:1-7). The sons of God are members of his family and, hence, are joint-heirs with Christ, inheriting with him the fulness of the Father (*Doctrine and Covenants* 93:17-23). Before gaining entrance to that glorious household, they must receive the higher priesthood (Moses 6:67-68), magnify their callings therein (*Doctrine and Covenants* 84:33-41), enter into the new and everlasting covenant of marriage (*Doctrine and Covenants* 131:1-4; 132), and be obedient in all things (*Doctrines of Salvation*, vol. 2, pp. 8-9, 37-41, 59, 64-65). Those who become the sons of God in this life (1 John 3:1-3) are the ones who by enduring in continued righteousness will be gods in eternity (*Doctrine and Covenants* 76:58).

The Biblical View

Are these Mormon teachings on the titles "sons of God" and "son of God" biblically correct? Is that really what the Bible means when it calls Jesus "the Son of God"?

The name "Son of God" is a title of honor and position given to Jesus 47 times in the Bible. Probably the most familiar is found in Galatians 2:20: "I am crucified with Christ: nevertheless I live; yet not I, but Christ liveth in me: and the life which I now live in the flesh I live by the faith of the Son of God, who loved me, and gave himself for me."

The apostle John used the title a good number of times to establish Jesus' divinity and therefore His right to the divine throne.

> Whosoever shall confess that Jesus is the Son of God, God dwelleth in him, and he in God (1 John 4:15).

> Who is he that overcometh the world, but he that believeth that Jesus is the Son of God? (1 John 5:5)

> He that believeth on the Son of God hath the witness in himself: he that believeth not God hath made him a liar; because he believeth not the record that God gave of his Son (1 John 5:10).

> He that hath the Son hath life; and he that hath not the Son of God hath not life (1 John 5:12).

> These things have I written unto you that believe on the name of the Son of God; that ye may know that ye have eternal life, and that ye may believe on the name of the Son of God (1 John 5:13).

> In this was manifested the love of God toward us, because that God sent his only begotten Son into the world, that we might live through him (1 John 4:9).

Not only does the Bible speak of Christ as the Son of God, but also of how through Him and an act of holy adoption, we can become sons of God:

> But as many as received him, to them gave he power to become the sons of God, even to them that believe on his name: which were born, not of blood, nor of the will of the flesh, nor of the will of man, but of God (John 1:12,13).

> But when the fulness of the time was come, God sent forth his Son, made of a woman, made under the law, to redeem them that were under the law, that we might receive the adoption of sons. And because ye are sons, God hath sent forth the Spirit of

his Son into your hearts, crying, Abba, Father. Wherefore thou art no more a servant, but a son; and if a son, then an heir of God through Christ (Galatians 4:4-7).

It's clear to see that Jesus is the Son of God because that is how the Bible, which is the inerrant Word of God, refers to Him (see Psalm 2:7; 89:26,27; Proverbs 30:4; Matthew 3:17; 11:27; 14:33; 16:15-17; 17:5; 26:63,64; Mark 1:1,11; 14:61,62; 15:39; Luke 1:32; 9:35; John 1:1-14; 3:16; etc.). There is a veritable avalanche of verses which teach clearly and plainly that Jesus is the Son of God. Some of them come from the Father Himself, while others are declarations by Jesus under solemn oath.

Now, this sonship does not mean, as the Mormons teach, that Jesus was physically fathered by God the Father through sexual relations with Mary. Nor does it mean that Jesus is not fully God and fully eternal. The Bible is clear about that. Jesus humbled Himself to become one of us. We can never realize how much Jesus gave up to come here to earth and suffer with us. That is the "mystery" of the incarnation: Jesus, "Emmanuel," "God with us."

Jesus is also the *only-begotten* Son of God (John 1:14,18; 3:16; 1 John 4:9). This means that His sonship relationship with the Father is utterly unique. Jesus is the only "natural born" Son of God. All the rest of us can be sons (or daughters) only by adoption through saving faith in Jesus (John 1:12; Romans 8:14-17). Thus, contrary to popular belief, the Bible does not teach that we are "all God's children," nor does it teach (as the Masons do) the "Fatherhood of God and the brotherhood of man." Those who do not receive Jesus Christ as their Lord and Savior are *not* children of God (John 8:44; Judges 19:22; 1 Samuel 2:12; 1 Kings 21:13).

Believers in Jesus Christ are children of God by adoption, but only Jesus is God's natural Son. This is essentially what is meant by Jesus being the Son of God. It is a unique term for the most unique Man who ever lived.

SONS OF PERDITION

The LDS Position

Mormonism teaches that the "sons of perdition" are the very lowest of the low. Some Mormon scholars argue that even Adolph

Hitler probably would not fall into this category because he never had the true light of the restored gospel revealed to him.

The first place the word *Perdition* appears in the LDS scriptures is in section 76 of the *Doctrine and Covenants*. Here it refers to Lucifer himself:

> And this we saw also, and bear record, that an angel of God who was in authority in the presence of God, who rebelled against the Only Begotten Son whom the Father loved and who was in the bosom of the Father, was thrust down from the presence of God and the Son, and was called Perdition, for the heavens wept over him . . . he was Lucifer, a son of the morning (vv. 25,26).

Individuals are brought into this sphere of curse in the *Book of Mormon:*

> But behold, it sorroweth me because of the fourth generation from this generation, for they are led away captive by him even as was the son of perdition; for they will sell me for silver and for gold, and for that which moth doth corrupt and which thieves can break through and steal. And in that day will I visit them, even in turning their works upon their own heads (3 Nephi 27:32).

> Yea, woe unto him that shall deny the revelations of the Lord, and that shall say the Lord no longer worketh by revelation, or by prophecy, or by gifts, or by tongues, or by healings, or by the power of the Holy Ghost! Yea, and wo unto him that shall say at that day, to get gain, that there can be no miracle wrought by Jesus Christ; for he that doeth this shall become like unto the son of perdition, for whom there was no mercy, according to the word of Christ (3 Nephi 29:6,7).

Again, Bruce R. McConkie in *Mormon Doctrine* explains the LDS view:

> Those in this life who gain a perfect knowledge of the divinity of the gospel cause, a knowledge that comes only by revelation from the Holy Ghost, and who then link themselves with Lucifer and come out in open rebellion, also become sons of perdition. Their destiny, following their resurrection, is to be cast

out with the devil and his angels, to inherit the same kingdom in a state where "their worm dieth not, and the fire is not quenched" (*Doctrine*, p. 746).

Joseph Smith said, "All sins shall be forgiven, except the sin against the Holy Ghost; for Jesus will save all except the sons of perdition (*Teachings*, p. 358).

The late LDS apostle, Mark E. Petersen, speaking at a stake conference in Bellevue, Washington, in the early 1980s, made a reference to one unnamed "son of perdition" living in the Issaquah area. A Mormon lady who was present asked the woman sitting next to her to whom he referred. She was told that it was an evil man named Ed Decker, who had left the church and joined the ranks of the devil.

Intrigued, the latter woman contacted me, listened to my story of finding the real Jesus, and she too gave her life to the Lord. The point of this story is that I and other outspoken former Mormons are the ones classified as "sons of perdition."

The Biblical View

Like so many of the LDS doctrines, a little bit of biblical truth is twisted to unorthodox purposes. Let's look at what the Bible actually says about the sons of perdition.

First, the word *perdition* is used as a substitute for *hell* or *destruction*:

> But they that will be rich fall into temptation and a snare, and into many foolish and hurtful lusts, which drown men in destruction and perdition (1 Timothy 6:9).

> But the heavens and the earth, which are now, by the same word are kept in store, reserved unto fire against the day of judgment and perdition of ungodly men (2 Peter 3:7).

Second, the word is used to describe the Antichrist, who will rise up in the last days and lead the final spiritual and political opposition to God.

> Let no man deceive you by any means: for that day shall not come, except there come a falling away first, and that man of

sin be revealed, the son of perdition; who opposeth and exalteth himself above all that is called God, or that is worshipped; so that he as God sitteth in the temple of God, shewing himself that he is God (2 Thessalonians 2:3,4).

Nowhere in the Bible do we read about people who are called "sons of perdition" in the same way as in Mormon theology. Perhaps the closest we can come is in the eighth chapter of John:

Jesus said unto them, If God were your Father, ye would love me: for I proceeded forth and came from God; neither came I of myself, but he sent me. Why do ye not understand my speech? even because ye cannot hear my word. Ye are of [your] father the devil, and the lusts of your father ye will do. He was a murderer from the beginning, and abode not in the truth, because there is no truth in him. When he speaketh a lie, he speaketh of his own: for he is a liar, and the father of it (John 8:42-44).

Even this declaration by Christ to the Pharisees, calling them sons of the devil, does not fit the conditions laid out for sons of perdition in Mormon theology.

It's interesting that the label "sons of perdition" is reserved in Mormonism for those who leave Mormonism for the truth of orthodox Christianity and return to share that truth and freedom with those still in the LDS church.

Those who vocally profess the saving grace of the Lord Jesus Christ need not fear the day of judgment. But those who have sat in an LDS temple receiving instruction in correct Mormon theology had better fear the day of judgment and the wrath of a God who says that His people shall not follow after other gods.

TALISMAN, JUPITER (Joseph Smith's)

A Jupiter talisman was found on the body of the murdered Joseph Smith. Its discovery and significance can be attributed to an LDS scholar, Reed Durham, and his paper, "Is There No Help for the Widow's Son?" (Martin Publishing, Nauvoo, IL, 1980, p. 22ff).

A talisman is a magical artifact, believed to possess certain virtue and power. Talismans can be made of cloth, parchment, or metal and are designed to be worn or carried by the sorcerer as a kind of sophisticated good-luck charm. These talismans are usually inscribed with either miniature magic circles and/or magic squares, and usually with sigils.

A sigil is a strange, often jagged line, which is made by tracing out the name of a demon, spirit, or genius (as they are sometimes called in high magic) on the magic square appropriate to that spirit. In the case of a Jupiter talisman, an owner would trace out the name on a Jupiter square, which would be four by four squares. The resulting tracing was then transposed onto the talisman and was believed to afford the magician absolute control over the demon.

Joseph Smith's talisman was a coin inscribed with a magic square in Hebrew on one side (4x4) and sigils on the other side (see Quinn, 1987, plate 28). Except for one character, it is identical to the magic talisman found in Francis Barrett's classic work *The Magus*, which was published and available to Smith (ibid., p. 69).

LDS author D. Michael Quinn notes that Smith's governing astrological sign was indeed Jupiter, so his using the Jupiter talisman made eminently good sense (ibid., caption to plate 28). It is ironic to note that the talisman Smith chose (there are many Jupiter talismans for different uses) was designed especially to give him success with women, and popularity and charm in general.

Considering Smith's involvement in polygamy with more than two dozen wives (to whom the church will admit—actually, there were more), it is no wonder that he appreciated such a magical aide. He needed to be popular with women in order to continue to add wives to his "celestial harem." Additionally, he probably needed all the charm he could muster to keep various irate husbands, brothers, and fathers from doing him grave bodily violence.

Quinn's research is especially damning because he notes that the inscription on the talisman owned by Smith indicated its use in ceremonies of spirit conjuration (see also *Occult*). The classic and formidable *grimoire* (magic work-text) *The Key of Solomon* defined the talisman's use *strictly for ceremonial magic*.

Now, ceremonial magic is just about the most advanced form of magic practiced in the past 1000 years. It is not a form of magic art for dabblers or dilettantes. *The Key of Solomon* is a ponderous and exacting manual of complex ceremonies for the most potent and dangerous forms of ceremonial magic.

It is highly unlikely that Smith would have either the understanding or access to such a talisman or wear it unless he himself was a ceremonial magician—*a wizard*. This would indicate, when added to the many other evidences, that Smith's involvement in the occult was both broad and profound. In those days, especially before the advent of the popular mass-market paperback books, to acquire and study these rare and dangerous volumes required real determination and skill (however misdirected). This evidence indicates that Smith was a dedicated and determined student of the black arts, perhaps even a master magician. And why shouldn't he have been? His entire family was steeped in the hell broth of magic (ibid., pp. 53-55).

With all this evidence against him, Smith can thank his "lucky stars" that he was not born during the time of the Mosaic law instead of the dispensation of grace. His prophetic career would have been cut mercifully shorter than it was. Had he shown up with his peep stones or his talisman in Moses' or Joshua's day, he would have been executed on the spot. The application of one single verse would have saved millions of Mormons from hell down through the years: "Thou shalt not suffer a witch to live" (Exodus 22:18).

TELESTIAL GLORY/KINGDOM

(See also *Degrees of Glory.*)

The LDS Position

The telestial kingdom is the lowest of the three degrees of glory: "And again, we saw the glory of the Telestial, which glory is that of the lesser, even as the glory of the stars differs from that of the glory of the moon in the firmament" (*Doctrine and Covenants* 76:81).

Those who shall spend their eternity in the telestial kingdom will be those who have lived the telestial law, which is defined as the law of the carnal world. The *Doctrine and Covenants* lists several requirements or conditions that will bring a person to this lowest degree of glory.

1. These are they who received not the gospel of Christ, neither the testimony of Jesus.

2. These are they who deny the Holy Spirit.

3. These are they who are thrust down to hell.

4. These are they who shall not be redeemed from the devil until the last resurrection, until the Lord, even Christ shall have finished his work.

5. These are they who receive not his fulness in the eternal world, but of the Holy Spirit through the ministration of the terrestrial [or next higher kingdom] (*Doctrine and Covenants* 76:82-86).

This list is enlarged later in the same revelation, showing that there are many levels of glory even within this same kingdom.

And the glory of the Telestial is one, even as the glory of the stars is one, for as one star differs from another star in glory, even so differs one from another in glory in the Telestial world.

1. These are they who are for Paul, and of Apollos, and of Cephas [and numerous others cited].

2. These are they who received not the gospel, neither the testimony of Jesus, neither the prophets, neither the everlasting covenant.

3. These are they who will not be gathered up with the saints, to be caught up into the church of the Firstborn and received into the cloud [they will not be in the first resurrection].

4. These are they who are liars, and sorcerers, and adulterers, and whoremongers, and whoever loves and makes a lie.

5. These are they who suffer the wrath of God on earth.

6. These are they who suffer the vengeance of eternal fire.

7. These are they who are cast down to hell and suffer the wrath of almighty God, until the fulness of times, when Christ shall have subdued all enemies under his feet, and shall have perfected his work (*Doctrine and Covenants* 76:98-106).

McConkie describes its occupants this way:

They will be the endless hosts of people of all ages who have lived after the manner of the world; who have been carnal, sensual, and devilish; who have chosen the vain philosophies of the world rather than accept the testimony of Jesus; who have been liars and thieves, sorcerers and adulterers, blasphemers and murderers (*Doctrine and Covenants* 76:81-112; Revelation 22:15). Their number will include "all the proud and all that do wickedly" (Malachi 4:1), for all such have lived a telestial law (*Doctrine*, p. 778).

LDS scripture further states that "they shall be judged according to their works and every man shall receive according to his own works, his own dominion, in the mansions which are prepared; and they shall be servants of the most High, but where God and Christ dwell they cannot come, worlds without end" (*Doctrine and Covenants* 76:111,112).

Basically, these are the great bulk of humanity who, during the millennial reign of Christ, will be sent from Earth or spirit prison to a physical place called hell and somehow proportionately suffer the buffetings of Satan for each of their ungodly deeds done while on Earth. They will then be raised up in the last resurrection, after the 1000 years of Christ's reign on Earth and be assigned to their own degree of glory in the telestial kingdom.

It is worth noting that Mormonism teaches the glory of even this lowly telestial kingdom is beyond human understanding (*Doctrine and Covenants* 76:89). This is the eternal kingdom, prepared with its mansions, for liars, murderers, thieves, whoremongers and sorcerers (to name a few).

This is the only hope of heaven for the Mormon lost in sin. Rather than reach out to the Savior for forgiveness and receive the promise of heaven with Christ, the sin-filled Mormon has this place of glory to look toward, beyond some individualized, purgatorial time in a loosely defined place called hell—a hell, we might add, that is rarely heard preached (if ever) by the vast majority of Mormons trusting in at least this telestial degree of glory for their eternal rest.

While God the Father and Christ are said not to visit this place, Mormons who are telestial kingdom bound are promised the ministry of the Holy Spirit and taught that God will send them ministering angels/personages from the terrestrial kingdom. It is as though the Holy Ghost is somehow not equal to God the Father or Christ in glory or holiness and can therefore mingle freely among these whoremongers and sorcerers who could not dare come into the presence of the Father or the Son.

The Biblical View

The Bible paints a far different picture than what this Mormon theology describes. With regard to our heavenly hopes, we are clearly told that "no whoremonger, nor unclean person, nor covetous man, who is an idolater, hath any inheritance in the kingdom of Christ and of God" (Ephesians 5:5). This directly contradicts the promises of Joseph Smith.

In fact, Paul continues in the very next sentences to warn the Ephesians to "let no man deceive you with vain words: for because of these things cometh the wrath of God upon the children of disobedience. Be not ye therefore partakers with them." What could be a clearer warning to the Mormon?

In Revelation 21, the apostle John describes his vision of the new heaven and new earth. At the end of that vision (v. 27) he adds, "And there shall in no wise enter into it any thing that defileth, neither whatsoever worketh abomination, nor maketh a lie." It is clear that John did not see the many supposed glories of the Mormon celestial, terrestrial, and telestial kingdoms. He saw *one* glorious heaven, and there were no eternal subdivisions being set up with mansions on high for any sinful man released from hell for good behavior.

TEMPLE GARMENTS

The LDS Position

Though never discussed in print, the temple garments of the LDS church are an essential feature of the temple endowment ritual. These garments are a form of underwear of a distinctive style.

They are white, and today come in either one- or two-piece styles and in several variations, both in terms of gender differences and in terms of methods of closure, fabric, etc. Essentially, they are like a T-shirt and long boxer shorts which extend slightly below the knee. They are marked with four stitched designs of supposedly spiritual significance: a Masonic square over the right breast, a compass over the left breast, a Masonic gauge or rule over the navel, and another over the right knee.

In older times they were available only in one-piece forms which were held together in front by white ribbon-like ties. A little over a generation ago they were much longer, extending to the ankles and wrists. This longer style seems to be the original form decreed by Joseph Smith.

Only Mormons who have been through the temple and are striving to be faithful to its covenants can or do wear this garment. This means that somewhere between 66 to 75 percent of Mormons do not wear it, nor do LDS children below the age of 18. It is given to the Mormon when he or she goes through the temple for the first time, after being washed with water and anointed with oil, prior to receiving his or her endowment (see also *Temple Ordinances*).

The garment is placed upon their naked body by a temple worker of the same gender, who declares:

> I place this garment upon you which you must wear throughout your life. It represents the garment given to Adam when he was found naked in the Garden of Eden, and is called the Garment of the Holy Priesthood. Inasmuch as you do not defile it, but are true and faithful to your covenants, it will be a shield and a protection to you against the power of the destroyer until you have finished your work here on earth (Chuck Sackett, *What's Going On in There?*, p. 20).

The "must wear throughout your life" has been interpreted with diminishing severity over the decades. Older former Mormons such as Thelma Geer have testified that prior generations were required to literally never be found with the garment off, even while bathing. It is to be worn underneath all other clothing, including other undergarments, and most devout Mormons do not even remove it for acts of marital intimacy.

Since the early 1980s a change in the policy on garments has occurred which permits men and women to abstain from wearing the garment if wearing it would expose it (or them) to public ridicule (i.e., underneath a jogging outfit or swimsuit). Still, LDS women especially are strongly forbidden from ever exposing any part of their body normally covered by the garment (i.e., midriff or upper thighs).

The garment is not to be disposed of as a rag when worn out or ruined in some way. The "sacred marks" mentioned above are to be first cut out of the garment and carefully burned. Then the garment may be discarded. All of this gives an aura of magic and mystery to the garment, and a great deal of LDS folklore has surrounded it (D. Michael Quinn, *Early Mormonism and the Magic World View*, p. 213).

Many Mormons do treat the garment as a kind of spiritual bullet-proof vest or a lucky rabbit's foot. Faith-promoting stories about faithful temple Mormons whose garments allegedly protected them from fires, bombs, bullets, or falling buildings abound. The fact that evidently the virtue or spiritual power of the garment is vitiated when the marks are cut out adds to this magical worldview.

The Biblical View

This sort of thing is treated in the Bible as superstitious nonsense. Although the Levitical priesthood in the Old Testament did have specially designed robes, they were utterly unlike the above-described garment (see Exodus 28–29). And even if there were some resemblances, this Levitical garment was done away with at the cross of Calvary (Hebrews 7:11-19).

There are three rather oblique references to a garment in the New Testament: the "wedding garment" which the guest was without in Matthew 22:11-14; and two in the highly apocalyptic Book of Revelation (Revelation 3:4; 16:15). Nowhere are any of these references called priesthood garments, nor is there any indication that they contain arcane markings.

The symbolic nature of Revelation makes it a tricky book from which to build doctrine, since it is quite possible that the garments it mentions are some sort of spiritual covering, not literal cloth. This is especially true since all the other references in the book to people clothed in special garments or "white robes" (Revelation 6:11; 7:9,13,14) obviously refer to disembodied souls (Revelation 6:9; 20:4) from the tribulation who are awaiting their resurrected bodies. How could a soul without a body wear a cloth garment?

This metaphoric usage becomes even more clear when one realizes the "whiteness" referred to comes from the robes being washed and made white in the blood of the Lamb (Revelation 7:14). A physical garment will not be made white by blood. This purity and whiteness comes from the spiritual cleansing power of the blood of Jesus—something which, ironically, the LDS church denies (see Zechariah 3:3-9).

TEMPLE ORDINANCES

Temple ordinances in Mormonism consist of certain prescribed rituals which normally may be done only within the secret confines of a consecrated LDS temple. Basically, they consist of the following:

1. Baptism for the Dead (see also *Baptism for the Dead*)

2. Washings—ceremonial washings of the body done on behalf of the living and the dead

3. Anointings—directly follow the washings, and the same body parts are anointed with oil as were washed

4. Endowments (more detail is given on all of these under *Endowments*)

5. Sealings (see also *Sealing Power*)

Mormons believe that these ordinances—which are needed for the fullest measure of LDS personal salvation—have been in existence from time immemorial, and were not invented by Joseph Smith. They also believe that these ordinances are essential for that full measure of salvation (called exaltation) which the LDS god offers:

All of these ordinances of exaltation are performed in the temples for both the living and the dead. *Their essential portions have been the same in all dispensations when the fulness of the sealing power has been exercised by the Lord's prophets (Doctrine and Covenants 124:28-41).*

They were given in modern times to the Prophet Joseph Smith by revelation, many things connected with them being translated by the Prophet from the papyrus on which the Book of Abraham was recorded (Book of Abraham, pp. 34-35) (*Doctrine*, p. 779, emphasis added).

Mormons are taught that these ordinances were given to Adam in the Garden of Eden. Indeed, the entire endowment ceremony revolves around the Garden of Eden and subsequent adventures of Adam and Eve. Mormons believe that most of the key men of God throughout the Old Testament had these ordinances and that they were reinstituted by Jesus Christ to the apostles (see *Doctrine and Covenants* 124:39,40). There is no mention of any such thing in the Bible or the *Book of Mormon*.

The problem is that if these were timeless rituals dating back before Christ to Abraham, Enoch, and Adam, why were so many essential parts of the ritual changed in 1990? (See also *Temples, Changes to the Ritual.*) If they were essential for Adam or Paul—or for that matter for Joseph Smith or Spencer W. Kimball—then why, all of a sudden, were *better than 30 percent of the ordinances* changed without explanation? Note the following verses from the *Book of Mormon* (emphases added).

Now, *the decrees of God are unalterable;* therefore, the way is prepared that whosoever will may walk therein and be saved (Alma 41:8).

For do we not read that *God is the same yesterday, today, and forever, and in him there is no variableness neither shadow of changing?* And now if ye have imagined up unto yourselves a god who doth vary, and in whom there is shadow of changing, then have ye imagined up unto yourselves a god who is not a God of miracles (Mormon 9:9,10).

And if there were miracles wrought then, why has God ceased to be a God of miracles and yet be an unchangeable Being? And behold, *I say unto you he changeth not; if so he would cease to be*

God; and he ceaseth not to be God, and is a God of miracles (Mormon 9:19).

For I know that God is not a partial God, *neither a changeable being; but he is unchangeable from all eternity to all eternity* (Moroni 8:18).

As if that weren't evidence enough that something is seriously wrong with the temple ordinances, then read this from the Old Testament: "For I am the LORD, I change not; therefore ye sons of Jacob are not consumed" (Malachi 3:6).

Perhaps the Lord is trying to tell the Mormons something about their church's ever-changing doctrine and practices?

TEMPLE RECOMMEND

Every Mormon who makes it to the temple has been determined worthy to attend. For the person who has been raised in the church, it generally comes at the time he or she is called to serve a mission or at the time of marriage. For missionaries, the process of gaining and renewing a temple recommend usually comes through the missionary system.

For the adult convert, it usually comes after a year or so of membership and when the local bishop determines the person or couple should go to the temple to "take out their endowments." Such couples usually go through a temple preparedness class (which, incidentally, does not discuss anything of the actual rituals and rites to be performed).

Once it has been determined by the bishop that the time has come, each person, couples included, will be interviewed by the bishop to determine temple worthiness. Questions are listed in internal documents and are basically the same throughout the church. Individual bishops will exercise their own judgment in emphasis and most have their own personal questions they may ask. Tithing, attendance at church meetings, and obedience to the Word of Wisdom are big on the list.

Once the member has passed review at the local level, arrangements are made at the stake presidency level, where the procedure is repeated. Once the approval has been given at that level, the recommend card is issued and the member(s) can now arrange for that first trip to the temple (see *Temple*), where they must present the card to gain admittance.

Temple recommends must be renewed annually. In most cases, it is tied in with the tithing settlement, where the member must meet with the local bishopric to show that all tithes and church recommended offerings have been honestly paid. If tithes have not been paid, the recommend will not be renewed.

The Biblical View

First, anyone would agree that paying tithes and offerings is a wonderful attribute. So is a life of sanctification and righteousness. But in the orthodox view these are done as Christians living a full Christian life, not as people doing these things *in order to* live a full Christian life (such as gaining attendance at a "holy" temple). Even in Mormonism, only a third of the members attain this "special worthiness" and the privilege of making it to the temple.

The Bible refers to temples almost 200 times, and in no single one is there a reference to tests of worthiness to enter into some magnificent, sacred building to do some secret ritual. In fact, what we do read is the exact reverse of what occurs in the LDS temple system:

> God that made the world and all things therein, seeing that he is Lord of heaven and earth, dwelleth not in temples made with hands; neither is worshipped with men's hands, as though he needed any thing, seeing he giveth to all life, and breath, and all things (Acts 17:24,25).

The Bible tells us that the true temple is not one made by man, but is in the heart of man: "Know ye not that ye are the temple of God, and that the Spirit of God dwelleth in you? If any man defile the temple of God, him shall God destroy; for the temple of God is holy, which temple ye are" (1 Corinthians 3:16,17).

Even the subject of temple recommends brings us full circle to the folly of man's penchant for creating his own gods—the products of a fallen people living within the foolishness of their vain imaginations.

TEMPLES

The LDS Position

The building of temples is one of the unique features of the LDS church among pseudo-Christian sects. Temples here are defined as consecrated places which are too sacred for the profane eye to see or the profane foot to enter. They are places where secret rituals are enacted on behalf of adherents to enable them to attain the keys to personal godhood.

In other words, LDS meetinghouses, which dot the streets of America, are open to the public—just as are the church buildings of Christian fellowships. Anyone, Mormon or otherwise, may enter. This is not the case with the LDS temples.

Temples are unique and quite expensive. While there are thousands of meetinghouses and stake centers all over the world, there are only about 50 temples (as of this writing) either built or under construction in the entire world. These temples, once they are dedicated, may be entered only by worthy Latter-day Saints. Their worthiness is determined by lengthy and penetrating interviews with their bishop and stake president. Only after they pass muster from these two local officials are they granted the coveted temple recommend (see also *Temple Recommend*). This is a card which will admit them to any LDS temple for a year from the date of issuance.

In some senses, the LDS temple might be thought of as the heart of the LDS experience. It is the hub from which flow so many of the peculiar doctrines and practices of the church. It is in temples that worthy LDS couples can be married for "time and all eternity" (see also *Time and All Eternity*). It is also in the temples that they learn their "new names" whereby they might be called out of the grave on the morning of the first resurrection and also gain admittance into the celestial kingdom. Young Mormons on the way to their missionary callings are clothed in their sacred temple garments for the first time in their initial temple visit (see also *Temple Garments*).

It is also in these temples that their work for the dead is done, which necessitates the Mormons' vast genealogical research program. Mormons believe that every dead person in human history eventually will have been "taken through" their temple rituals by proxy.

Thus, a large part of what makes Mormonism unique radiates from the temple and its rituals. Indeed, it is only through the temple ritual that a Mormon has any hope of becoming a god or goddess.

What goes on inside the temples is too involved to detail here (see also *Baptism for the Dead; Endowments; Temple Ordinances*). Still, we should examine in a broad sense how the Mormons fit (however badly) their peculiar notion of temple "worship" into a biblical framework.

First, it is important to note that the concept of temples came comparatively late in the evolution of LDS doctrine. Because of this, there is no mention of temple worship anywhere in the *Book of Mormon*, which was produced fairly early in the history of the church (c. 1830).

The first temple was built by the Mormon church in Kirtland, Ohio, some six years after the church was founded. Even though this temple was built, Joseph Smith and his followers didn't exactly seem to know what to do with it. The modern temple ordinances practiced today were never performed in it. Numerous strange, mystical manifestations took place within its walls, however, including a supposed hierophany of Jesus and various pseudo-pentecostal manifestations (glossolalia, visions of angels, singing in the spirit, etc.) [*History*, 2:416-32].

The Latter-day Saints under Joseph Smith were driven out of Kirtland and fled first to Missouri and finally to Illinois. There, in their settlement in Nauvoo, they purposed to build a second temple. The Kirtland temple still stood, but they no longer occupied it.

It was in this Nauvoo period that the idea of a temple ritual or endowment began to develop. Right after Smith took the Master Mason's degree in Nauvoo (March 16, 1842), he began teaching a secret endowment ritual which was extremely similar to Freemasonry. This began in May of 1842.

Finally, just before Smith's murder in 1844, endowment rituals began to be widely performed among the leading Mormons—even though the Nauvoo temple was far from finished. The idea of secret initiation rituals in a supposedly Christian church was quite a novel idea at the time and, as we shall see, it was totally unsupported biblically.

The Biblical View

To be sure, there were temples in the Old Testament. Indeed, the tabernacle in the wilderness (and later, Solomon's temple) formed the very heart of Israel's Mosaic sacrificial system. But there is only the most superficial resemblance between Jewish Old Testament temples and LDS temples—either in architecture, design, or rituals performed within them. It is also important to note that no Christian temples are ever mentioned in the New Testament (i.e., temples built especially by Christians for rituals as part of the worship of God).

A detailed examination of the Mosaic temple rites is far beyond the scope of this book. They can, however, be simply summarized in a short statement: A special priesthood existed to offer bloody animal sacrifices to atone for the sins of the people.

The Mosaic tabernacle consisted of an outer court with a huge altar for burnt offerings and a laver for the priests to wash themselves. In the center of the court was a small tent. Within the tent were two chambers: the holy place and the most holy place. The former was separated from the latter by a veil. Only the high priest could enter the most holy place. It contained the Ark of the Covenant.

Outside the veil, but in the tent's holy place, were the table of shewbreads, the altar of incense, and the seven-branched candelabra illuminating them all. Only members of the Levitical priesthood were allowed in the holy place.

Understand that there is virtually no resemblance between this design and the LDS temple, except that both have a veil. Even there, the similarity quickly vanishes because the veil of the temple was a thick, woven tapestry through which only one man could walk, and that only once a year on the Day of Atonement. The veil of the LDS temples is a thin, silky partition which one can almost see through. It is pierced with holes, and thousands of temple Mormons probably pass through the veils in the various temples every day. It is part of the endowment ritual.

It should also be noted that after the sacrifice of Christ on the cross, the temple veil was rent and the holy of holies became open to every believer. Today in the LDS temples the veil is back in place, again separating man from God by religious procedure.

Further, there is no Ark of the Covenant nor mercy seat beyond the veil in LDS temples—only a nice, spacious room which looks more like a hotel lobby done in beiges and whites.

Additionally, and most importantly, there is no blood sacrifice offered in the LDS temple ceremony—ever! This is vital, because the whole point of having a priesthood is to offer sacrifices. By definition, that is what a priest does. Since Jesus did away with blood sacrifices by His atoning death—a fact even Mormons acknowledge—what does the LDS priesthood sacrifice? Certainly nothing in the temple!

The simple fact is that there is virtually no similarity between the rituals of the Mosaic tabernacle and the Mormon temple. There is no biblical record of people learning secret handshakes or passwords in the tabernacle. There is no record of anyone getting baptized for the dead. There is no biblical record of anyone getting married for time and all eternity. Finally, the idea of the temple being a place where only a select few could enter was not part of the Old Testament temple. Any Jew could (indeed had to) enter the outer court to bring his sacrificial lamb and have it slain and offered as an immolation for the remission of sins. He did not need some kind of "temple recommend" to get in the door.

The sole function of the Old Testament temple was to teach the people that without the shedding of blood, there is no remission of sins (see Hebrews 9:22). This cannot be said of the temples of Mormonism. Indeed, the idea of Jesus' all-sufficient sacrifice is barely mentioned. There is simply no reason to think that the LDS temple has a biblical basis. It is merely the dream of a sinful prophet enchanted with the timeless mummery of Masonry.

TEMPLES, CHANGES TO THE RITUAL

Tax time brought more than the usual amount of stress to devout temple Mormons in 1990. In about the middle of April reports began filtering out of the LDS community that the highly sacred (and secretive) temple endowment ceremonies were changed substantially without any evident explanation.

The LDS church, officially silent on the changes at first, has just issued an official statement confirming that some changes had been made. It is important to remember that these rituals, which are secret to all but the elite few Mormons worthy enough to enter the temple, are performed word-perfectly and are believed to be essential to the Mormon attaining godhood.

Interestingly enough, the changes are primarily in areas where books like *The God Makers* by myself and Dave Hunt, *What's Going On in There?* by Chuck Sackett, and my book, *The Mormon*

Dilemma, had recently exposed the occult or Freemasonic content of the rites.

In 1982 *The God Makers* film reenacted some of the most occult elements in the endowment. The later film, *The Temple of the God Makers*, went even deeper. Tellingly, many of the scenes shown are the very ones now inexplicably missing. The changes include the elimination of the following:

1. The chanting of the words *pay lay ale*, which temple patrons were told came from the ancient "Adamic language" and meant "O God, hear the words of my mouth."

2. A portion of the ceremony in which a Protestant preacher is portrayed as a hireling of Lucifer. He is paid to preach the gospel of salvation by the grace and omnipresence and omnipotence of God the Father to "Adam and his posterity."

3. The penalty signs which portray the temple patron having their throat slit, their heart ripped out, or their belly torn open for revealing the secrets of the temple rite.

4. Women in the temple having to veil their faces in prayer.

5. Women in the temple swearing a covenant to obey their husbands as God.

6. The Masonic "five points of fellowship" and the embrace with "the Lord" through the veil in order to gain admittance to the Celestial Room and the presence of Heavenly Father.

7. The use of female veil workers at the veil, representing mother goddesses, to embrace the women temple patrons and bring them through to the Celestial Room.

Imagine the intense shock which would come from walking into the quiet, solemn confines of the temple and discovering that rites which you had been told were the highest, holiest, most spiritually important and perfectly restored ceremonies you could do on this Earth, had abruptly been changed. These were supposedly restored from the actual, pure temple rituals that Christ Himself performed to the letter of the law. If these ordinances were divinely revealed, what possible justification could there be for changing them?

Some radical changes have been occurring in the LDS church. All of a sudden, the church which claimed to have the "one, the only true truth" was backing down on many of the issues Christian apologists were crying out against.

The Mormon church has been building temples at an ever-growing rate, yet ever since the public revelation of the heretical acts within those temples in books, movies, and on nationwide radio and television, fewer and fewer Mormons have been anxious to return a second time. The church had to do something to stop the quiet discontent growing among its members. The image of holy purification and dedication had become overshadowed by images of eerie occult rites. Empty temples were the result.

Why were the changes made? If Joseph Smith taught that all Protestant ministers were corrupt (and he did), then why take something perfectly correct and true by LDS standards out of the temple rite? If *pay lay ale* really means "O God, hear the words of my mouth," then what could possibly need changing about such a nice, pious prayer?

The disturbing reality is that the only reason to change these vital ceremonies is because the accusations of Christian critics were true. If the endowment was perfect before for getting Mormons their godhood, then why change it? If it wasn't perfect before, then the changes become understandable—but that means that 160 years of Mormons went to their graves trusting in a broken endowment full of occult and Masonic eccentricities and a broken "plan of salvation."

We need to rejoice in the ground gained by the Lord here and to pray that these changes will cause some Mormons to step back a moment and think these issues through. If they do, they will discover that the entire LDS church falls like a house of cards before the clear light of reason and the Bible.

It is obvious that the Mormon church does not want to wear the label of a cult, but the very word *cult* describes a group at stress with the mainstream. Our work has been to turn up that stress volume and break people away and back into mainstream Christianity.

Beware: The LDS leadership will do all in its power to attempt to step into mainstream, ecumenical Christianity during the nineties, and it will remove every stress factor necessary in order to do it. Remember, however, that no matter how hard these Mormon leaders work to clean up their act, it is still an act—a counterfeit faith.

TERRESTRIAL GLORY/KINGDOM

(See also *Degrees of Glory.*)

The second highest degree of glory in Mormonism is called the terrestrial glory or terrestrial kingdom. It differs from the celestial glory "even as that of the moon differs from the sun in firmament" (*Doctrine and Covenants* 76:71). McConkie explains: "In effect they bask, as does the moon, in reflected glory, for there are restrictions and limitations placed upon them" (*Mormon Doctrine*, p. 784).

With only some 30 percent of all Mormons going to the temple and stepping into that celestial pathway, it is assumed that the vast majority of Mormons will spend eternity in this kingdom. Those Mormons who attain this level of glory remain unmarried for all eternity. They do not become gods or receive exaltation. Their earthly marriages, not sealed in an LDS temple, end upon death. "For these angels did not abide my law; therefore they cannot be enlarged, but remain separately and singly, without exaltation, in their saved condition to all eternity; and from henceforth are not gods but are angels of God forever and ever" (*Doctrine and Covenants* 132:17).

Their calling will be to "minister for those who are worthy of a far more and an exceeding, and an eternal weight of glory" (*Doctrine and Covenants* 132:16). Some will also be called to minister to those less-fortunate souls who have ended up in the even lower kingdom, the telestial kingdom (*Doctrine and Covenants* 76:86).

McConkie describes such Mormons this way: "Members of the Church of Jesus Christ of Latter-day Saints who have testimonies of Christ and the divinity of the great latter-day work and who are not valiant, but who are instead lukewarm in their devotion to the Church and to righteousness" (*Mormon Doctrine*, p. 784).

Basically, a Mormon falling short of celestial glory would not be worthy of a temple recommend, would not be living the Word of Wisdom, would not be a full tithe payer, would not be attending meetings regularly, yet would have a testimony of the truthfulness of the church, its prophet, and its message.

Yet, this kingdom is not reserved only for all these "good, but not great" Mormons, but for honorable and just non-Mormons as well. LDS scripture gives us a clear list of seven types of people who will achieve this degree of glory.

1. Behold, these are they who died without law;

2. And also they who are the spirits of men kept in [spirit] prison whom the Son visited, and preached the gospel unto them, that they might be judged according to men in the flesh;

3. Who received not the testimony of Jesus in the flesh, but afterward received it.

4. These are they who are honorable men of the earth, who were blinded by the craftiness of men.

5. These are they who receive of his glory, but not of his fulness.

6. These are they who receive of the presence of the Son, but not the fulness of the Father. (Wherefore, they are bodies terrestrial, and not bodies celestial, and differ in glory as the moon differs from the sun.)

7. These are they who are not valiant in the testimony of Jesus; wherefore, they obtain not the crown over the kingdom of our God (*Doctrine and Covenants* 76:72-79).

The vast majority of members of the LDS church look to this kingdom as their eternal place of glory. One would guess that their number is probably close to 75 to 80 percent of the entire church membership. Most Mormons know in their hearts that if they are to truly be judged for their own works, even their secret acts, they cannot possibly be worthy of godhood.

The promise of a glorious kingdom, marvelous beyond man's understanding (*Doctrine and Covenants* 76:114) for even lukewarm service to the church is like a soothing ointment to the frustrations of those who fail at true perfection. Since this takes the less-than-worthy Mormon off the hook, there is little chance that the average Mormon feels the need to deal with a personal relationship with Jesus Christ. There is no teaching that prompts any such Mormon into dealing with his/her sin nature and the need for the covering of Christ's gift at Calvary. Admittance into the terrestrial kingdom is all dependent upon the individual Mormon's personal level of obedience to the laws and ordinances of the LDS gospel.

Mormon leaders teach that Jesus was an elder brother who pointed the way for others to earn perfection and exaltation. If a member doesn't succeed, there is no need to worry. The terrestrial kingdom is still there and glorious beyond imagination.

This whole doctrine flies in the face of biblical reality. The laws and ordinances of such a man-made religion are a snare of the devil. Paul explained that we are complete only in Christ, not in ourselves. When we trust in Jesus, we are forgiven all trespasses. Paul says that Jesus has blotted "out the handwriting of ordinances that was against us, which was contrary to us, and took it out of the way, nailing it to His cross" (Colossians 2:14).

Because of this doctrine, many Mormons are unreachable with the true gospel of grace. Most in this situation know very little of the Bible and even less of the other three LDS scriptures. To discuss theological points raises warning signs that often prompt the Mormon to slam the door shut on any witness.

Fear is a factor because terrestrial-bound Mormons are comfortable in their lack of knowledge. They rely on the subjective testimony of "I know it is true." To shake that testimony is to loosen an anchor they really don't want to cut loose from.

Since the Mormon is operating in the subjective, however, give your own testimony of how you were saved and set free from sin and how you have "blessed assurance." If there is one thing that a terrestrial-bound Mormon does not have, it is the assurance of God's special love for him or her personally. That knowledge and peace is worth all the terrestrial glories out there.

TESTIMONY OF THE THREE WITNESSES

The amazing story of Joseph Smith being led by an angel to the gold plates of the *Book of Mormon* (and the restoration of the fullness of the everlasting gospel) is a legend of classic proportion.

That God and Jesus physically appeared to modern man is news enough for the human mind, but to give man a book with His holy and untarnished Word was more than the world could hope for, short of the Second Coming of Christ.

Were it true and provable, it would be news that should have shaken the very foundations of the Earth. But, of course, the gold plates from which the book was supposedly translated were said to be taken back, and the world had left only the testimony of the translator and a few very close associates. Their witness appears in the front of the *Book of Mormon* and is used to this day to confirm the truth of the validity of the *Book of Mormon* (emphasis added):

Be it known unto all nations, kindreds, tongues, and people, unto whom this work shall come: *that we, through the grace of God the Father, and our Lord Jesus Christ, have seen the plates which contain this record,* which is a record of the people of Nephi, and also of the Lamanites, their brethren, and also of the people of Jared, who came from the tower of which hath been spoken. And we also know that they have been translated by the gift and power of God, for his voice hath declared it unto us; wherefore we know of a surety that the work is true. *And we also testify that we have seen the engravings which are upon the plates;* and they have been shown unto us by the power of God, and not of man. And we declare with words of soberness, that *an angel of God came down from heaven, and he brought and laid before our eyes, that we beheld and saw the plates,* and the engravings thereon; and we know that it is by the grace of God the Father, and our Lord Jesus Christ, that we beheld and bear record that these things are true. And it is marvelous in our eyes. Nevertheless, the voice of the Lord commanded us that we should bear record of it; wherefore, to be obedient unto the commandments of God, we bear testimony of these things. And we know that if we are faithful in Christ, we shall rid our garments of the blood of all men, and be found spotless before the judgment-seat of Christ, and shall dwell with him eternally in the heavens. And the honor be to the Father, and to the Son, and to the Holy Ghost, which is one God. Amen.

Oliver Cowdery
David Whitmer
Martin Harris

An angel allegedly appeared with the plates and these three men said they saw the angel, the plates, and the engravings which were upon the plates. To all appearances this is a strong witness, particularly when you realize that later another group gave what is called the *Testimony of the Eight Witnesses.*

But there is more to this than meets the eye. Let us look at each of the men who gave their testimony.

Oliver Cowdery

Oliver Cowdery was the church's second elder, often called the "second president." The early-day companion of Joseph Smith, he was scribe for the *Book of Mormon,* present at the "restoration of the priesthood," and as close to the real truth as any man (*Pearl of Great Price,* Joseph Smith—History 2:72-76).

Yet in 1838 in Kirtland, Oliver confronted Joseph Smith with the charge of adultery with Fanny Alger, and with lying and teaching false doctrines (Private Letter to Brother Warren Cowdery, by Oliver Cowdery, January 21, 1838).

Joseph Smith denied this and charged Cowdery with being a liar (*History of the Church,* vol. 3, pp. 16-18, *Elder's Journal,* Joseph Smith, July 1838). Church records show Miss Alger was Smith's first "spiritual wife." Oliver was telling the truth (*Historical Record,* 1886, vol. 5, p. 233).

Cowdery was excommunicated for this and other "crimes" (*History of the Church,* vol. 3, pp. 16-18). Later, as a Methodist, he denied the *Book of Mormon* ("Improvement Era," January 1969, p. 56, "Oliver Cowdery—The Man Outstanding," Joseph Greehalgh, 1965, p. 28) and publicly confessed his sorrow and shame for his connection with Mormonism (*The True Origin of the Book of Mormon,* Charles Shook, 1914, pp. 58-59).

While the Mormon church claims Cowdery rejoined them in the fall of 1848 (*Historical Record,* 1886, vol. 5, p. 201), they also accused him later that year with trying to "raise up the Kingdom again" with the apostate, William E. McLellin (*The Mormon Frontier, Diary of Hosea Stout,* vol. 2, p. 336).

Oliver Cowdery was publicly charged by Joseph Smith and leading Mormons with stealing, lying, perjury, counterfeiting, adultery, and being the leader of a gang of "scoundrels of the deepest degree" (Senate Document 189, February 15, 1841, pp. 6-9, *Comprehensive History of the Church,* B.H. Roberts, vol. 1, pp. 438-39).

David Whitmer

David Whitmer claimed he saw the plates only "by the eye of faith" (*Palmyra Reflector,* March 19, 1831). He later told of finding the plates lying in a field, and later still told Orson Pratt that they were on a table with all sorts of brass plates, gold plates, the Sword of Laban, the "Director" and the Urim and Thummim (*Millennial Star,* vol. XL, pp. 771-72).

During the summer of 1837, while in Kirtland, Whitmer pledged his new loyalty to a prophetess (as did Martin Harris and Oliver Cowdery) who used a black seer stone and danced herself into "trances" (*Biographical Sketches,* Lucy Smith, pp. 211-13).

This was the beginning of the end for him. The end came in 1847 in his declaration to Oliver Cowdery that he (Whitmer) was to be the prophet of the New Church of Christ and Cowdery a counselor (letter to Oliver Cowdery by David Whitmer, September 8, 1847, printed in the "Ensign of Liberty," 5/1848, p. 93; also see "Ensign of Liberty," 8/1849, pp. 101-04).

In the meantime, he was excommunicated and roughly put out. His and Cowdery's families were, in fact, driven into the streets and robbed by the Mormons while Whitmer and Cowdery were away trying to arrange a place to flee (John Whitmer's *History of the Church*, p. 22).

Cursed by leaders such as Sidney Rigdon, Whitmer was denounced by the prophet Joseph Smith as a "dumb beast to ride" and "an ass to bray out cursings instead of blessings" (*History of the Church*, vol. 3, p. 228).

Martin Harris

Martin Harris was first a Quaker, then a Universalist, next a Restorationist, then a Baptist, next a Presbyterian, and then a Mormon (*Mormonism Unveiled*, E.D. Howe, 1834, pp. 260-61).

After his excommunication in 1837, Harris changed his religion eight more times, going from the Shakers to one Mormon splinter group then the next, and back to the main group in 1842 ("Improvement Era," March 1969, p. 63; *Journal of Discourses*, vol. 7, p. 164, Brigham Young). Yet in 1846 Harris was preaching among the Saints in England for the apostate leader, James J. Strang (*Church Chronology*, Andrew Jensen, 1899, p. 31; *Millennial Star*, vol. 8, November 15, 1846, pp. 124-28).

Harris proclaimed that his testimony for Shakerism was greater than it was for Mormonism. The Shaker's "Sacred Roll and Book" was also said to be delivered by an angel (*Martin Harris—Witness and Benefactor*, Brigham Young University, 1955 Thesis, Wayne C. Gunnell, p. 52; *The Braden and Kelly Debate*, p. 173).

Harris's later testimony that he saw the plates by "the eyes of faith and not with the natural eyes" should eliminate him automatically as a witness (*Gleanings by the Way*, J.A. Clark, pp. 256-57).

In the *Elder's Journal* for August 1838, Joseph Smith denounced Harris as "so far beneath contempt that to notice him would be too great a sacrifice for a gentleman to make. The Church exerted some restraint on him, but now he has given loose to all kinds of abominations, lying, cheating, swindling, and all kinds of debauchery."

Now that you've been introduced to the three witnesses, let me ask just one question: Would you bet your eternal soul on their testimony?

TIME AND ALL ETERNITY

"Time and all eternity" is a unique LDS phrase and is basically used to describe the quality of the special marriage covenant into which worthy temple Mormons enter in LDS temples. This is known as temple marriage or the new and everlasting covenant of marriage (see also *New and Everlasting Covenant; Celestial Glory/ Kingdom*).

Mormons believe that marriages performed outside of the temple and the special sealing power of the Melchizedek priesthood will dissolve upon death (see also *Sealing Power*). Contrary to the clear teaching of the Bible, however (see Matthew 22:30), Mormons are taught that marriages sealed in the temple by the power of the priesthood will endure past death into eternity if the couple are true and faithful in all their covenants. Hence the expression "time" (marriage in this life) "and all eternity" (marriage into the eternities).

This is the central tenet of the law of eternal progression (see also *Law of Eternal Progression*). LDS leaders teach not only that the family unit will continue into eternity, but also that the couple will become a god and goddess pair (although she will have to share him with other goddess wives in the LDS polygamous celestial glory). They will be allowed to keep the *worthy* children they have conceived while on earth, and also add to them many other "spirit children" in celestial glory. These spirit children will go on to populate an entire new world, so there must be millions of them.

The numerous biblical, logical, and logistical problems of this doctrine—which is so central to LDS theology—are dealt with under the entry *Law of Eternal Progression*. Suffice it to say that it is an offense against God and it is beyond reason to believe such a doctrine, however charming it might appear at first glance. It reduces God to a minor cog in a kind of gargantuan cosmic pyramid scheme, and it is *not* biblical.

TRINITY

The LDS Position

Mormons are taught that the historic Christian position on the Trinity (three Persons in one God) is false. Instead, they believe that the first vision of Joseph Smith and subsequent "revelations" from Smith reveal that God the Father and God the Son are two separate gods.

They believe that the Godhead is like the First Presidency of the church: a president and two counselors, the president being first in authority. God the Father is the president, and the Son and Holy Spirit are His two counselors. They regard the Trinity as a pagan heresy, much like the Jehovah's Witnesses do (except from the other extreme). While the Witnesses are radical monotheists, the Mormons believe in a plurality of Gods—the Godhead being the most obvious example of that plurality.

Mormons commonly ask this question regarding the Trinity: "How can the Father, Jesus, and the Holy Spirit be one Being, when at Jesus' baptism and when he has prayed to God, it shows the separation of the three?"

God does expect us to be able to give a reasonable, and (more importantly) scriptural answer to questions like that. The first problem is that most Mormons don't understand what Christians profess about the Trinity.

This ignorance is well-reflected in this strange statement from a sermon of LDS Prophet Joseph Smith on June 16, 1844:

> Many men say there is one God: the Father, the Son, and the Holy Ghost are only one God [sic] I say that is a strange God anyhow—three in one, and one in three! It is a curious organization. . . . All are to be crammed into one God, according to sectarianism. It would make the biggest God in all the world. He would be a wonderfully big God—he would be a giant or a monster (*Teachings*, p. 372).

Even Gilbert Scharffs, the author of *The Truth About "The God Makers,"* didn't have a good handle on what orthodox Christianity holds to be true. Because of this, Mormons keep setting up "straw men" to knock down, which doesn't prove anything.

Although Mormons don't think Christians believe that God the Father and God the Son are two separate Persons, *we do!* They think we somehow have "crammed" (to use Joseph Smith's term) three gods into a celestial trash compactor and crushed them into one indistinguishable glob. Christian teaching for millennia has been that there are three distinct Persons in one God. That is important to bear in mind.

Thus, God the Son is a Person and God the Father is a Person. There is nothing illogical about one Person talking to another, as when Jesus prayed; or about a Person commending another Person, as when God the Father spoke at Jesus' baptism.

We see in Joseph Smith's remark above, in embryo form, the entire audacious error of Mormonism's approach to the Trinity. Joseph assumes, rather arrogantly, that if he cannot comprehend a concept of God, it must be wrong. He also mocks the "bigness" of God. That is half of the problem of LDS doctrine on God. It just cannot handle the bigness of God!

The Biblical View

The biblical God *is* "a wonderfully big God." He is indeed "the biggest God in all the world." Joseph Smith mocks the very greatness of the God of the Bible. This may be one of the many reasons why the Lord struck down Smith just 11 days after he uttered this blasphemy. The major problem Mormons have is that their God just isn't big enough.

If your God is big enough to set the planets, the stars, and the galaxies in motion (Isaiah 45:12); if He is big enough to hang the mighty constellations of the Pleiades up like Christmas ornaments (Job 9:9; 38:31); if He is big enough to know the very number of hairs on every head of five-billion-plus human beings (Luke 12:7); then He is certainly big enough to be three separate Persons in one God.

The LDS question assumes that it is odd that, if there is one God, the Persons within the Godhead should wish to communicate with one another. Yet God declared very early on that it was not good for man to be alone (Genesis 2:18), and it is evident that Adam was made in the image of God (Genesis 1:27). From this we can deduce that God Himself is a social Being. If it is not good for man to be alone, it is certainly not good for God to be alone. Of course, He was never alone, even before He made us.

The three Persons of the Trinity have enjoyed perfect communion and fellowship from all eternity. There was never a time when God was "lonely" for the very simple reason that there was never a time when He was alone. All three Persons of the Trinity have existed *as one God* from all eternity. That is why each of the Persons in the Trinity is essential to God's very nature; there are three Persons in one God.

We need to explain to the Mormon why the Trinity is a necessary component of biblical Christianity. There are two reasons:

1. The Bible declares repeatedly that there is *only one God* (Deuteronomy 6:4; 1 Kings 8:60; Isaiah 42:8; 43:10,11; 44:6-8; 45:5,6; 46:5,9; Mark 12:32; John 17:3; 1 Corinthians 8:6; Galatians 3:20; Ephesians 4:6; 1 Timothy 2:5; Hebrews 6:13; 1 John 5:7).

2. Yet, it also tells us that *Jesus is God* (John 1:1-14; 8:58; 10:30; Colossians 1:15-19; 2:9; 1 Timothy 3:16; 1 John 2:22; 4:1-3; Revelation 1:7,8; 22:13-16) and also that the *Holy Spirit is God* (Genesis 1:2; Job 33:4; Isaiah 11:2; 40:13; 61:1; Acts 5:3,4; 13:2-4; 15:28; 16:6; 20:23).

Thus, we are left with an apparent contradiction: one God or three Gods. Since we know the Word of God cannot contradict itself (Numbers 23:19; 2 Samuel 7:28; Psalm 119:160; Malachi 3:6; 1 Peter 1:25; 2 Peter 1:19), there must be some problem with the way we are interpreting the text. The only safe rule in such an instance is to allow the Bible to interpret the Bible.

One helpful passage is the famous "Great Commission" text, Matthew 28:19: "Go ye therefore, and teach all nations, baptizing them in the name [singular: one name] of the Father, and of the Son, and of the Holy Ghost."

We find the Trinity even in the Old Testament. Isaiah 48:12 says:

> Hearken unto me, O Jacob and Israel, my called; *I am he; I am the first and I also am the last* [this is obviously God speaking; there can be no other "first and last"]. Mine hand also hath laid the foundation of the earth, and my right hand hath spanned the heavens: when I call unto them, they stand up together. All ye, assemble yourselves, and hear; which among them hath declared these things? The LORD hath loved him: he will do his pleasure on Babylon, and his arm shall be on the Chaldeans. I, even I, have

spoken; yea, I have called him: I have brought him, and he shall make his way prosperous. Come ye near unto me, hear ye this; I have not spoken in secret from the beginning; from the time that it was, there am I: *and now the Lord GOD, and his Spirit, hath sent me* (Isaiah 48:12-16, emphasis added).

Now notice here, we have all three members of the Trinity in the space of a few short verses, and this from the supposedly "anti-Trinitarian" Old Testament. Also, again note that both the Lord GOD [i.e., translated from the Hebrew *YHWH Elohim*, the LDS names for the Son and the Father, mentioned as one Person] and His Spirit have sent me [i.e., the Son, Jesus].

Another common LDS anti-Trinity proof text is drawn from Jesus' high priestly prayer in John 17:

And now I am no more in the world, but these are in the world, and I come to thee. Holy Father, keep through thine own name those whom thou hast given me, *that they may be one*, as we are (v. 11).

That they all *may be one*; as thou, Father, art in me, and I in thee, that they also may be one in us: that the world may believe that thou hast sent me. And the glory which thou gavest me I have given them; that they *may be one*, even as we are one (vv. 21,22).

At first glance this might seem pretty convincing. It does seem to say that Jesus wants the oneness of His disciples to be as the oneness which He and the Father experience. The LDS apologist will say that God didn't mash all the disciples together into one person, but that they remained distinct and separate human beings, and that this proves the Father and Jesus are just like two different human beings, only exalted.

Once again, though, this shows the lack of understanding Mormons have of what Christians actually believe. We *do* believe that the Father and Jesus are two distinct Persons. Therefore, the Mormon notion of people or gods being crushed together is fallacious.

Still, it must be asked, What is the Lord talking about in those verses? When the Bible is allowed to interpret itself, the answer is immediately crystal clear. Paul explains it this way:

> For as we have many members in one body, and all members have not the same office: so we, being many, are one body in Christ, and every one members one of another (Romans 12:4,5).

> For as the body is one, and hath many members, and all the members of that one body, being many, are one body: so also is Christ. For by one Spirit are we all baptized into one body, whether we be Jews or Gentiles, whether we be bond or free; and have been all made to drink into one Spirit. . . . But now are they many members, yet but one body (1 Corinthians 12:12,13,20; see also Ephesians 4:4; Colossians 3:15).

The oneness Christ prayed for is *the oneness of the body of Christ.* Christians are baptized by one Spirit into one body—Christ's body. This text is not talking about one denomination (one true church), or else Christ's prayer would have been a joke for centuries. It refers to the oneness of the body of believers.

This is the meaning of the prayer of the Lord. It is inconceivable to think that the Father would fail to answer His Son's final prayer before His death on the cross. Thus, Christ's prayer *was* answered, but with a oneness which is just as spiritual, just as powerful, and just as irresistible as the oneness of the Triune God (Romans 8:35-39).

This is deep material—no one denies that. It is sometimes helpful in talking to Mormons, once you have advanced past the scriptural stage, to try and share some metaphors which often can provide additional insight.

Dr. Norman Geisler, a Bible scholar, makes a simple analogy. He says that God is three "Who's" in one "What." In other words, Who God is *is* Father, Son and Spirit; but what God is *is* one God. God is one God who *is* Father, Son, and Spirit.

Look at a room. A room is composed of three dimensions, height, width, and depth, yet it is one room. Take away the room's height, and it ceases to be a room.

These are understandable things with which we are all familiar, yet they are only shadows of the true glory of God in His fullness. The story is told of St. Augustine wrestling with the problem of the Trinity. He supposedly was walking along a beach one night and saw a child with a small bucket trying to pour ocean water into it with his hands. Augustine remarked to the boy that he could never get the ocean into his little bucket.

The boy replied, so the story goes, "Then why are you trying to comprehend the fullness of the mystery of the Godhead?" and walked away.

The Bible says that there is but one God; and the Father, Son, and Spirit are all that God—three distinct Persons in one Essence. That is what the Bible says and, ultimately, that is why we must believe it. "LORD, my heart is not haughty, nor mine eyes lofty: neither do I exercise myself in great matters, or in things too high for me. Surely I have behaved and quieted myself, as a child that is weaned of his mother: my soul is even as a weaned child" (Psalm 131:1,2).

UNPARDONABLE SIN

LDS theology holds that it is possible to commit the unpardonable sin. Its commission consists in possessing the full light of the "restored gospel" of Mormonism, and then turning one's back on that light and rejecting it through apostasy or other serious sins such as unrepentant murder, adultery, or homosexuality. It is understood that one would probably have to be a temple Mormon who had taken out his endowments and been sealed for time and all eternity in order to have the ability to commit this sin. Bruce R. McConkie elaborates:

> Commission of the unpardonable sin consists in crucifying unto oneself the Son of God afresh and putting him to open shame (Hebrews 6:4-8; *Doctrine and Covenants* 76:34,35). To commit this unpardonable crime a man *must receive the gospel, gain from the Holy Ghost by revelation the absolute knowledge of the divinity of Christ, and then deny "the new and everlasting covenant by which he was sanctified, calling it an unholy thing, and doing despite to the Spirit of grace"* (*Teachings*, p. 128.) He thereby commits murder by assenting unto the Lord's death, that is, having a perfect knowledge of the truth he comes out in open rebellion and places himself in a position wherein he would have crucified Christ knowing perfectly the while that he was the Son of God. Christ is thus crucified afresh and put to open shame (*Doctrine and Covenants* 132:27) (*Doctrine*, p. 816, emphasis added).

In his usual melodramatic, egomaniacal way, Joseph Smith

defined "unpardonable sin" to be a rejection of Smith's own prophetic calling and the desire to do him harm:

> *What must a man do to commit the unpardonable sin?* . . .
> He must receive the Holy Ghost, have the heavens opened unto him, and know God, and then sin against him. After a man has sinned against the Holy Ghost, there is no repentance for him. He has got to say that the sun does not shine while he sees it; he has got to deny Jesus Christ when the heavens have been opened unto him, and to deny the plan of salvation with his eyes open to the truth of it; and from that time he begins to be an enemy. *This is the case with many apostates of The Church of Jesus Christ of Latter-day Saints.*
> *When a man begins to be an enemy to this work he hunts me, he seeks to kill me, and never ceases to thirst for my blood.* He gets the spirit of the devil . . . *the same spirit that they had who crucified the Lord of Life* . . . the same spirit that sins against the Holy Ghost. You cannot save such persons; you cannot bring them to repentance; they make open war, like the devil, and awful is the consequence (*Teachings*, p. 358, emphasis added).

All this means is that in addition to adulterers, murderers, and homosexuals who do not repent, anyone who has become a bornagain Christian and leaves the LDS church has essentially committed the Mormon version of the unpardonable sin. This is more especially the case with former temple Mormons and with those ex-Mormons who now seek to evangelize their former LDS family and friends out of the church and into the arms of Jesus Christ.

It is very ironic that obedience to Jesus' command of John 3:3—that man must be born again to see the kingdom of God—is interpreted as the unpardonable sin in the Church of Jesus Christ of Latter-day Saints. To the Christian, the unpardonable sin is blasphemy against the Holy Ghost (which is covered in the section by that title).

URIM AND THUMMIM

The LDS Position

The "Urim and Thummim" are two mysterious objects mentioned briefly in the Bible, and then subsequently made much of by

LDS founder Joseph Smith. The terms, which are plural in the Hebrew, are translated as "lights and perfections," which of course gives little help in understanding what they were.

Joseph Smith, like most cultists, never hesitated to rush in where angels fear to tread. Thus, he came up with some exotic explanations for what the Urim and Thummim were. Naturally, he claimed to possess them.

The LDS approach to these mysterious devices is quite unique. Their beliefs make it sound as if there are a baker's dozen of these Urim and Thummim floating around.

> Because of the sacred nature of these holy instruments, they have not been viewed by most men, and even the times and circumstances under which they have been held by mortals are not clearly set forth. Undoubtedly they were in use before the flood, but the first scriptural reference to them is in connection with the revelations given the Brother of Jared (Ether 3:21-28). Abraham had them in his day (Abraham 3:1-4), and Aaron and the priests in Israel had them from generation to generation (Exodus 28:30; Leviticus 8:8; Numbers 27:21; Deuteronomy 33:8; 1 Samuel 28:6; Ezra 2:63; Nehemiah 7:65). There is no record that Lehi brought a Urim and Thummim to this continent, but King Mosiah had one prior to the discovery of the Book of Ether, and it was handed down from prophet to prophet [*Doctrine*, p. 818].

There is no biblical basis for any of this. There was no high priesthood of Aaron before the Book of Exodus, and there certainly is no indication that there were any high priests in the New World, which is where the bulk of the *Book of Mormon* material supposedly takes place. None of the immigrants allegedly coming over with Lehi in the *Book of Mormon* were Levites, which meant they could not be of the house of Aaron. They could not biblically hold any priesthood office.

Joseph Smith himself was not a Levite, nor a member of the house of Aaron, nor were most of the "characters" mentioned by McConkie in the above paragraph. Thus, none of them had any right to possess the Urim and Thummim.

It also must be mentioned that Smith was deeply involved with several sinful practices, including sexual immorality and sorcery—to say nothing of teaching his people to worship a false god. This would, if anything, make him worse off spiritually than Saul was in 1 Samuel 28 when God refused to answer him "by Urim." Yet by that time Saul had not yet consulted the infamous "witch of Endor."

There is some confusion about whether the alleged Urim and Thummim which Smith possessed was the same thing as his seer stone:

> Joseph Smith received the same Urim and Thummim had by the Brother of Jared for it was the one expressly provided for the translation of the Jaredite and Nephite records (*Doctrine and Covenants* 10:1; 17:1; Ether 3:22-28). It was separate and distinct from the one had by Abraham and the one had by the priests in Israel. The Prophet also had a seer stone which was separate and distinct from the Urim and Thummim, and which (speaking loosely) has been called by some a Urim and Thummim (*Doctrines of Salvation*, vol. 3, pp. 222-26) [ibid.].

As has been shown elsewhere in this volume, Smith's use of the seer stones (see also *Occult; Peep Stones; Seer Stones*) was highly occult in nature. Thus, even to mention them in the same breath with the Urim and Thummim would border on blasphemy.

There is one final, bizarre Mormon doctrine concerning the Urim and Thummim which needs to be mentioned. This is the almost-science-fiction idea that the Earth itself will become one:

> The existence and use of the Urim and Thummim as an instrument of revelation will continue among exalted beings in eternity. From the inspired writings of the Prophet we learn that angels "reside in the presence of God, on *a globe like a sea of glass and fire, where all things for their glory are manifest, past, present, and future,* and are continually before the Lord. *The place where God resides is a great Urim and Thummim.*
>
> *This earth,* in its sanctified and immortal state, will be made like unto crystal and *will be a Urim and Thummim* to the inhabitants who dwell thereon, whereby all things pertaining to an inferior kingdom, or all kingdoms of a lower order, will be manifest to those who dwell on it; and this earth will be Christ's. Then the *white stone* mentioned in Revelation 2:17, *will become a Urim and Thummim to each individual who receives one,* whereby things pertaining to a higher order of kingdoms will be made known (*Doctrine and Covenants* 130:6-11) (*Doctrine,* p. 819, emphasis in original).

Of course, there is zero biblical support for any of this. Smith had no right to use the Urim and Thummim, even if he had actually possessed them. There is no evidence historically that he ever did, beyond his own testimony. They have disappeared down that same black hole with the gold plates, the Sword of Laban, and the rest of the "sacred" LDS artifacts. Thus this, like the rest of Mormonism, must collapse under its own deceitful weight.

The Biblical View

From the biblical picture, one thing is clear. The Urim and Thummim were part of the ritual garb which the high priest of Israel wore. They were placed in the "breastplate of judgment" (Exodus 28:30), which was a kind of massive jewel setting designed to be worn over the breast of the high priest. In Exodus 28:15-21, we learn that it was to have four rows of precious stones, three stones in each. Each of these 12 stones was to have a name of one of the 12 tribes of Israel engraved upon it.

Verse 29 of the same chapter makes it clear that this was an utterly unique breastplate and was to be worn only by the high priest. Behind the plate was evidently some sort of pouch or pocket. In here were placed the Urim and Thummim. Verse 30 bears out this unique quality of these artifacts: "And thou shalt put in the breastplate of judgment the Urim and the Thummim; and they shall be upon Aaron's heart, when he goeth in before the LORD: and Aaron shall bear the judgment of the children of Israel upon his heart before the LORD continually."

Thus, there was a tremendous and weighty responsibility in bearing the Urim and Thummim. It was not something to be taken lightly. Later on in the Old Testament, the function of these objects became clearer. This verse explains that the Urim and Thummim seemed to have been used for seeking counsel from the Lord:

> And the LORD said unto Moses, Take thee Joshua the son of Nun, a man in whom is the spirit, and lay thine hand upon him; and set him before Eleazar the priest, and before all the congregation; and give him a charge in their sight. And thou shalt put some of thine honour upon him, that all the congregation of the children of Israel may be obedient. And he shall stand before Eleazar the priest, who shall ask counsel for him after the judgment of Urim before the LORD: at his word shall they go out, and

at his word they shall come in, both he, and all the children of Israel with him, even all the congregation (Numbers 27:18-21).

The Urim and Thummim seem to have been passed from one high priest to another, and Joshua as the new leader of Israel was given the right to seek advice from them. Some Bible scholars speculate that they might have been two stones of different colors. They might have been used like drawing lots. A question would be asked of the Lord, and the high priest would draw his hand into the pouch. Whichever of the two stones emerged, that would be the Lord's answer—either yes or no—depending upon the color. Yet no one knows for certain how they worked.

One more important fact we can learn from the Bible is that the Urim and Thummim did not always function, especially if the person attempting to use them was in deep sin. This was the case with Saul, toward the end of his life: "And when Saul saw the host of the Philistines, he was afraid, and his heart greatly trembled. And when Saul enquired of the LORD, the LORD answered him not, neither by dreams, nor by Urim, nor by prophets" (1 Samuel 28:5,6).

Later on, in Ezra 2:63, the Urim and Thummim (or at least the Urim, which may have been a short way of speaking of both devices) were inquired of to determine which priests truly had pure, unpolluted lineage so that they would be permitted to eat of the holy things (see also Nehemiah 7:65). After this, the Urim and Thummim disappear from the Bible. They are last seen in the return of the people from Babylonian captivity and are never mentioned in the New Testament.

VIRGIN BIRTH, VIRGIN MARY

The LDS Position

Was the Virgin Mary really a virgin? Not according to Mormonism.

Remember that the Mormon church teaches that God is an exalted man, with body parts and passions. *Doctrine and Covenants* 130:22 states: "The Father has a body of flesh and bones as tangible as man's; the Son also." He is said to physically live with His many wives near the star Kolob, where he procreates spirit children with his wives through natural means. Mormonism teaches that this god came down to earth in the flesh and was the physical father of Jesus. These basic doctrines are so far out of the realm of orthodoxy that one should not have to read further to know that Mormonism could not be Christian.

Read what the Mormon leaders say about God, our Savior, and the Virgin Mary:

> If none but gods will be permitted to multiply immortal children, it follows that each God must have one or more wives. God, the Father of our spirits, became the Father of our Lord Jesus Christ according to the flesh (Orson Pratt, *The Seer*, p. 158).

> The fleshly body of Jesus required a Mother as well as a Father. Therefore, the Father and Mother of Jesus, according to the flesh, must have been associated together in the capacity of Husband and Wife; hence the Virgin Mary must have been, for the time being, the lawful wife of God the Father: we use the term

lawful Wife, because it would be blasphemous in the highest degree to say that He overshadowed her or begat the Savior unlawfully (Orson Pratt, *The Seer*, p. 158).

Inasmuch as God was the first husband to her, it may be that He only gave her to be the wife of Joseph while in the mortal state, and that He intended after the resurrection to again take her as one of his own wives to raise up immortal spirits in eternity (Orson Pratt, *The Seer*, p. 158).

The man Joseph, the husband of Mary, did not, that we know of, have more than one wife, but Mary the wife of Joseph had another husband (Brigham Young, *Journal of Discourses*, 11:268).

They tell us the Book of Mormon states that Jesus was begotten of the Holy Ghost. I challenge that statement. The Book of Mormon teaches No Such Thing! Neither does the Bible (Joseph Fielding Smith, tenth prophet of the Mormon Church, in *Doctrines of Salvation*, vol. 1, p. 18).

Christ was begotten of God. He was *not* born without the aid of man and that man was God (*Doctrines of Salvation*, vol. 1, p. 18).

The birth of the Savior was as natural as are the births of our children; it was the result of natural action. He partook of flesh and blood—was begotten of his Father, as we are of our fathers (Brigham Young, *Journal of Discourses*, 8:115).

In relation to the way in which I look upon the works of God and his creatures, I will say that I was naturally begotten; so was my father, and also my Savior Jesus Christ. According to the Scriptures, he is the first begotten of his father in the flesh, and there was nothing unnatural about it (Heber C. Kimball, *Journal of Discourses*, 8:211).

When the Virgin Mary conceived the child Jesus, the Father had begotten him in his own likeness. He was not begotten by the Holy Ghost. . . . What a learned idea! Jesus, our elder brother was begotten in the flesh by the same character that was in the garden of Eden, and who is our Father in Heaven. [He really does mean Adam.] Now remember from this time forth, and forever, that Jesus Christ was not begotten by the Holy Ghost. I will repeat a little anecdote. I was in conversation with a certain learned professor upon this subject when I replied to this idea— "If the son was begotten by the Holy Ghost, it would be very dangerous to baptize and confirm females and give the Holy Ghost to them, lest he should beget children to be palmed off on the Elders by the people, bringing the Elders into great difficulties."... But what do the people in Christendom, with the Bible in their hands, know about this subject? Comparatively nothing (Brigham Young, *Journal of Discourses* 1:50,51).

God the Father is a perfected, glorified, holy Man, an immortal Personage. And Christ was born into the world as the literal Son of this Holy Being; he was born in the same personal, real, and literal sense that any mortal son is born to a mortal father. There is nothing figurative about his paternity; he was begotten, conceived and born in the normal and natural course of events, for he is the son of God, and that designation means what it says (Bruce R. McConkie, *Mormon Doctrine*, p. 742).

Christ is the Son of Man, meaning that his Father (the Eternal God) is a Holy Man. "In the language of Adam, Man of Holiness" is the name of God (ibid., p. 742).

But the Holy Ghost is not the Father of Christ—and when the Child was born, he was "the Son of the Eternal Father" (ibid., p. 743).

These name-titles all signify that our Lord is the only Son of the Father in the flesh. Each of the words is to be understood literally. Only means only, begotten means begotten, and Son means son. Christ was begotten by an Immortal Father in the same way that mortal men are begotten by mortal fathers (ibid., p. 546).

The Biblical View

To believe this Mormon doctrine is to believe that the Bible is a lie. What does the Word of God say about Mary and the virgin birth?

And he said, Hear ye now, O house of David; Is it a small thing for you to weary men, but will ye weary my God also? Therefore the Lord himself shall give you a sign; Behold, a virgin shall conceive, and bear a son, and shall call his name Immanuel (Isaiah 7:13,14).

Then said Mary unto the angel, How shall this be, seeing I know not a man? And the angel answered and said unto her, The

Holy Ghost shall come upon thee, and the power of the Highest shall overshadow thee: therefore also that holy thing which shall be born of thee shall be called the Son of God (Luke 1:34,35).

Now the birth of Jesus Christ was on this wise: When as his mother Mary was espoused to Joseph, before they came together, she was found with child of the Holy Ghost (Matthew 1:18).

Could it be any plainer, any simpler? One may ask, "How can the Mormons teach such things? How can they be blinded from the simplicity of the true gospel to accept such nonbiblical fantasy?" The Word of God answers their questions: "But if our gospel be hid, it is hid to them that are lost: in whom the god of this world hath blinded the minds of them which believe not, lest the light of the glorious gospel of Christ, who is the image of God, should shine unto them (2 Corinthians 4:3,4).

Who else but the father of all lies would take joy in defaming the name of Christ, in humanizing the birth of the Savior?

WORD OF WISDOM

The LDS "word of wisdom" is probably one of the most widely used precepts of Mormonism. It is also probably the most misquoted and misused of all of Joseph Smith's "revelations."

If you ask a Mormon missionary about the word of wisdom, he or she will tell you that it is a revelation that was far ahead of its time.

Presented as section 89 of the *Doctrine and Covenants*, it supposedly was a revelation given to Joseph Smith at Kirtland, Ohio, on February 27, 1833, enjoining the church to abstain from certain foods and to exercise moderation in the use of other foods. Here it is in its entirety, paragraphed and italicized by topic to best highlight the parts of the revelation:

> [1]A Word of Wisdom, for the benefit of the council of high priests assembled in Kirtland, and the church, and also the saints in Zion—[2]To be sent greeting; not by commandment or constraint, but by revelation and the word of wisdom, showing forth the order and will of God in the temporal salvation of all saints in the last days—[3]Given for a principle with promise, adapted to the capacity of the weak and the weakest of all saints, who are or can be called saints.
>
> [4]Behold, verily, thus saith the Lord unto you: In consequence of evils and designs which do and will exist in the hearts of conspiring men in the last days, I have warned you, and forewarn you, by giving unto you this word of wisdom by revelation—[5]*That*

inasmuch as any man drinketh wine or strong drink among you, behold it is not good, neither meet in the sight of your Father, only in assembling yourselves together to offer up your sacraments before him. 6And, behold, this should be wine, yea, pure wine of the grape of the vine, of your own make. 7And, again, strong drinks are not for the belly, but for the washing of your bodies.

8And again, *tobacco is not for the body, neither for the belly, and is not good for man, but is an herb for bruises and all sick cattle,* to be used with judgment and skill. 9And again, *hot drinks are not for the body or belly.*

10And again, verily I say unto you, *all wholesome herbs God hath ordained for constitution, nature, and use of man*—11*Every herb in the season thereof, and every fruit in the season thereof;* all these to be used with prudence and thanksgiving.

12Yea, *flesh of beasts and of the fowls of the air,* I, the Lord, have ordained for the use of man with thanksgiving; nevertheless *they are to be used sparingly;* 13*And it is pleasing unto me that they should not be used, only in times of winter, or of cold, or famine.*

14*All grain is ordained for the use of man and of beasts, to be the staff of life, not only for man but for the beasts of the field, and the fowls of heaven, and all wild animals that run or creep on the earth;* 15And these hath God made for the use of man only in times of famine and excess of hunger. 16*All grain is good for the food of man;* as also the fruit of the vine; that which yieldeth fruit, whether in the ground or above the ground—

17Rye for the fowls and for swine, and for all beasts of the field, and barley for all useful animals, and for mild drinks, as also other grain.

18Obedience to the commandments, shall receive health in their navel and marrow to their bones; 19And shall find wisdom and great treasures of knowledge, even hidden treasures; 20And shall run and not be weary, and shall walk and not faint. 21And I, the Lord, give unto them a promise, that the destroying angel shall pass by them, as the children of Israel, and not slay them. Amen.

This edict was not met with great rejoicing. Most of the men smoked and enjoyed a drink or two; women were taken to having tea in the afternoons. Remember, a good many converts were coming into the fold from England, where drinking tea was more common than wearing shoes.

During this same time, Joseph Smith was conducting the "School of the Prophet," and those men attending were often a bit more than energetically given to smoking and chewing. Brigham Young commented on the reason Smith went to the Lord in the matter:

> When they assembled together in this room . . . the first thing they did was light their pipes, and while smoking, talk about the great things of the kingdom, and spit all over the room, and as soon as the pipe was out of their mouths a large chew of tobacco would then be taken. Often, when the prophet entered the room to give the school instructions he would find himself in a cloud of tobacco smoke. This, and the complaints of his wife at having to clean so filthy a floor, made the prophet think on the matter, and he inquired of the Lord (Brigham Young, *Journal of Discourses* 12:158).

The prophet himself was not immune from the problems associated with breaking the word of wisdom, which at first was not a commandment from God. Fawn Brodie wrote of the problem that even Smith had with the curse of tobacco and strong drink (Fawn Brodie, *No Man Knows My History*, pp. 166-67).

Shortly after this revelation came the establishment of the high council of the church in February 1834. At one of the earliest meetings of this council, over which the presidency of the church presided, the question was asked "whether disobedience to the word of wisdom was a transgression sufficient to deprive an official member from holding office in the Church after having it sufficiently taught him?"

After a vigorous discussion, Joseph Smith gave the following decision which was unanimously accepted by the council: "No official member in this Church is worthy to hold an office after having the word of wisdom properly taught him; and he, the official member, neglecting to comply with and obey it" (*Far West Record*, April 7, 1838, p. 111).

Since the actual words of the revelation did not mention coffee or tea, there continued to be some wider interpretation of where the boundaries lay. Was it a real commandment or just a strong suggestion? Did the hot drinks part mean coffee and tea? What about iced tea or cold coffee? The problems and controversies continued on and were still present when Brigham Young became the second president of the church. Young did not vacillate on the issue as had Smith:

> In the name of the Lord Jesus Christ, I command the Elders of Israel—those who have been in the habit of getting drunk—to cease drinking strong drink from this time henceforth. But some may think they need it as soon as they go out of this house. Let me be your physician in this matter. So long as you are able to walk and attend to your business, it is folly to say that you need ardent spirits to keep you alive. The constitution that a person has should be nourished and cherished; and whenever we take anything into the system to force and stimulate it beyond its natural capacity, it shortens life. I am physician enough to know that. When you are tired and think you need a little spirituous liquor, take some bread and butter or bread and milk, and lie down and rest. Do not labor so hard as to deem it requisite to get half drunk in order to keep up your spirits. If you will follow this counsel, you will be full of life and health, and you will increase your intelligence, your joy, and comfort (*Journal of Discourses* 7:337).

> Now, Elders of Israel, if you have the right to chew tobacco, you have a privilege I have not; if you have a right to drink whiskey, you have a right that I have not; if you have a right to transgress the Word of Wisdom, you have a right that I have not (*Journal of Discourses* 12:30).

> I know that some say the revelations upon these points are not given by way of commandment. Very well, but we are commanded to observe every word that proceeds from the mouth of God (*Journal of Discourses* 13:3).

> This Word of Wisdom prohibits the use of hot drinks and tobacco. I have heard it argued that tea and coffee are not mentioned therein; that is very true; but what were the people in the habit of taking as hot drinks when the revelation was given? Tea and coffee. We were not in the habit of drinking water very hot, but tea and coffee—the beverages in common use. And the Lord said hot drinks are not good for the body nor the belly, liquor is not good for the body nor the belly, but for the washing of the body, etc. Tobacco is not good, save for sick cattle, and for bruises and sores, its cleansing properties being then very useful (*Journal of Discourses* 13:277).

Today, the word of wisdom is a kind of rod of faith for the Latter-day Saints. Every worthy church member must be in obedience to it in order to advance in office or be found worthy to gain a temple recommend and entrance to the temple and its promise of celestial glory and godhood. Yet the scope of the commandment seems to have narrowed a bit to include only alcohol, tobacco, and caffeine products, as well as a vague call to exercise moderation in all things.

Bruce R. McConkie describes the commandment this way:

Three types of things are prohibited to man by the Word of Wisdom: tobacco, strong drinks, and hot drinks. By strong drinks is meant alcoholic beverages; hot drinks, according to the Prophet's own statement, mean tea and coffee. Accordingly the negative side of the Word of Wisdom is a command to abstain from tea, coffee, tobacco, and liquor.

Abstinence from these four things has been accepted by the Church as a measuring rod to determine in part the personal worthiness of church members. When decisions are made relative to the granting of temple recommends or approving brethren for church positions or ordinations, inquiry is made relative to these four items.

Obviously the standard of judgment must be uniform throughout the Church, and local officers are not at liberty to add other items to this list. However, there are many other substances which have a harmful effect on the human body, though such particular things are not specifically prohibited by the Word of Wisdom. Certainly the partaking of cola drinks, though not included within the measuring standard here set out, is in violation of the spirit of the Word of Wisdom. Harmful drugs of any sort are in a like category (*Doctrine*, p. 845).

Still, it is interesting to note that the Saints do not consider much of the Word of Wisdom to be relevant. For example, in verse 5 they were commanded to use wine only for communion. This was consistent with section 20 of the *Doctrine and Covenants* where it was "the duty of the elders, priests, teachers, deacons, and members of the church of Christ—An apostle is an elder, and it is his calling to baptize; and to ordain other elders, priests, teachers, and deacons; *and to administer bread and wine* the emblems of the flesh and blood of Christ" (vv. 38-40).

While they were later instructed that they must not buy sacrament wine from strangers, and anything used with an eye single to

His glory was acceptable to use in communion, the Lord seemed to be fairly open about the use of both wine and strong drink. In fact, He appeared to be looking forward to that day when He would join in:

> Listen to the voice of Jesus Christ, your Lord, your God, and your Redeemer, whose word is quick and powerful. For, behold, I say unto you, that it mattereth not what ye shall eat or what ye shall drink when ye partake of the sacrament, if it so be that ye do it with an eye single to my glory . . . remembering unto the Father my body which was laid down for you, and my blood which was shed for the remission of your sins. Wherefore, a commandment I give unto you, that *you shall not purchase wine neither strong drink of your enemies; wherefore, you shall partake of none except it is made new among you;* yea, in this my Father's kingdom which shall be built up on the earth. Behold, this is wisdom in me; wherefore, marvel not, for the hour cometh that I will drink of the fruit of the vine with you on the earth (*Doctrine and Covenants* 27:1-5, emphasis added).

Again, in verses 12 and 13, both meat and poultry are to be used sparingly and only in times of winter, or of cold, or of famine. And in verse 17, man is to eat wheat and feed the corn to the ox. Yet, Mormons today use meat and poultry year-round as main staples of their diets and use corn and corn products far more than they feed it to oxen.

We certainly do not fault the Mormons for doing exactly what we all do. But remember, they claim to be specifically ordered of God by divine revelation to obey the whole commandment, not to pick and choose certain parts only.

I agree that a man will be far healthier should he abstain from those things listed above. We would all be healthier if we ate less red meat. Today, even much of the poultry we eat is tainted with bad things. But none of these things would keep a person out of the kingdom of God. It's like these are traps set out to take away the unwary Mormon. God doesn't play games of that sort. The Bible has something to say about these ordinances that are set against us.

> And you, being dead in your sins and the uncircumcision of your flesh, hath he quickened together with him, having forgiven you all trespasses; blotting out the handwriting of ordinances that was against us, which was contrary to us, and took it

out of the way, nailing it to his cross; and having spoiled principalities and powers, he made a shew of them openly, triumphing
over them in it. Let no man therefore judge you in meat, or in
drink, or in respect of an holyday, or of the new moon, or of the
sabbath days: which are a shadow of things to come; but the body
is of Christ (Colossians 2:13-17).

ZION

In the early days of the LDS church, "Zion" was the name given to the physical place where the saints resided. Many of the converts who came to join the church immigrated from England. The LDS church was a gathering-in type of movement. The Mormons sang LDS hymns that called out to "Come to Zion, Come to Zion."

From 1831 until 1838, Kirtland, Ohio, was called Zion—the gathering place for the Latter-day Saints that also served as its central headquarters. The city had a significant role in the early history of the church (*Encyclopedia of Mormonism*, vol. 2, pp. 793-98).

When the Saints left Ohio, the new city of Saints and the headquarters for the church became Nauvoo, Illinois, from 1839 until 1846. In the final days of Joseph Smith's life, Nauvoo was one of the largest cities in the region. English and Canadian converts fled in great number to the new Zion. In fact, many of the Saints still in the East also fled to Zion (ibid., vol. 3, pp. 987-93).

In *Doctrine and Covenants* 57, Joseph Smith gave the revelation that Independence, in Jackson County, Missouri, was the "land of promise and the place for the city of Zion" (v. 2). It was to be the site for the New Jerusalem and the American place from where the millennium church would operate.

After the death of Smith, Zion again was moved as Brigham Young began the exodus to the Great Salt Lake. Mormons came to the newest (and final) Zion, heeding the biblical admonishment to literally "come out from among them."

And what concord hath Christ with Belial? or what part hath he that believeth with an infidel? And what agreement hath the temple of God with idols? for ye are the temple of the living God; as God hath said, I will dwell in them, and walk in them; and I will be their God, and they shall be my people. Wherefore come out from among them, and be ye separate, saith the Lord, and touch not the unclean thing; and I will receive you, and will be a Father unto you, and ye shall be my sons and daughters, saith the Lord Almighty (2 Corinthians 6:15-18).

What the Mormons failed to see was that Paul's admonishment was a spiritual one to the church at Corinth, and is still a spiritual one to the church today. No Latter-day Saints in the first century were immigrating to a geographical place called Zion. The term was an Old Testament place name which often signified the people more than the place.

Obviously, the LDS church of today has dropped the call to physically come to Zion; it uses the broader, Old Testament definition of *Zion* to mean the people. And no wonder. It sure is a whole lot easier to explain.

NOTES

Foreword by Hank Hanegraaff

1. Ed Decker was an active participant in the Mormon church's "Every member a missionary" program.

2. *The Pearl of Great Price*, Joseph Smith—History 1:18-19.

3. According to Joseph Smith, the word *Mormon* "means, literally, more good." Smith wrote that *mor* is simply a contraction of the word *more* and that *mon* is the Egyptian word for "good." Quoted in Fawn M. Brodie, *No Man Knows My History: The Life of Joseph Smith the Mormon Prophet* (New York: Alfred A Knopf, 1945), p. 276; cf. Joseph Smith, Jr., *History of the Church*, 7 vols. (Salt Lake City: Deseret Book Co., 1978, reprint), 5:400.

4. Described as two stones in silver bows called the Urim and Thummim in *The Pearl of Great Price*, Joseph Smith—History 1:35; cf. v. 62.

5. *The Book of Mormon* contains an apocryphal account of the ancient inhabitants of the Americas. They were divided into three groups: the Jaredites, the Nephites, and the Lamanites. The Lamanites are purportedly the principal ancestors of the American Indians.

6. *Doctrine and Covenants* 27:12-13.

7. It should be noted that Moroni, for some inexplicable reason, did *not* achieve godhood, but had merely become a resurrected angel.

8. *The Book of Mormon*, introduction.

9. According to Mormonism, the "stick of Judah" is the Bible and the "stick of Joseph" is *The Book of Mormon*. The joining of these "sticks" symbolizes the joining of the two writings.

10. Smith, *History of the Church* 4:461; cf. *The Book of Mormon*, introduction.

11. See, for example, *Journal of Discourses* 7:290-91.

12. *Doctrine and Covenants* 130:22.

13. Eighth Article of Faith.

14. See Bruce R. McConkie, *Mormon Doctrine*, 2d ed. (Salt Lake City: Bookcraft, 1966), pp. 546-47.

15. Brigham Young in *Journal of Discourses* 4:218.

16. Orson Hyde in *Journal of Discourses* 1:123.

17. Current Mormon president Howard W. Hunter, for example, is sealed to at least two wives.

SUGGESTED "OFFICIAL"
MORMON BIBLIOGRAPHY

Achieving a Celestial Marriage course manual, Church Educational System CDFR60-CDFR61, Department of Seminaries and Institutes of Religion, Salt Lake City, 1976.

The Book of Mormon, The Corporation of the President of the Church of Jesus Christ of Latter-day Saints, Salt Lake City.

Discourses of Brigham Young, comp. by John A. Widtsoe, Deseret Books, Salt Lake City, 1977.

Doctrine and Covenants, The Corporation of the President of the Church of Jesus Christ of Latter-day Saints, Salt Lake City.

Encylopedia of Mormonism, volumes 1-4, New York: McMillan Publishing Co., 1992.

Ensign magazines (various issues), The Corporation of the President of the Church of Jesus Christ of Latter-day Saints, Salt Lake City.

General Handbook of Instructions, The Corporation of the President of the Church of Jesus Christ of Latter-day Saints, Salt Lake City, No. 21, 1976.

Spencer W. Kimball, *The Miracle of Forgiveness*, Salt Lake City: Bookcraft, 1969.

LDS Hymn Book, The Corporation of the President of the Church of Jesus Christ of Latter-day Saints, Salt Lake City, 1966.

Bruce R. McConkie, *Mormon Doctrine*, Salt Lake City: Bookcraft, 1966.

LeGrand Richards, *A Marvelous Work and a Wonder*, Salt Lake City: Deseret Books, 1950.

Joseph F. Smith, *Gospel Doctrine*, Salt Lake City: Deseret Books, 1977.

Joseph Fielding Smith, *Answers to Gospel Questions* (5 volumes), Salt Lake City: Deseret Books, 1979.

Joseph Fielding Smith, *Doctrines of Salvation* (3 volumes), Salt Lake City: Bookcraft, 1976.

Joseph Smith, Jr., et al. *The History of the Church* (6 volumes), Salt Lake City: Deseret Books.

James E. Talmage, *The Articles of Faith*, The Church of Jesus Christ of Latter-day Saints, Salt Lake City, 1977.

_____, *The Great Apostasy*, Salt Lake City: Deseret Books, 1968.

_____, *The House of the Lord*, Salt Lake City: Deseret Books, 1978.

_____, *Jesus the Christ*, Salt Lake City: Deseret Books, 1962.

Teachings of the Prophet Joseph Smith, ed. by Joseph Fielding Smith, Salt Lake City: Deseret Books, 1976.

The Pearl of Great Price, The Corporation of the President of the Church of Jesus Christ of Latter-day Saints, Salt Lake City.

Uniform System for Teaching the Gospel, The Corporation of the President of the Church of Jesus Christ of Latter-day Saints, Salt Lake City. 1985.

"What the Mormons Think of Christ" (pamphlet) 1982, The Church of Jesus Christ of Latter-day Saints.

NON-MORMON BOOKS FREQUENTLY REFERENCED IN THIS HANDBOOK

D. Michael Quinn, *Early Mormonism and the Magic World View*, Salt Lake City: Signature Books, 1987.

Chuck Sackett, *What's Going On in There?* Thousand Oaks, CA: Sword of the Shepherd Ministries, 1982.

SUBJECT INDEX

D

E

F

G

H

I

J

T

Other Harvest House Books
by *Ed Decker*

The God Makers
What You Need to Know About Mormons
What You Need to Know About Masons
The God Makers II
Fast Facts on False Teachings

You may write to Ed Decker at:

Saints Alive in Jesus
P.O. Box 1076
Issaquah, WA 98027